::studysync®

Reading & Writing Companion

GRADE 6 UNITS

Alex Davis

Turning Points • Ancient Realms

Facing Challenges • Our Heroes

::studysync

studysync.com

Send all inquiries to:
BookheadEd Learning, LLC
610 Daniel Young Drive
Sonoma, CA 95476

8 9 LMN 20 19 18 C

::studysync®

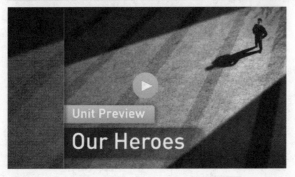

GETTING STARTED

Welcome to the StudySync Reading and Writing Companion! In this booklet, you will find a collection of readings based on the theme of the unit you are studying. As you work through the readings, you will be asked to answer questions and perform a variety of tasks designed to help you closely analyze and understand each text selection. Read on for an explanation of

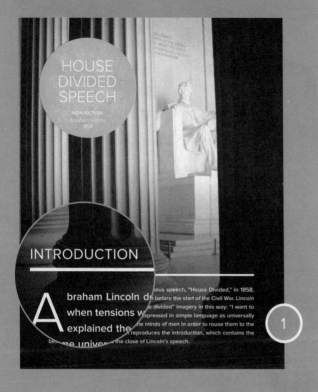

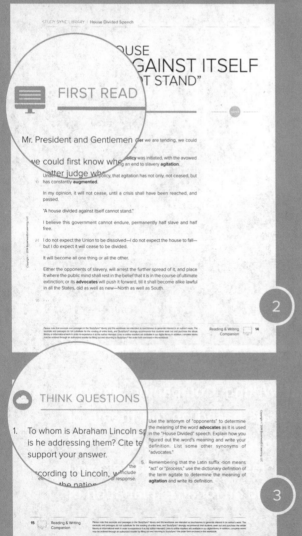

1 INTRODUCTION

An Introduction to each text provides historical context for your reading as well as information about the author. You will also learn about the genre of the excerpt and the year in which it was written.

2 FIRST READ

During your first reading of each excerpt, you should just try to get a general idea of the content and message of the reading. Don't worry if there are parts you don't understand or words that are unfamiliar to you. You'll have an opportunity later to dive deeper into the text.

Many times, while working through the Think Questions after your first read, you will be asked to **annotate** or **make annotations** about what you are reading. This means that you should use the "Notes" column to make comments or jot down any questions you may have about the text. You may also want to note any unfamiliar vocabulary words here.

3 THINK QUESTIONS

These questions will ask you to start thinking critically about the text, asking specific questions about its purpose, and making connections to your prior knowledge and reading experiences. To answer these questions, you should go back to the text and draw upon specific evidence that you find there to support your responses. You will also begin to explore some of the more challenging vocabulary words used in the excerpt.

4 CLOSE READ & FOCUS QUESTIONS

After you have completed the First Read, you will then be asked to go back and read the excerpt more closely and critically. Before you begin your Close Read, you should read through the Focus Questions to get an idea of the concepts you will want to focus on during your second reading. You should work through the Focus Questions by making annotations, highlighting important concepts, and writing notes or questions in the "Notes" column. Depending on instructions from your teacher, you may need to respond online or use a separate piece of paper to start expanding on your thoughts and ideas.

5 WRITING PROMPT

Your study of each excerpt or selection will end with a writing assignment. To complete this assignment, you should use your notes, annotations, and answers to both the Think and Focus Questions. Be sure to read the prompt carefully and address each part of it in your writing assignment.

6 EXTENDED WRITING PROJECT

After you have read and worked through all of the unit text selections, you will move on to a writing project. This project will walk you through steps to plan, draft, revise, edit, and finally publish an essay or other piece of writing about one or more of the texts you have studied in the unit. Student models and graphic organizers will provide guidance and help you organize your thoughts as you plan and write your essay. Throughout the project, you will also study and work on specific writing skills to help you develop different portions of your writing.

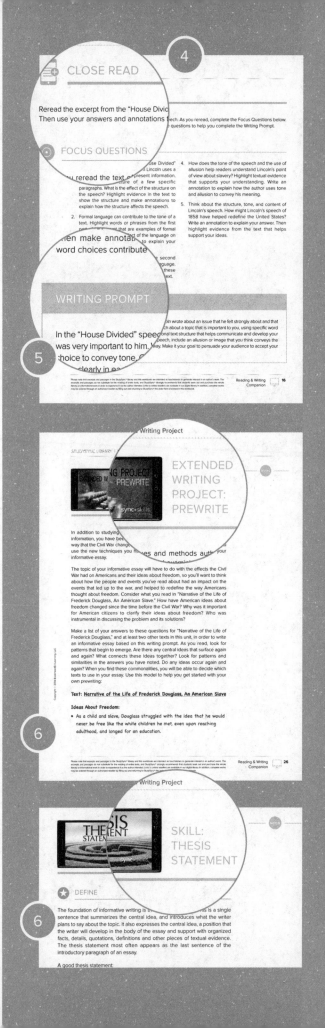

✸✸studysync®

Reading & Writing Companion

What happens when life changes direction?

Turning Points

Turning Points

TEXTS

TEXTS

EXTENDED WRITING PROJECT

HATCHET

FICTION

Gary Paulsen
1987

INTRODUCTION

n this gripping tale of survival by author Gary Paulsen, 13 year-old Brian is left stranded in the Canadian wilderness after his pilot has a heart attack and their plane crashes in a lake. The excerpt describes the day after the crash.

"Nothing. It kept coming back to that. He had nothing."

 FIRST READ

Excerpt from Chapter 5

1   They would look for him, look for the plane. His father and mother would be frantic. They would tear the world apart to find him. Brian had seen searches on the news, seen movies about lost planes. When a plane went down they mounted **extensive** searches and almost always they found the plane within a day or two. Pilots all filed flight plans—a detailed plan for where and when they were going to fly, with all the courses explained. They would come, they would look for him. The searchers would get government planes and cover both sides of the flight plan filed by the pilot and search until they found him.

2   Maybe even today. They might come today. This was the second day after the crash. No. Brian frowned. Was it the first day or the second day? They had gone down in the afternoon and he had spent the whole night out cold. So this was the first real day. But they could still come today. They would have started the search immediately when Brian's plane did not arrive.

3   Yeah, they would probably come today.

4   Probably come in here with **amphibious** planes, small bushplanes with floats that could land right here on the lake and pick him up and take him home.

5   Which home? The father home or the mother home. He stopped the thinking. It didn't matter. Either on to his dad or back to his mother. Either way he would probably be home by late night or early morning, home where he could sit down and eat a large, cheesy, juicy burger with tomatoes and double fries with ketchup and a thick chocolate shake.

6   And there came hunger.

7   Brian rubbed his stomach. The hunger had been there but something else— fear, pain—had held it down. Now, with the thought of the burger, the

Please note that excerpts and passages in the StudySync® library and this workbook are intended as touchstones to generate interest in an author's work. The excerpts and passages do not substitute for the reading of entire texts, and StudySync® strongly recommends that students seek out and purchase the whole literary or informational work in order to experience it as the author intended. Links to online resellers are available in our digital library. In addition, complete works may be ordered through an authorized reseller by filling out and returning to StudySync® the order form enclosed in this workbook.

Reading & Writing Companion   **5**

Copyright © BookheadEd Learning, LLC

emptiness roared at him. He could not believe the hunger, had never felt it this way. The lake water had filled his stomach but left it hungry, and now it demanded food, screamed for food.

8   And there was, he thought, absolutely nothing to eat.

9   Nothing.

10 What did they do in the movies when they got stranded like this? Oh, yes, the hero usually found some kind of plant that he knew was good to eat and that took care of it. Just ate the plant until he was full or used some kind of cute trap to catch an animal and cook it over a slick little fire and pretty soon he had a full eight-course meal.

11 The trouble, Brian thought, looking around, was that all he could see was grass and brush. There was nothing **obvious to** eat and aside from about a million birds and the beaver he hadn't seen animals to trap and cook, and even if he got one somehow he didn't have any matches so he couldn't have a fire. . .

12 Nothing.

13 It kept coming back to that. He had nothing.

14 Well, almost nothing. As a matter of fact, he thought, I don't know what I've got or haven't got. Maybe I should try and figure out just how I stand. It will give me something to do—keep me from thinking of food. Until they come to find me.

15 Brian had once had an English teacher, a guy named Perpich, who was always talking about being positive, thinking positive, staying on top of things. That's how Perpich had put it—stay positive and stay on top of things. Brian thought of him now—wondered how to stay positive and stay on top of this. All Perpich would say is that I have to get **motivated**. He was always telling kids to get motivated.

16 Brian changed position so he was sitting on his knees. He reached into his pockets and took out everything he had and laid it on the grass in front of him.

17 It was pitiful enough. A quarter, three dimes, a nickel, and two pennies. A fingernail clipper. A billfold with a twenty dollar bill—"In case you get stranded at the airport in some small town and have to buy food," his mother had said—and some odd pieces of paper.

18   And on his belt, somehow still there, the hatchet his mother had given him. He had forgotten it and now reached around and took it out and put it in the grass. There was a touch of rust already forming on the cutting edge of the blade and he rubbed it off with his thumb.

19   That was it.

20   He frowned. No, wait—if he was going to play the game, might as well play it right. Perpich would tell him to quit messing around. Get motivated. Look at *all* of it, Robeson.

21   He had on a pair of good tennis shoes, now almost dry. And socks. And jeans and underwear and a thin leather belt and a T-shirt with a windbreaker so torn it hung on him in tatters.

22   And a watch. He had a digital watch still on his wrist but it was broken from the crash—the little screen blank—and he took it off and almost threw it away but stopped the hand motion and lay the watch on the grass with the rest of it.

23   There. That was it.

24   No, wait. One other thing. Those were all the things he had, but he also had himself. Perpich used to drum that into them—"You are your most valuable **asset**. Don't forget that. *You* are the best thing you have."

25   Brian looked around again. I wish you were here, Perpich. I'm hungry and I'd trade everything I have for a hamburger.

Excerpted from Hatchet *by Gary Paulsen, published by Simon & Schuster.*

 THINK QUESTIONS

1.   State one or more details from the text to support your understanding of Brian's family situation— either from ideas that are directly stated or ideas that you have inferred from clues in the text.

2.   How do Brian's thoughts, feelings, and reactions change as a response to what has happened to him? Cite textual evidence in your answer.

3.   How does the media affect Brian's perception of what a plane crash is like? Use evidence from the text in support of your answer.

4.   Use context to determine the meaning of the word **motivated** as it is used in *Hatchet*. Write your definition of "motivated" and tell how you arrived at it.

5.   Remembering that the Greek prefix *amphi-* means "both" and the Greek root *bios* means "life," use the context clues provided in the passage to determine the meaning of **amphibious**. Write your definition of "amphibious" and tell how you arrived at it.

CLOSE READ

Reread the excerpt from *Hatchet*. As you reread, complete the Focus Questions below. Then use your answers and annotations from the questions to help you complete the Writing Prompt.

FOCUS QUESTIONS

1. Explain how the author uses the first four paragraphs to indicate Brian's realization of the severity of his situation. Highlight evidence from the text and make annotations to explain your choices.

2. Paragraph 6 consists of a single four-word sentence fragment. Why would Paulsen only include these four words in the paragraph? What do they reveal about Brian's situation? Make inferences about the text and its deeper meaning. Support your answer with textual evidence and make annotations to explain your answer choices.

3. Paragraph 10 makes a brief detour from the action as the narrator reveals Brian's thoughts about a certain kind of movie. Why is this detour a valuable addition to the narrative? Why does he think of movies at this moment? Highlight textual evidence and make annotations to explain your choices.

4. In Paragraph 14 and in the final paragraph of the excerpt, the author shows Brian's thoughts in the first person, using the pronoun *I*, as if you could read Brian's mind. What impact does this technique have in contrast to the rest of the excerpt, where Brian is called *he*? Highlight textual evidence and make annotations to explain your ideas.

5. Perpich is an important character in this excerpt despite the fact that he is not directly part of the action. Why is he important? Even though Perpich is not physically with Brian, what impact does he have on him at this life-changing moment? How does the point of view help reveal this? Highlight evidence from the text and make annotations to support your explanation.

WRITING PROMPT

How does the point of view from which Gary Paulsen tells *Hatchet* help you understand Brian's actions, thoughts, and feelings? Why do you think Paulsen chose to use Brian's third-person limited point of view rather than either Brian's first-person point of view or a third-person objective point of view? Use your understanding of point of view to think about how the story would have been different if you had read it from those other points of view. Support your writing with evidence from the text.

GUTS:
THE TRUE STORIES BEHIND HATCHET AND THE BRIAN BOOKS

NON-FICTION
Gary Paulsen
2001

INTRODUCTION

Gary Paulsen is a prolific writer of novels, short stories, plays, and magazine articles. He is best known for his series of five books about the wilderness adventures of teenager Brian Robeson, beginning with *Hatchet*. In his nonfiction work *Guts*, Paulsen shares his own real-life adventures that led to his writing *Hatchet* and other books. In this excerpt, Paulsen reflects on an experience as a volunteer emergency worker that left him with a haunting memory.

"There was, of course, hope—there is always hope."

FIRST READ

From Chapter 1: Heart Attacks, Plane Crashes and Flying

1 Perhaps the single most catastrophic event in Brian's life in *Hatchet* is when the pilot dies of a heart attack. This forces Brian to fly the plane and land—in little more than an "aimed" crash—in a lake, where he swims free and saves himself.

2 Before I was fortunate enough to become successful as a writer, I worked at home, writing as much as I could between construction jobs. Because I had so much downtime, I added my name to a list of volunteers available to answer emergency ambulance calls. My wife and I lived then in a small prairie town in the middle of farm country, near the confluence of two major highways. The volunteer service was small, and all we had was one old ambulance donated by a city that had bought new ones. But we were the only service available for thousands of square miles.

3 We answered calls to highway wrecks, farm accidents, poisonings, gunshot accidents and many, many heart attacks. I would go out on the calls alone or with another man who also worked at home.

4 I saw at least a dozen heart attack victims in the first year. Sadly, most of them were dead before I arrived. The distances we had to cover were so great that we simply could not get there in time to save them. If we did arrive before they died, we had to wait an hour or more for the "flight for life" chopper from the nearest city. Often it arrived too late.

5   When I came to write *Hatchet*, I remembered one call to a small ranch some sixty miles northeast of Colorado Springs. It was early in the morning when the siren cut loose, and I ran half-dressed for my old truck, drove to the garage where the ambulance was kept and answered the phone hanging on the wall.

6   "Please come quick!" a woman said. "It's my Harvey. He's having chest pains."

7   She gave me the location of the ranch and I took off. It should have taken me a full twenty minutes to get there because of the roughness of the gravel roads but I arrived in fourteen by driving like a maniac.

8   It was just getting light as I ran into the house carrying our emergency bag, and I could smell what was happening as soon as I entered the kitchen. The lights were on and a man of about fifty was sitting at the kitchen table. His face was gray and he was holding his left shoulder with his right hand. He looked at me and smiled sheepishly, as if to apologize for the inconvenience, and started to say something but then stopped and looked again at the floor in what soldiers call the thousand-yard stare. His wife, a thin woman in jeans and a sweatshirt, stood by him, and she gave me what we called the Look— an expression that meant *Thank God you're here please save him please save him please save him*.

9   But the smell of methane was very strong and the gray look was very bad and as I reached for him to put him on his back, he jolted as if hit by electricity, stiffened in the kitchen chair and fell sideways to the floor. His eyes looked into mine. Directly into my eyes.

10 "Call the hospital and tell them to bring the chopper now," I said, and knelt to help him, but he was hit with another jolt that stiffened him and his eyes opened wide and the smell grew much stronger and I knew he was gone. There was, of course, hope—there is always hope. Even when I was called to car accidents and saw children I knew were dead, I would keep working on them because I could not bring myself to accept their death—the hope would not allow it—and I worked on this man now though the smell came up and the skin grew cold. I kept at the CPR because the woman kept giving me the Look and I could not give up hope. But minutes passed and then half an hour before I heard the sound of the rotors—which was very good time, though much too late for this man—and I kept working on him though I knew he was dead and I had seen him die, seen him move from his life into his death, and though I had seen death many times before, I had not seen it in this way. Not in the way his eyes looked into mine while the life left him.

Please note that excerpts and passages in the StudySync® library and this workbook are intended as touchstones to generate interest in an author's work. The excerpts and passages do not substitute for the reading of entire texts, and StudySync® strongly recommends that students seek out and purchase the whole literary or informational work in order to experience it as the author intended. Links to online resellers are available in our digital library. In addition, complete works may be ordered through an authorized reseller by filling out and returning to StudySync® the order form enclosed in this workbook.

Reading & Writing
Companion

11

11   Years later, when I came to write *Hatchet* and the scene where the pilot is dying, I remembered this man of all the men I saw dead from heart attacks and car wrecks and farm accidents. I remembered him and his eyes and I put him in the plane next to Brian because he was, above all things, real, and I wanted the book to be real. But I did not sleep well that night when I wrote him into the book and I will not sleep well tonight thinking of his eyes.

Excerpted from *Guts: The True Stories Behind Hatchet and the Brian Books* by Gary Paulsen, published by Laurel-Leaf Books.

 THINK QUESTIONS

1. What does the excerpt tell you about Gary Paulsen's life before he became a successful writer? Cite textual evidence in your answer.

2. From the text, what conclusions can you draw about Gary Paulsen as a person? Cite evidence from the text to support your answer.

3. What details does Gary Paulsen use to describe the appearance and expression of the wife of the heart attack victim? Why might Paulsen include these details? Cite evidence from the text to support your answer.

4. Use context clues to determine the meaning of the word **catastrophic** as it is used in *Guts: True Stories Behind* Hatchet *and the Brian Books*. Write your definition of "catastrophic" and tell how you arrived at it. Then check your meaning against the definition given in a dictionary.

5. Use context clues to determine the meaning of the word **sheepishly** as it is used in the excerpt. Write your definition of "sheepishly" and tell how you arrived at it. Then check your definition in a dictionary and revise if necessary.

CLOSE READ

Reread the excerpt from *Guts: The True Stories Behind* Hatchet *and the Brian Books*. As you reread, complete the Focus Questions below. Then use your answers and annotations from the questions to help you complete the Writing Prompt.

 ## FOCUS QUESTIONS

1. A single paragraph may have a distinct central or main idea, separate from that of the text as a whole. What is the central idea of the first paragraph of *Guts: The True Stories Behind* Hatchet *and the Brian Books*? What details does the author include to help you determine the central idea? Highlight textual evidence to support your answer and annotate to explain your ideas.

2. In paragraph 3, Paulsen uses the word "accident" twice. The word "accident" comes from a Latin prefix, *ad-*, and a Latin root word, *cadere*. The prefix *ad-* means "toward or to," while the root *cadere* means "to fall." Given this knowledge and the context of the paragraph, what is the meaning of "accident"? Highlight clues in the text that helped you determine it.

3. In paragraph 9, how do the details the author includes support the central idea of Chapter 1? Highlight textual evidence and annotate to explain your ideas.

4. Summarize Chapter 1 of *Guts* in your own words, making sure to include the most important events or ideas without adding your personal opinions. Highlight textual evidence and annotate to explain your ideas.

5. How is the event at the ranch near Colorado Springs significant for Paulsen, and how does it become a turning point in his life? Highlight evidence from the text to support your answer and annotate to explain your ideas.

WRITING PROMPT

Reread the excerpt from *Guts: The True Stories Behind* Hatchet *and the Brian Books*, stating the central idea of the text and at least three details that support it. Note how the author uses language, particularly words with Greek and Latin roots and affixes, such as "catastrophic." How does this contribute to or support the central idea? Then, use your understanding of the central idea to describe what can happen when life changes direction. Remember to write clearly, using complete sentences and supporting your ideas with evidence from the text.

Please note that excerpts and passages in the StudySync® library and this workbook are intended as touchstones to generate interest in an author's work. The excerpts and passages do not substitute for the reading of entire texts, and StudySync® strongly recommends that students seek out and purchase the whole literary or informational work in order to experience it as the author intended. Links to online resellers are available in our digital library. In addition, complete works may be ordered through an authorized reseller by filling out and returning to StudySync® the order form enclosed in this workbook.

Reading & Writing Companion   **13**

ISLAND OF THE BLUE DOLPHINS

FICTION
Scott O'Dell
1960

INTRODUCTION

Based on a true story, Scott Odell's *Island of the Blue Dolphins* tells the tale of twelve-year-old Karana and her brother Ramo, who are accidentally left behind on their island home after the rest of their tribe leaves. When Ramo is killed by a pack of wild dogs, Karana must learn to survive alone. In this excerpt, Karana has just wounded the leader of the dog pack.

"I fitted an arrow and pulled back the string, aiming at his head."

FIRST READ

Excerpt from Chapter 15

1 There were no tracks after the rain, but I followed the trail to the pile of rocks where I had seen them before. On the far side of the rocks I found the big gray dog. He had the broken arrow in his chest and he was lying with one of his legs under him.

2 He was about ten **paces** from me so I could see him clearly. I was sure that he was dead, but I lifted the spear and took good aim at him. Just as I was about to throw the spear, he raised his head a little from the earth and then let it drop.

3 This surprised me greatly and I stood there for a while not knowing what to do, whether to use the spear or my bow. I was used to animals playing dead until they suddenly turned on you or ran away.

4 The spear was the better of the two weapons at this distance, but I could not use it as well as the other, so I climbed onto the rocks where I could see him if he ran. I placed my feet carefully. I had a second arrow ready should I need it. I fitted an arrow and pulled back the string, aiming at his head.

5 Why I did not send the arrow I cannot say. I stood on the rock with the bow pulled back and my hand would not let it go. The big dog lay there and did not move and this may be the reason. If he had gotten up I would have killed him. I stood there for a long time looking down at him and then I climbed off the rocks.

6 He did not move when I went up to him, nor could I see him breathing until I was very close. The head of the arrow was in his chest and the broken **shaft** was covered with blood. The thick fur around his neck was matted from the rain.

Please note that excerpts and passages in the StudySync® library and this workbook are intended as touchstones to generate interest in an author's work. The excerpts and passages do not substitute for the reading of entire texts, and StudySync® strongly recommends that students seek out and purchase the whole literary or informational work in order to experience it as the author intended. Links to online resellers are available in our digital library. In addition, complete works may be ordered through an authorized reseller by filling out and returning to StudySync® the order form enclosed in this workbook.

Reading & Writing Companion   **15**

7   I do not think that he knew I was picking him up, for his body was **limp**, as if he were dead. He was very heavy and the only way I could lift him was by kneeling and putting his legs around my shoulders.

8   In this manner, stopping to rest when I was tired, I carried him to the headland.

9   I could not get through the opening under the fence, so I cut the bindings and lifted out two of the whale ribs and thus took him into the house. He did not look at me or raise his head when I laid him on the floor, but his mouth was open and he was breathing.

10 The arrow had a small point, which was **fortunate**, and came out easily though it had gone deep. He did not move while I did this, nor afterwards as I cleaned the wound with a peeled stick from a coral bush. This bush has poisonous berries, yet its wood often heals wounds that nothing else will.

11 I had not gathered food for many days and the baskets were empty, so I left water for the dog and, after mending the fence, went down to the sea. I had no thought that he would live and I did not care.

12 All day I was among the rocks gathering shellfish and only once did I think of the wounded dog, my enemy, lying there in the house, and then to wonder why I had not killed him.

13 He was still alive when I got back, though he had not moved from the place where I had left him. Again I cleaned the wound with a coral twig. I then lifted his head and put water in his mouth, which he swallowed. This was the first time that he had looked at me since the time I had found him on the trail. His eyes were sunken and they looked out at me from far back in his head.

14 Before I went to sleep I gave him more water. In the morning I left food for him when I went down to the sea, and when I came home he had eaten it. He was lying in the corner, watching me. While I made a fire and cooked my supper, he watched me. His yellow eyes followed me wherever I moved.

15 That night I slept on the rock, for I was afraid of him, and at dawn as I went out I left the hole under the fence open so he could go. But he was there when I got back, lying in the sun with his head on his paws. I had speared two fish, which I cooked for my supper. Since he was very thin, I gave him one of them, and after he had eaten it he came over and lay down by the fire, watching me with his yellow eyes that were very narrow and slanted up at the corners.

16 Four nights I slept on the rock, and every morning I left the hole under the fence open so he could leave. Each day I speared a fish for him and when I got home he was always at the fence waiting for it. He would not take the fish

from me so I had to put it on the ground. Once I held out my hand to him, but at this he backed away and showed his teeth.

17 On the fourth day when I came back from the rocks early he was not there at the fence waiting. A strange feeling came over me. Always before when I returned, I had hoped that he would be gone. But now as I crawled under the fence I did not feel the same.

18 I called out, "Dog, Dog," for I had no other name for him.

19 I ran toward the house, calling it. He was inside. He was just getting to his feet, stretching himself and yawning. He looked first at the fish I carried and then at me and moved his tail.

20 That night I stayed in the house. Before I fell asleep I thought of a name for him, for I could not call him Dog. The name I thought of was Rontu, which means in our language Fox Eyes.

Excerpted from Island of the Blue Dolphins *by Scott O'Dell, published by Sandpiper.*

 THINK QUESTIONS

1. Why does Karana, the narrator, decide not to shoot the wounded dog? Cite textual evidence to support your answer.

2. Do you think Karana has hunted with a bow and arrow before? Note evidence in the text that supports your answer.

3. Why does the dog back away and show his teeth when Karana goes up to feed him? Cite textual evidence to support your answer.

4. Use context to determine the meaning of the word **fortunate** as it is used in *Island of the Blue Dolphins*. Write your definition of "fortunate" and tell how you arrived at it. How might the word "fortunate" be related to the word "fortune"?

5. Use context clues to determine the meaning of **limp** as it is used in *Island of the Blue Dolphins*. Write your definition and note any clues that helped you to define the word. How does its relationship to other words in the sentence help you to figure out its meaning?

Please note that excerpts and passages in the StudySync® library and this workbook are intended as touchstones to generate interest in an author's work. The excerpts and passages do not substitute for the reading of entire texts, and StudySync® strongly recommends that students seek out and purchase the whole literary or informational work in order to experience it as the author intended. Links to online resellers are available in our digital library. In addition, complete works may be ordered through an authorized reseller by filling out and returning to StudySync® the order form enclosed in this workbook.

Reading & Writing Companion   **17**

CLOSE READ

Reread the excerpt from *Island of the Blue Dolphins*. As you reread, complete the Focus Questions below. Then use your answers and annotations from the questions to help you complete the Writing Prompt.

FOCUS QUESTIONS

1. Reread paragraphs 1 through 4. What evidence can be found in the text that suggests hunting is an important skill for Karana and others who once lived on the island? Make annotations to explain your answer.

2. Reread paragraphs 14 through 16. What evidence in the text helps to communicate the dog's feelings about Karana and the situation? Highlight evidence of the dog's actions and reactions, and make annotations to explain what they show about the dog's perspective.

3. Reread paragraphs 13 through 15. How does the author use a description of the gray dog's eyes to show the progress of his recovery in the selection? Cite textual evidence in your response.

4. Remember that Karana's brother Ramo was killed by a group of wild dogs, yet Karana seems to be uncertain about her true feelings for the gray dog she tried to kill. Highlight textual evidence that supports this statement. Why might she feel so uncertain about her true feelings?

5. What happens between Karana and the dog at the end of the selection? How do their feelings toward one another change? How might both of their lives change direction after this? Cite textual evidence to support your answer.

WRITING PROMPT

Island of the Blue Dolphins is written using first-person point of view, and everything we learn about the events in the story come from the observations of Karana, the main character. In third-person omniscient point of view, on the other hand, the narrator of the story is an observer rather than a character, and reveals the thoughts and feelings of every character in the story. How would telling Karana's encounter with the wild dog from the third person omniscient point of view reveal more information about the thoughts and feelings of both characters? Use your understanding of text evidence and point of view to arrive at your answer. Support your writing with evidence from the text.

DRAGONWINGS

FICTION
Lawrence Yep
1975

INTRODUCTION

Laurence Yep's *Dragonwings* tells the story of eight-year-old Moon Shadow, who sails from China early in the 20th century to join his father Windrider in San Francisco. Though working at a laundry, Windrider is a genius who dreams of flying. The excerpt describes the boy's yearning to be with his father.

"I knew as little about my father as I knew about the land of the Golden Mountain."

 FIRST READ

Excerpt from: The Land of the Demons
(February—March, 1903)

1   Ever since I can remember, I had wanted to know about the Land of the Golden Mountain, but my mother had never wanted to talk about it. All I knew was that a few months before I was born, my father had left our home in the Middle Kingdom, or China, as the white demons call it, and traveled over the sea to work in the demon land. There was plenty of money to be made among the demons, but it was also dangerous. My own grandfather had been **lynched** about thirty years before by a mob of white demons almost the moment he had set foot on their shores.

2   Mother usually said she was too busy to answer my questions. It was a fact that she was overworked, for Grandmother was too old to help her with the heavy work, and she had to try to do both her own work and Father's on our small farm. The rice had to be grown from seeds, and the seedlings transplanted to the paddies, and the paddies tended and harvested. Besides this, she always had to keep one eye on our very active pig to keep him from rooting in our small vegetable patch. She also had to watch our three chickens, who loved to wander away from our farm.

3   Any time I brought up the subject of the Golden Mountain, Mother suddenly found something going wrong on our farm. Maybe some seedlings had not been planted into their underwater beds properly, or perhaps our pig was eating the wrong kind of garbage, or maybe one of our chickens was dirtying our doorway. She always had some good excuse for not talking about the Golden Mountain. I knew she was afraid of the place, because every chance we got, she would take me into the small temple in our village and we would pray for Father's safety, though she would never tell me what she was afraid of. It was a small satisfaction to her that our prayers had worked so far. Mother was never stingy about burning incense for Father.

4   I was curious about the Land of the Golden Mountain mainly because my father was there. I had, of course, never seen my father. And we could not go to live with him for two reasons. For one thing, the white demons would not let wives join their husbands on the Golden Mountain because they did not want us settling there permanently. And for another thing, our own **clans** discouraged wives from leaving because it would mean an end to the money the husbands sent home to their families—money which was then spent in the Middle Kingdom. The result was that the wives stayed in the villages, seeing their husbands every five years or so if they were lucky though sometimes there were longer separations, as with Mother and Father.

5   We had heavy debts to pay off, including the cost of Father's ticket. And Mother and Grandmother had decided to invest the money Father sent to us in buying more land and livestock. At any rate, there was no money to spare for Father's visit back home. But my mother never complained about the hard work or the loneliness. As she said, we were the people of the Tang, by which she meant we were a tough, hardy, patient race. (We did not call ourselves Chinese, but the people of the Tang, after that famous **dynasty** that had helped settle our area some eleven hundred years ago. It would be the same as if an English demon called himself a man of the *Tudors*, the dynasty of *Henry VIII and* of *Elizabeth I*—though demon names sound so drab compared to ours.)

6   But sometimes Mother's patience wore thin. It usually happened when we walked over to the small side room in the Temple, where classes were also held. Like many other people, Mother and Grandmother could neither read nor write; but for a small fee, the village schoolmaster would read one of Father's weekly letters to us or write a letter at our **dictation**. In the evening after dinner, we would join the line of people who had a husband or brothers or sons overseas. There we would wait until it was our turn to go inside the Temple, and Mother would nervously turn the letter over and over again in her hands until Grandmother would tell her she was going to wear out the letter before we could read it.

7   To tell the truth, I knew as little about my father as I knew about the Land of the Golden Mountain. But Mother made sure that I knew at least one important thing about him: He was a maker of the most marvelous kites. Everyone in the village said he was a master of his craft, and his kites were often treasured by their owners like family **heirlooms**. As soon as I was big enough to hold the string, Mother took me out to the hill near our village where we could fly one of Father's kites. Just the two of us would go.

8   But you won't appreciate my father's skill if you think flying a kite—any kind of a kite—is just putting a bunch of paper and sticks up into the air. I remember the first time we went to fly a kite. There was nothing like the thrill

Please note that excerpts and passages in the StudySync® library and this workbook are intended as touchstones to generate interest in an author's work. The excerpts and passages do not substitute for the reading of entire texts, and StudySync® strongly recommends that students seek out and purchase the whole literary or informational work in order to experience it as the author intended. Links to online resellers are available in our digital library. In addition, complete works may be ordered through an authorized reseller by filling out and returning to StudySync® the order form enclosed in this workbook.

Reading & Writing Companion   21

NOTES

when my kite first leaped up out of Mother's hands into the air. Then she showed me how to pull and tug and guide the kite into the winds. And when the winds caught the kite, it shot upward. She told me then how the string in my hand was like a leash and the kite was like a hound that I had sent hunting, to flush a sunbeam or a stray **phoenix** out of the clouds.

Excerpted from *Dragonwings* by Lawrence Yep, published by HarperCollins Publishers.

THINK QUESTIONS

1. Refer to one or more details from the text to support your understanding of how Moon Shadow feels about the Land of the Golden Mountain—both from ideas that are directly stated and ideas that you have inferred from clues in the text.

2. Citing evidence from the text, write two or three sentences describing how Moon Shadow's mother displays strength.

3. Write two or three sentences exploring what Moon Shadow knows about his father.

4. Use context clues to determine the meaning of the word **lynched** as it is used in *Dragonwings*. Write your definition of lynched and tell how you arrived at it.

5. Use the context clues provided in the passage to determine the suggested meaning of **heirloom**. Describe the feeling that a reader might associate with "heirloom" as it is used in this context. What other words might have similar meanings and similar feelings associated with them?

CLOSE READ

Reread the excerpt from *Dragonwings*. As you reread, complete the Focus Questions below. Then use your answers and annotations from the questions to help you complete the Writing Prompt.

FOCUS QUESTIONS

1. As you reread the text of *Dragonwings*, remember that the story is told by eight-year-old Moon Shadow. Readers see and experience things from his point of view. In the excerpt, what details in paragraphs 1, 4, and 5 reveal Moon Shadow's point of view about the Land of the Golden Mountain and the people there? What are his ideas based on? Highlight evidence in the text, and explain how the words and phrases you've chosen reveal Moon Shadow's thoughts about the land and its people.

2. In paragraphs 2, 3, and 5, Moon Shadow describes his family's life on a small farm in China. What can you infer about their exposure to the world? How does this reality contrast with Moon Shadow's knowledge about the Land of the Golden Mountain in paragraph 1? Highlight textual evidence and make annotations to explain your choices.

3. An author may use words with particular connotations to draw an emotional response from the reader. Which words or phrases in paragraph 7 draw positive responses? How do these word choices help you understand Moon Shadow's feelings about his father? Highlight textual evidence and make annotations to explain how the word or phrase is being used.

4. In paragraph 8, which words or phrases does the author use to describe Moon Shadow's memory of flying his first kite? Highlight textual evidence and make annotations to replace words with positive connotations with words that are neutral in their associations. How would the impact of this scene on the reader be different if Yep had used more neutral words in paragraph 8?

5. Use your understanding of connotation and denotation in this excerpt to identify how the author's choice of the word "demon" has an impact on the selection, and explain what this impact is. Highlight evidence from the text and make annotations that will help support your ideas.

WRITING PROMPT

In *Dragonwings*, how do the word choices the author makes have an impact on the reader's understanding of Moon Shadow and his world? What do they reveal about Moon Shadow' point of view? Use your understanding of connotation and denotation to explain Moon Shadow's thoughts and feelings. Support your writing with evidence from the text.

Please note that excerpts and passages in the StudySync® library and this workbook are intended as touchstones to generate interest in an author's work. The excerpts and passages do not substitute for the reading of entire texts, and StudySync® strongly recommends that students seek out and purchase the whole literary or informational work in order to experience it as the author intended. Links to online resellers are available in our digital library. In addition, complete works may be ordered through an authorized reseller by filling out and returning to StudySync® the order form enclosed in this workbook.

Reading & Writing Companion   **23**

THE FATHER OF CHINESE AVIATION

NON-FICTION
Rebecca Maksel
2008

INTRODUCTION

I n 1903, Orville and Wilbur Wright made aviation history by becoming the first to build and fly a powered airplane. Their success fascinated Feng Ru, a Chinese immigrant and self-taught engineer living in California. Feng soon established an airplane manufacturing company in Oakland and completed his first plane in 1908. A few years later, he returned to China and continued his pioneering efforts in aviation there. Today, Feng Ru is known as the "Father of Chinese Aviation."

"Upon hearing of the Wright brothers' success, Feng turned his attention to aviation..."

FIRST READ

Feng Ru made history on the California coast, then introduced airplanes to his native land.

1   At twilight on a Tuesday evening in September 1909, Feng Ru prepared to test an airplane of his own design above the gently rolling hills of Oakland, California. It was just six years after Orville and Wilbur Wright took to the skies at Kill Devil Hills, North Carolina, and only a year after their first public flights.

2   "The big bi-plane, with its four starting wheels tucked beneath it like the talons of a bird, sailed slowly in an elliptical course around the crest of the hill nearly back to the starting point," reported the *Oakland Enquirer* in its September 23 edition. For an astonishing 20 minutes Feng circled the Piedmont area, never more than 12 feet off the ground. Suddenly, a bolt holding the propeller to the shaft snapped, sending Feng tumbling to earth, bruised but otherwise unharmed.

3   While Feng Ru is little known in the United States, his fame in China is equivalent to the Wright brothers'. Middle and high schools are named in his honor, and his childhood home is a museum; China even considers its space program to be based upon the foundations of Feng's work.

4   Feng immigrated to the U.S. from China sometime between 1894 and 1898, when he was in his early teens, and immediately set to work doing odd jobs at a Chinese mission in San Francisco. "He was staggered by America's power and prosperity. He understood that industrialization made the country great, and felt that industrialization could do the same for China," says historian Patti Gully, who has co-authored a book on the contributions of Chinese living outside their country to the development of aviation in China. "So he went east to learn all he could about machines, working in shipyards, power plants, machine shops, anywhere he could acquire mechanical knowledge."

NOTES

5   Feng became well known for developing alternate versions of the water pump, the generator, the telephone, and the wireless telegraph, some of which were used by San Francisco's Chinese businessmen. But upon hearing of the Wright brothers' success, Feng turned his attention to aviation, laboriously translating into Chinese anything he could find on the Wrights, Glenn Curtiss and, later, French aircraft designer Henri Farman.

6   By 1906, Feng decided to return to California to establish an aircraft factory, building airplanes of his own design. San Francisco's massive earthquake and resulting fire forced him to relocate to Oakland instead, where, funded by local Chinese businessmen, Feng erected his workshop—a 10- by eight-foot shack. Jammed into this small space were tools, books, journals, mechanical projects, aircraft parts—and Feng himself, who rarely finished work before 3 a.m.

7   In this tiny spot, the self-taught engineer established the Guangdong Air Vehicle Company in 1909, and completed his first airplane that year, according to the American Institute of Aeronautics and Astronautics. During one test flight, Feng lost control of his airplane (not an unusual occurrence), which plunged into his workshop, setting it ablaze. Feng and his three assistants moved operations to an Oakland hayfield, referred to by the *New York Times* and the *Washington Post* as "a hidden retreat."

8   "They posted guards at the perimeters of the field to discourage the curious," says Gully, "and talked to visitors through a crack in the wall."

9   So anxious was Feng to keep his invention secret that he had the engine castings made by different East Coast machine shops, then assembled the parts himself. His discretion paid off; Feng's successful test flights were covered by mainstream press, and his work was praised by revolutionary Sun Yat-sen. By 1911, as the *New York Times* reported on February 21: "[Feng] will leave here for his native land to-morrow, taking with him a biplane of the Curtiss type, in which he intends to make exhibition flights. It is believed that he will be the first aviator to rise from the ground in China. . . . The machine he is taking to China is of his own construction. The aviator is financed by six of his countrymen, residents of Oakland, who will accompany him on the trip. The first flights will be tried at Hongkong and Canton."

10 Feng was leaving just in time: anti-Chinese sentiment was on the rise in the American West, and the Oregonian reported of the pilot's latest flight: "Immigration officials and customs inspectors are today said to be gnashing their teeth. They find it hard enough to keep the Chinese out now, without having them dropping in on flying machines."

11 When Feng arrived in Hong Kong on March 21, 1911, by custom he should have headed immediately toward his ancestral village to pay his respects.

NOTES

But even with his family urging him to come home, the preoccupied inventor was so obsessed with his airplane that it took him two months to fulfill his duties.

12   On August 26, 1912, Feng was killed while performing an aerial exhibition before a crowd of 1,000 spectators. "He was performing in a plane of his own design and manufacture," says Gully. "He was flying at about 120 feet and had traveled about five miles before the accident. I've read a report that he put his machine into an extreme climb, but his engine seemed to fail and the aircraft fell to the ground. It sounds like a classic stall, but of course no one knew about such things in those days. His aircraft smashed into a bamboo grove, and his injuries included a pierced lung. As he lay dying, he reportedly told his assistants, 'Your faith in the progress of your cause is by no means to be affected by my death.'"

13   The Republic of China gave Feng Ru a full military funeral, awarding him the posthumous rank of a major general. At Sun Yat-Sen's request, the words "Chinese Aviation Pioneer" were engraved upon Feng's tombstone.

First appeared on airspacemag.com on August 13, 2008.

 THINK QUESTIONS

1. Cite textual evidence that Feng Ru was extremely devoted to his work of creating airplanes.

2. State two or three details from the text to support the idea that Feng Ru was indeed "The Father of Chinese Aviation."

3. Based on textual evidence, support the idea that being in the United States helped Feng Ru pursue his dream of designing and building an airplane.

4. Remembering that the Latin root *avi* means "bird," use this knowledge, in addition to the context, to determine the meaning of the word **aviation** as it is used in "The Father of Chinese Aviation." Write your definition of "aviation" and tell how you got it.

5. Remembering that the Latin suffix *-ence* means "an instance, act, or condition of," use the suffix, the root, and context clues provided in the passage to determine the meaning of **occurrence**. Write your definition of occurrence and tell how you arrived at it.

CLOSE READ

Reread the article "The Father of Chinese Aviation." As you reread, complete the Focus Questions below. Then use your answers and annotations from the questions to help you complete the Writing Prompt.

 ## FOCUS QUESTIONS

1. What information does paragraph 3 provide to support the idea that Feng Ru is honored in his native China? Highlight textual evidence in the paragraph and make annotations to support your answer.

2. Based on the details given in paragraphs 6 and 7, describe the difficult conditions that Feng worked in. Highlight textual evidence to support your ideas and make annotations to explain your answer choices.

3. What central idea about taking risks can be inferred from paragraphs 6 and 7 of the article? Highlight textual evidence and make annotations to explain your idea.

4. What central idea about racism can be logically inferred from paragraph 10 of the article? Highlight textual evidence and write annotations to explain your idea.

5. Paragraph 4 says that Feng Ru "was staggered by America's power and prosperity." Compare the denotation and connotation of the word *staggered*. What is the emotional impact of the word? Explain the impact that American industrialization had on Feng Ru's life. What other events influenced Feng Ru's work? Highlight textual evidence in the paragraph to support your answer.

WRITING PROMPT

The central idea of a text tells you what it is mostly about. The supporting details help you understand the central idea. Use your understanding of textual evidence to help you find the central idea that emerges in the article "The Father of Aviation." Provide two or more pieces of evidence from the text to support your idea. Is the idea explicit in the text, or did you need to infer it?

I NEVER HAD IT MADE

NON-FICTION

Jackie Robinson

1972

INTRODUCTION

n 1947, Jackie Robinson, a talented baseball player and man of great character, made history as the first African American baseball player to "break the color line" and play in modern Major League Baseball. In this excerpt from his autobiography, Robinson reflects back on his experience and its impact on

"I had become the first black player in the major leagues."

FIRST READ

From the Preface: Today

1 I guess if I could choose one of the most important moments in my life, I would go back to 1947, in the Yankee Stadium in New York City. It was the opening day of the world series and I was for the first time playing in the series as a member of the Brooklyn Dodgers team. It was a history-making day. It would be the first time that a black man would be allowed to participate in a world series. I had become the first black player in the major leagues.

2 I was proud of that and yet I was uneasy. I was proud to be in the hurricane eye of a significant breakthrough and to be used to prove that a sport can't be called national if blacks are barred from it. Branch Rickey, the president of the Brooklyn Dodgers, had rudely awakened America. He was a man with high ideals, and he was also a shrewd businessman. Mr. Rickey had shocked some of his fellow baseball tycoons and angered others by deciding to smash the unwritten law that kept blacks out of the big leagues. He had chosen me as the person to lead the way.

3 It hadn't been easy. Some of my own teammates refused to accept me because I was black. I had been forced to live with snubs and rebuffs and rejections. Within the club, Mr. Rickey had put down rebellion by letting my teammates know that anyone who didn't want to accept me could leave. But the problems within the Dodgers club had been minor compared to the opposition outside. It hadn't been that easy to fight the resentment expressed by players on other teams, by the team owners, or by bigoted fans screaming "n——." The hate mail piled up. There were threats against me and my family and even out-and-out attempts at physical harm to me.

4 Some things counterbalanced this ugliness. Black people supported me with total loyalty. They supported me morally: they came to sit in a hostile audience in unprecedented numbers to make the turnstiles hum as they never had

before at ballparks all over the nation. Money is America's God, and business people can dig black power if it coincides with green power, so these fans were important to the success of Mr. Rickey's "Noble Experiment."

5   Some of the Dodgers who swore they would never play with a black man had a change of mind, when they realized I was a good ballplayer who could be helpful in their earning a few thousand more dollars in world series money. After the initial resistance to me had been crushed, my teammates started to give me tips in how to improve my game. They hadn't changed because they liked me any better; they had changed because I could help fill their wallets.

6   My fellow Dodgers were not decent out of self-interest alone. There were heartwarming experiences with some teammates; there was Southern-born Pee Wee Reese, who turned into a staunch friend. And there were others.

7   Mr. Rickey stands out as the man who inspired me the most. He will always have my admiration and respect. Critics had said, "Don't you know that your precious Mr. Rickey didn't bring you up out of the black leagues because he loved you? Are you stupid enough not to understand that the Brooklyn club profited hugely because of what your Mr. Rickey did?"

8   Yes, I know that. But I also know what a big gamble he took. A bond developed between us that lasted long after I had left the game. In a way I feel I was the son he had lost and he was the father I had lost.

9   There was more than just making money at stake in Mr. Rickey's decision. I learned that his family was afraid that his health was being undermined by the resulting pressures and that they pleaded with him to abandon the plan. His peers and fellow baseball moguls exerted all kinds of influence to get him to change his mind. Some of the press condemned him as a fool and a demagogue. But he didn't give in.

10 In a very real sense, black people helped make the experiment succeed. Many who came to the ball park had not been baseball fans before I began to play in the big leagues. Suppressed and repressed for so many years, they needed a victorious black man as a symbol. It would help them believe in themselves. But black support of the first black man in the majors was a complicated matter. The breakthrough created as much danger as it did hope. It was one thing for me out there on the playing field to be able to keep my cool in the face of insults. But it was another for all those black people sitting in the stands to keep from overreacting when they sensed a racial slur or an unjust decision. . . . I learned from Rachel, who had spent hours in the stands, that clergymen and laymen had held meetings in the black community to spread the word. We all knew about the help of the black press. Mr. Rickey and I owed them a great deal.

11   Children from all races came to the stands. The very young seemed to have no hangup at all about my being black. They just wanted me to be good, to deliver, to win. The inspiration of their innocence is amazing. I don't think I'll ever forget the small, shrill voice of a tiny white kid who, in the midst of a racially tense atmosphere during an early game in a Dixie town, cried out, "Attaboy, Jackie." It broke the tension and it made me feel I had to succeed.

12   The black and the young were my cheering squads. But also there were people—neither black nor young—people of all races and faiths and in all parts of the country, people who couldn't care less about my race.

13   Rachel was even more important to my success. I know that every successful man is supposed to say that without his wife he could never have accomplished success. It is gospel in my case. Rachel shared those difficult years that led to this moment and helped me through all the days thereafter. She has been strong, loving, gentle, and brave, never afraid to either criticize or comfort me.

Excerpted from *I Never Had It Made* by Jackie Robinson, published by HarperCollins Publishers.

 THINK QUESTIONS

1. Refer to one or more details from the text to support your understanding of why Jackie Robinson feels uneasy about opening day of the world series—both from ideas that are directly stated and ideas that you have inferred from clues in the text.

2. Use details from the text to write two or three sentences describing the different ways people treated Jackie Robinson.

3. Write two or three sentences exploring who Jackie Robinson credits with contributing to his success and why. Support your answer with textual evidence.

4. Use context to determine the meaning of the word **shrewd** as it is used in *I Never Had It Made*. Write your definition of **shrewd** and tell how you arrived at it. Then, use a dictionary or thesaurus to find the precise definition of the word, and revise your original definition as needed.

5. Use the context clues provided in the passage to determine the meaning of the word **inspiration** as it is used in *I Never Had It Made*. Write your definition of **inspiration** and tell how you arrived at it.

CLOSE READ

Reread the excerpt from *I Never Had It Made*. As you reread, complete the Focus Questions below. Then use your answers and annotations from the questions to help you complete the Writing Prompt.

FOCUS QUESTIONS

Question 3 asks you to use documents located on the web. Ask your teacher for URLs to find these documents. You can find it on YouTube or through another source.

1. In paragraph 3, Robinson describes his treatment by teammates and players on other teams. What can you infer about their view of African Americans in baseball? How does this treatment contrast with the responses of children in paragraph 11? How does this information contribute to your understanding of what Robinson experienced? Highlight evidence in the text to support your ideas and write annotations to explain your choices.

2. An author may use figurative language to express strong emotions or to add interest to the text. Which words or phrases in the text show the range of emotions Robinson experienced? Highlight your evidence and annotate to explain how each word or phrase is important.

3. View the video clip "Rachel Robinson: Meeting Branch Rickey". Which parts of the text does the video elaborate on? What new information about the relationship between Robinson and Branch Rickey did you learn from the video? Highlight your evidence and annotate to show what more you understand about Robinson and Branch Rickey after viewing the video.

4. In paragraph 11, use your understanding of text structure to explain the cause and effect relationship Robinson presents and how it contributes to the development of ideas. Highlight evidence in the text to support your ideas and write annotations to explain your choices.

5. Remember that the story is told by Jackie Robinson. Readers see and experience things through this one individual. In the text, what details in paragraphs 2, 4, and 10 reveal why Robinson's selection as the first black player in the major leagues was significant and contribute to the development of the ideas in the text? What impact did his selection have on the American culture? What did this change mean for different groups of people? Highlight evidence in the text and make annotations to explain why Robinson's selection is historically important.

WRITING PROMPT

Compare and contrast the video clip about Jackie Robinson's role in the Civil Rights Movement and the excerpt from *I Never Had It Made*. How are the two alike, and how do they differ? Be sure to comment on how each medium is structured and the kinds of language each one features. Does figurative language play a role in both? If not, does any element of the video fill the same role as the figures of speech in the text? How do the video and text support the overall message of what constitutes a turning point in life? Support your writing with evidence from the text and video.

Please note that excerpts and passages in the StudySync® library and this workbook are intended as touchstones to generate interest in an author's work. The excerpts and passages do not substitute for the reading of entire texts, and StudySync® strongly recommends that students seek out and purchase the whole literary or informational work in order to experience it as the author intended. Links to online resellers are available in our digital library. In addition, complete works may be ordered through an authorized reseller by filling out and returning to StudySync® the order form enclosed in this workbook.

Reading & Writing Companion   33

WARRIORS DON'T CRY

NON-FICTION

Melba Pattillo Beals
1994

INTRODUCTION

I n 1954, the Supreme Court decision *Brown* v. *the Board of Education of Topeka, Kansas* declared that segregation was unconstitutional and schools must be integrated. To thwart the efforts of the Arkansas governor to keep the first nine black students, including Melba Pattillo Beals, out of Central High School, President Eisenhower sent federal troops to Little Rock to make sure the students got in safely. In this excerpt, Beals describes how the soldiers escorted them through the

"The soldiers did not make eye contact as they surrounded us..."

 FIRST READ

 NOTES

1   The next morning, Wednesday, September 25, at 8 A.M., as we turned the corner near the Bateses' home, I saw them, about fifty uniformed soldiers of the 101st. Some stood still with their rifles at their sides, while others manned the jeeps parked at the curb. Still other troops walked about holding walkie-talkies to their ears. As I drew nearer to them I was fascinated by their well-shined boots. Grandma had always said that well-kept shoes were the mark of a disciplined individual. Their guns were also glistening as though they had been polished, and the creases were sharp in the pant legs of their uniforms.

2   I had heard all those newsmen say "Screaming Eagle Division of the 101st", but those were just words. I was seeing human beings, flesh-and-blood men with eyes that looked back at me. They resembled the men I'd seen in army pictures on TV and on the movie screen. Their faces were white, their expressions blank.

3   There were lots of people of both races standing around, talking to one another in whispers. I recognized some of the ministers from our churches. Several of them nodded or smiled at me. I was a little concerned because many people, even those who knew me well, were staring as though I were different from them.

4   Thelma and Minnijean stood together inspecting the soldiers close up while the other students milled about. I wondered what we were waiting for. I was told there was an assembly at Central with the military briefing the students.

5   Reporters hung from trees, perched on fences, stood on cars and darted about with their usual urgency. Cameras were flashing on all sides. There was an **eerie** hush over the crowd, not unlike the way I'd seen folks behave outside the home of the deceased just before a funeral.

Copyright © BookheadEd Learning, LLC

6　There were tears in Mother's eyes as she whispered good-bye. "Make this day the best you can," she said.

7　"Let's bow our heads for a word of prayer." One began to say some comforting words. I noticed tears were streaming down the faces of many of the adults. I wondered why they were crying and just at that moment when I had more hope of staying alive and keeping safe than I had since the **integration** began.

8　"Protect those youngsters and bring them home. Flood the Holy Spirit into the hearts and minds of those who would attack our children."

9　"Yes, Lord," several voices echoed.

10　One of the soldiers stepped forward and beckoned the driver of a station wagon to move it closer to the driveway. Two jeeps moved forward, one in front of the station wagon, one behind. Guns were mounted on the hoods of the jeeps.

11　We were already a half hour late for school when we heard the order "Move out" and the leader motioned us to get into the station wagon. As we collected ourselves and walked toward the caravan, many of the adults were crying openly. When I turned to wave to Mother Lois, I saw tears streaming down her cheeks. I couldn't go back to comfort her.

12　Sarge, our driver, was friendly and pleasant. He had a Southern accent, different from ours, different even from the one Arkansas whites had. We rolled away from the curb lined with people waving at us. Mama looked even more **distraught**. I remembered I hadn't kissed her good-bye.

13　Our convoy moved through streets lined with people on both sides, who stood as though they were waiting for a parade. A few friendly folks from our community waved as we passed by. Some of the white people looked totally horrified, while others raised their fists to us. Others shouted ugly words.

14　We pulled up to the front of the school. Groups of soldiers on guard were lined at intervals several feet apart. A group of twenty or more was running at breakneck speed up and down the street in front of Central High School, their rifles with bayonets pointed straight ahead. Sarge said they were doing crowd control—keeping the mob away from us.

15　About twenty soldiers moved toward us, forming an olive-drab square with one end open. I glanced at the faces of my friends. Like me, they appeared to be impressed by the **imposing** sight of military power. There was so much to see, and everything was happening so quickly. We walked through the open end of the square. Erect, rifles at their sides, their faces stern, the soldiers did not make eye contact as they surrounded us in a protective cocoon. After a long moment, the leader motioned us to move forward.

16   I felt proud and sad at the same time. Proud that I lived in a country that would go this far to bring justice to a Little Rock girl like me, but sad that they had to go to such great lengths. Yes, this is the United States, I thought to myself. There is a reason that I salute the flag. If these guys just go with us this first time, everything's going to be okay.

17   We began moving forward. The eerie silence of that moment would be forever etched into my memory. All I could hear was my own heartbeat and the sound of boots clicking on the stone.

18   Everyone seemed to be moving in slow motion as I peered past the raised **bayonets** of the 101st soldiers. I walked on the concrete path toward the front door of the school, the same path the Arkansas National Guard had blocked us from days before. We approached the stairs, our feet moving in unison to the rhythm of the marching click-clack sound of the Screaming Eagles. Step by step we climbed upward-where none of my people had ever before walked as a student. We stepped up the front door of Central High School and crossed the threshold into that place where angry segregationist mobs had forbidden us to go.

Excerpted from *Warriors Don't Cry* by Melba Pattillo Beals, published by Washington Square Press.

THINK QUESTIONS

1. Refer to one or more details from the text to support your understanding of why soldiers are escorting Beals and other students—both from ideas that are directly stated and ideas that you have inferred from clues in the text.

2. Write two or three sentences exploring how the presence of the students affected different individuals in the crowd in different ways. Cite evidence from the text in your sentences.

3. Cite evidence from the text that shows how Beals feels about being escorted through the crowds.

4. Use context clues to determine the meaning of the word **distraught** as it is used in *Warriors Don't Cry*. Write your definition of *distraught* and tell how you arrived at it. Then, use a dictionary to confirm the precise pronunciation of "distraught." Why might this word be challenging to pronounce if a reader is not familiar with it?

5. Using context clues provided in the passage, define **bayonets** and explain how you got your definition. Then, use a dictionary to determine the precise meaning and pronunciation of the word. Are the precise meaning and pronunciation what you expected? Explain.

Please note that excerpts and passages in the StudySync® library and this workbook are intended as touchstones to generate interest in an author's work. The excerpts and passages do not substitute for the reading of entire texts, and StudySync® strongly recommends that students seek out and purchase the whole literary or informational work in order to experience it as the author intended. Links to online resellers are available in our digital library. In addition, complete works may be ordered through an authorized reseller by filling out and returning to StudySync® the order form enclosed in this workbook.

Reading & Writing Companion   37

CLOSE READ

Reread the excerpt from *Warriors Don't Cry*. As you reread, complete the Focus Questions below. Then use your answers and annotations from the questions to help you complete the Writing Prompt.

FOCUS QUESTIONS

1. Reread paragraph 2 of the text. How does Beals portray the difference between hearing about a historical event on the news and actually living through it? Highlight words and phrases that show the contrast, and write annotations that explain these differences. How does paragraph 5 build on this contrast?

2. In paragraph 12 of the text, Beals makes a point to mention that she hadn't kissed her mother good-bye. Why was it important for her to share this with readers? What can you infer from this detail? Why is this information significant? Cite evidence from the text to support your answer.

3. Throughout the text, Beals never lets readers forget that soldiers are guarding her and her fellow classmates. Cite evidence from the text to explain what these soldiers represent. How do these details contribute to the central idea of the text?

4. Explain why the last two paragraphs of the selection are significant to the time order structure that Beals has laid out in the text. How might their impact change if Beals had begun her story with these paragraphs and then described what happened before them? Highlight parts of the text that support your answer.

5. Why was the experience of crossing the threshold into Central High School a life-changing event for Beals and other African Americans? What impact did her experiences on that day have on her feelings about her country? Highlight textual evidence to support your answer.

WRITING PROMPT

Identify the central idea of the excerpt and describe how the author's use of a sequential text structure helps her develop that central idea effectively. Then choose two to three paragraphs from the text and explain the essential role that each one plays in the text structure. What does each paragraph contribute to the sequence of events that Beals describes? How do your selected paragraphs add memorable facts and details to her account of this turning point in her life? What conclusion can you draw about her experience? Be sure to support your ideas with textual evidence.

Reading & Writing Companion

THE STORY OF MY LIFE

NON-FICTION
Helen Keller
1903

INTRODUCTION

Serious illness at the age of 19 months left Helen Keller both blind and deaf. Serving as an inspiration to millions, Keller overcame those handicaps and went on to become a renowned author and social activist. In this passage from her autobiography, six-year-old Helen meets the person who will change her

"'Light! give me light!' was the wordless cry of my soul."

 FIRST READ

Excerpt from Chapter IV

1 The most important day I remember in all my life is the one on which my teacher, Anne Mansfield Sullivan, came to me. I am filled with wonder when I consider the immeasurable contrasts between the two lives which it connects. It was the third of March, 1887, three months before I was seven years old.

2 On the afternoon of that eventful day, I stood on the porch, dumb, expectant. I guessed vaguely from my mother's signs and from the hurrying to and fro in the house that something unusual was about to happen, so I went to the door and waited on the steps. The afternoon sun penetrated the mass of honeysuckle that covered the porch, and fell on my upturned face. My fingers lingered almost unconsciously on the familiar leaves and blossoms which had just come forth to greet the sweet southern spring. I did not know what the future held of marvel or surprise for me. Anger and bitterness had preyed upon me continually for weeks and a deep languor had succeeded this passionate struggle.

3 Have you ever been at sea in a dense fog, when it seemed as if a tangible white darkness shut you in, and the great ship, tense and anxious, **groped** her way toward the shore with plummet and sounding-line, and you waited with beating heart for something to happen? I was like that ship before my education began, only I was without compass or sounding-line, and had no way of knowing how near the harbour was. "Light! give me light!" was the wordless cry of my soul, and the light of love shone on me in that very hour.

4 I felt approaching footsteps. I stretched out my hand as I supposed to my mother. Some one took it, and I was caught up and held close in the arms of her who had come to **reveal** all things to me, and, more than all things else, to love me.

5   The morning after my teacher came she led me into her room and gave me a doll. The little blind children at the Perkins **Institution** had sent it and Laura Bridgman had dressed it; but I did not know this until afterward. When I had played with it a little while, Miss Sullivan slowly spelled into my hand the word "d-o-l-l." I was at once interested in this finger play and tried to imitate it. When I finally succeeded in making the letters correctly I was flushed with childish pleasure and pride. Running downstairs to my mother I held up my hand and made the letters for doll. I did not know that I was spelling a word or even that words existed; I was simply making my fingers go in monkey-like imitation. In the days that followed I learned to spell in this uncomprehending way a great many words, among them pin, hat, cup and a few verbs like sit, stand and walk. But my teacher had been with me several weeks before I understood that everything has a name.

6   One day, while I was playing with my new doll, Miss Sullivan put my big rag doll into my lap also, spelled "d-o-l-l" and tried to make me understand that "d-o-l-l" applied to both. Earlier in the day we had had a tussle over the words "m-u-g" and "w-a-t-e-r." Miss Sullivan had tried to impress it upon me that "m-u-g" is mug and that "w-a-t-e-r" is water, but I persisted in **confounding** the two. In despair she had dropped the subject for the time, only to renew it at the first opportunity. I became impatient at her repeated attempts and, seizing the new doll, I dashed it upon the floor. I was keenly delighted when I felt the fragments of the broken doll at my feet. Neither sorrow nor regret followed my passionate outburst. I had not loved the doll. In the still, dark world in which I lived there was no strong **sentiment** or tenderness. I felt my teacher sweep the fragments to one side of the hearth, and I had a sense of satisfaction that the cause of my discomfort was removed. She brought me my hat, and I knew I was going out into the warm sunshine. This thought, if a wordless sensation may be called a thought, made me hop and skip with pleasure.

7   We walked down the path to the well-house, attracted by the fragrance of the honeysuckle with which it was covered. Some one was drawing water and my teacher placed my hand under the spout. As the cool stream gushed over one hand she spelled into the other the word water, first slowly, then rapidly. I stood still, my whole attention fixed upon the motions of her fingers. Suddenly I felt a misty consciousness as of something forgotten--a thrill of returning thought; and somehow the mystery of language was revealed to me. I knew then that "w-a-t-e-r" meant the wonderful cool something that was flowing over my hand. That living word awakened my soul, gave it light, hope, joy, set it free! There were barriers still, it is true, but barriers that could in time be swept away.

8   I left the well-house eager to learn. Everything had a name, and each name gave birth to a new thought. As we returned to the house every object which I touched seemed to quiver with life. That was because I saw everything with

Reading & Writing
Companion

NOTES

the strange, new sight that had come to me. On entering the door I remembered the doll I had broken. I felt my way to the hearth and picked up the pieces. I tried vainly to put them together. Then my eyes filled with tears; for I realized what I had done, and for the first time I felt repentance and sorrow.

9 I learned a great many new words that day. I do not remember what they all were; but I do know that mother, father, sister, teacher were among them-- words that were to make the world blossom for me, "like Aaron's rod, with flowers." It would have been difficult to find a happier child than I was as I lay in my crib at the close of that eventful day and lived over the joys it had brought me, and for the first time longed for a new day to come.

THINK QUESTIONS

1. How did Helen Keller's disabilities affect her before her teacher, Anne Sullivan, arrived? Support your answer with evidence from the text.

2. Did Anne Sullivan give Helen the doll simply as a present, or as a way to start her education? Refer to text evidence to support your answer.

3. Why is the episode at the well such a significant moment in Keller's life? Support your answer with details from the text.

4. Use context clues to determine the meaning of the word **reveal** as it is used in *The Story of My Life*. Write your definition of reveal and tell how you arrived at it.

5. The Latin root *in-* + *statuere* means "to set up." Use this information and context in the passage to determine the meaning of **institution**. Write your definition of institution and tell how you arrived at it.

CLOSE READ

Reread the excerpt from *The Story of My Life*. As you reread, complete the Focus Questions below. Then use your answers and annotations from the questions to help you complete the Writing Prompt.

FOCUS QUESTIONS

1. Writers of informational text often use the exact, or denotative, meaning of a word to construct literal meaning. In an autobiography, writers sometimes use the connotative meaning of a word when they tell about emotional moments in their own lives. In the sixth paragraph of *The Story of My Life*, Helen Keller recalls the "passionate outburst" she had when she took a doll Anne Sullivan had given her and dashed it to the floor. Keller also uses the word *passionate* in the second paragraph. Does this use of the word have a positive or negative connotation? Use textual evidence to support your answer.

2. In paragraph 2, Keller uses the word "languor" to describe the way she felt just before Anne Sullivan arrived. Use context clues in the sentence to define the word **languor**. Then use this text evidence to decide if the word has a more positive or more negative connotation as it is used here. Use a dictionary or thesaurus to confirm your definition. What word or words might have a similar meaning, but a different connotation?

3. The word *flushed* is a word that can have multiple denotative meanings: to drive from cover or from a hiding place; to turn red or blush; to clean or empty; a sudden feeling of emotion, such as excitement, pride, or anger. What meaning of the word *flushed* does Helen Keller use in the fifth paragraph? Does it have a positive or a negative connotation? Use evidence from the text to support your answer.

4. Most authors of informational text use a specific text structure to organize and present information. What text structure does Keller use throughout this excerpt? Cite textual evidence and annotate to support your answer.

5. In paragraph 7, Sullivan holds one of Keller's hands under a running waterspout and traces letters spelling "water" on Keller's other hand. How did this moment change Keller? How does this event support the central idea that Anne Sullivan opened up the world to Helen Keller? Highlight textual evidence and annotate to support your answer.

WRITING PROMPT

Keller experiences a change of emotions between paragraphs 6 and 8. How does the author's use of connotation in the text help the reader understand her change in feelings? How does her change relate to the central idea in the text? Support your writing with evidence from the text. Be sure to include words with positive and negative connotations from the paragraphs as textual evidence.

Please note that excerpts and passages in the StudySync® library and this workbook are intended as touchstones to generate interest in an author's work. The excerpts and passages do not substitute for the reading of entire texts, and StudySync® strongly recommends that students seek out and purchase the whole literary or informational work in order to experience it as the author intended. Links to online resellers are available in our digital library. In addition, complete works may be ordered through an authorized reseller by filling out and returning to StudySync® the order form enclosed in this workbook.

Reading & Writing Companion **43**

ELEVEN

FICTION
Sandra Cisneros
1991

INTRODUCTION

When her teacher insists that an ugly red sweater belongs to Rachel, the eleven year-old has exceptional thoughts, but can't share them. Even so, it's evident that the protagonist of Sandra Cisnero's short story has insight beyond her years.

"I'm eleven and it's my birthday today and I'm crying like I'm three..."

 FIRST READ

 NOTES

1   What they don't understand about birthdays and what they never tell you is that when you're eleven, you're also ten, and nine, and eight, and seven, and six, and five, and four, and three, and two, and one. And when you wake up on your eleventh birthday you expect to feel eleven, but you don't. You open your eyes and everything's just like yesterday, only it's today. And you don't feel eleven at all. You feel like you're still ten. And you are—underneath the year that makes you eleven.

2   Like some days you might say something stupid, and that's the part of you that's still ten. Or maybe some days you might need to sit on your mama's lap because you're scared, and that's the part of you that's five. And maybe one day when you're all grown up maybe you will need to cry like if you're three, and that's okay. That's what I tell Mama when she's sad and needs to cry. Maybe she's feeling three.

3   Because the way you grow old is kind of like an onion or like the rings inside a tree trunk or like my little wooden dolls that fit one inside the other, each year inside the next one. That's how being eleven years old is.

4   You don't feel eleven. Not right away. It takes a few days, weeks even, sometimes even months before you say Eleven when they ask you. And you don't feel smart eleven, not until you're almost twelve. That's the way it is.

5   Only today I wish I didn't have only eleven years rattling inside me like pennies in a tin Band-Aid box. Today I wish I was one hundred and two instead of eleven because if I was one hundred and two I'd have known what to say when Mrs. Price put the red sweater on my desk. I would've known how to tell her it wasn't mine instead of just sitting there with that look on my face and nothing coming out of my mouth.

NOTES

6 "Whose is this?" Mrs. Price says, and she holds the red sweater up in the air for all the class to see. "Whose? It's been sitting in the coatroom for a month."

7 "Not mine," says everybody. "Not me."

8 "It has to belong to somebody," Mrs. Price keeps saying, but nobody can remember. It's an ugly sweater with red plastic buttons and a collar and sleeves all stretched out like you could use it for a jump rope. It's maybe a thousand years old and even if it belonged to me I wouldn't say so.

9 Maybe because I'm skinny, maybe because she doesn't like me, that stupid Sylvia Saldivar says, "I think it belongs to Rachel." An ugly sweater like that, all raggedy and old, but Mrs. Price believes her. Mrs. Price takes the sweater and puts it right on my desk, but when I open my mouth nothing comes out.

10 "That's not, I don't, you're not . . . Not mine," I finally say in a little voice that was maybe me when I was four.

11 "Of course it's yours," Mrs. Price says, "I remember you wearing it once." Because she's older and the teacher, she's right and I'm not.

12 Not mine, not mine, not mine, but Mrs. Price is already turning to page thirty-two, and math problem number four. I don't know why but all of a sudden I'm feeling sick inside, like the part of me that's three wants to come out of my eyes, only I squeeze them shut tight and bite down on my teeth real hard and try to remember today I am eleven, eleven. Mama is making a cake for me for tonight, and when Papa comes home everybody will sing Happy birthday, happy birthday to you.

13 But when the sick feeling goes away and I open my eyes, the red sweater's still sitting there like a big red mountain. I move the red sweater to the corner of my desk with my ruler. I move my pencil and books and eraser as far from it as possible. I even move my chair a little to the right. Not mine, not mine, not mine.

14 In my head I'm thinking how long till lunchtime, how long till I can take the red sweater and throw it over the schoolyard fence, or leave it hanging on a parking meter, or bunch it up into a little ball and toss it in the alley. Except when math period ends Mrs. Price says loud and in front of everybody, "Now, Rachel, that's enough," because she sees I've shoved the red sweater to the tippy-tip corner of my desk and it's hanging all over the edge like a waterfall, but I don't care.

15 "Rachel," Mrs. Price says. She says it like she's getting mad. "You put that sweater on right now and no more nonsense."

16 "But it's not—"

17 "Now!" Mrs. Price says.

18 This is when I wish I wasn't eleven, because all the years inside of me—ten, nine, eight, seven, six, five, four, three, two, and one—are pushing at the back of my eyes when I put one arm through one sleeve of the sweater that smells like cottage cheese, and then the other arm through the other and stand there with my arms apart like if the sweater hurts me and it does, all itchy and full of germs that aren't mine.

19 That's when everything I've been holding in since this morning, since when Mrs. Price put the sweater on my desk, finally lets go, and all of a sudden I'm crying in front of everybody. I wish I was invisible but I'm not. I'm eleven and it's my birthday today and I'm crying like I'm three in front of everybody. I put my head down on the desk and bury my face in my stupid clown-sweater arms. My face all hot and spit coming out of my mouth because I can't stop the little animal noises from coming out of me, until there aren't any more tears left in my eyes, and it's just my body shaking like when you have the hiccups, and my whole head hurts like when you drink milk too fast.

20 But the worst part is right before the bell rings for lunch. That stupid Phyllis Lopez, who is even dumber than Sylvia Saldivar, says she remembers the red sweater is hers! I take it off right away and give it to her, only Mrs. Price pretends like everything's okay.

21 Today I'm eleven. There's a cake Mama's making for tonight, and when Papa comes home from work we'll eat it. There'll be candles and presents and everybody will sing Happy birthday, happy birthday to you, Rachel, only it's too late.

22 I'm eleven today. I'm eleven, ten, nine, eight, seven, six, five, four, three, two, and one, but I wish I was one hundred and two. I wish I was anything but eleven, because I want today to be far away already, far away like a runaway balloon, like a tiny o in the sky, so tiny-tiny you have to close your eyes to see it.

Please note that excerpts and passages in the StudySync® library and this workbook are intended as touchstones to generate interest in an author's work. The excerpts and passages do not substitute for the reading of entire texts, and StudySync® strongly recommends that students seek out and purchase the whole literary or informational work in order to experience it as the author intended. Links to online resellers are available in our digital library. In addition, complete works may be ordered through an authorized reseller by filling out and returning to StudySync® the order form enclosed in this workbook.

Reading & Writing Companion   47

THINK QUESTIONS

1. How does Rachel feel about the red sweater that is placed on her desk? Respond with textual evidence from the story as well as ideas that you have inferred from clues in the text.

2. According to Rachel, why does Sylvia say the sweater belongs to Rachel? Support your answer with textual evidence.

3. Write two or three sentences exploring why Mrs. Price responds as she does when Phyllis claims the sweater. Support your answer with textual evidence.

4. Use context clues to determine the meaning of the word **raggedy** as it is used in *Eleven*. Write your definition of "raggedy" and tell how you arrived at it.

5. Remembering that the Latin prefix *non-* means "not, or the reverse of," use the context clues provided in the passage to determine the meaning of **nonsense**. Write your definition of "nonsense" and tell how you arrived at it.

CLOSE READ

Reread the short story "Eleven." As you reread, complete the Focus Questions below. Then use your answers and annotations from the questions to help you complete the Writing Prompt.

FOCUS QUESTIONS

1. As you reread the text of "Eleven," remember that the story is told by the main character, eleven-year-old Rachel. In the first four paragraphs of the story, Rachel uses the second-person point of view by referring to readers as "you." Why do you think the author of the story chose to structure the story that way? Highlight details in the text and make annotations that support your thinking.

2. Beginning in paragraph 5, Rachel begins to tell readers the story from a first person point of view. Why does she do this? How does the change affect the structure of the story? Highlight evidence from the text and make annotations that support your thinking.

3. Reread paragraph 12. What figure of speech does the author use in this paragraph? What does this figure of speech mean? Make annotations to explain how you interpret this figure of speech, and highlight evidence from the text that supports your interpretation.

4. The author uses a figure of speech called a *simile* to compare two things that seem dissimilar, but that share certain qualities. Reread paragraph 19 and explain why "my whole head hurts like when you drink milk too fast" is an effective simile. Annotate your ideas using evidence from the text.

5. In the last paragraph, Rachel repeats an idea that she told readers at the beginning of the story. What idea does she repeat? How does this add to your understanding of Rachel and her experience? Why has this experience been a turning point for her? Highlight textual evidence and make annotations to explain your choices.

WRITING PROMPT

In "Eleven," Sandra Cisneros focuses the narrative on an embarrassing moment in the life of the main character. Analyze how that choice contributes to the overall development of the plot. What do we learn about Rachel through her description of this event that we might not otherwise know? How does the way Cisneros structures the story help build sympathy for Rachel? How do figures of speech such as similes contribute to the descriptions of Rachel and reveal her ideas about her world? How does the event support Rachel's theory that people are all the ages they've ever been? Support your writing with evidence from the text. Be sure to cite specific examples of similes and other figures of speech that contribute to your ideas.

Please note that excerpts and passages in the StudySync® library and this workbook are intended as touchstones to generate interest in an author's work. The excerpts and passages do not substitute for the reading of entire texts, and StudySync® strongly recommends that students seek out and purchase the whole literary or informational work in order to experience it as the author intended. Links to online resellers are available in our digital library. In addition, complete works may be ordered through an authorized reseller by filling out and returning to StudySync® the order form enclosed in this workbook.

Reading & Writing Companion **49**

THE PIGMAN

FICTION

Paul Zindel

1968

INTRODUCTION

While making prank calls soliciting donations to an imaginary charity, high school friends John and Lorraine dial the number of Mr. Angelo Pignati. The Pigman, as they come to know him, eagerly prolongs the conversation and agrees to donate money, inviting the youths to come by his house and pick up a check. In doing so, John and Lorraine discover a lonely, eccentric man with whom they might just develop a friendship.

"There were blue, black, yellow, orange, striped, green, and rainbow-colored pigs."

FIRST READ

From Chapter 5

1   "We should all go to the zoo tomorrow," Mr. Pignati said, again out of nowhere.

2   "Mr. Pignati," I said with an air of impatience, "Miss Truman and I have many other stops to make today. I mean, where would the L & J Fund be if we simply sat around . . . all day and went to zoos?"

3   "Yes," Lorraine said. "We really shouldn't have stayed this long."

4   "Oh, I'm sorry," Mr. Pignati said, and I couldn't help feeling sorry. His smile and bright eyes faded in front of us, and he got awkwardly to his feet. "Let me get the check," he said, and his voice was so depressed I thought he was really going to cry.

5   "You don't really have to—" Lorraine started, but he looked bewildered.

6   "Of course, that's what we came for," I said to make it look real at least. Lorraine shot me a look of outrage.

7   "Of course," he said.

8   We watched him go down another hall to a room that had black curtains on the doorway. I mean, there was no door, just these curtains. He disappeared through them. When he finally came back out, he seemed to be very tired, and he started writing the check.

9   "Whom should I make it out to?" he asked.

10   Lorraine gulped and went speechless.

11   "Cash will be fine. Make it out to cash," I found myself saying.

Please note that excerpts and passages in the StudySync® library and this workbook are intended as touchstones to generate interest in an author's work. The excerpts and passages do not substitute for the reading of entire texts, and StudySync® strongly recommends that students seek out and purchase the whole literary or informational work in order to experience it as the author intended. Links to online resellers are available in our digital library. In addition, complete works may be ordered through an authorized reseller by filling out and returning to StudySync® the order form enclosed in this workbook.

Reading & Writing Companion   51

12   He handed me the check, and my hand shook a little. It wasn't that I was scared or anything, but it was an awful lot of money.

13   "On behalf of the L & J Fund I accept this check."

14   "Oh, *yes*," Lorraine echoed, and I could tell she was furious with me because her eyes were starting to flit all over the place again.

15   "Do you think you might like to go to the zoo with me *someday*?" Mr. Pignati asked just as I knew Lorraine was getting ready to flee out of the house.

16   "I always go to the zoo." The old man laughed. "I love animals. My wife and I both love animals, but . . . I've been going to the zoo by myself lately. I always go. Every day."

17   "You love animals . . . ?" Lorraine muttered, her left hand opening the front door just a crack.

18   There was a dreadful pause.

19   "Oh, I forgot to show you my pigs!" he exclaimed, the gleam returning to his eyes. "You didn't see my pigs, did you?"

20   There came another terrible pause.

21   "No . . . we didn't see . . . your pigs," I said.

22   He gestured us back into the living room and then moved down the hall to the room at the far end—the one with the black curtains hanging on the side of the entrance. Lorraine didn't want to follow him, but I dragged her behind me until we got to the doorway.

23   "Ohh-h-h!" Lorraine stammered.

24   The room was dark because its two windows were covered with faded paper shades. It was a real dump except for the table and chairs at the far end of it. The table had pigs all over it. And the shelves had pigs all over them. There were pigs all over the place. It was ridiculous. I never saw so many pigs. I don't mean the live kind; these were phony pigs. There were glass pigs and clay pigs and marble pigs.

25   Lorraine reached her hand out.

26   "Touch them," he told her. "Don't be afraid to pick them up." It was a big change from my mother who always lets out a screech if you go near anything, so I couldn't help liking this old guy even if he was sort of weird.

27 There were pigs that had *Made in Japan* on them. Some were from Germany and Austria and Switzerland. There were pigs from Russia and lots of pigs from Italy, naturally. There were little pigs and big pigs. Ugly ones and cute ones. There were blue, black, yellow, orange, striped, green, and rainbow-colored pigs. Pigs, pigs, pigs!

28 "Don't you like them?" he asked.

29 "Oh, everybody loves pigs," I said.

30 "My wife collects pigs. I got her started on it when I gave her one to remind her of me—before we got married."

31 "Oh?"

32 "This one," he said, lifting a large white pig with an ugly smile on its face, "this one was the first one I got her. She thought it was very funny. Pig. *Pig*nati. Do you get it?"

33 "Yes, Mr. Pignati. We get it."

From Chapter Six

34 John had called the Pigman and made arrangements for us to meet him in front of the zoo at ten o'clock in the morning. We didn't want to be seen walking around our neighborhood with him, but the zoo was far enough away so we knew we'd be safe once we got there.

35 John and I arrived around nine thirty and sat down on the benches at the entrance. The sea-lion pool is right there, and that kept John busy while I was combing my hair and polishing my Ben Franklin sunglasses. I don't wear all crazy clothes, but I do like my Ben Franklin sunglasses because everyone looks at me when I wear them. I used to be afraid to have people look at me, but ever since I met John I seem to wear little things that make them look. He wears phony noses and moustaches and things like that. He's even got a big pin that says "MY, YOU'RE UGLY," and he wears that once in awhile.

36 I really didn't want to go to the zoo. I don't like seeing all those animals and birds and fish behind bars and glass just so a lot of people can stare at them. And I particularly hate the Baron Park Zoo because the attendants there are not intelligent. They really aren't. The thing that made me stop going to the zoo a few years ago was the way one attendant fed the sea lions. He climbed up on the big diving platform in the middle of the pool and unimaginatively just dropped the fish into the water. I mean, if you're going to feed sea lions, you're not supposed to plop the food into the tank. You can tell by the

expressions on their faces that the sea lions are saying things like "Don't dump the fish in!"

37   "Pick the fish up one by one and throw them into the air so we can chase after them."

38   "Throw the fish in different parts of the tank!"

39   "Let's have fun!"

40   "Make a game out of it!"

41   If my mother had ever let me have a dog, I think it would have been the happiest dog on earth. I know just how the minds of animals work—just the kind of games they like to play. The closest I ever came to having a pet was an old mongrel that used to hang around the neighborhood. I thought there was nothing wrong with sitting on the front steps and petting him, but my mother called the ASPCA, and I know they killed him.

42   At ten o'clock sharp, Mr. Pignati arrived.

43   "Hi!" he said. His smile stretched clear across his face. "Hope I'm not late?"

44   "Right on time, Mr. Pignati. Right on time," John answered.

Excerpted from The Pigman *by Paul Zindel, published by HarperCollins Publishers.*

THINK QUESTIONS

1. How would you describe the narrators of *The Pigman*? Cite textual evidence to support your answer.

2. How does John react to the pigs when he first sees them in Mr. Pignati's room? Cite a sentence from the text to support your answer.

3. How does Lorraine feel about accepting Mr. Pignati's check? Cite a sentence from the text to support your answer.

4. Use context to determine the meaning of the word **behalf** as it is used in *The Pigman*. Write your definition of "behalf" and tell how you arrived at it.

5. Remembering that the Latin prefix *un-* means "not," the Latin suffix *-ive* means "of, relating to," and the Latin suffix *-ly* indicates an adverb, use the context clues provided in the passage to determine the meaning of **unimaginatively**. Write your definition of "unimaginatively" and tell how you arrived at it.

CLOSE READ

Reread the excerpt from *The Pigman*. As you reread, complete the Focus Questions below. Then use your answers and annotations from the questions to help you complete the Writing Prompt.

FOCUS QUESTIONS

1. What is John's view of Mr. Pignati? Does it change over the course of the text? Highlight evidence in the text and make annotations to support your answer.

2. In Chapter 5, why does John accept Mr. Pignati's check? Highlight textual evidence that supports your ideas, and write annotations to explain your answer choices.

3. In paragraph 14, John says that Lorraine was "furious" with him. What do the connotations of the word *furious* tell you about Lorraine's feelings that a synonym such as *angry* or *upset* wouldn't tell you? Highlight evidence in the text and make annotations to support your answer.

4. In paragraph 35, Lorraine presents her view of John. How has John changed Lorraine's way of behaving? Highlight evidence that shows Lorraine's point of view on the subject. Write annotations to explain your choices.

5. Write two or three sentences describing what you learn from the text about Mr. Pignati's character traits. How was meeting John and Lorraine a life-changing event for Mr. Pignati? Highlight textual evidence that supports your answer, and annotate to explain your ideas.

WRITING PROMPT

How do the two points of view from which *The Pigman* is narrated help you to better understand the characters in the story? How is this more effective than if the story were told from only one point of view? Give specific examples, and support your writing with evidence from the text.

Please note that excerpts and passages in the StudySync® library and this workbook are intended as touchstones to generate interest in an author's work. The excerpts and passages do not substitute for the reading of entire texts, and StudySync® strongly recommends that students seek out and purchase the whole literary or informational work in order to experience it as the author intended. Links to online resellers are available in our digital library. In addition, complete works may be ordered through an authorized reseller by filling out and returning to StudySync® the order form enclosed in this workbook.

Reading & Writing Companion   **55**

THE ROAD NOT TAKEN

POETRY
Robert Frost
1915

INTRODUCTION

studysync tv

Robert Frost's classic poem is generally interpreted as a nod to non-conformism, but some see it differently. When asked about the *sigh* in the last stanza, Frost wrote to a friend, "It was my rather private jest at the expense of those who might think I would yet live to be sorry for the way I had

"I took the one less traveled by..."

 FIRST READ

 NOTES

1 Two roads **diverged in** a yellow wood,
2 And sorry I could not travel both
3 And be one traveler, long I stood
4 And looked down one as far as I could
5 To where it bent in the **undergrowth;**

6 Then took the other, as just as fair,
7 And having perhaps the better **claim,**
8 Because it was grassy and wanted wear;
9 Though as for that the passing there
10 Had worn them really about the same,

11 And both that morning equally lay
12 In leaves no step had **trodden** black.
13 Oh, I kept the first for another day!
14 Yet knowing how way leads on to way,
15 I doubted if I should ever come back.

16 I shall be telling this with a sigh
17 Somewhere ages and ages **hence:**
18 Two roads diverged in a wood, and I—
19 I took the one less traveled by,
20 And that has made all the difference.

THINK QUESTIONS

1. What evidence in the text of the poem shows you that the speaker is uncertain about which road to choose?

2. What do lines 16–20 tell you about how the speaker imagines his future? Explain using evidence from the text to support your answer.

3. How does the speaker feel about the road he didn't take? Cite textual evidence to support your answer.

4. Use context clues to determine the meaning of the word **trodden** as it is used in "The Road Not Taken." Write your definition of "trodden" and state the clue(s) from the text you used to determine your answer.

5. The word **diverged** is used in lines 1 and 18. What meaning of "diverged" would you guess from line 1, and how would its use in lines 18–19 help you confirm the meaning?

CLOSE READ

Reread the poem "The Road Not Taken." As you reread, complete the Focus Questions below. Then use your answers and annotations from the questions to help you complete the Writing Prompt.

FOCUS QUESTIONS

1. How does the poetic structure Frost uses help to unify the poem? Highlight textual evidence and make annotations to explain your ideas.

2. Highlight examples of imagery in stanza 1. What effect does this create for the reader? Cite specific textual evidence and make annotations to support your response.

3. In stanza 4, how is the poet's use of repetition effective? Highlight evidence from the text and write annotations to support your ideas.

4. What can you infer about the speaker's thoughts and feelings in this poem? Highlight evidence from the text and write annotations to support your findings.

5. The "road" in Frost's poem serves as a symbol of the journey of life. What message does Frost want the reader to understand about this journey? How is this a turning point? What can you infer about the speaker's thoughts and feelings about life's journey in this poem? Highlight evidence from the text and write annotations to support your findings.

WRITING PROMPT

How does Robert Frost's use of poetic structure and poetic elements in "The Road Not Taken" support the poem's meaning in both the print and audio versions of the poem? Explain what you believe the poem means, and how the poem's meaning is shaped by at least one aspect of poetic structure and at least one poetic element. Examine whether or not you experience these differently when you listen to the audio version, and whether hearing the poem read aloud changes your understanding of its meaning. Introduce your response with a thesis statement, and support your ideas with clearly organized details and quotations from the text.

Please note that excerpts and passages in the StudySync® library and this workbook are intended as touchstones to generate interest in an author's work. The excerpts and passages do not substitute for the reading of entire texts, and StudySync® strongly recommends that students seek out and purchase the whole literary or informational work in order to experience it as the author intended. Links to online resellers are available in our digital library. In addition, complete works may be ordered through an authorized reseller by filling out and returning to StudySync® the order form enclosed in this workbook.

Reading & Writing Companion   59

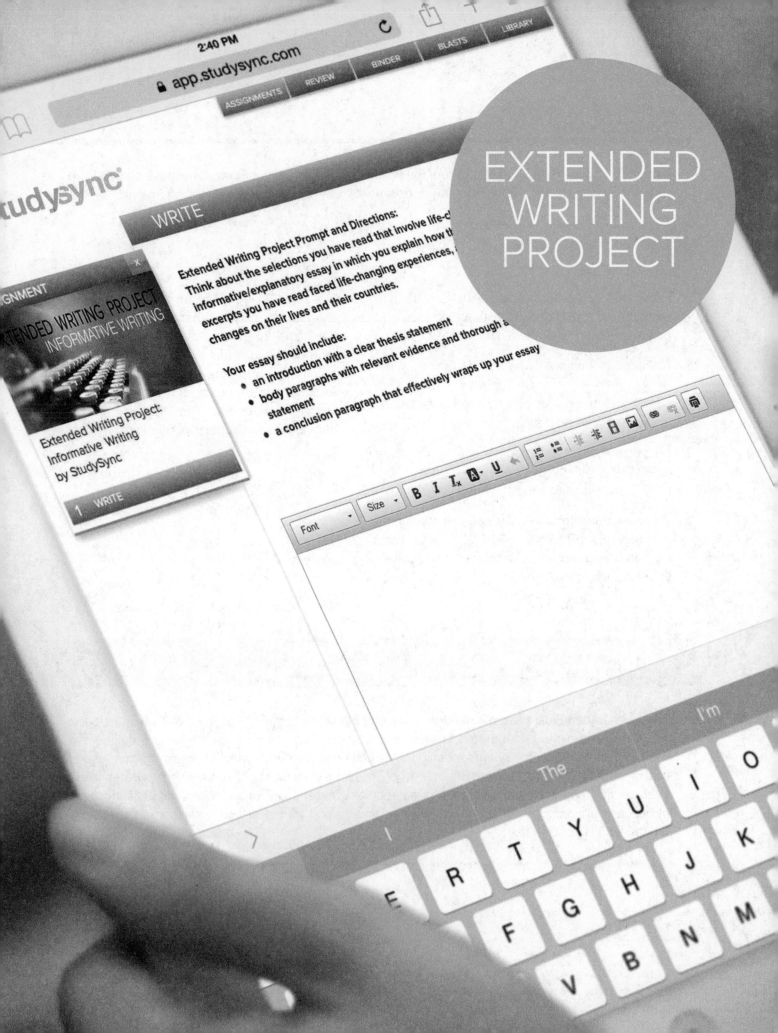

EXTENDED WRITING PROJECT

studysync®

2:40 PM

app.studysync.com

ASSIGNMENTS   REVIEW   BINDER   BLASTS   LIBRARY

WRITE

Extended Writing Project Prompt and Directions:
Think about the selections you have read that involve life-ch...
informative/explanatory essay in which you explain how th...
excerpts you have read faced life-changing experiences, ...
changes on their lives and their countries.

Your essay should include:

- an introduction with a clear thesis statement
- body paragraphs with relevant evidence and thorough a...
  statement
- a conclusion paragraph that effectively wraps up your essay

EXTENDED WRITING PROJECT
INFORMATIVE WRITING

Extended Writing Project:
Informative Writing
by StudySync

1   WRITE

Font   Size   B I I_x A U

INFORMATIVE/ EXPLANATORY WRITING

WRITING PROMPT

Think about the selections you have read that involve life-changing experiences. Write an informative/explanatory essay in which you explain how three individuals in three of the excerpts you have read faced life-changing experiences, and analyze the impact of these changes on their lives and their countries.

Your essay should include:

- an introduction with a clear thesis statement
- body paragraphs with relevant evidence and thorough analysis to support your thesis statement
- a conclusion paragraph that effectively wraps up your essay

Informative/explanatory writing examines a specific topic and presents ideas and information about it in a logical, organized way. Informative/ explanatory writing can explain, define, classify, compare, inform, or describe. Some examples of informative/explanatory writing include: scientific studies, research reports, newspaper or encyclopedia articles, and non-fiction texts such as biographies and histories.

Strong informative/explanatory writing introduces a thesis statement, which is a statement that presents the writer's central (or main) idea about the topic. The writer then develops that thesis statement with relevant supporting details such as facts and examples. The organizational structure of the writing fits the topic, and precise language and clear explanations help the reader understand the information. Transition words not only make the writing flow smoothly but also clarify the relationships among ideas. Though informative/ explanatory writing draws a conclusion based on the facts and information, the writing is unbiased, meaning that the writer does not state his/her own opinion.

Please note that excerpts and passages in the StudySync® library and this workbook are intended as touchstones to generate interest in an author's work. The excerpts and passages do not substitute for the reading of entire texts, and StudySync® strongly recommends that students seek out and purchase the whole literary or informational work in order to experience it as the author intended. Links to online resellers are available in our digital library. In addition, complete works may be ordered through an authorized reseller by filling out and returning to StudySync® the order form enclosed in this workbook.

Reading & Writing Companion   61

The features of informative/explanatory writing include:

- a logical organizational structure
- an introduction with a clear thesis statement
- relevant supporting details
- precise language and domain-specific vocabulary
- citations of sources
- a concluding statement

As you continue with this Extended Writing Project, you'll receive more instructions and practice to help you craft each of the elements of informative/explanatory writing in your own essay.

 STUDENT MODEL

Before you get started on your own informative/explanatory essay, begin by reading this essay that one student wrote in response to the writing prompt. As you read this Student Model, highlight and annotate the features of informative/explanatory writing that the student included in the essay.

The Power of Change

Turning points in life are often difficult and challenging times. This idea is explored in the memoir *Warriors Don't Cry* by Melba Pattillo Beals, the autobiography *I Never Had It Made* by Jackie Robinson, and the article "The Father of Chinese Aviation" by Rebecca Maksel. Melba Pattillo Beals, Jackie Robinson, and Feng Ru all faced life-changing experiences and, in doing so, changed their countries.

Melba Pattillo Beals helped improve education for all African American students. She was a student who chose to be one of the first African Americans to integrate Central High in Little Rock, Arkansas. On the morning of September 25, 1957, Beals was greeted by "fifty uniformed soldiers" (Beals). They were there to keep her, along with eight other African American students, safe on the first day of school. The threat of violence was very real. Even some adults who supported the students cried openly with fear. Still, Beals was determined to take forward steps for both herself and her people. "Step by step we climbed upward— where none of my people had ever before walked as a student" (Beals). In the face of threats, Beals and the other courageous African American students with her on that day paved the way for new racial attitudes in the United States.

Like Beals, Jackie Robinson also charted new territory for his race. He became the first African American to play major league baseball. In his autobiography, Robinson discussed some of the difficulties he faced. Because he was black, Robinson was not immediately accepted by the team. He had to "live with snubs and rebuffs and rejections" (Robinson). However, the resentment from players on other teams was even worse than from his own team members. Like Beals, he faced threats of violence and "even out-and-out attempts at physical harm" (Robinson). Despite the threats, many African Americans came out to support him. In time, acceptance for Robinson increased, and he took his place as the first of many African American ballplayers. Robinson recognized that this was an important step for African Americans. He was proud, Robinson said, "to prove that a sport can't be called national if blacks are barred from it." Robinson helped change the attitudes of major league baseball. He also helped change the attitudes of his country.

Like Beals and Robinson, Feng Ru's hard work and courage changed his own country—China. Feng Ru was an immigrant to the United States. He was also a self-taught engineer. As a young man, he learned "all he could about machines, working in shipyards, power plants, machine shops" (Maksel). After awhile, he became fascinated with the new field of aviation. In 1906, he started his own "aircraft factory, building airplanes of his own design" (Maksel). However, testing new aircraft was dangerous. During a test flight, Feng lost control of the plane "which plunged into his workshop, setting it ablaze" (Maksel). Although this would not be his last crash, he did not give up his experiments. He returned to China to bring his knowledge of aviation to that country. Feng Ru died in a crash in his homeland, but to this day, he is heralded as the "father of Chinese aviation" (Maksel).

Beals, Robinson, and Feng Ru each faced obstacles and danger. Beals faced an angry mob. Robinson faced threats of violence. Feng Ru faced death itself. However, all three acted with courage, and their determination had an impact on their countries as a whole. Each individual's choices led to a greater good.

Please note that excerpts and passages in the StudySync® library and this workbook are intended as touchstones to generate interest in an author's work. The excerpts and passages do not substitute for the reading of entire texts, and StudySync® strongly recommends that students seek out and purchase the whole literary or informational work in order to experience it as the author intended. Links to online resellers are available in our digital library. In addition, complete works may be ordered through an authorized reseller by filling out and returning to StudySync® the order form enclosed in this workbook.

Reading & Writing Companion   **63**

THINK QUESTIONS

1. Which sentence in the first two paragraphs most clearly states what the entire essay will be about?

2. In the second paragraph, what evidence does the writer use to support the statement that "Melba Pattillo Beals helped improve education for all African American students"?

3. In the final paragraph of the essay, what conclusions does the writer make about these three individuals and their experiences? Write two or three sentences that sum up in your own words the writer's conclusion.

4. Thinking about the writing prompt, which selections or other resources would you like to use to create your own informative/explanatory essay?

5. Based on what you have read, listened to or researched, how would you answer the question: *What happens when life changes direction?* Explain what you believe are some challenges associated with life changes.

EXTENDED WRITING PROJECT
PREWRITE

PREWRITE

WRITING PROMPT

Think about the selections you have read that involve life-changing experiences. Write an informative/explanatory essay in which you explain how three individuals in three of the excerpts you have read faced life-changing experiences, and analyze the impact of these changes on their lives and their countries.

Your essay should include:

- an introduction with a clear thesis statement
- body paragraphs with relevant evidence and thorough analysis to support your thesis statement
- a conclusion paragraph that effectively wraps up your essay

In addition to studying techniques authors use to convey information, you have been reading and learning about stories that feature life-changing experiences. In the Extended Writing Project, you will use informational writing techniques to compose your own informative/explanatory essay.

Since the topic of your informative/explanatory essay will have to do with the impact of life-changing experiences, you'll want to consider how the people you've read about have been impacted by the turning points in their lives. Think back to what you read about Jackie Robinson in *I Never Had It Made*: What important life decision did Robinson face? What were the circumstances of the decision? How easy was the decision to make? What happened as a result of his decision? What did the decision teach him about life? How did his experiences and his reactions to them impact his country?

Please note that excerpts and passages in the StudySync® library and this workbook are intended as touchstones to generate interest in an author's work. The excerpts and passages do not substitute for the reading of entire texts, and StudySync® strongly recommends that students seek out and purchase the whole literary or informational work in order to experience it as the author intended. Links to online resellers are available in our digital library. In addition, complete works may be ordered through an authorized reseller by filling out and returning to StudySync® the order form enclosed in this workbook.

Reading & Writing Companion   65

Make a list of the answers to these questions for Robinson and at least two other individuals you've read about in this unit. As you write down your ideas, look for patterns that begin to emerge. Do the experiences have anything in common? Do you notice ideas that are repeated? Looking for these patterns may help you solidify the ideas you want to discuss in your essay. Use this model to help you get started with your own prewriting:

Text: *I Never Had It Made,* by Jackie Robinson

Life Decision: Robinson decided to fight to be the first African American player in major league baseball.

What Happened: He faced discrimination from both his fellow ballplayers and fans.

In the face of resentment and threats, he proved to be a remarkable baseball player. Eventually, many of the players on his team accepted him, and he drew strength from his relationships with Mr. Rickey and his wife, Rachel.

SKILL:
THESIS
STATEMENT

DEFINE

The **thesis statement** is the most important sentence in an informative/explanatory essay because it introduces what the writer is going to say about the essay's topic. The thesis statement expresses the writer's central or main idea about that topic, a position the writer will develop in the body of the essay. The thesis statement usually appears in the essay's introductory paragraph and is often the introduction's last sentence. The rest of the paragraphs in the essay all support the thesis statement with facts, evidence, and examples.

IDENTIFICATION AND APPLICATION

A thesis statement:

- makes a clear statement about the writer's central idea
- lets the reader know what to expect in the body of the essay
- responds fully and completely to an essay prompt
- is presented in the introduction paragraph

MODEL

The following is the introduction paragraph from the Student Model, "The Power of Change":

> *Turning points in life are often difficult and challenging times. This idea is explored in the memoir* Warriors Don't Cry *by Melba Pattillo Beals, the autobiography* I Never Had It Made *by Jackie Robinson, and the article* "The Father of Chinese Aviation" *by Rebecca Maksel.* **Melba Pattillo Beals, Jackie Robinson, and Feng Ru all faced life-changing experiences and, in doing so, changed their countries.**

Notice the bold-faced thesis statement. This student's thesis statement responds to the prompt. It reminds readers of the topic of the essay—the impact of life-changing experiences. It also specifically states the writer's central or main idea about that topic. The writer asserts that Beals, Robinson, and Feng Ru all faced these kinds of amazing experiences, and that both they and their countries were affected by them.

 PRACTICE

Write a thesis statement for your informative/explanatory essay that introduces your central idea in relation to the essay prompt. When you are finished, trade with a partner and offer each other feedback. How clear was the writer's central idea? Is it obvious what this essay will focus on? Does your thesis statement specifically address the prompt? Offer each other suggestions, and remember that they are most helpful when they are constructive.

SKILL:
ORGANIZE
INFORMATIVE
WRITING

⭐ DEFINE

The purpose of writing an informative/explanatory text is to inform readers, so authors need to organize and present their ideas, facts, details, and other information in a logical way. Experienced authors carefully choose an **organizational structure** that best suits their material. They often use an outline or other graphic organizer to determine which organizational structure will help them express their ideas effectively.

For example, scientific reports and studies often use a cause and effect structure. This mirrors the information scientists need to relay—the experiment and the results of the experiment. Historians and memoirists often use a chronological structure, discussing events in the order they occurred. Other organizational structures include: **comparison-contrast, problem-solution, definition, classification,** and **order of importance.**

⋯ IDENTIFICATION AND APPLICATION

- When selecting an organizational structure, writers must consider the purpose of their writing. They often ask themselves questions about the kind of information they are writing about. They might consider:
  › "What is the central idea I'd like to convey?"
  › "Would it make sense to relay events in the order they occurred?"
  › "Is there a specific problem discussed in the texts? What solutions seem likely answers to the problem?"
  › "Is there a natural cause and effect relationship in my information?"
  › "Can I compare and contrast different events or individuals' responses to events?"
  › "Am I teaching readers how to do something?"

NOTES

- Writers often use word choice to create connections and transitions between ideas and to suggest the organizational structure being used:
  › Sequential order: *first, next, then, finally, last, initially, ultimately*
  › Cause and effect: *because, accordingly, as a result, effect, so*
  › Compare and contrast: *like, unlike, also, both, similarly, although, while, but, however*

- Sometimes, within the overall structure, writers may find it necessary to organize individual paragraphs using other structures - a definition paragraph in a chronological structure, for instance. This should not affect the overall organization.

- Sometimes a writer may include special formatting elements in an informative/explanatory text if these are useful in clarifying organization. These elements may include headings, or phrases in bold that announce the start of a section of text. Headings are usually included only if called for in a prompt or when needed to guide a reader through a long or complex text.

 ## MODEL

The writer of the Student Model understood from her prewriting that she was mostly comparing and contrasting the life-changing experiences of three different figures in history.

In this excerpt from the introduction of the Student Model, the writer makes the organizational structure clear with her word choice:

> *Like Beals and Robinson, Feng Ru's hard work and courage changed his own country—China.*

The writer uses the word "like" to identify something the three subjects (Beals, Robinson, and Feng Ru) had in common.

The writer of the Student Model, "The Power of Change," knew that she was comparing and contrasting crucial turning points in the lives of three historic figures. She used a three-column chart to organize her ideas during her prewriting process. She color-coded the information so that it was clear what either two or all three of the figures had in common. What was unique to each individual is unmarked.

MELBA PATTILLO BEALS	JACKIE ROBINSON	FENG RU
One of Little Rock 9	Changed their country	Determination
Threat of danger	Played major league baseball	Built planes of his own design
Integrated Central High	Had courage	Changed their country
African American	The first to integrate an institution	Self-taught
Changed their country	Team did not initially support him	Asian
Many people were against it	Determination	Threat of danger
Had courage	African American community supported him	Brought aviation to homeland of China
The first to integrate an institution	African American	Had courage
Determination	Threat of danger	
Death threats	Death threats	
African American community supported her		

 PRACTICE
_____

Using an *Organize Informative/Explanatory Writing* Three-Column Chart like the one you have just studied, fill in the information you've gathered during your prewriting process.

SKILL:
SUPPORTING
DETAILS

 DEFINE

In informative/explanatory writing, writers develop their thesis statement with relevant information called **supporting details.** Relevant information can be any fact, definition, concrete detail, example, or quotation that is important to the reader's understanding of the topic and closely related to the thesis, or central idea. Supporting details can be found in a variety of places, but they must develop the thesis statement in order to be considered relevant and necessary:

- Facts important to understanding the topic
- Research related to the thesis statement
- Quotations from texts or from individuals such as experts or eyewitnesses
- Conclusions of scientific findings and studies
- Definitions from reference material

Writers can choose supporting details from many sources. Encyclopedias, research papers, newspaper articles, graphs, memoirs, biographies, criticism, documentaries, and online references can all provide relevant information for source material. Though information is plentiful and the source material varied, the writer must be careful to evaluate the quality of information to determine what information is most important and most closely related to the thesis statement. If the information doesn't support the topic or if the information doesn't strengthen the writer's point, it is not relevant.

 IDENTIFICATION AND APPLICATION

Step 1:

Review your thesis statement. To identify relevant supporting details, ask this question: What is my central or main idea about this topic? A writer might be making a statement about rainforests, for example:

We all have a responsibility to save the rainforests.

Step 2:

Ask what a reader needs to know about the topic in order to understand the central idea. In order to understand a statement about *saving* the rainforests, much less the reader's *responsibility* towards them, a reader must first know something about the rainforests. Why do they need saving? In a sentence following, the writer explains this:

They are in *danger* due to our shared use of their resources.

He or she then supplies the reason why:

Rainforests are being harvested for their resources at a rate too fast for them to replenish themselves.

What could that possibly mean to a reader? The writer gives more information:

We use vast amounts of its resources for fuel and clothes.

Step 3:

Look for facts, quotations, research, and the conclusions of others. They will strengthen the thesis statement. It is a building process. Build your information onto the information you gave in the sentence before. Identify supporting details. Carefully evaluate their relevance to your main idea. Ask yourself:

- Is this information necessary to the reader's understanding of the topic?
- Does this information help to prove my point?
- Does this information relate closely to my thesis statement?
- Is there stronger evidence that makes the same point?

 MODEL

In the following excerpt from Jackie Robinson's autobiography *I Never Had It Made*, Robinson develops the idea that Mr. Rickey's motives to let Jackie play in the major leagues were not primarily monetary.

Mr. Rickey stands out as the man who inspired me the most. He will always have my admiration and respect. Critics had said, "Don't you know that your precious Mr. Rickey didn't bring you up out of the black leagues because he loved you? Are you stupid enough not to understand that the Brooklyn club profited hugely because of what your Mr. Rickey did?"

Please note that excerpts and passages in the StudySync® library and this workbook are intended as touchstones to generate interest in an author's work. The excerpts and passages do not substitute for the reading of entire texts, and StudySync® strongly recommends that students seek out and purchase the whole literary or informational work in order to experience it as the author intended. Links to online resellers are available in our digital library. In addition, complete works may be ordered through an authorized reseller by filling out and returning to StudySync® the order form enclosed in this workbook.

Reading & Writing Companion   **73**

NOTES

Yes, I know that. But I also know what a big gamble he took. A bond developed between us that lasted long after I had left the game. In a way I feel I was the son he had lost and he was the father I had lost.

There was more than just making money at stake in Mr. Rickey's decision. I learned that his family was afraid that his health was being undermined by the resulting pressures and that they pleaded with him to abandon the plan. His peers and fellow baseball moguls exerted all kinds of influence to get him to change his mind. Some of the press condemned him as a fool and a demagogue. But he didn't give in.

In paragraph 1, Robinson addresses what the critics said about Mr. Rickey's motives being all about money. He counters with supporting details about Mr. Rickey in paragraphs 2 and 3.

In paragraph 2, Robinson states that he and Mr. Rickey had a bond. This may be true, but Robinson does not provide much concrete evidence here.

Robinson's most compelling evidence of Mr. Rickey's pure motives appears in paragraph 3. He says Mr. Rickey's family worried about his health, Mr. Rickey was pressured by his peers, and he was called a fool by the press. These are three significant and relevant details. They certainly help prove that Mr. Rickey's motives were not strictly monetary.

 PRACTICE

Using sources, write a few supporting details for your informative/explanatory essay that will help develop your thesis statement. List your details on a *Supporting Details* Relevancy Graphic Organizer to determine how strong your supporting details are. Then trade your details with a partner when you are finished. Offer feedback about the details. Engage in a peer review to determine which details are most relevant and strengthen your thesis statement.

PLAN

Copyright © BookheadEd Learning, LLC

WRITING PROMPT

Think about the selections you have read that involve life-changing experiences. Write an informative/explanatory essay in which you explain how three individuals in three of the excerpts you have read faced life-changing experiences, and analyze the impact of these changes on their lives and their countries.

Your essay should include:

- an introduction with a clear thesis statement
- body paragraphs with relevant evidence and thorough analysis to support your thesis statement
- a conclusion paragraph that effectively wraps up your essay

Review the information you listed in your *Organize Informative/Explanatory Writing* Three-Column Chart listing three individuals and the details about the life-changing event or events they experienced. Review the impact of this event on their lives and their country. This organized information, your thesis statement, and your *Supporting Details* Relevancy Graphic Organizer will help you to create a road map to use for writing your essay.

Consider the questions you answered in your prewriting assignment as you develop your main paragraph topics and their supporting details in the road map:

- What important life decision did each person face?
- What were the circumstances of each person's decision?
- How easy was the decision to make?
- What happened as a result of each of these decisions?

- What did these decisions teach the individuals who made them about life?
- How did these experiences and decisions impact the society and country in which these individuals lived?

Use this model to get started with your road map. In each category, write a brief description of the information you plan to include in your informative/explanatory essay. Write your thesis statement, the topics of each of your paragraphs, and the most relevant supporting details in each paragraph:

Essay Road Map

Thesis statement:

Paragraph 1 Topic:

    Supporting Detail #1:

    Supporting Detail #2:

Paragraph 2 Topic:

    Supporting Detail #1:

    Supporting Detail #2:

Paragraph 3 Topic:

    Supporting Detail #1:

    Supporting Detail #2:

SKILL:
INTRODUCTIONS

 DEFINE
_____

The **introduction** is the opening paragraph or section of a nonfiction text. In an informative/explanatory text, the introduction provides readers with important information by **introducing the topic** and **stating the thesis** that will be developed in the body of the text. A strong introduction also generates interest in the topic by engaging readers in an interesting or attentive way.

 IDENTIFICATION AND APPLICATION
_____

- In informative or explanatory writing, the introduction identifies the topic of the writing by explicitly stating what the text will be about. The writer may also use the introduction to provide some necessary background information about the topic to help the reader understand the information that is to come.

- In addition to the topic, the introduction includes the central, or main, idea that the writer will include in the text. This central idea is the **thesis.** A strong statement of the thesis serves as a guide for the remainder of the work. It lets the reader know what the focus of the essay is. The thesis statement should indicate the point the writer will make and the people or source materials he or she will discuss. Note, however, that a thesis is not always stated explicitly within the text. A writer might instead hint at the thesis through details and ideas in the introduction.

- It is customary to build interest in the topic by beginning the introduction with a **"hook,"** or a way to grab the reader's attention. This awakens the reader's natural curiosity and encourages him or her to read on. Hooks can ask open-ended questions, make connections to the reader or to life, or introduce a surprising fact.

Please note that excerpts and passages in the StudySync® library and this workbook are intended as touchstones to generate interest in an author's work. The excerpts and passages do not substitute for the reading of entire texts, and StudySync® strongly recommends that students seek out and purchase the whole literary or informational work in order to experience it as the author intended. Links to online resellers are available in our digital library. In addition, complete works may be ordered through an authorized reseller by filling out and returning to StudySync® the order form enclosed in this workbook.

Reading & Writing
Companion

77

MODEL

Take a look at the introduction of Jackie Robinson's *I Never Had It Made:*

> **I guess if I could choose one of the most important moments in my life, I would go back to 1947, in the Yankee Stadium in New York City.** It was the opening day of the world series and I was for the first time playing in the series as a member of the Brooklyn Dodgers team. **It was a history-making day.** It would be the first time that a black man would be allowed to participate in a world series. **I had become the first black player in the major leagues.**

Jackie Robinson starts readers off with a **hook**. The opening sentence transports the reader back in time, and the reader is left to wonder, "What important thing happened in 1947?" This is an effective hook because the reader will be inclined to read on to discover the answer to this question.

The remainder of the first paragraph in this passage of *I Never Had It Made* goes on to introduce the topic: Robinson was the first black man to play major league baseball. This information appears at the end of the introductory paragraph and is explicitly stated: "I had become the first black player in the major leagues."

The **central idea,** however, is only hinted at in the introduction. The main idea of this passage is that as "the first black player in the major leagues," Jackie Robinson had to overcome many challenges, but by doing so, he changed the course of sports history. However, there is no explicitly stated **thesis** here, because this is an excerpt from Robinson's autobiography, which is longer and more complex than an essay someone might write for school. The **thesis** for the entire book would be much longer than a sentence. Instead, Robinson hints at this idea in the introduction when he states, "It was a history-making day."

PRACTICE

Write an introduction for your informative/explanatory essay that includes a hook, the topic, and the thesis statement. When you are finished, trade with a partner and offer each other feedback. How strong is the language of your partner's thesis statement? How clear is the topic? Were you hooked? Offer each other suggestions, and remember that they are most helpful when they are constructive.

SKILL: BODY PARAGRAPHS AND TRANSITIONS

 DEFINE

Body paragraphs are the section of the essay between the introduction and conclusion paragraphs. This is where you support your thesis statement by developing your main points with evidence from the text and analysis. Typically, each body paragraph will focus on one main point or idea to avoid confusing the reader. The main point of each body paragraph must support the thesis statement.

It's important to structure your body paragraph clearly. One strategy for structuring the body paragraph for an informational essay is the following:

Topic sentence: The topic sentence is the first sentence of your body paragraph and clearly states the main point of the paragraph. It's important that your topic sentence develop the main assertion or statement you made in your thesis statement.

Evidence #1: It's important to support your topic sentence with evidence. Evidence can be relevant facts, definitions, concrete details, quotations, or other information and examples.

Analysis/Explanation #1: After presenting evidence to support your topic sentence, you will need to analyze that evidence and explain how it supports your topic sentence and, in effect, your thesis statement.

Evidence #2: Continue to develop your topic sentence with a second piece of evidence.

Analysis/Explanation #2: Analyze this second piece of evidence and explain how it supports your topic sentence and, in effect, your thesis.

Concluding sentence: After presenting your evidence you need to wrap up your main idea and transition to the next paragraph in your conclusion sentence.

Transitions are connecting words and phrases that clarify the relationships among ideas in a text. Transitions work at three different levels: within a sentence, between paragraphs, and to indicate organizational structure.

Authors of informative/explanatory texts use transitions to help readers recognize the overall organizational structure. Transitions also help readers make connections among ideas within and across sentences and paragraphs. Also, by adding transition words or phrases to the beginning or end of a paragraph, authors guide readers smoothly through the text.

In addition, transition words and phrases help authors make connections between words within a sentence. Conjunctions such as *and, or,* and *but* and prepositions such as *with, beyond, inside,* show the relationships between words. Transitions help readers understand how words fit together to make meaning.

 IDENTIFICATION AND APPLICATION

- Body paragraphs are the section of the essay between the introduction and conclusion paragraphs. The body paragraphs provide the evidence and analysis/explanation needed to support the thesis statement. Typically, writers develop one main idea per body paragraph.
  › A topic sentence clearly states the main idea of that paragraph.
  › Evidence consists of relevant facts, definitions, concrete details, quotations, or other information and examples.
  › Analysis and explanation are needed to explain how the evidence supports the topic sentence.
  › The conclusion sentence wraps up the main point and transitions to the next body paragraph.

- Transition words are a necessary element of a successful piece of informative/explanatory writing.
  › Transition words help readers understand the text structure of an informative/explanatory text. Here are some transition words that are frequently used in three different text structures:
    › Cause-effect: *because, accordingly, as a result, effect, so, for, since*
    › Compare-contrast: *like, unlike, also, both, similarly, although, while, but, however, whereas, conversely, meanwhile, on the contrary, and yet, still*
    › Chronological order: *first, next, then, finally, last, initially, ultimately*

- Transition words help readers understand the flow of ideas and concepts in a text. Some of the most useful transitions are words that indicate that the ideas in one paragraph are building on or adding to those in another. Examples include: *furthermore, therefore, in addition, moreover, by extension, in order to,* etc.

MODEL

The Student Model uses a body paragraph structure to develop the main ideas presented in the thesis statement and also includes transitions to help the reader understand the relationship among ideas in the text.

Read the body paragraphs from the Student Model, "The Power of Change." Look closely at the structure and note the transition words in bold. Think about the purpose of the information presented. Does it effectively develop the main points made in each topic sentence? How do the transition words help you to understand the similarities and differences between these three individuals and their experiences?

> **Melba Pattillo Beals helped improve education for all African American students.** She was a student who chose to be one of the first African Americans to integrate Central High in Little Rock, Arkansas. On the morning of September 25, 1957, Beals was greeted by "fifty uniformed soldiers" (Beals). They were there to keep her, along with eight other African American students, safe on the first day of school. The threat of violence was very real. Even some adults who supported the students cried openly with fear. Still, Beals was determined to take forward steps for both herself and her people. "Step by step we climbed upward—where none of my people had ever before walked as a student" (Beals). **In the face of threats, Beals and the other courageous African American students with her on that day paved the way for new racial attitudes in the United States.**
>
> **Like** Beals, Jackie Robinson **also** charted new territory for his race. He became the first African American to play major league baseball. In his autobiography, Robinson discussed some of the difficulties he faced. **Because** he was black, Robinson was not immediately accepted by the team. He had to "live with snubs and rebuffs and rejections" (Robinson). **However,** the resentment from players on other teams was even worse than from his own team members. **Like** Beals, he faced threats of violence and "even out-and-out attempts at physical harm" (Robinson). **Despite** the threats, many

Please note that excerpts and passages in the StudySync® library and this workbook are intended as touchstones to generate interest in an author's work. The excerpts and passages do not substitute for the reading of entire texts, and StudySync® strongly recommends that students seek out and purchase the whole literary or informational work in order to experience it as the author intended. Links to online resellers are available in our digital library. In addition, complete works may be ordered through an authorized reseller by filling out and returning to StudySync® the order form enclosed in this workbook.

Reading & Writing Companion   **81**

African Americans came out to support him. In time, acceptance for Robinson increased, and Jackie took his place as the first of many African American ballplayers. Robinson recognized that this was an important step for African Americans. He was proud, Robinson said, "to prove that a sport can't be called national if blacks are barred from it." Robinson helped change the attitudes of major league baseball. He **also** helped change the attitudes of his country.

Like Beals and Robinson, Feng Ru's hard work and courage changed his own country—China. Feng Ru was an immigrant to the United States. He was **also** a self-taught engineer. As a young man, he learned "all he could about machines, working in shipyards, power plants, machine shops" (Maksel). **After awhile,** he became fascinated with the new field of aviation. In 1906, he started his own "aircraft factory, building airplanes of his own design" (Maksel). **However,** testing new aircraft was dangerous. **During** a test flight, Feng lost control of the plane "which plunged into his workshop, setting it ablaze" (Maksel). **Although** this would not be his last crash, he did not give up his experiments. He returned to China to bring his knowledge of aviation to that country. Feng Ru died in a crash in his homeland, but to this day, he is heralded as the "father of Chinese aviation" (Maksel).

Body paragraph 1 of the Student Model begins by stating, "Melba Pattillo Beals helped improve education for all African American students." This **topic sentence** clearly establishes the main idea this body paragraph will develop. The writer will attempt to show how Beals improved education.

This topic sentence is immediately followed by **evidence.** The writer uses the example that Beals "chose to be one of the first African Americans to integrate Central High" and includes a direct quote from the excerpt to support the topic sentence.

Directly after the quote "fifty uniformed soldiers" (Beals), the writer **explains** the danger associated with the decision to integrate. The writer then presents a second piece of evidence, emphasizing the determination Beals demonstrated, to further develop the main point established in the topic sentence.

The paragraph concludes by stating that "In the face of threats, Beals and the other courageous African American students with her on that day paved the way for new racial attitudes in the United States." This **conclusion sentence** wraps up the paragraph and makes a clear statement about the impact of Beals's decision.

Copyright © BookheadEd Learning, LLC

All three body paragraphs use **transitional words** strategically to show relationships among the ideas in each body paragraph. The first sentence of the second body paragraph states "**Like** Beals, Jackie Robinson **also.**" The transitional words "like" and "also" make it clear that the writer is highlighting the similarities between Beals and Robinson.

The writer also uses transition words such as "however", "because", and "despite" within the body paragraphs themselves to help guide the reader as he or she transitions from one sentence to the next.

 ## PRACTICE

Write one body paragraph for your literary analysis that compares or contrasts the texts selected for your essay. Make sure your paragraph follows the suggested format, starting with a topic sentence. When you are finished, trade with a partner and offer each other feedback. How effective is the topic sentence at stating the main point of the paragraph? How strong is the textual evidence used to support the topic sentence? What is being compared and contrasted in the paragraph? Do transition words help make the compare-and-contrast relationship clear? Offer each other suggestions, and remember that they are most helpful when they are constructive.

Please note that excerpts and passages in the StudySync® library and this workbook are intended as touchstones to generate interest in an author's work. The excerpts and passages do not substitute for the reading of entire texts, and StudySync® strongly recommends that students seek out and purchase the whole literary or informational work in order to experience it as the author intended. Links to online resellers are available in our digital library. In addition, complete works may be ordered through an authorized reseller by filling out and returning to StudySync® the order form enclosed in this workbook.

Reading & Writing Companion 83

CONCLUSIONS

sync•skills

SKILL: CONCLUSIONS

 DEFINE

The **conclusion** is the final paragraph or section of a nonfiction text. In an informative/explanatory text, the conclusion brings the discussion to a close. It follows directly from the introduction and body of the text by referring back to the main ideas presented there. A conclusion should reiterate the thesis statement and summarize the main ideas covered in the body of the text. Depending on the type of text, a conclusion might also include a recommendation or solution, a call to action, or an insightful statement. Many conclusions try to connect with readers by encouraging them to apply what they have learned from the text to their own lives.

 IDENTIFICATION AND APPLICATION

- An effective informative conclusion reinforces the thesis statement.

- An effective informative conclusion briefly mentions or reviews the strongest supporting facts or details. This reminds readers of the most relevant information and evidence in the work.

- The conclusion leaves the reader with a final thought. In informative writing, this final thought may:

  › Answer a question posed by the introduction
  › Ask a question on which the reader can reflect
  › Ask the reader to take action on an issue
  › Present a last, compelling example
  › Convey a memorable or inspiring message
  › Spark curiosity and encourage readers to learn more

MODEL

In the concluding paragraph of the student model "The Power of Change," the writer reinforces the thesis statement, reminds the reader of relevant details, and ends with a final thought.

> **Beals, Robinson, and Feng Ru each faced obstacles and danger.** Beals faced an angry mob. Robinson faced threats of violence. Feng Ru faced death itself. However, **all three acted with courage,** and their determination **had an impact on their countries as a whole.** Each individual's **choices led to a greater good.**

According to the thesis statement, Melba Pattillo Beals, Jackie Robinson, and Feng Ru all faced crucial life-changing experiences, and these changes had an impact on the countries in which they lived. The first line of the conclusion mentions all three historical figures again and reminds the reader of the challenges they faced. Relevant facts in the next few sentences highlight the specific danger each person confronted. Then the writer states that "their determination had an impact on their countries as a whole." This sentence emphasizes the significant changes each person brought about. It explicitly supports the thesis statement of the essay. Finally, the writer broadens the topic to connect with life today. The writer states, "Each individual's life choices led to a greater good." This is an effective final thought. It represents information that the reader can connect with in his or her own life.

PRACTICE

Write a conclusion for your informative/explanatory essay. When you are finished, trade with a partner and offer each other feedback. How effectively did the writer reinforce the thesis statement in the conclusion? With what final thought did the writer leave the reader? Offer each other suggestions, and remember that they are most helpful when they are constructive.

DRAFT

WRITING PROMPT

Think about the selections you have read that involve life-changing experiences. Write an informative/explanatory essay in which you explain how three individuals in three of the excerpts you have read faced life-changing experiences, and analyze the impact of these changes on their lives and their countries.

Your essay should include:

- an introduction with a clear thesis statement
- body paragraphs with relevant evidence and thorough analysis to support your thesis statement
- a conclusion paragraph that effectively wraps up your essay

You've already made progress toward writing your own informative/explanatory text. You've thought about your purpose, audience, and topic. You've carefully examined the unit's texts and selected your three individuals. Based on your analysis of textual evidence, you've identified what you want to say about life-changing experiences. You've decided how to organize information, and gathered supporting details. Now it's time to write a draft of your essay.

Use your essay road map and your other prewriting materials to help you as you write. Remember that informative/explanatory writing begins with an introduction and presents a thesis statement. Body paragraphs develop the thesis statement with supporting ideas, details, quotations, and other relevant information and explanations drawn from or based on the texts. Transitions help the reader understand the relationships among ideas and to follow the flow of information. A concluding paragraph restates or reinforces your thesis statement. An effective conclusion can also do more—it can leave a lasting impression on your readers.

Copyright © BookheadEd Learning, LLC

Finally, remember that correct use of language is necessary if your readers are going to understand your descriptions and ideas. Your language should be precise, rather than too vague or general, to help your readers follow information and learn about your topic. In some cases, you may want to use specialized vocabulary or domain-specific words, if appropriate, to fit your topic. It is always important to check that you use words that are grammatically correct. One important thing to consider is whether you are using pronouns correctly: if your pronouns do not agree in number or person, or if they shift around throughout the essay, readers may be confused.

When drafting, ask yourself these questions:

- How can I improve my hook to make it more appealing?
- What can I do to clarify my thesis statement?
- What textual evidence—including relevant facts, strong details, and interesting quotations —supports the thesis statement?
- Have I chosen an organizational structure that makes information clear, and that helps readers understand my topic?
- How have I used transitions to clarify the relationships among my ideas?
- Would more precise language or different details about these extraordinary individuals make the text more exciting and vivid? How well have I communicated what these individuals experienced and achieved?
- What final thought do I want to leave with my readers?

Before you submit your draft, read it over carefully. You want to be sure that you've responded to all aspects of the prompt.

Please note that excerpts and passages in the StudySync® library and this workbook are intended as touchstones to generate interest in an author's work. The excerpts and passages do not substitute for the reading of entire texts, and StudySync® strongly recommends that students seek out and purchase the whole literary or informational work in order to experience it as the author intended. Links to online resellers are available in our digital library. In addition, complete works may be ordered through an authorized reseller by filling out and returning to StudySync® the order form enclosed in this workbook.

Reading & Writing Companion   **87**

EXTENDED WRITING PROJECT
REVISE

REVISE

WRITING PROMPT

Think about the selections you have read that involve life-changing experiences. Write an informative/explanatory essay in which you explain how three individuals in three of the excerpts you have read faced life-changing experiences, and analyze the impact of these changes on their lives and their countries.

Your essay should include:
- an introduction with a clear thesis statement
- body paragraphs with relevant evidence and thorough analysis to support your thesis statement
- a conclusion paragraph that effectively wraps up your essay

You have written a draft of your informative/explanatory text. You have also received input from your peers about how to improve it. Now you are going to revise your draft.

Here are some recommendations to help you revise.

- Review the suggestions made by your peers.
- Focus on maintaining a formal style. A formal style suits your purpose—giving information about a serious topic. It also fits your audience—students, teachers, and other readers interested in learning more about your topic.
  - › As you revise, eliminate any slang.
  - › Remove any first-person pronouns such as "I," "me," or "mine" or instances of addressing readers as "you." These are more suitable to a writing style that is informal, personal, and conversational.

> › Check that you have used all pronouns correctly, including reflexive and intensive pronouns. Remember that the same kinds of pronouns (ending in -*self* or -*selves*) can be either reflexive or intensive.
> › If you include your personal opinions, remove them. Your essay should be clear, direct, and unbiased.

• After you have revised elements of style, think about whether there is anything else you can do to improve your essay's information or organization.

> › Do you need to add any new textual evidence to fully support your thesis statement or engage the interest of readers?
> › Did one of your three individuals say something special that you forgot to quote? Quotations can add life to your essay.
> › Can you substitute a more precise word for a word that is general or dull?
> › Consider your organization. Would your essay flow better if you strengthened the transitions between paragraphs?
> › How effective is your conclusion? Do you want to strengthen it by leaving your readers with a final message?

Please note that excerpts and passages in the StudySync® library and this workbook are intended as touchstones to generate interest in an author's work. The excerpts and passages do not substitute for the reading of entire texts, and StudySync® strongly recommends that students seek out and purchase the whole literary or informational work in order to experience it as the author intended. Links to online resellers are available in our digital library. In addition, complete works may be ordered through an authorized reseller by filling out and returning to StudySync® the order form enclosed in this workbook.

Reading & Writing Companion   89

SKILL: SOURCES
AND CITATIONS

 DEFINE

Sources are the documents and information that an author uses to research his or her writing. Some sources are **primary sources.** A primary source is a first-hand account of thoughts or events by the individual who experienced them. Other sources are **secondary sources.** A secondary source analyzes and interprets primary sources. **Citations** are notes that give information about the sources an author used in his or her writing. Citations are required whenever authors quote others' words or refer to others' ideas in their writing. Citations let readers know who originally came up with those words and ideas.

IDENTIFICATION AND APPLICATION

• Sources can be primary or secondary in nature. Primary sources are first-hand accounts, artifacts, or other original materials. Examples of primary sources include:

  › Letters or other correspondence
  › Photographs
  › Official documents
  › Diaries or journals
  › Autobiographies or memoirs
  › Eyewitness accounts and interviews
  › Audio recordings and radio broadcasts
  › Works of art
  › Artifacts

• Secondary sources are usually text. Secondary sources are the written interpretation and analysis of primary source materials. Some examples of secondary sources include:

  › Encyclopedia articles
  › Textbooks

NOTES

- › Commentary or criticisms
- › Histories
- › Documentary films
- › News analyses

- Whether sources are primary or secondary, they must be credible and accurate. Writers of informative/explanatory texts look for sources from experts in the topic they are writing about.
  - › When researching online, they look for URLs that contain ".gov" (government agencies), ".edu" (colleges and universities), and ".org" (museums and other non-profit organizations).
  - › Writers also use respected print and online news and information sources.

- When a writer uses sources, he or she usually tells their titles and authors in the introduction to the writing. Notice that the writer of the Student Model names the authors and titles of the selections included in his or her essay in the introduction to "The Power of Change." However, when many sources have been used, or in a formal research report, writers usually also include a Works Cited list at the end of their writing. A Works Cited list includes all the information available about the sources the writer used. You will learn more about preparing a Works Cited list in a later unit.

- Anytime a writer uses words from another source exactly as they are written, the words must appear in quotation marks. Quotation marks show that the words are not the author's own words but are borrowed from another source. In the Student Model, the writer uses quotation marks around words taken directly from the source *Warriors Don't Cry:*

  "Step by step we climbed upward—where none of my people had ever before walked as a student" (Beals).

- A writer includes a citation to give credit to any source, whether primary or secondary, that is quoted exactly. There are several different ways to cite a source. In the Student Model, the writer tells readers exactly what selections are being included in the essay in the introduction. The title and author of each source is

  - › One way is to put the author's last name in parenthesis at the end of the sentence in which the quote appears. This is what the writer of the Student Model does after the quotation above.
  - › Another way to give credit is to cite the author's name in the context of the sentence. For example, in the student model essay, the writer indicates that Robinson himself says these quoted words from *I Never had it Made.*

He was proud, Robinson said, "to prove that a sport can't be called national if blacks are barred from it."

- Citations are also necessary when a writer borrows ideas from another source, even if the writer paraphrases, or puts those ideas in his or her own words. Citations credit the source, but they also help readers discover where they can learn more.

- When writers use and cite sources in research reports, they usually include a Works Cited list at the very end of their writing. A Works Cited list gives complete information about every work.

 MODEL

In this excerpt from the student model essay, the writer uses quotations from secondary source material and includes parenthetical citations.

> *Like Beals and Robinson, Feng Ru's hard work and courage changed his own country—China. Feng Ru was an immigrant to the United States. He was also a self-taught engineer. As a young man, he learned* **"all he could about machines, working in shipyards, power plants, machine shops"** *(Maksel). After awhile, he became fascinated with the new field of aviation. In 1906, he started his own* **"aircraft factory, building airplanes of his own design" (Maksel).** *However, testing new aircraft was dangerous. During a test flight, Feng lost control of the plane* **'which plunged into his workshop, setting it ablaze" (Maksel).** *Although this would not be his last crash, he did not give up his experiments. He returned to China to bring his knowledge of aviation to that country. Feng Ru died in a crash in his homeland, but to this day, he is heralded as the* **"father of Chinese aviation" (Maksel).**

Notice that each sentence begins with the writer's own words. When the writer uses portions of text from the source material, those specific portions of text appear in quotations. The student has cited material with the author's last name in parenthesis after each quotation.

The quotations in this paragraph all come from an article written by Rebecca Maksel. Because the article is written by Maksel about Feng Ru, a historical figure, and not by Feng Ru himself, this is a secondary source. All references to the secondary source are cited to give credit to the author.

PRACTICE

Write citations for quoted information in your informative/explanatory essay. When you are finished, trade with a partner and offer each other feedback. How successful was the writer in citing sources for the essay? How well did the writer incorporate sources? Did he or she always include them in parentheses at the end of a sentence, or were they sometimes included in the context of the sentence? Did the writer paraphrase some ideas, putting them in his or her own words? If so, did the writer remember to credit the original source of the paraphrased idea? Offer each other suggestions, and remember that they are most helpful when they are constructive.

Please note that excerpts and passages in the StudySync® library and this workbook are intended as touchstones to generate interest in an author's work. The excerpts and passages do not substitute for the reading of entire texts, and StudySync® strongly recommends that students seek out and purchase the whole literary or informational work in order to experience it as the author intended. Links to online resellers are available in our digital library. In addition, complete works may be ordered through an authorized reseller by filling out and returning to StudySync® the order form enclosed in this workbook.

Reading & Writing Companion

93

EDIT, PROOFREAD, AND PUBLISH

WRITING PROMPT

Think about the selections you have read that involve life-changing experiences. Write an informative/explanatory essay in which you explain how three individuals in three of the excerpts you have read faced life-changing experiences, and analyze the impact of these changes on their lives and their countries.

Your essay should include:

- an introduction with a clear thesis statement
- body paragraphs with relevant evidence and thorough analysis to support your thesis statement
- a conclusion paragraph that effectively wraps up your essay

You have revised your informative/explanatory essay and received input from your peers on that revision. Now it's time to edit and proofread your essay to produce a final version. As you reread your work, think about whether there's anything more you can do to improve it. Keep these questions in mind as you edit your writing, making additional changes as needed:

- Have I included my peers' valuable suggestions?
- Is the style and tone of my writing appropriate for my audience throughout my essay?
- Have I informed my readers about the life-changing experiences of three individuals and explained the impact of those experiences?
- Have I introduced my thesis statement clearly, developed it with strong textual evidence, and reinforced it in my conclusion?
- Does my organizational structure make the information flow smoothly? Do transitions clarify the relationships among my ideas?

- Will any of my ideas, facts, or examples be improved if I substitute a more precise word for one that is vague or general?
- Have I accurately cited my sources?

When you are satisfied with the content, style, and organization of your work, proofread your writing carefully for errors. For example, have you used correct punctuation for quotations and citations? Make sure that pronouns agree with their antecedents, and that you have used reflexive and intensive pronouns correctly. Also check that you have eliminated any sentence fragments. Be sure to correct any misspelled words.

Once you have made all your corrections, you are ready to submit and publish your work. You can distribute your writing to family and friends, hang it on a bulletin board, or post it on a blog. If you publish online, create links to your sources and citations. That way, readers can follow-up on what they've learned from your informative/explanatory essay and read more on their own.

studysync®

Reading & Writing Companion

How does history inform and inspire us?

Ancient Realms

Ancient Realms

TEXTS

TEXTS

EXTENDED WRITING PROJECT

articles find
claims
Newsela

409

Text Fulfillment
through
StudySync

Please note that excerpts and passages in the StudySync® library and this workbook are intended as touchstones to generate interest in an author's work. The excerpts and passages do not substitute for the reading of entire texts, and StudySync® strongly recommends that students seek out and purchase the whole literary or informational work in order to experience it as the author intended. Links to online resellers are available in our digital library. In addition, complete works may be ordered through an authorized reseller by filling out and returning to StudySync® the order form enclosed in this workbook.

Reading & Writing
Companion   **99**

HATSHEPSUT: HIS MAJESTY, HERSELF

NON-FICTION
Catherine M. Andronik
2001

INTRODUCTION

In Egypt's eighteenth dynasty, during the mid-to-late 1400s BCE, a long pattern of male dominance was interrupted when Hatshepsut, the widow of Pharaoh Tuthmosis II, and daughter of Tuthmosis, took the throne. Hatshepsut's reign lasted twenty-two years, during which time she built great monuments, sent an expedition to the little-known land of Punt, and handed over a peaceful Egypt to her nephew, Tuthmosis III, who subsequently attempted to erase Hatshepsut's

"Hatshepsut had no choice: she had to call herself pharaoh, or king—a male title."

 FIRST READ

 NOTES

1   Hatshepsut, royal daughter of **Pharaoh** Tuthmosis and his Great Wife Ahmose, grew up in an Egypt that was peaceful, **prosperous**, and respected throughout the known world.

2   Despite this prosperity, all but one of Hatshepsut's siblings died. Fatal diseases were common, deadly creatures such as scorpions flourished in the Egyptian desert, accidents happened, and a doctor's treatment was often more superstitious than scientific. When the time came for Pharaoh Tuthmosis to name an **heir** to his throne, only one son remained: Tuthmosis, son of Mutnofret, a woman of the pharaoh's harem. When he became pharaoh, young Tuthmosis would have little choice but to marry a woman of the royal blood. Marriages between close relatives were customary within ancient Egypt's royal family, so Hatshepsut was destined to become her half brother's wife. As the sole child of the pharaoh and the God's Wife, Hatshepsut was her dynasty's last hope to keep the royal bloodlines of Egypt intact.

3   Hatshepsut's father, Pharaoh Tuthmosis I, died at the relatively old age of fifty. His secret tomb, the first underground chamber to be hidden in the towering cliffs of the Valley of the Kings, just northwest of Thebes, had been excavated years in advance. The fine sarcophagus (sar-KOFF-ah-guss), or stone coffin, which would hold his body was also ready. The pharaoh's mummy was carefully prepared, as befitted a great and beloved king. After seventy days, with solemn ceremony, Tuthmosis was laid in a tomb filled with all the choice food and drink, games and furniture, clothing and jewelry, and the little clay servant figures, called shawabtis (shah-WAHB-tees), that he could possibly need in the afterlife.

4   Following her father's death, Hatshepsut married her half brother, and the young man was crowned Pharaoh Tuthmosis II. Hatshepsut may have been only about twelve years old. As queen, she received a variety of new titles. Her favorite was God's Wife. Tuthmosis II and Hatshepsut had one child, a daughter named Neferure (neh-feh-ROO-ray).

NOTES

5   The reign of Tuthmosis II was unremarkable. It was also brief, for he was a sickly young man. Within a few years of his coronation, Hatshepsut's husband had died.

6   With the death of Tuthmosis II, Egypt was left without a king to ensure that the many gods would look kindly upon the fragile desert land. Maat was a delicate thing, and without a pharaoh to tend to its preservation, it was in danger of collapsing.

7   Although Hatshepsut had been Tuthmosis II's Great Wife, he'd had other wives in his harem, including one named Isis. Isis had borne the pharaoh a baby boy, who was also named Tuthmosis. Since Isis was not royal, neither was her baby. But like his father, he could grow up to be pharaoh if he married a princess of the royal blood: his half sister, Neferure.

8   Until Tuthmosis III was mature enough to be crowned pharaoh what Egypt needed was a regent, an adult who could take control of the country. The regent would have to be someone familiar with palace life and protocol. He would need to conduct himself with the proper authority around the royal advisors. He should be prepared to wield power if it became necessary, and he should feel comfortable around visiting dignitaries from other lands. He needed to know his place among the priests of the various gods.

9   It was a job Hatshepsut, perhaps just fifteen years old, had been training for since her earliest days by her father's side. Women had acted as regents for infants at other times in Egypt's history, and the gods had not frowned upon them.

10   So until Tuthmosis III was ready to be crowned as pharaoh, the acting ruler of Egypt would be his aunt, the royal widow of the king, Hatshepsut.

11   At first, little Tuthmosis III was considered the pharaoh, with Hatshepsut just his second-in-command. But a small child could not be an effective ruler. As Hatshepsut settled into her role as regent, she gradually took on more and more of the royal decision-making. She appointed officials and advisors; dealt with the priests; appeared in public ceremonies first behind, then beside, and eventually in front of her nephew. Gradually, over seven years, her power and influence grew. In the end, Hatshepsut was ruling Egypt in all but name.

12   There is no reliable record of exactly when or how it happened, but at some point, Hatshepsut took a bold and unprecedented step: She had herself crowned pharaoh with the large, heavy, red-and-white double crown of the two Egypts, north and south. Since all pharaohs took a throne name, a sort of symbolic name, upon their coronation, Hatshepsut chose Maatkare (maht-KAH-ray). Maat, that crucial cosmic order, was important to Hatshepsut. Egypt

required a strong pharaoh to ensure maat. Hatshepsut could be that pharaoh—even if she did happen to be a woman.

13 A few women had tried to rule Egypt before, but never with such a valid hclaim to the throne or at such a time of peace and prosperity. When Queens Nitocris and Sobekneferu had come to the throne in earlier dynasties, Egypt had been suffering from political problems, and there had been no male heirs. These women had not ruled long or well, and neither had had the audacity to proclaim herself pharaoh. Hatshepsut would be different.

14 There was no word in the language of ancient Egypt for a female ruler; a queen was simply the wife of a king. Hatshepsut had no choice: she had to call herself pharaoh, or king—a male title. She was concerned with preserving and continuing traditional order as much as possible, so to the people of Egypt she made herself look like a man in her role as pharaoh. In ceremonies, she wore a man's short kilt instead of a woman's long dress, much as she had as a child. Around her neck she wore a king's broad collar. She even fastened a false golden beard to her chin. When she wrote about herself as pharaoh, sometimes she referred to herself as he, other times as she. This would be very confusing for historians trying to uncover her identity thousands of years later.

15 Since Hatshepsut could not marry a queen, her daughter Neferure acted as God's Wife in public rituals. It was good training for Neferure, who would in time be expected to marry her half brother, Tuthmosis III, and be his royal consort. But Hatshepsut never seems to have considered that her daughter could succeed her as pharaoh.

16 Hatshepsut might have had to look and act like a man in public, but she never gave up feminine pleasures. Archaeologists have uncovered bracelets and alabaster cosmetic pots with Hatshepsut's cartouche (kar-TOOSH), or hieroglyphic name symbol, inscribed on each. Both men and women in Egypt used **cosmetics**. They needed creams and oils to keep their skin and hair from drying out under the brutal desert sun. And the kohl, a kind of makeup made from powdered lead that people applied around their eyes, did more than make them attractive; it also helped block out the sun's glare. But Hatshepsut was especially particular about her appearance. One inscription describes her as "more beautiful than anything."

17 With the exception of one military campaign against Nubia, Hatshepsut's reign was peaceful. Instead of expanding Egypt's borders through war and conquest, Hatshepsut built **monuments** within her country to proclaim its power. Her masterpiece was the magnificent temple at the site known today as Deir el-Bahri. The temple was dedicated to Amen, the god who was supposed to be the divine father of every pharaoh, the god to whom

Please note that excerpts and passages in the StudySync® library and this workbook are intended as touchstones to generate interest in an author's work. The excerpts and passages do not substitute for the reading of entire texts, and StudySync® strongly recommends that students seek out and purchase the whole literary or informational work in order to experience it as the author intended. Links to online resellers are available in our digital library. In addition, complete works may be ordered through an authorized reseller by filling out and returning to StudySync® the order form enclosed in this workbook.

Reading & Writing Companion   103

NOTES

Hatshepsut felt she owed her good fortune. The temple at Deir el-Bahri was said to be Hatshepsut's own mortuary temple. The building is set into the side of a mountain and rises gracefully in three beautifully proportioned tiers, each supported by columns like those to be seen centuries later in Greek temples. Its design was far ahead of its time. Hatshepsut called it Djeser-Djeseru (JEH-sir jeh-SEH-roo)—"Holy of Holies."

18 On the walls of this temple, Hatshepsut had artists carve and paint her biography. According to the story told on the walls of Djeser-Djeseru, she had been chosen as pharaoh by the gods themselves, even before her birth. Perhaps, even after years on the throne, she still felt a need to justify a woman's right to rule. The gods in the pictures on the temple walls do not seem to care whether Hatshepsut is a man or a woman—in fact, some of the paintings show her as a boy.

 THINK QUESTIONS

1. Before Hatshepsut became pharaoh, what practice does the text say she had for the job? Include evidence from the text to support your answer.

2. How was Hatshepsut's reign different from the reigns of the two earlier queens who had ruled Egypt? Use evidence from the text to support your answer.

3. What evidence does the text give to support the idea that Hatshepsut cared about her appearance?

4. Use context to determine the meaning of the word **cosmetics** as it is used in *Hatshepsut, His Majesty, Herself*. Write your definition of "cosmetics" and tell how you got it. How are the words "creams," "oils," and "kohl" in the following sentences related to the vocabulary word? How does this relationship help you better understand the meaning of "cosmetics"?

5. Remembering that the Latin suffix -ous means "having, characterized by," use the context clues provided in the passage to determine the meaning of **prosperous.** Write your definition of "prosperous" and tell how you got it. In your answer, identify any words you know that seem to be related to "prosperous," and explain how these relationships helped you infer the word's meaning.

CLOSE READ

Reread the excerpt from *Hatshepsut: His Majesty, Herself*. As you reread, complete the Focus Questions below. Then use your answers and annotations from the questions to help you complete the Writing Prompt.

FOCUS QUESTIONS

1. The focus of *Hatshepsut: His Majesty, Herself* is on an individual, Hatshepsut. The first two paragraphs introduce her. What information does the second paragraph give about the special destiny that awaited Hatshepsut? Why was that her destiny? Highlight textual evidence and make annotations to explain your ideas.

2. Paragraphs 8–11 talk about what a regent in ancient Egypt was expected to be like, and they describe Hatshepsut's behavior as regent. What details show that Hatshepsut successfully did what a regent was expected to do? Highlight evidence from the text and make annotations to support your explanation.

3. What does the way Hatshepsut became pharaoh show about her character? Highlight details from the text and make annotations to show how they provide evidence for your answer.

4. Paragraph 14 provides many details about ways in which Hatshepsut made herself look like a man in public. Highlight two or more of those details. Why did she choose to appear like a man in public? Highlight textual evidence and make annotations to explain your answer.

5. Paragraphs 17–18 provide examples of the ways in which Hatshepsut used her reign to declare Egypt's power. What do the choices Hatshepsut made say about her a ruler? Highlight textual evidence and make annotations to explain your answer.

WRITING PROMPT

How is a historical figure like Hatshepsut relevant today? In what ways can she be considered an inspiration for both boys and girls? What specific events or situations in Hatshepsut's life does the author use to introduce, illustrate, and elaborate on her character and values? Write a clear and well-organized explanation that examines why Hatshepsut continues to be relevant. Develop the topic and support your ideas with facts, details, quotations, or other evidence from the text .

Please note that excerpts and passages in the StudySync® library and this workbook are intended as touchstones to generate interest in an author's work. The excerpts and passages do not substitute for the reading of entire texts, and StudySync® strongly recommends that students seek out and purchase the whole literary or informational work in order to experience it as the author intended. Links to online resellers are available in our digital library. In addition, complete works may be ordered through an authorized reseller by filling out and returning to StudySync® the order form enclosed in this workbook.

Reading & Writing Companion   **105**

BOOK OF THE DEAD

NON-FICTION
circa 1550 BCE

INTRODUCTION

Book of the Dead is the title given to the surviving collection of funerary texts composed by ancient Egyptian scribes. Generally found on pyramids, tombs, coffins and scrolls of papyrus, the hymns, spells, and prayers found in the book provided guidance to the newly dead for negotiating the important but difficult journey to the afterlife. The "Negative Confession" was to be recited just before a dead person's heart was weighed on the scales of the Hall of Ma'at

"I have wronged none, I have done no evil."

 FIRST READ

 NOTES

The Negative Confession

From the Papyrus of Ani:

1. Hail, Usekh-nemmt, who comest forth from Anu, I have not committed sin.
2. Hail, Hept-khet, who comest forth from Kher-aha, I have not committed robbery with violence.
3. Hail, Fenti, who comest forth from Khemenu, I have not stolen.
4. Hail, Am-khaibit, who comest forth from Qernet, I have not slain men and women.
5. Hail, Neha-her, who comest forth from Rasta, I have not stolen grain.
6. Hail, Ruruti, who comest forth from heaven, I have not **purloined** offerings.
7. Hail, Arfi-em-khet, who comest forth from Suat, I have not stolen the property of God.
8. Hail, Neba, who comest and goest, I have not uttered lies.
9. Hail, Set-qesu, who comest forth from Hensu, I have not carried away food.
10. Hail, Utu-nesert, who comest forth from Het-ka-Ptah, I have not uttered curses.
11. Hail, Qerrti, who comest forth from Amentet, I have not committed adultery, I have not lain with men.
12. Hail, Her-f-ha-f, who comest forth from thy cavern, I have made none to weep.
13. Hail, Basti, who comest forth from Bast, I have not eaten the heart.
14. Hail, Ta-retiu, who comest forth from the night, I have not attacked any man.
15. Hail, Unem-snef, who comest forth from the execution chamber, I am not a man of **deceit**.
16. Hail, Unem-besek, who comest forth from Mabit, I have not stolen **cultivated** land.

Please note that excerpts and passages in the StudySync® library and this workbook are intended as touchstones to generate interest in an author's work. The excerpts and passages do not substitute for the reading of entire texts, and StudySync® strongly recommends that students seek out and purchase the whole literary or informational work in order to experience it as the author intended. Links to online resellers are available in our digital library. In addition, complete works may be ordered through an authorized reseller by filling out and returning to StudySync® the order form enclosed in this workbook.

Reading & Writing Companion 107

NOTES

17. Hail, Neb-Maat, who comest forth from Maati, I have not been an eavesdropper.

18. Hail, Tenemiu, who comest forth from Bast, I have not **slandered** [no man].

19. Hail, Sertiu, who comest forth from Anu, I have not been angry without just cause.

20. Hail, Tutu, who comest forth from Ati (the Busirite Nome), I have not debauched the wife of any man.

21. Hail, Uamenti, who comest forth from the Khebt chamber, I have not debauched the wife of [any] man.

22. Hail, Maa-antuf, who comest forth from Per-Menu, I have not polluted myself.

23. Hail, Her-uru, who comest forth from Nehatu, I have terrorized none.

24. Hail, Khemiu, who comest forth from Kaui, I have not **transgressed** [the law].

25. Hail, Shet-kheru, who comest forth from Urit, I have not been wroth.

26. Hail, Nekhenu, who comest forth from Heqat, I have not shut my ears to the words of truth.

27. Hail, Kenemti, who comest forth from Kenmet, I have not **blasphemed**.

28. Hail, An-hetep-f, who comest forth from Sau, I am not a man of violence.

29. Hail, Sera-kheru, who comest forth from Unaset, I have not been a stirrer up of strife.

30. Hail, Neb-heru, who comest forth from Netchfet, I have not acted with undue haste.

31. Hail, Sekhriu, who comest forth from Uten, I have not pried into matters.

32. Hail, Neb-abui, who comest forth from Sauti, I have not multiplied my words in speaking.

33. Hail, Nefer-Tem, who comest forth from Het-ka-Ptah, I have wronged none, I have done no evil.

34. Hail, Tem-Sepu, who comest forth from Tetu, I have not worked witchcraft against the king.

35. Hail, Ari-em-ab-f, who comest forth from Tebu, I have never stopped [the flow of] water.

36. Hail, Ahi, who comest forth from Nu, I have never raised my voice.

37. Hail, Uatch-rekhit, who comest forth from Sau, I have not cursed God.

38. Hail, Neheb-ka, who comest forth from thy cavern, I have not acted with **arrogance**.

39. Hail, Neheb-nefert, who comest forth from thy cavern, I have not stolen the bread of the gods.

40. Hail, Tcheser-tep, who comest forth from the shrine, I have not carried away the khenfu cakes from the Spirits of the dead.

41. Hail, An-af, who comest forth from Maati, I have not snatched away the bread of the child, nor treated with **contempt** the god of my city.

42. Hail, Hetch-abhu, who comest forth from Ta-she (the Fayyum), I have not slain the cattle belonging to the god.

 THINK QUESTIONS

1. Using textual evidence, explain why this text is called "The Negative Confession."

2. Cite details from the text to explain how these confessions convey the values of the Egyptians.

3. Using textual evidence, support the idea that the speaker seeks to avoid punishment in the afterlife.

4. Use context clues to determine the meaning of the word **purloined** as it is used in confession Number 6 in *Book of the Dead*. Write your definition of "purloined," and tell how you arrived at it.

5. Noting that many of the confessions address the speaker's words as well as his actions, use the context clues provided in the passage to infer the meaning of **blasphemed**. Write your definition of "blasphemed," and tell how you arrived at it. Check your definition against an online or print dictionary and revise as needed.

Please note that excerpts and passages in the StudySync® library and this workbook are intended as touchstones to generate interest in an author's work. The excerpts and passages do not substitute for the reading of entire texts, and StudySync® strongly recommends that students seek out and purchase the whole literary or informational work in order to experience it as the author intended. Links to online resellers are available in our digital library. In addition, complete works may be ordered through an authorized reseller by filling out and returning to StudySync® the order form enclosed in this workbook.

Reading & Writing Companion **109**

CLOSE READ

Reread the excerpt from *Book of the Dead*. As you reread, complete the Focus Questions below. Then use your answers and annotations from the questions to help you complete the Writing Prompt.

FOCUS QUESTIONS

1. What do confessions 15, 17, and 26 have in common? What do they tell you about the laws of the Egyptian gods? Highlight textual evidence and write annotations to explain your response.

2. What idea about theft can be inferred from the confessions? What do the statements about theft suggest about the text's central idea? Highlight specific confessions from the text that provide evidence and write annotations to explain your response.

3. What idea about anger and the inability to control one's emotions can be inferred from the confessions? What do the statements about anger suggest about the text's central idea? Cite textual evidence and write annotations to explain your response.

4. The sin of arrogance is well documented in ancient texts. Which confessions are related to arrogance or pride against the gods? Highlight textual evidence and write annotations that explain your choices.

5. How do confessions 27, 37, 39, and 42 support the ideas stated in confession 41? How do they help inform the reader's understanding of the laws of the Egyptian gods? Cite specific evidence from the text, and write annotations to explain your response.

WRITING PROMPT

Reread confessions 12 to 42 of "The Negative Confession." Analyze the details, choosing eight confessions, with details that together suggest a similar central idea. Summarize the central idea in your own words, and use textual evidence that supports your thinking.

THE BOOK OF EXODUS

NON-FICTION
circa 1400 BCE

INTRODUCTION

The second book of the Pentateuch, the Book of Exodus chronicles the Israelites' escape from slavery in Egypt and their difficult passage through the wilderness to the land of Canaan. After leading his people to safety, Moses climbed Mt. Sinai, where God spoke to him from the heavens and established a covenant. The two stone tablets that Moses brought down, inscribed with the Ten Commandments, went on to become the basis for Judaic law.

"...Moses spoke, and God answered him in thunder."

NOTES

 FIRST READ

Chapter 18

1 Jethro, the priest of Mid'ian, Moses' father-in-law, heard of all that God had done for Moses and for Israel his people, how the LORD had brought Israel out of Egypt. **2** Now Jethro, Moses' father-in-law, had taken Zippo'rah, Moses' wife, after he had sent her away, **3** and her two sons, of whom the name of the one was Gershom (for he said, "I have been a sojourner in a foreign land"), **4** and the name of the other, Elie'zer (for he said, "The God of my father was my help, and delivered me from the sword of Pharaoh"). **5** And Jethro, Moses' father-in-law, came with his sons and his wife to Moses in the wilderness where he was encamped at the mountain of God. **6** And when one told Moses, "Lo, your father-in-law Jethro is coming to you with your wife and her two sons with her," **7** Moses went out to meet his father-in-law, and did obeisance and kissed him; and they asked each other of their welfare, and went into the tent. **8** Then Moses told his father-in-law all that the LORD had done to Pharaoh and to the Egyptians for Israel's sake, all the hardship that had come upon them in the way, and how the LORD had delivered them. **9** And Jethro rejoiced for all the good which the LORD had done to Israel, in that he had delivered them out of the hand of the Egyptians.

10 And Jethro said, "Blessed be the LORD, who has delivered you out of the hand of the Egyptians and out of the hand of Pharaoh. **11** Now I know that the LORD is greater than all gods, because he delivered the people from under the hand of the Egyptians, when they dealt arrogantly with them." **12** And Jethro, Moses' father-in-law, offered a burnt offering and sacrifices to God; and Aaron came with all the elders of Israel to eat bread with Moses' father-in-law before God.

13 On the morrow Moses sat to judge the people, and the people stood about Moses from morning till evening. **14** When Moses' father-in-law saw all that he was doing for the people, he said, "What is this that you are doing for the people? Why do you sit alone, and all the people stand about you from morning till evening?" **15** And Moses said to his father-in-law, "Because the

NOTES

people come to me to **inquire** of God; **16** when they have a dispute, they come to me and I decide between a man and his neighbor, and I make them know the **statutes** of God and his decisions." **17** Moses' father-in-law said to him, "What you are doing is not good. **18** You and the people with you will wear yourselves out, for the thing is too heavy for you; you are not able to perform it alone. **19** Listen now to my voice; I will give you counsel, and God be with you! You shall represent the people before God, and bring their cases to God; **20** and you shall teach them the statutes and the decisions, and make them know the way in which they must walk and what they must do. **21** Moreover choose able men from all the people, such as fear God, men who are trustworthy and who hate a bribe; and place such men over the people as rulers of thousands, of hundreds, of fifties, and of tens. **22** And let them judge the people at all times; every great matter they shall bring to you, but any small matter they shall decide themselves; so it will be easier for you, and they will bear the **burden** with you. **23** If you do this, and God so commands you, then you will be able to endure, and all these people also will go to their place in peace."

24 So Moses gave heed to the voice of his father-in-law and did all that he had said. **25** Moses chose able men out of all Israel, and made them heads over the people, rulers of thousands, of hundreds, of fifties, and of tens. 26 And they judged the people at all times; hard cases they brought to Moses, but any small matter they decided themselves. 27 Then Moses let his father-in-law depart, and he went his way to his own country.

Chapter 19

1 On the third new moon after the people of Israel had gone forth out of the land of Egypt, on that day they came into the wilderness of Sinai. **2** And when they set out from Reph'idim and came into the wilderness of Sinai, they **encamped** in the wilderness; and there Israel encamped before the mountain. **3** And Moses went up to God, and the LORD called to him out of the mountain, saying, "Thus you shall say to the house of Jacob, and tell the people of Israel: **4** You have seen what I did to the Egyptians, and how I bore you on eagles' wings and brought you to myself. **5** Now therefore, if you will obey my voice and keep my **covenant,** you shall be my own possession among all peoples; for all the earth is mine, **6** and you shall be to me a kingdom of priests and a holy nation. These are the words which you shall speak to the children of Israel."

7 So Moses came and called the elders of the people, and set before them all these words which the LORD had commanded him. **8** And all the people answered together and said, "All that the LORD has spoken we will do." And Moses reported the words of the people to the LORD. **9** And the LORD said to Moses, "Lo, I am coming to you in a thick cloud, that the people may hear when I speak with you, and may also believe you for ever."

16 On the morning of the third day there were thunders and lightnings, and a thick cloud upon the mountain, and a very loud trumpet blast, so that all the people who were in the camp trembled. **17** Then Moses brought the people out of the camp to meet God; and they took their stand at the foot of the mountain. **18** And Mount Sinai was wrapped in smoke, because the LORD descended upon it in fire; and the smoke of it went up like the smoke of a kiln, and the whole mountain quaked greatly. **19** And as the sound of the trumpet grew louder and louder, Moses spoke, and God answered him in thunder. **20** And the LORD came down upon Mount Sinai, to the top of the mountain; and the LORD called Moses to the top of the mountain, and Moses went up.

Chapter 20

1 And God spoke all these words, saying,

2 "I am the LORD your God, who brought you out of the land of Egypt, out of the house of bondage.

3 "You shall have no other gods before me.

4 "You shall not make for yourself a graven image, or any likeness of anything that is in heaven above, or that is in the earth beneath, or that is in the water under the earth; **5** you shall not bow down to them or serve them; for I the LORD your God am a jealous God, visiting the iniquity of the fathers upon the children to the third and the fourth generation of those who hate me, **6** but showing steadfast love to thousands of those who love me and keep my commandments.

7 "You shall not take the name of the LORD your God in vain; for the LORD will not hold him guiltless who takes his name in vain.

8 "Remember the Sabbath day, to keep it holy. **9** Six days you shall labor, and do all your work; **10** but the seventh day is a Sabbath to the LORD your God; in it you shall not do any work, you, or your son, or your daughter, your manservant, or your maidservant, or your cattle, or the sojourner who is within your gates; **11** for in six days the LORD made heaven and earth, the sea, and all that is in them, and rested the seventh day; therefore the LORD blessed the Sabbath day and hallowed it.

12 "Honor your father and your mother, that your days may be long in the land which the LORD your God gives you.

13 "You shall not kill.

14 "You shall not commit adultery.

15 "You shall not steal.

16 "You shall not bear false witness against your neighbor.

17 "You shall not covet your neighbor's house; you shall not covet your neighbor's wife, or his manservant, or his maidservant, or his ox, or his ass, or anything that is your neighbor's."

18 Now when all the people perceived the thunderings and the lightnings and the sound of the trumpet and the mountain smoking, the people were afraid and trembled; and they stood afar off, **19** and said to Moses, "You speak to us, and we will hear; but let not God speak to us, lest we die." **20** And Moses said to the people, "Do not fear; for God has come to prove you, and that the fear of him may be before your eyes, that you may not sin." **21** And the people stood afar off, while Moses drew near to the thick darkness where God was. **22** And the LORD said to Moses, "Thus you shall say to the people of Israel: 'You have seen for yourselves that I have talked with you from heaven.

 THINK QUESTIONS

1. What crucial advice does Jethro provide, and how does it affect Moses and the Israelites? Cite relevant textual evidence in your answer.

2. The Lord declares that he wants to make the Israelites his "possession among all peoples." What does the Lord mean? What will the Israelites need to do in order to become the Lord's "possession"? Cite textual evidence to support your explanation.

3. How do the people respond when God comes to them on the mountain? Why do they respond that way? Cite textual evidence in your answer.

4. Use context clues to determine the meaning of the word **inquire** as it is used in the Book of Exodus. Write your definition of "inquire," and tell how you arrived at it.

5. Remembering that the Latin prefix *en-* means "to cause to be," use the context clues provided in the passage to determine the meaning of **encamped.** Write your definition of "encamped," and tell how you arrived at it.

Please note that excerpts and passages in the StudySync® library and this workbook are intended as touchstones to generate interest in an author's work. The excerpts and passages do not substitute for the reading of entire texts, and StudySync® strongly recommends that students seek out and purchase the whole literary or informational work in order to experience it as the author intended. Links to online resellers are available in our digital library. In addition, complete works may be ordered through an authorized reseller by filling out and returning to StudySync® the order form enclosed in this workbook.

Reading & Writing Companion   **115**

CLOSE READ

Reread the excerpt from the Book of Exodus. As you reread, complete the Focus Questions below. Then use your answers and annotations from the questions to help you complete the Writing Prompt.

FOCUS QUESTIONS

1. Highlight details from the text in Chapter 18, verses 1–6, that introduce and illustrate Jethro's visit. What details explain Jethro's role in Moses' life? Make annotations and cite evidence from the text to explain your response.

2. How do the events described in verses 3–6 of Chapter 19 help readers understand that Moses has a special role to play in the history of the Israelites? Highlight textual evidence and annotate your ideas.

3. Highlight details in Chapter 19, verses 16–20, that describe the physical surroundings of Moses and the Israelites. What impact do the details have on these individuals? How do they help the reader interpret the events being described? Highlight textual evidence and annotate your ideas.

4. Reread Chapter 20, verses 8–11. Highlight and annotate the verse that states a central idea and the verses that provide supporting details. Then jot down reasons to explain your choices. Cite evidence from the text to explain your response.

5. Discuss the historical significance of the Ten Commandments that God delivers to Moses. How do they serve to inform the people of Israel? Throughout the ages, how have they continued to inform others? Highlight textual evidence and annotate your ideas.

WRITING PROMPT

Use your understanding of informational text elements to determine how individuals, ideas, and events interact in the Book of Exodus. Choose an important individual, event, or idea from the text and demonstrate how one influences the other elements. How does this interaction ultimately lead to the delivery of the Ten Commandments? Cite specific textual evidence to support your ideas.

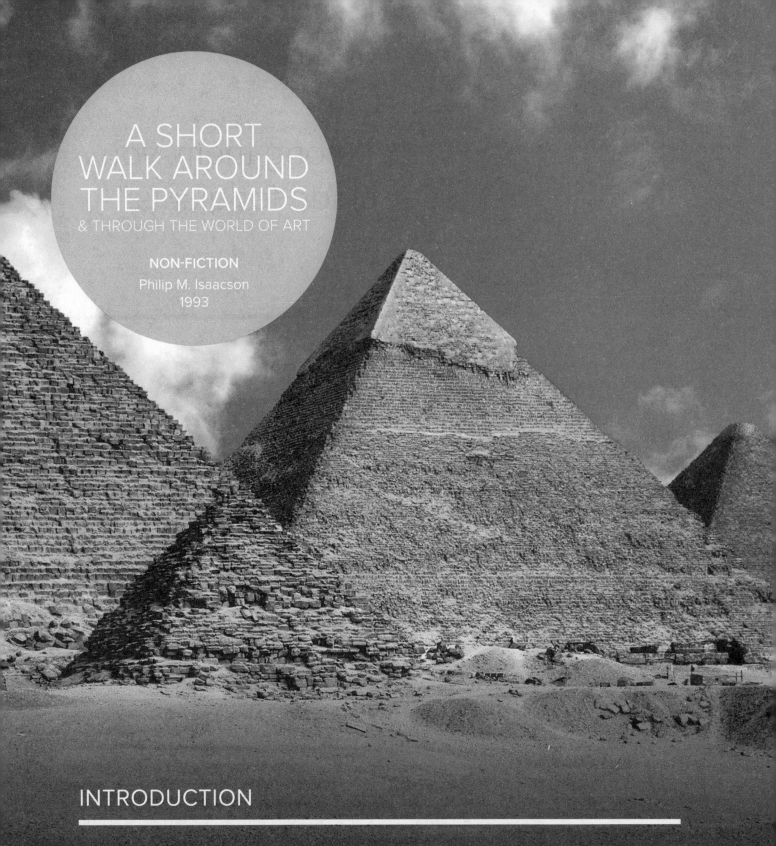

A SHORT WALK AROUND THE PYRAMIDS

& THROUGH THE WORLD OF ART

NON-FICTION

Philip M. Isaacson
1993

INTRODUCTION

Philip Isaacson's book shows the rewards of looking closely at art. He explains how color and style affect the way images are perceived, and reinforces his assertions with illustrations. Here he shows readers how to look at the pyramids and several sculptures in the way an artist would.

"When you walk among them, you walk in a place made for giants."

 FIRST READ

A SIMPLE FORM

1 At Giza, a few miles north of Saqqara, sit three great pyramids, each named for the king—or Pharaoh—during whose reign it was built. No other buildings are so well known, yet the first sight of them sitting in their field is breathtaking. When you walk among them, you walk in a place made for giants. They seem too large to have been made by human beings, too perfect to have been formed by nature, and when the sun is overhead, not solid enough to be attached to the sand. In the minutes before sunrise, they are the color of faded roses, and when the last rays of the desert sun touch them, they turn to amber. But whatever the light, their broad **proportions**, the beauty of the limestone, and the care with which it is fitted into place create three unforgettable works of art.

2 What do we learn about art when we look at the pyramids?

3 First, when all of the things that go into a work—its **components**—complement one another, they create an object that has a certain spirit, and we can call that spirit harmony. The pyramids are **harmonious** because limestone, a warm, quiet material, is a cordial companion for a simple, logical, pleasing shape. In fact, the stone and the shape are so comfortable with each other that the pyramids seem inevitable—as though they were bound to have the form, color, and texture that they do have.

4 The pyramids also show us that simple things must be made with care. The fine workmanship that went into the building of the pyramids is a part of their beauty. Complicated shapes may conceal poor work—such shapes distract our eye—but in something as simple as a pyramid, there is no way to hide flaws. Because any flaw would mar its beauty, the craftsmanship must be perfect.... Any building less beautifully designed or made with less skill would have looked awkward in the company of the dignified old structures near it.

5   Finally, pyramids show us that a light helps to shape our feelings about art. As the sun moves above the desert, the pyramids seem to change. As they do, our feelings about them also change. In the early morning they sit squarely on the horizon, and we feel that they have become the kings for which they were named; by midday they have become restless and change into silver-white clouds; and at dusk they settle down and regain their power.

6   The pyramids will always work their magic on us. Their forms, so simple and reasonable, and their great size lift us high above the ordinary moments in our lives.

SCULPTURE

7   As we have seen, art does not have to be complicated to be wonderful. Still, art can be more complicated, often much more complicated, than the pyramids at Saqqara and Giza.

8   We are looking at a piece of sculpture—the head of a horse carved in marble the color of cream. But it's more than a horse. It represents the Greek goddess of the moon, Selene, as she drops from the night into a dark sea. The horse was carved about 435 B.C. for a temple on a hill in the ancient city of Athens.

9   The temple is called the Parthenon, and the horse was part of a group of figures made especially for its east pediment, a large stone triangle fitted just under the roof. The Parthenon, high on a hill, catches the first light of morning. The carvers wanted the sight of that golden light washing across the horse and a line of other gods to be unforgettable. And so they coaxed the images of their gods out of the marble with such tenderness that they gave the world an example of ideal beauty....

10 The traditional art of African nations is a wonderful part of the world's art. Like the art of all people who live in groups called tribes—the people of the Pacific islands, the Native Americans, the Eskimos, the Indians of the Northwest Coast of Canada—it was once called **primitive** art. But it isn't primitive. It isn't primitive in its shape or in the way it is made or in the deep feelings it expresses. There doesn't seem to be a good short name for the traditional art of tribal societies, but that's not important. We should enjoy it, as we enjoy all art, because of its form, its color, its materials, and its beautiful workmanship, and for what we may know of the people who made it....

11 Most of the things that we have considered so far have three dimensions: height, width, and thickness. They have been buildings and sculpture, solid things that we can reach out and touch. Some are very simple forms. Others are more complicated. Sculpture that doesn't look real we called **abstract** and said it sometimes stood for things that we can see and sometimes for things we can only sense. All that we have seen has given us a sense of

NOTES

harmony and has touched our emotions. We found harmony when design, materials, and craftsmanship joined to become an agreeable whole. And we learned that harmony alone does not make a wonderful work of art. Art must also stir our emotions, and it can do this in many ways. The three great pyramids did this through their colossal size and their dramatic seat on the edge of the desert. The Elgin Marbles and the Kota figure achieved it by carrying the deep spiritual feelings of their artists to us.

Excerpted from *A Short Walk Around the Pyramids & Through the World of Art* by Philip M. Isaacson, published by Alfred A. Knopf.

THINK QUESTIONS

1. What is the author's opinion regarding the pyramids at Giza? Use textual evidence to support your answer.

2. According to the author, what three things do spectators learn about art when looking at the pyramids? Support your answer with evidence from the text.

3. Why does the author think that "primitive" is not a good description for the traditional art of tribal societies? Cite textual evidence to support your answer.

4. Use context to determine the meaning of the word **components** as it is used in *A Walk Around the Pyramids & Through the World of Art*. Write your definition of "components," and tell how you arrived at it. Then, use a dictionary to check your meaning and revise it, if necessary.

5. Use context clues to determine the meaning of the word **abstract** as it is used in *A Walk Around the Pyramids & Through the World of Art*. Write your definition of "abstract," and tell how you arrived at it.

CLOSE READ

Reread the excerpt from *A Walk Among the Pyramids*. As you reread, complete the Focus Questions below. Then use your answers and annotations from the questions to help you complete the Writing Prompt.

FOCUS QUESTIONS

1. In paragraph 3, Isaacson writes that limestone is a "cordial companion" for the simple, logical shape of the pyramids. This technique—in which the author describes an object as having human qualities—is called personification. If necessary, consult an online or print dictionary to determine the definition of "cordial." Then annotate ideas that help you explain Isaacson's meaning within the context of his argument. Identify and highlight specific evidence from the text that supports your response.

2. In paragraph 4, Isaacson uses the contrasting words "complicated" and "simple" to make a point about craftsmanship. Highlight evidence from the text that helps you explain how the relationship between these words supports Isaacson's argument, and make annotations noting your ideas.

3. In paragraph 6, Isaacson concludes his argument about the pyramids by stating that the great size of the pyramids lifts viewers "high above the ordinary moments" of their lives. How does this concluding statement both support and extend Isaacson's argument? Identify and highlight specific evidence from the text that supports your ideas.

4. In paragraph 9, what claim does Isaacson make about Greek sculpture? Highlight specific evidence from the text that he offers, and use the annotation tool to note the supporting reason for his claim that he implies.

5. How can examples of "unforgettable works of art" like the pyramids, both inform and inspire us? Cite specific evidence from the text that supports your ideas.

WRITING PROMPT

Isaacson makes the argument that the pyramids at Giza serve as timeless instructors to the masses about the elements of great art. Do you find Isaacson's argument about the qualities and impact of the pyramids persuasive? Why or why not? Explain Isaacson's argument, including the relationship between his claim, reasons, and evidence. Use your understanding of argument and claim to evaluate Isaacson's text. Support your writing with evidence from the text.

Please note that excerpts and passages in the StudySync® library and this workbook are intended as touchstones to generate interest in an author's work. The excerpts and passages do not substitute for the reading of entire texts, and StudySync® strongly recommends that students seek out and purchase the whole literary or informational work in order to experience it as the author intended. Links to online resellers are available in our digital library. In addition, complete works may be ordered through an authorized reseller by filling out and returning to StudySync® the order form enclosed in this workbook.

Reading & Writing Companion   **121**

AESOP'S FABLES

FICTION
Aesop
circa 600 BCE

INTRODUCTION

There are facts and fictions surrounding the person known as Aesop. Said to be an African slave freed for his wit and intelligence, and reportedly thrown to his death over a precipice by the people of Delphi, Aesop is credited with creating hundreds of fables, though none of his actual writings survive. What can't be disputed is that the short, charming tales of wisdom and folly have left an indelible mark on Western culture. In this selection of seven fables, not all have explicit morals; some you have to figure out.

"The Ants inquired of him, 'Why did you not treasure up food during the summer?'"

FIRST READ

NOTES

The Swollen Fox

1 A VERY HUNGRY FOX, seeing some bread and meat left by shepherds in the hollow of an oak, crept into the hole and made a hearty meal. When he finished, he was so full that he was not able to get out, and began to groan and lament his fate. Another Fox passing by heard his cries, and coming up, inquired the cause of his complaining. On learning what had happened, he said to him, "Ah, you will have to remain there, my friend, until you become such as you were when you crept in, and then you will easily get out."

The Flies And The Honey-Pot

2 A NUMBER of Flies were attracted to a jar of honey which had been overturned in a housekeeper's room, and placing their feet in it, ate greedily. Their feet, however, became so smeared with the honey that they could not use their wings, nor release themselves, and were suffocated. Just as they were expiring, they exclaimed, "O foolish creatures that we are, for the sake of a little pleasure we have destroyed ourselves." Pleasure bought with pains, hurts.

The Hen And The Golden Eggs

3 A COTTAGER and his wife had a Hen that laid a golden egg every day. They supposed that the Hen must contain a great lump of gold in its inside, and in order to get the gold they killed it. Having done so, they found to their surprise that the Hen differed in no respect from their other hens. The foolish pair, thus hoping to become rich all at once, **deprived** themselves of the gain of which they were assured day by day.

The Miser

4 A MISER sold all that he had and bought a lump of gold, which he buried in a hole in the ground by the side of an old wall and went to look at daily. One of his workmen observed his frequent visits to the spot and decided to watch his movements. He soon discovered the secret of the hidden treasure, and

Please note that excerpts and passages in the StudySync® library and this workbook are intended as touchstones to generate interest in an author's work. The excerpts and passages do not substitute for the reading of entire texts, and StudySync® strongly recommends that students seek out and purchase the whole literary or informational work in order to experience it as the author intended. Links to online resellers are available in our digital library. In addition, complete works may be ordered through an authorized reseller by filling out and returning to StudySync® the order form enclosed in this workbook.

Reading & Writing Companion **123**

digging down, came to the lump of gold, and stole it. The Miser, on his next visit, found the hole empty and began to tear his hair and to make loud lamentations. A neighbor, seeing him overcome with grief and learning the cause, said, "Pray do not grieve so; but go and take a stone, and place it in the hole, and fancy that the gold is still lying there. It will do you quite the same service; for when the gold was there, you had it not, as you did not make the slightest use of it."

The Fox And The Woodcutter

5   A FOX, running before the hounds, came across a Woodcutter felling an oak and begged him to show him a safe hiding-place. The Woodcutter advised him to take shelter in his own hut, so the Fox crept in and hid himself in a corner. The huntsman soon came up with his hounds and inquired of the Woodcutter if he had seen the Fox. He declared that he had not seen him, and yet pointed, all the time he was speaking, to the hut where the Fox lay hidden. The huntsman took no notice of the signs, but believing his word, hastened forward in the chase. As soon as they were well away, the Fox departed without taking any notice of the Woodcutter: whereon he called to him and reproached him, saying, "You ungrateful fellow, you owe your life to me, and yet you leave me without a word of thanks." The Fox replied, "Indeed, I should have thanked you **fervently** if your deeds had been as good as your words, and if your hands had not been traitors to your speech."

The Ants And The Grasshopper

6   THE ANTS were spending a fine winter's day drying grain collected in the summertime. A Grasshopper, **perishing** with famine, passed by and earnestly begged for a little food. The Ants inquired of him, "Why did you not treasure up food during the summer?' He replied, "I had not leisure enough. I passed the days in singing." They then said in **derision**: "If you were foolish enough to sing all the summer, you must dance supperless to bed in the winter."

The Wolf In Sheep's Clothing

7   ONCE UPON A TIME a Wolf **resolved** to disguise his appearance in order to secure food more easily. Encased in the skin of a sheep, he pastured with the flock deceiving the shepherd by his costume. In the evening he was shut up by the shepherd in the fold; the gate was closed, and the entrance made thoroughly secure. But the shepherd, returning to the fold during the night to obtain meat for the next day, mistakenly caught up the Wolf instead of a sheep, and killed him instantly.

8   Harm seek. Harm find.

THINK QUESTIONS

1. How are the moral lessons in "The Swollen Fox" and "The Honey Pot" alike? Cite textual evidence in your answer and explain how you got it.

2. Use textual evidence to explain why Aesop might have used animals as characters to teach moral lessons.

3. How are the cottager and his wife in "The Hen and the Golden Eggs" similar to the miser in "The Miser?" What lesson is Aesop teaching in both fables? Cite passages in the text that support your answer.

4. Use context to determine the meaning of the word **deprived** as it is used in the fable "The Hen and the Golden Eggs." Write your definition of "deprived" and tell how you got it. Then, use a dictionary to check your definition.

5. The Latin suffix -ly, which means "in what manner," is used in English for many adverbs. Use your knowledge of the suffix and the context clues provided in the passage to determine the meaning of **fervently**. Write your definition of "fervently" and tell how you got it. Then, check your definition in a dictionary. How does your definition differ from the official one?

CLOSE READ

Reread the excerpts from *Aesop's Fables*. As you reread, complete the Focus Questions below. Then use your answers and annotations from the questions to help you complete the Writing Prompt.

FOCUS QUESTIONS

1. Reread "The Ants and the Grasshopper." Highlight the human characteristics that Aesop gives the insects in this fable. What kind of people would these insects be? Make annotations about what Aesop might be trying to express through this personification, and how it supports the fable's moral, or theme.

2. State the message of "The Hen and the Golden Eggs" as a moral, as if you were Aesop and were adding it as a last sentence for the fable. Highlight and cite evidence in the text that points to the moral.

3. Reread "The Miser" and make annotations to explain how placing the stone in the hole helps convey the fable's theme. Use evidence from the text and make annotations noting evidence that supports your thinking.

4. Reread "The Fox and the Woodcutter." Why do you think the author chose to personify a fox in this fable, and what kind of person do you think the fox represents? What does the Fox want the woodcutter to learn from this experience? State your answer in the form of a theme, and cite specific evidence from the text in your answer.

5. The moral of "The Wolf in Sheep's Clothing" is, "Harm seek. Harm find." Explain this moral in your own words. Cite textual evidence in your answer and make annotations that support your explanation of the moral.

WRITING PROMPT

Though written centuries ago, how do the morals and themes of Aesop's fables continue to inspire and inform readers even today? Consider the themes in the fables you have read, along with the thoughts, words, and actions of the characters, and the author's use of personification to support and express themes. Explain how these are still relevant to an audience of readers today. Respond by developing and supporting your ideas with textual evidence from at least three of the fables you have read.

THE LIGHTNING THIEF

FICTION
Rick Riordan
2005

INTRODUCTION

studysynctv

Greek gods come to life in Rick Riordan's fantasy novel, *The Lightning Thief*. After being kicked out of boarding school, again, twelve-year-old Percy Jackson learns that his father is Poseidon, God of the Sea. Before long, Percy and his friends are off on a dangerous mission to find Zeus's missing lightning bolt, which must be returned before Mount Olympus erupts into war. Here, Percy questions his mother about the father who abandoned him, and then reflects on the odd things that seem to happen to him wherever he goes.

"She never exactly said, but I knew why the beach was special to her."

 FIRST READ

From Chapter 3

1 Our rental cabin was on the south shore, way out at the tip of Long Island. It was a little pastel box with faded curtains, half sunken into the dunes. There was always sand in the sheets and spiders in the cabinets, and most of the time the sea was too cold to swim in.

2 I loved the place.

3 We'd been going there since I was a baby. My mom had been going even longer. She never exactly said, but I knew why the beach was special to her. It was the place where she'd met my dad.

4 As we got closer to Montauk, she seemed to grow younger, years of worry and work disappearing from her face. Her eyes turned the color of the sea.

5 We got there at sunset, opened all the cabin's windows, and went through our usual cleaning routine. We walked on the beach, fed blue corn chips to the seagulls, and munched on blue jelly beans, blue saltwater taffy, and all the other free samples my mom had brought from work.

6 I guess I should explain about the blue food.

7 See, Gabe had once told my mom there was no such thing. They had this fight, which seemed like a really small thing at the time. But ever since, my mom went out of her way to eat blue. She baked blue birthday cakes. She mixed blueberry smoothies. She bought blue-corn tortilla chips and brought home blue candy from the shop. This—along with keeping her maiden name, Jackson, rather than calling herself Mrs. Ugliano—was proof that she wasn't totally suckered by Gabe. She did have a **rebellious** streak, like me.

8   When it got dark, we made a fire. We roasted hot dogs and marshmallows. Mom told me stories about when she was a kid, back before her parents died in the plane crash. She told me about the books she wanted to write someday, when she had enough money to quit the candy shop.

9   Eventually, I got up the nerve to ask about what was always on my mind whenever we came to Montauk—my father. Mom's eyes went all misty. I figured she would tell me the same things she always did, but I never got tired of hearing them.

10   "He was kind, Percy," she said. "Tall, handsome, and powerful. But gentle, too. You have his black hair, you know, and his green eyes."

11   Mom fished a blue jelly bean out of her candy bag. "I wish he could see you, Percy. He would be so proud."

12   I wondered how she could say that. What was so great about me? A **dyslexic, hyperactive** boy with a D+ report card, kicked out of school for the sixth time in six years.

13   "How old was I?" I asked. "I mean . . . when he left?"

14   She watched the flames. "He was only with me for one summer, Percy. Right here at this beach. This cabin."

15   "But . . . he knew me as a baby."

16   "No, honey. He knew I was expecting a baby, but he never saw you. He had to leave before you were born."

17   I tried to square that with the fact that I seemed to remember . . . something about my father. A warm glow. A smile.

18   I had always assumed he knew me as a baby. My mom had never said it outright, but still, I'd felt it must be true. Now, to be told that he'd never even seen me . . .

19   I felt angry at my father. Maybe it was stupid, but I **resented** him for going on that ocean voyage, for not having the guts to marry my mom. He'd left us, and now we were stuck with Smelly Gabe.

20   "Are you going to send me away again?" I asked her. "To another boarding school?"

21   She pulled a marshmallow from the fire.

22   "I don't know, honey." Her voice was heavy. "I think . . . I think we'll have to do something."

23   "Because you don't want me around?" I regretted the words as soon as they were out.

24   My mom's eyes welled with tears. She took my hand, squeezed it tight. "Oh, Percy, no. I—I have to, honey. For your own good. I have to send you away."

25   Her words reminded me of what Mr. Brunner had said—that it was best for me to leave Yancy.

26   "Because I'm not normal," I said.

27   "You say that as if it's a bad thing, Percy. But you don't realize how important you are. I thought Yancy Academy would be far enough away. I thought you'd finally be safe."

28   "Safe from what?"

29   She met my eyes, and a flood of memories came back to me—all the weird, scary things that had ever happened to me, some of which I'd tried to forget.

30   During third grade, a man in a black trench coat had stalked me on the playground. When the teachers threatened to call the police, he went away growling, but no one believed me when I told them that under his broad-brimmed hat, the man only had one eye, right in the middle of his head.

31   Before that—a really early memory. I was in preschool, and a teacher accidentally put me down for a nap in a cot that a snake had slithered into. My mom screamed when she came to pick me up and found me playing with a limp, scaly rope I'd somehow managed to strangle to death with my meaty toddler hands.

32   In every single school, something creepy had happened, something unsafe, and I was forced to move.

33   I knew I should tell my mom about the old ladies at the fruit stand, and Mrs. Dodds at the art museum, about my weird **hallucination** that I had sliced my math teacher into dust with a sword. But I couldn't make myself tell her. I had a strange feeling the news would end our trip to Montauk, and I didn't want that.

34   "I've tried to keep you as close to me as I could," my mom said. "They told me that was a mistake. But there's only one other option, Percy—the place your

father wanted to send you. And I just . . . I just can't stand to do it."

35   "My father wanted me to go to a special school?"

36   "Not a school," she said softly. "A summer camp."

37   My head was spinning. Why would my dad—who hadn't even stayed around long enough to see me born—talk to my mom about a summer camp? And if it was so important, why hadn't she ever mentioned it before?

38   "I'm sorry, Percy," she said, seeing the look in my eyes. "But I can't talk about it. I—I couldn't send you to that place. It might mean saying good-bye to you for good."

39   "For good? But if it's only a summer camp . . ."

40   She turned toward the fire, and I knew from her expression that if I asked her any more questions she would start to cry.

Excerpted from *The Lightning Thief* by Rick Riordan, published by Miramax Books/ Hyperion Books for Children.

THINK QUESTIONS

1. How does Percy describe himself? Is his view of himself largely positive or negative? Cite textual evidence to support your response.

2. How do Percy's beliefs about why he attends boarding school differ from those of his mother? Use textual evidence to support your response.

3. What does Percy discover about his father? In what way does that cause him to feel conflicted? Support your response with textual evidence.

4. Use context to determine the meaning of the word **rebellious** as it is used in *The Lightning Thief*. Write your definition of "rebellious" and tell how you arrived at it.

5. Remembering that the Greek prefix *dys-* means "difficult" and the Greek root *lex* means "words," use the context clues provided in the passage to determine the meaning of **dyslexic**. Write your definition of "dyslexic" and tell how you arrived at it. Then check your definition against a print or online dictionary and revise it, if necessary.

Please note that excerpts and passages in the StudySync® library and this workbook are intended as touchstones to generate interest in an author's work. The excerpts and passages do not substitute for the reading of entire texts, and StudySync® strongly recommends that students seek out and purchase the whole literary or informational work in order to experience it as the author intended. Links to online resellers are available in our digital library. In addition, complete works may be ordered through an authorized reseller by filling out and returning to StudySync® the order form enclosed in this workbook.

Reading & Writing Companion   **131**

CLOSE READ

Reread the excerpt from *The Lightening Thief*. As you reread, complete the Focus Questions below. Then use your answers and annotations from the questions to help you complete the Writing Prompt.

FOCUS QUESTIONS

1. In paragraph 7, what can you infer about Percy's mother's relationship with her husband Gabe? What does this tell you about her character? Highlight textual evidence that supports your inference, and make annotations to note specific reasons for it.

2. Look for several examples of information about Percy that are directly stated by the author in paragraph 12. Use these examples, along with Percy's narration, to make an inference about Percy's character. Highlight the textual evidence on which you base your inference, and annotate ideas that explain it.

3. As you reread paragraphs 9–19, analyze how Percy's point of view regarding his father differs from his mother's. Highlight specific textual evidence from the paragraphs that helps you contrast the two points of view, and annotate your ideas on why the differences exist.

4. Paragraph 31 describes how as a preschooler, Percy strangles a snake in his cot. This scene alludes, or refers, to the Greek hero Hercules, who is famed for doing the same thing. Hercules, who is half human and half god, is also known for his great strength and the completion of a series of 12 seemingly impossible labors or tasks. Highlight evidence from the text that refers to this allusion, and make annotations to note what the information about Hercules helps you infer about Percy.

5. Closely read the last seven paragraphs. What inferences are you able to make about the "summer camp" that Percy's dad wants to send Percy to? Highlight textual evidence and annotate ideas that support your response.

WRITING PROMPT

Because *The Lightning Thief* is told from Percy's first-person point of view, the reader starts out just as much in the dark about what might be happening in his life as he is. Write an essay that analyzes how that fact affects the way readers experience the story. How does this point of view build drama and suspense? How do inferences help the reader gain an understanding of events that even Percy might not have? Support your analysis with textual evidence.

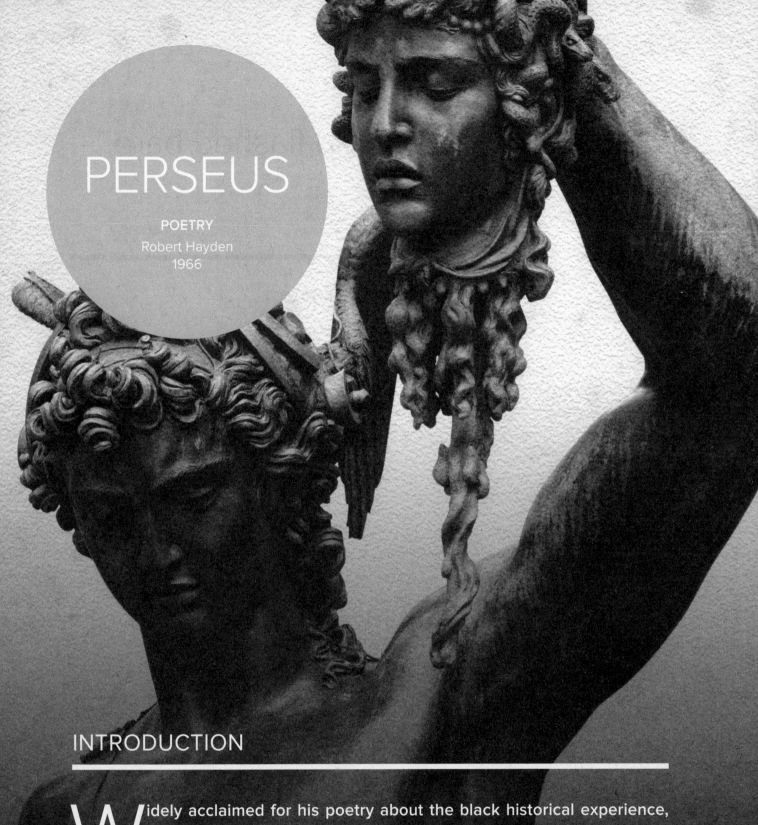

PERSEUS

POETRY
Robert Hayden
1966

INTRODUCTION

Widely acclaimed for his poetry about the black historical experience, Robert Hayden was the first African American to serve as Consultant in Poetry to the Library of Congress. Here, Hayden offers a new perspective on the Greek mythical hero Perseus. Gazing down on the severed head of Medusa, the snake-haired Gorgon, Perseus has a moment of self-reflection, and

"I struck. The shield flashed bare."

 FIRST READ

1 Her sleeping head with its great **gelid** mass
2 of serpents **torpidly** astir?
3 burned into the mirroring shield—?
4 a **scathing** image **dire**
5 as hated truth the mind accepts at last
6 and **festers** on?
7 I struck. The shield flashed bare.

8 Yet even as I lifted up the head?
9 and started from that place?
10 of gazing silences and terrored stone,
11 I thirsted to destroy.?
12 None could have passed me then—
13 no garland-bearing girl, no priest?
14 or staring boy—and lived.

"Perseus". Copyright © 1966 by Robert Hayden, from COLLECTED POEMS OF ROBERT HAYDEN by Robert Hayden, edited by Frederick Glaysher. Copyright © 1985 by Emma Hayden. Used by permission of Liveright Publishing Corporation.

THINK QUESTIONS

1. What does line 10 tell you about the setting of Medusa's resting place? Explain using evidence from the text to support your answer.

2. How is Perseus able to behead the snake-haired Medusa without turning to "terrored stone"? Cite textual evidence to support your answer.

3. After Perseus kills Medusa, what "hated truth" does he acknowledge about himself? Cite textual evidence to support your answer.

4. The word **gelid** is used in line 1 to describe the serpents on Medusa's head. What meaning of "gelid" would you infer from lines 1 and 2? Write your definition of "gelid" and tell how you arrived at it. Then, check your meaning against a print or online dictionary and revise if necessary.

5. Use context to infer the meaning of the word **torpidly** as it is used in "Perseus." Write your definition of "torpidly" here and state the clue(s) from the text you used to determine the meaning.

CLOSE READ

Reread the poem "Perseus." As you reread, complete the Focus Questions below. Then use your answers and annotations from the questions to help you complete the Writing Prompt.

FOCUS QUESTIONS

1. Use context clues to define the word **mass** as it is used in line 1 of the poem. Highlight the context clues and annotate to write your definition of the word and explore its connotations, or emotional connections. Then, analyze why the poet uses this word rather than a synonym. Support your ideas with evidence from the text.

2. What do you notice about the structure of the sentences that make up the first stanza? Highlight textual evidence and make annotations to help you explain how this structure impacts the tone this portion of the poem conveys.

3. Explain the poet's use of the phrase "gazing silences" in line 10. Cite textual evidence by highlighting clues that explain its meaning, and make annotations to explore the connotations of the words. (You may wish to use a dictionary or thesaurus to compare the connotations of some of the synonyms.) Support your ideas about why the phrase is effective with evidence from the poem.

4. How do the examples Perseus provides in lines 13 and 14 impact the meaning of what he is telling his audience at the end of the poem? How do they fit in with the poem's tone? Highlight specific examples of words and phrases, and make annotations to support your thinking. Cite textual evidence to support your ideas.

5. How do Perseus's actions call into question the qualities one historically associates with the idea of a hero? What lessons can be learned from Perseus's actions? How do they inform us? Support your ideas with textual evidence.

WRITING PROMPT

More than anything, "Perseus" shares with readers the inner struggle of a hero who finds that he is perhaps more like his bloodthirsty enemy than he realized. Trace the tone conveyed throughout the poem. How does the tone of the poem help readers better understand Perseus's conflict? How does the poet's choice of words and phrases, in both their denotative and connotative meanings, support this tone and help readers compare and contrast both sides of a hero? Support your writing with specific examples from the text.

Please note that excerpts and passages in the StudySync® library and this workbook are intended as touchstones to generate interest in an author's work. The excerpts and passages do not substitute for the reading of entire texts, and StudySync® strongly recommends that students seek out and purchase the whole literary or informational work in order to experience it as the author intended. Links to online resellers are available in our digital library. In addition, complete works may be ordered through an authorized reseller by filling out and returning to StudySync® the order form enclosed in this workbook.

Reading & Writing Companion 135

HEROES EVERY CHILD SHOULD KNOW: PERSEUS

FICTION
Hamilton Wright Mabie
1914

INTRODUCTION

Perseus, the son of a mortal woman, Danaë, and Zeus, the king of the gods, faced challenges from the day he was born. Locked in a wooden chest, the infant and his mother were set adrift in the sea. They washed up safely on a remote island, where a fisherman took them in. Eventually, Perseus grew into a fine, able-bodied young man. One fateful day, he was visited by the goddess Athena, who had chosen him for the task of killing her bitter enemy Medusa, the snake-haired Gorgon whose gaze would turn a beholder to stone. Perseus was all too willing to take on the mission, even if it meant dying in the process.

"I will go, though I die in going."

 FIRST READ

From Chapter I: Perseus

1   Then Athene smiled and said:

2   "Be patient, and listen; for if you forget my words, you will indeed die. You must go northward to the country of the Hyperboreans, who live beyond the pole, at the sources of the cold north wind, till you find the three Grey Sisters, who have but one eye and one tooth between them. You must ask them the way to the Nymphs, the daughters of the Evening Star, who dance about the golden tree, in the Atlantic island of the west. They will tell you the way to the Gorgon, that you may slay her, my enemy, the mother of monstrous beasts. Once she was a maiden as beautiful as morn, till in her pride she sinned a sin at which the sun hid his face; and from that day her hair was turned to vipers, and her hands to eagle's claws; and her heart was filled with shame and rage, and her lips with bitter venom; and her eyes became so terrible that whosoever looks on them is turned to stone; and her children are the winged horse and the giant of the golden sword; and her grandchildren are Echidna the witch-adder, and Geryon the three-headed tyrant, who feeds his herds beside the herds of hell. So she became the sister of the Gorgons, the daughters of the Queen of the Sea. Touch them not, for they are **immortal;** but bring me only Medusa's head."

3   "And I will bring it!" said Perseus; "but how am I to escape her eyes? Will she not freeze me too into stone?"

4   "You shall take this polished shield," said Athene, "and when you come near her look not at her yourself, but at her image in the brass; so you may strike her safely. And when you have struck off her head, wrap it, with your face turned away, in the folds of the goatskin on which the shield hangs. So you will bring it safely back to me, and win to yourself **renown,** and a place among the heroes who feast with the Immortals upon the peak where no winds blow."

5   Then Perseus said, "I will go, though I die in going. But how shall I cross the seas without a ship? And who will show me my way? And when I find her, how shall I slay her, if her scales be iron and brass?"

6   Now beside Athene appeared a young man more light-limbed than the stag, whose eyes were like sparks of fire. By his side was a **scimitar** of diamond, all of one clear precious stone, and on his feet were golden sandals, from the heels of which grew living wings.

7   Then the young man spoke: "These sandals of mine will bear you across the seas, and over hill and dale like a bird, as they bear me all day long; for I am Hermes, the far-famed Argus-slayer, the messenger of the Immortals who dwell on Olympus."

8   Then Perseus fell down and worshipped, while the young man spoke again:

9   "The sandals themselves will guide you on the road, for they are divine and cannot stray; and this sword itself the Argus-slayer, will kill her, for it is divine, and needs no second stroke. Arise, and gird them on, and go forth."

10   So Perseus arose, and girded on the sandals and the sword.

11   And Athene cried, "Now leap from the cliff and be gone."

12   But Perseus lingered.

13   "May I not bid farewell to my mother and to Dictys? And may I not offer burnt offerings to you, and to Hermes the far-famed Argus- slayer, and to Father Zeus above?"

14   "You shall not bid farewell to your mother, lest your heart **relent** at her weeping. I will comfort her and Dictys until you return in peace. Nor shall you offer burnt offerings to the Olympians; for your offering shall be Medusa's head. Leap, and trust in the armour of the Immortals."

15   Then Perseus looked down the cliff and shuddered; but he was ashamed to show his dread. Then he thought of Medusa and the renown before him, and he leapt into the empty air.

16   And behold, instead of falling he floated, and stood, and ran along the sky. He looked back, but Athene had vanished, and Hermes; and the sandals led him on northward ever, like a crane who follows the spring toward the Ister fens.

17   So Perseus started on his journey, going dry-shod over land and sea; and his heart was high and joyful, for the winged sandals bore him each day a seven days' journey. And he turned neither to the right hand nor the left, till he came to the Unshapen Land, and the place which has no name.

18   And seven days he walked through it on a path which few can tell, till he came to the edge of the everlasting night, where the air was full of feathers, and the soil was hard with ice; and there at last he found the three Grey Sisters, by the shore of the freezing sea, nodding upon a white log of driftwood, beneath the cold white winter moon; and they chanted a low song together, "Why the old times were better than the new."

19   There was no living thing around them, not a fly, not a moss upon the rocks. Neither seal nor sea gull dare come near, lest the ice should clutch them in its claws. The surge broke up in foam, but it fell again in flakes of snow; and it frosted the hair of the three Grey Sisters, and the bones in the ice cliff above their heads. They passed the eye from one to the other, but for all that they could not see; and they passed the tooth from one to the other, but for all that they could not eat; and they sat in the full glare of the moon, but they were none the warmer for her beams. And Perseus pitied the three Grey Sisters; but they did not pity themselves.

20   So he said, "Oh, venerable mothers, wisdom is the daughter of old age. You therefore should know many things. Tell me, if you can, the path to the Gorgon."

21   Then one cried, "Who is this who **reproaches** us with old age?" And another, "This is the voice of one of the children of men."

22   Then one cried, "Give me the eye, that I may see him"; and another, "Give me the tooth, that I may bite him." But Perseus, when he saw that they were foolish and proud, and did not love the children of men, left off pitying them. Then he stepped close to them, and watched till they passed the eye from hand to hand. And as they groped about between themselves, he held out his own hand gently, till one of them put the eye into it, fancying that it was the hand of her sister. Then he sprang back, and laughed, and cried:

23   "Cruel and proud old women, I have your eye; and I will throw it into the sea, unless you tell me the path to the Gorgon, and swear to me that you tell me right."

24   Then they wept, and chattered, and scolded; but in vain. They were forced to tell the truth, though, when they told it, Perseus could hardly make out the road.

25   "You must go," they said, "foolish boy, to the southward, into the ugly glare of the sun, till you come to Atlas the Giant, who holds the heaven and the earth apart. And you must ask his daughters, the Hesperides, who are young and foolish like yourself. And now give us back our eye, for we have forgotten all the rest."

NOTES

26 So Perseus gave them back their eye. And he leaped away to the southward, leaving the snow and the ice behind. And the terns and the sea gulls swept laughing round his head, and called to him to stop and play, and the dolphins gambolled up as he passed, and offered to carry him on their back. And all night long the sea nymphs sang sweetly. Day by day the sun rose higher and leaped more swiftly into the sea at night, and more swiftly out of the sea at dawn; while Perseus skimmed over the billows like a sea gull, and his feet were never wetted; and leapt on from wave to wave, and his limbs were never weary, till he saw far away a mighty mountain, all rose-red in the setting sun. Perseus knew that it was Atlas, who holds the heavens and the earth apart.

27 He leapt on shore, and wandered upward, among pleasant valleys and waterfalls. At last he heard sweet voices singing; and he guessed that he was come to the garden of the Nymphs, the daughters of the Evening Star. They sang like nightingales among the thickets, and Perseus stopped to hear their song; but the words which they spoke he could not understand. So he stepped forward and saw them dancing, hand in hand around the charmed tree, which bent under its golden fruit; and round the tree foot was coiled the dragon, old Ladon the sleepless snake, who lies there for ever, listening to the song of the maidens, blinking and watching with dry bright eyes.

28 Then Perseus stopped, not because he feared the dragon, but because he was bashful before those fair maids; but when they saw him, they too stopped, and called to him with trembling voices:

29 "Who are you, fair boy? Come dance with us around the tree in the garden which knows no winter, the home of the south wind and the sun. Come hither and play with us awhile; we have danced alone here for a thousand years, and our hearts are weary with longing for a playfellow."

30 "I cannot dance with you, fair maidens; for I must do the errand of the Immortals. So tell me the way to the Gorgon, lest I wander and perish in the waves."

31 Then they sighed and wept; and answered:

32 "The Gorgon! she will freeze you into stone."

33 "It is better to die like a hero than to live like an ox in a stall. The Immortals have lent me weapons, and they will give me wit to use them."

34 Then they sighed again and answered: "Fair boy, if you are bent on your own ruin, be it so. We know not the way to the Gorgon; but we will ask the giant Atlas above upon the mountain peak." So they went up the mountain to Atlas their uncle, and Perseus went up with them. And they found the giant kneeling, as he held the heavens and the earth apart.

35 They asked him, and he answered mildly, pointing to the sea board with his mighty hand, "I can see the Gorgons lying on an island far away, but this youth can never come near them, unless he has the hat of darkness, which whosoever wears cannot be seen."

36 Then cried Perseus, "Where is that hat, that I may find it?"

37 But the giant smiled. "No living mortal can find that hat, for it lies in the depths of Hades, in the regions of the dead. But my nieces are immortal, and they shall fetch it for you, if you will promise me one thing and keep your faith."

38 Then Perseus promised; and the giant said, "When you come back with the head of Medusa, you shall show me the beautiful horror, that I may lose my feeling and my breathing, and become a stone for ever; for it is weary labour for me to hold the heavens and the earth apart."

39 Then Perseus promised, and the eldest of the Nymphs went down, and into a dark cavern among the cliffs, out of which came smoke and thunder, for it was one of the mouths of hell.

40 And Perseus and the Nymphs sat down seven days and waited trembling, till the Nymph came up again; and her face was pale, and her eyes dazzled with the light for she had been long in the dreary darkness; but in her hand was the magic hat.

41 Then all the Nymphs kissed Perseus, and wept over him a long while; but he was only impatient to be gone. And at last they put the hat upon his head, and he vanished out of their sight.

42 But Perseus went on boldly, past many an ugly sight, far away into the heart of the Unshapen Land, till he heard the rustle of the Gorgons' wings and saw the glitter of their **brazen** talons; and then he knew that it was time to halt, lest Medusa should freeze him into stone.

43 He thought awhile with himself, and remembered Athene's words. He arose aloft into the air, and held the mirror of the shield above his head, and looked up into it that he might see all that was below him.

44 And he saw the three Gorgons sleeping. He knew that they could not see him, because the hat of darkness hid him; and yet he trembled as he sank down near them, so terrible were those brazen claws.

45 Two of the Gorgons were foul as swine, and lay sleeping heavily, with their mighty wings outspread; but Medusa tossed to and fro restlessly, and as she tossed Perseus pitied her. But as he looked, from among her tresses the vipers' heads awoke, and peeped up with their bright dry eyes, and showed

NOTES

their fangs, and hissed; and Medusa, as she tossed, threw back her wings and showed her brazen claws.

46 Then Perseus came down and stepped to her boldly, and looked steadfastly on his mirror, and struck with Herpe stoutly once; and he did not need to strike again.

47 Then he wrapped the head in the goat-skin, turning away his eyes, and sprang into the air aloft, faster than he ever sprang before.

48 For Medusa's wings and talons rattled as she sank dead upon the rocks; and her two foul sisters woke, and saw her lying dead.

49 Into the air they sprang yelling, and looked for him who had done the deed. They rushed, sweeping and flapping, like eagles after a hare; and Perseus's blood ran cold as he saw them come howling on his track; and he cried, "Bear me well now, brave sandals, for the hounds of Death are at my heels!"

50 And well the brave sandals bore him, aloft through cloud and sunshine, across the shoreless sea; and fast followed the hounds of Death. But the sandals were too swift, even for Gorgons, and by nightfall they were far behind, two black specks in the southern sky, till the sun sank and he saw them no more.

THINK QUESTIONS

1. Refer to one or more details from the text to explain what Athene asks Perseus to do and how Athene and Hermes equip Perseus for the task.

2. Citing evidence from the text, write two or three sentences explaining how Perseus continues to receive help from others in the accomplishment of his quest.

3. Cite textual evidence to describe how Perseus feels when he first gazes on the sleeping Medusa, as well as how and why these feelings change.

4. Use context clues to determine the meaning of the word **renown** as it is used in *Heroes Every Child Should Know: Perseus*. Write your definition of "renown" and tell how you arrived at it. Then, use a thesaurus or other reference book to identify at least one synonym for "renown." How do these synonyms help clarify the word's meaning?

5. The Latin prefix *in-* means "not," the root *mort* means "death," and the suffix *-al* means "characterized by." Use these root and affix meanings, along with context clues provided in the passage, to determine the meaning of **immortal.** Write your definition of "immortal" and tell how you got it.

CLOSE READ

Reread the excerpt from *Heroes Every Child Should Know: Perseus*. As you reread, complete the Focus Questions below. Then use your answers and annotations from the questions to help you complete the Writing Prompt.

FOCUS QUESTIONS

1. Summarize the scene between Perseus, Atlas, and his nieces (paragraphs 27–41). Why is it important to the development of the plot? Identify specific phrases or sentences that play an important role in the overall plot. Support your response with specific evidence from the text.

2. Paragraph 45 uses the word **brazen** to describe Medusa's claws. Another definition of *brazen* is "without shame." How does this other definition apply to Medusa? Does it help justify Perseus's actions against Medusa? Discuss the multiple meanings of the word "brazen" as it is used here, and cite specific evidence from the text in your response.

3. In what ways does Perseus's ultimate escape from the Gorgons resolve the story's conflict? Highlight textual evidence and make annotations noting ideas that help you evaluate the closure the resolution provides.

4. How do the ideas of being mortal or immortal affect the plot of the myth? Discuss the meanings of these words and make annotations to trace the development of these ideas in the story. Cite specific evidence from the text in your response.

5. How is the plot of the myth of Perseus similar to and different from that of the narrative poem "Perseus"? Highlight specific evidence from both texts that helps you compare and contrast them, and annotate to explain why those words or phrases show the similarities and differences of the two plots.

WRITING PROMPT

Compare and contrast how the shared plot events in the poem "Perseus" and the myth Heroes Every Child Should Know: Perseus affect the character of Perseus, as well as how he changes as a result. In your response, analyze what Perseus learns about himself in each text, along with how that realization impacts the resolution shared with readers. Remember to support your writing with evidence from the text.

Please note that excerpts and passages in the StudySync® library and this workbook are intended as touchstones to generate interest in an author's work. The excerpts and passages do not substitute for the reading of entire texts, and StudySync® strongly recommends that students seek out and purchase the whole literary or informational work in order to experience it as the author intended. Links to online resellers are available in our digital library. In addition, complete works may be ordered through an authorized reseller by filling out and returning to StudySync® the order form enclosed in this workbook.

Reading & Writing Companion   **143**

BLACK SHIPS BEFORE TROY:
THE STORY OF THE ILIAD

FICTION
Rosemary Sutcliff
1993

INTRODUCTION

The ancient Greeks and Trojans fought for 10 long years over Helen, but why? What forces brought Paris, a Trojan prince, and Helen, the most beautiful women in the world, together in the first place? Author Rosemary Sutcliffe's book tells the story of the Trojan War, which had its origins in a golden

"All she did—it seemed a small thing—was to toss down on the table a golden apple."

FIRST READ

Excerpt From "The Golden Apple"

1   In the high and far-off days when men were heroes and walked with the gods, Peleus, king of the Myrmidons, took for his wife a sea **nymph** called Thetis, Thetis of the Silver Feet. Many guests came to their wedding feast, and among the mortal guests came all the gods of high Olympus.

2   But as they sat feasting, one who had not been invited was suddenly in their midst: Eris, the goddess of **discord,** had been left out because wherever she went she took trouble with her; yet here she was, all the same, and in her blackest mood, to **avenge** the insult.

3   All she did—it seemed a small thing—was to toss down on the table a golden apple. Then she breathed upon the guests once, and vanished.

4   The apple lay gleaming among the piled fruits and the brimming wine cups; and bending close to look at it, everyone could see the words "To the fairest" traced on its side.

5   Then the three greatest of the goddesses each claimed that it was hers. Hera claimed it as wife to Zeus, the All-father, and queen of all the gods. Athene claimed that she had the better right, for the beauty of wisdom such as hers surpassed all else. Aphrodite only smiled, and asked who had a better claim to beauty's prize than the goddess of beauty herself.

6   They fell to arguing among themselves; the argument became a quarrel, and the quarrel grew more and more bitter, and each called upon the assembled guests to judge between them. But the other guests refused, for they knew well enough that whichever goddess they chose to receive the golden apple, they would make enemies of the other two.

Please note that excerpts and passages in the StudySync® library and this workbook are intended as touchstones to generate interest in an author's work. The excerpts and passages do not substitute for the reading of entire texts, and StudySync® strongly recommends that students seek out and purchase the whole literary or informational work in order to experience it as the author intended. Links to online resellers are available in our digital library. In addition, complete works may be ordered through an authorized reseller by filling out and returning to StudySync® the order form enclosed in this workbook.

Reading & Writing Companion   **145**

7   In the end, the three took the quarrel home with them to Olympus. The other gods took sides, some with one and some with another, and the ill will between them dragged on for a long while. More than long enough, in the world of men, for a child born when the quarrel first began to grow to manhood and become a warrior or a herdsman. But the immortal gods do not know time as mortals know it.

8   Now on the northeast coast of the Aegean Sea, there was a city of men. Troy was its name, a great city surrounded by strong walls, and standing on a hill hard by the shore. It had grown rich on the tolls that its kings demanded from merchant ships passing up the nearby straits to the Black Sea cornlands and down again. Priam, who was now king, was lord of wide realms and long-maned horses, and he had many sons about his hearth. And when the quarrel about the golden apple was still raw and new, a last son was born to him and his wife Queen Hecuba, and they called him Paris.

9   There should have been great rejoicing, but while Hecuba still carried the babe within her, the **soothsayers** had foretold that she would give birth to a firebrand that should burn down Troy. And so, when he was born and named, the king bade a servant carry him out into the wilderness and leave him to die. The servant did as he was bid; but a herdsman searching for a missing calf found the babe and brought him up as his own.

10 The boy grew tall and strong and beautiful, the swiftest runner and the best archer in all the country around. So his boyhood passed among the oak woods and the high hill-pastures that rose toward Mount Ida. And there he met and fell in love with wood nymph called Oenone, who loved him in return. She had the gift of being able to heal the wounds of mortal men, no matter how sorely they were hurt.

11 Among the oak woods they lived together and were happy—until one day the three jealous goddesses, still quarreling about the golden apple, chanced to look down from Olympus, and saw the beautiful young man herding his cattle on the slopes of Mount Ida. They knew, for the gods know all things, that he was the son of Priam, king of Troy, though he himself did not know it yet; but the thought came to them that he would not know who they were, and therefore he would not be afraid to judge between them. They were growing somewhat weary of the argument by then.

12 So they tossed the apple down to him, and Paris put up his hands and caught it. After it the three came down, landing before him so lightly that their feet did not bend the mountain grasses, and bade him choose between them, which was the fairest and had best right to the prize he held in his hand.

13 First Athene, in her gleaming armor, fixed him with sword-gray eyes and promised him supreme wisdom if he would name her.

14 Then Hera, in her royal robes as queen of heaven, promised him **vast** wealth and power and honour, if she awarded her the prize.

15 Lastly, Aphrodite drew near, her eyes as blue as deep-sea water, her hair like spun gold wreathed around her head, and, smiling honey-sweet, whispered that she would give him a wife as fair as herself, if he tossed the apple to her.

16 And Paris forgot the other two with their offers of wisdom and power, forgot also, for that moment, dark-haired Oenone in the shadowed oak woods; and he gave the golden apple to Aphrodite.

17 Then Athene and Hera were angry with him for refusing them the prize, just as the wedding guests had known that they would be; and both of them were angry with Aphrodite. But Aphrodite was well content, and set about keeping her promise to the herdsman who was a king's son.

Excerpted from *Black Ships Before Troy* by Rosemary Sutcliff, published by Frances Lincoln Children's Books.

 THINK QUESTIONS

1. How did the argument about which goddess was the "fairest" begin? Support your answer with evidence from the text.

2. Why did the goddesses consider Paris a good choice to judge the contest between them? Cite textual evidence that supports your answer.

3. What does Paris's choice for the winner of the contest help you infer about him? Indicate the textual evidence you used to make your inference.

4. Use context to determine the meaning of the word **nymph** as it is used in *Black Ships Before Troy*. Write your definition of "nymph" and tell how you arrived at it.

5. The Latin affix *dis-* means "away" or "apart," and the root *cord* means "heart." Use these meanings, along with context clues, to determine the meaning of the word **discord** as it is used in *Black Ships Before Troy*. Write your definition of "discord" and tell how you got it.

Please note that excerpts and passages in the StudySync® library and this workbook are intended as touchstones to generate interest in an author's work. The excerpts and passages do not substitute for the reading of entire texts, and StudySync® strongly recommends that students seek out and purchase the whole literary or informational work in order to experience it as the author intended. Links to online resellers are available in our digital library. In addition, complete works may be ordered through an authorized reseller by filling out and returning to StudySync® the order form enclosed in this workbook.

Reading & Writing Companion   **147**

CLOSE READ

Reread the excerpt from *Black Ships Before Troy*. As you reread, complete the Focus Questions below. Then use your answers and annotations from the questions to help you complete the Writing Prompt.

FOCUS QUESTIONS

1. Paragraph 2 introduces Eris, the goddess of discord. In what way does her title help you understand her actions? Highlight evidence from the text that indicates the motive, or reason, she has for behaving that way. Then use textual evidence from paragraphs 4 and 5 to analyze why she challenges the goddesses to what is essentially a beauty contest. Highlight details and make annotations that support your thinking.

2. In paragraph 7, the narrative pauses to describe the actions of the Greek gods on Olympus. What information is conveyed here, and why is this section important to the story? Highlight relevant evidence from the text and make annotations to explain what the information indicates.

3. Foreshadowing, or hinting at an event that may happen further on in a story, is a plot device often used to structure a story. Paragraph 7 states that in the time the gods spent quarreling about the goddesses and the golden apple, a child could have grown up and "become a warrior or a herdsman." Highlight textual evidence in paragraphs 8 and 9 that indicate that the statement foreshadows something about Paris's life. Make annotations to explain your ideas.

4. Readers of *Black Ships Before Troy* could likely follow the plot of the story without the mention of Oenone in paragraph 10. What does knowledge of her presence add to your understanding of Paris and his actions in the final paragraphs of the myth? Annotate ideas and highlight relevant evidence from the text to support your answer.

5. Compare and contrast how the goddess Athene is presented in the selections *Black Ships Before Troy* and *Heroes Every Child Should Know: Perseus*. From both texts, what can you infer about this goddess? Annotate ideas and highlight relevant evidence from both texts to support your answer.

WRITING PROMPT

Black Ships Before Troy is essentially a series of three events: a wedding between a goddess and a mortal, a challenge that an envious goddess poses to three more powerful goddesses, and a judgment made by a mortal prince/herdsman. Analyze how the structure of the text helps connect and develop these three events. How does one event inform the other? In your analysis, give examples of how specific parts of the text connect and contribute to the development of the plot. Remember to support your ideas with textual evidence throughout your writing.

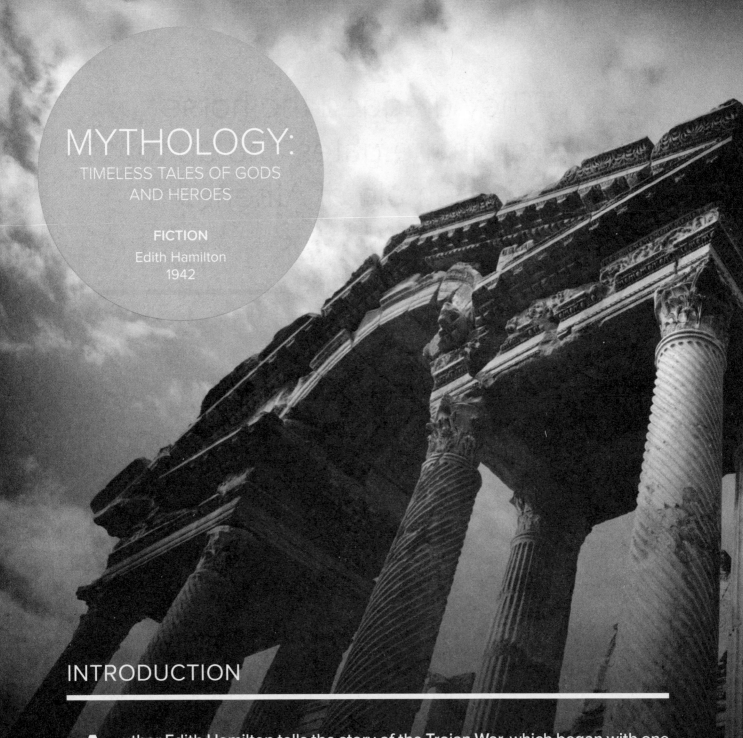

MYTHOLOGY:
TIMELESS TALES OF GODS AND HEROES

FICTION
Edith Hamilton
1942

INTRODUCTION

Author Edith Hamilton tells the story of the Trojan War, which began with one psychological trick and ended with another. According to the myth, Eris, the goddess of discord, played on the vanity and jealousy of three other goddesses—Hera, Aphrodite, and Athena—by leaving a golden apple for "the fairest." Paris, a Trojan, decided in favor of Aphrodite, and in exchange Aphrodite made Helen, the beautiful wife of the Greek king, Menelaus, fall in love with Paris. Outraged, the Greeks declared war on Troy. Ten years later, as the war dragged on, the Greeks devised a trick of their own, now known as the Trojan Horse.

"They dragged the horse through the gates and up to the temple of Athena."

 FIRST READ

From Part Four, Chapter Two: The Fall of Troy

1 [The Greeks] saw clearly by now that unless they could get their Army into the city and take the Trojans by surprise, they would never conquer. Almost ten years had passed since they had first laid siege to the town, and it seemed as strong as ever. The walls stood uninjured. They had never suffered a real attack. The fighting had taken place, for the most part, at a distance from them. The Greeks must find a secret way of entering the city, or accept defeat. The result of this new determination and new vision was the stratagem of the wooden horse. It was, as anyone would guess, the creation of Odysseus' wily mind.

2 He had a skillful worker in wood make a huge wooden horse which was hollow and so big that it could hold a number of men. Then he persuaded— and had a great deal of difficulty in doing so—certain of the chieftains to hide inside it, along with himself, of course. They were all terror-stricken except Achilles' son Neoptolemus, and indeed what they faced was no slight danger. The idea was that all the other Greeks should strike camp, and apparently put out to sea, but they would really hide beyond the nearest island where they could not be seen by the Trojans. Whatever happened they would be safe; they could sail home if anything went wrong. But in that case the men inside the wooden horse would surely die.

3 Odysseus, as can be readily believed, had not overlooked this fact. His plan was to leave a single Greek behind in the deserted camp, primed with a tale calculated to make the Trojans draw the horse into the city—and without investigating it. Then, when night was darkest, the Greeks inside were to leave their wooden prison and open the city gates to the Army, which by that time would have sailed back, and be waiting before the wall.

4   A night came when the plan was carried out. Then the last day of Troy dawned. On the wall the Trojan watchers saw with astonishment two sights, each as startling as the other. In front of the Scaean gates stood an enormous figure of a horse, such a thing as no one had ever seen, an **apparition** so strange that it was vaguely terrifying, even though there was no sound or movement coming from it. No sound or movement anywhere, indeed. The noisy Greek camp was hushed; nothing was stirring there. And the ships were gone. Only one conclusion seemed possible: The Greeks had given up. They had sailed for Greece; they had accepted defeat. All Troy **exulted.** Her long warfare was over; her sufferings lay behind her.

5   The people flocked to the abandoned Greek camp to see the sights: here Achilles had sulked so long; there Agamemnon's tent had stood; this was the quarters of the trickster, Odysseus. What rapture to see the places empty, nothing in them now to fear. At last they drifted back to where that monstrosity, the wooden horse, stood, and they gathered around it, puzzled what to do with it. Then the Greek who had been left behind in the camp discovered himself to them. His name was Sinon, and he was a most plausible speaker. He was seized and dragged to Priam, weeping and protesting that he no longer wished to be a Greek. The story he told was one of Odysseus' masterpieces. Pallas Athena had been exceedingly angry, Sinon said, at the theft of the Palladium, and the Greeks in terror had sent to the oracle to ask how they could appease her. The oracle answered: "With blood and with a maiden slain you calmed the winds when first you came to Troy. With blood must your return be sought. With a Greek life make expiation." He himself, Sinon told Priam, was the wretched victim chosen to be sacrificed. All was ready for the awful rite, which was to be carried out just before the Greeks' departure, but in the night he had managed to escape and hidden in a swamp had watched the ships sail away.

6   It was a good tale and the Trojans never questioned it. They pitied Sinon and assured him that he should **henceforth** live as one of themselves. So it befell that by false cunning and pretended tears those were conquered whom great Diomedes had never overcome, nor savage Achilles, nor ten years of warfare, nor a thousand ships. For Sinon did not forget the second part of his story. The wooden horse had been made, he said, as a votive offering to Athena, and the reason for its immense size was to discourage the Trojans from taking it into the city. What the Greeks hoped for was that the Trojans would destroy it and so draw down upon them Athena's anger. Placed in the city, it would turn her favor to them and away from the Greeks. The story was clever enough to have had by itself, in all probability, the desired effect but Poseidon, the most bitter of all the gods against Troy, contrived an addition which made the issue certain. The priest Laocoön, when the horse was first discovered, had been urgent with the Trojans to destroy it. "I fear the Greeks even when they bear gifts," he said. Cassandra, Priam's daughter, had echoed

Please note that excerpts and passages in the StudySync® library and this workbook are intended as touchstones to generate interest in an author's work. The excerpts and passages do not substitute for the reading of entire texts, and StudySync® strongly recommends that students seek out and purchase the whole literary or informational work in order to experience it as the author intended. Links to online resellers are available in our digital library. In addition, complete works may be ordered through an authorized reseller by filling out and returning to StudySync® the order form enclosed in this workbook.

Reading & Writing
Companion   151

his warning, but no one ever listened to her and she had gone back to the palace before Sinon appeared. Laocoön and his two sons heard his story with suspicion, the only doubters there. As Sinon finished, suddenly over the sea came two fearful serpents swimming to the land. Once there, they glided straight to Laocoön. They wrapped their huge coils around him and the two lads and they crushed the life out of them. Then they disappeared within Athena's temple.

7   There could be no further hesitation. To the horrified spectators Laocoön had been punished for opposing the entry of the horse which most certainly no one else would now do. All the people cried,

8   "Bring the carven image in.
Bear it to Athena,
Fit gift for the child of Zeus."

9   Who of the young but hurried forth?
Who of the old would stay at home?
With song and rejoicing they brought death in,
Treachery and destruction.

10   They dragged the horse through the gates and up to the temple of Athena. Then, rejoicing in their good fortune, believing the war ended and Athena's favor restored to them, they went to their houses in peace as they had not for ten years.

11   In the middle of the night the door in the horse opened. One by one the chieftains let themselves down. They stole to the gates and threw them wide, and into the sleeping town marched the Greek Army. What they had first to do could be carried out silently. Fires were started in buildings throughout the city. By the time the Trojans were awake, before they realized what had happened, while they were struggling into their armor, Troy was burning. They rushed out to the street one by one in confusion. Bands of soldiers were waiting there to strike each man down before he could join himself to others. It was not fighting, it was butchery. Very many died without ever a chance of dealing a blow in return. In the more distant parts of the town the Trojans were able to gather together here and there and then it was the Greeks who suffered. They were borne down by desperate men who wanted only to kill before they were killed. They knew that the one safety for the conquered was to hope for no safety. This spirit often turned the victors into the **vanquished.** The quickest-witted Trojans tore off their own armor and put on that of the dead Greeks, and many a Greek thinking he was joining friends discovered too late that they were enemies and paid for his error with his life. On top of the houses they tore up the roofs and hurled the beams down upon the Greeks. An entire tower standing on the roof of Priam's palace was

Copyright © BookheadEd Learning, LLC

lifted from its foundations and toppled over. Exulting the defenders saw it fall and **annihilate** a great band who were forcing the palace doors. But the success brought only a short respite.

Excerpted from Mythology: Timeless Tales of Gods and Heroes by Edith Hamilton, published by Grand Central Publishing.

 THINK QUESTIONS

1. What did the Greeks rely on more to defeat the Trojans—cleverness or power? Explain, citing evidence from the text to support your choice.

2. Using textual evidence, write two or three sentences that explain why Odysseus found it difficult to persuade the Greek chieftains to go along with his plan.

3. What were the two parts of Sinon's lie to the Trojans, and why was each part important? Cite textual evidence in your answer.

4. Use context clues to determine the meaning of the word **exulted** as it is used in _Mythology: Timeless Tales of Gods and Heroes_. Write your definition of "exulted" and tell how you arrived at it. Then, use a dictionary to determine the precise part of speech and pronunciation of "exulted" and write what you found.

5. Remembering that the Latin suffix _-tion_ means "the state or condition of" and the Latin root _apparare_ means "to appear," use the context clues provided in the passage to determine the meaning of **apparition.** Write your definition of "apparition" and tell how you arrived at it.

Please note that excerpts and passages in the StudySync® library and this workbook are intended as touchstones to generate interest in an author's work. The excerpts and passages do not substitute for the reading of entire texts, and StudySync® strongly recommends that students seek out and purchase the whole literary or informational work in order to experience it as the author intended. Links to online resellers are available in our digital library. In addition, complete works may be ordered through an authorized reseller by filling out and returning to StudySync® the order form enclosed in this workbook.

Reading & Writing Companion **153**

CLOSE READ

Reread the excerpt from *Mythology: Timeless Tales of Gods and Heroes.* As you reread, complete the Focus Questions below. Then use your answers and annotations from the questions to help you complete the Writing Prompt.

 FOCUS QUESTIONS

1. In the first paragraph on page 39, the author describes the city of Troy, the main setting of this excerpt. How does this description compare to the description of Troy in *Black Ships Before Troy?* Cite textual evidence showing that the setting of the two stories is the same.

2. At the end of the first paragraph of the excerpt, we learn that the idea for the Trojan horse was "the creation of Odysseus' wily mind." How does this sentence convey the meaning of the word "wily"? What other evidence in the passage can you find that support Odysseus being described this way? Highlight text and make annotations to support your response.

3. The tale that Sinon tells includes a reference to winning the support of Athene by bringing the horse into Troy. How does this detail affect the Greeks' decision? What does this tell you about the relationship between mortals and gods at this time, and how does their relationship compare to that portrayed in *Black Ships Before Troy?* Cite textual evidence from both excerpts to support your response.

4. The next-to-last paragraph of the text is very short, but it is important to the development of the plot. How does this paragraph advance the plot? In what way does the Trojans' response in this paragraph build suspense? Highlight evidence from the text and make annotations to note details that support your answer.

5. The last paragraph of the story is a long, detailed battle scene. How do the descriptive details contribute to your understanding of what happens? How does the Trojan War relate to *Black Ships Before Troy,* another selection in this unit? Highlight specific evidence from the text and make annotations to note your ideas.

WRITING PROMPT

The previous excerpt in this unit, *Black Ships Before Troy,* and this excerpt tell the beginning and ending of a long, complicated tale. Many events happened in the middle of the story to bring the plot line from a wedding feast to a bloody battle. Using clues and characters from both excerpts, write a summary of what you think might have happened from the time Paris makes his choice to the beginning of the long war. What caused the war, who were the key players, and what was the role of the gods and goddesses in the story plot? Be sure to reference events from both excerpts to tie your story together.

THE HERO SCHLIEMANN:
THE DREAMER WHO DUG FOR TROY

NON-FICTION
Laura Amy Schlitz
2006

INTRODUCTION

Author Laura Amy Schlitz's engaging book tells the story of German businessman and archaeologist Heinrich Schliemann, who was born to explore. As a boy, Schliemann thrilled over Homer's stories in *The Iliad* and *The Odyssey*. As a young man in the import trade, he traveled the globe, learning to speak fourteen languages along the way. By age forty-six, the wealthy Schliemann was ready to fulfill a boyhood dream—finding the lost city of Troy

"He was digging into a wall when he caught a glimpse of shining gold."

FIRST READ

From Chapter V

1   When Heinrich began digging at Hissarlik, he had very little idea what he was doing. He knew that he wanted to dig into the mound and find a city of the Bronze Age, but he didn't know what a Bronze Age city would look like. His guide was Homer—he was looking for **artifacts** and **architecture** that matched the descriptions in Homer's poetry. This was not a scientific approach.

2   The thrust of his plan was to dig—deep. At the top of the mound, he expected to find a Roman city, then a Greek city underneath, then a Greek city from the time of Homer, and, just below that, the walled city of *The Iliad*. Instead of carefully sifting through the mound, layer by layer, he decided to dig out vast trenches—rather as if he were removing slices from a cake. Since Homer's Troy was ancient, Heinrich expected to find it near the bottom.

3   And so he dug, violently and impatiently. Frank Calvert advised him to proceed with care, to sift through what he was throwing away, but Heinrich was not a cautious man. He whacked away at the mound as if it were a piñata.

4   Modern **archaeologists** do not dig like this. They remove the earth gently and keep detailed records of what they find. If they find an artifact that isn't what they're hoping to find, they don't discard the artifact: they change their ideas. Instead of looking *for* something, they examine whatever comes to light. Heinrich, of course, was looking for Homer's Troy. "Troy...was sacked twice," modern archaeologists remark, "once by the Greeks and once by Heinrich Schliemann." It is generally agreed that Schliemann did more damage than the Greeks.

. . .

NOTES

5   It was not until 1873 that Heinrich found the riches his heart craved. According to Heinrich, the treasure was found on the last morning of May. He was digging into a wall when he caught a glimpse of shining gold. Some instinct told him there was a rich treasure hidden within the wall, and he resolved to dig it out for himself. He announced to his workers that it was his birthday (it wasn't) and told them to take the day off. He summoned Sophia to his side and told her to fetch her red shawl. Together, the husband-and-wife team worked to dig the artifacts out of the wall. There were thousands of precious objects: helmets and swords, **vessels** of gold and silver, shields, lances, vases, cauldrons, and jewelry. There were more than eight thousand gold rings; there were earrings and bracelets and necklaces and diadems.

6   Sophia bundled the treasure in her shawl and carried it back to their living quarters. Once they were alone together, Heinrich decked his beautiful wife in the golden **diadem** that had once kissed the brow of Helen of Troy.

7   This is a good story. It is still found in books, but it is not true. For one thing, Sophia Schliemann was not with her husband on May 31. Her father had recently died, and she had gone to Athens for the funeral. As early as December 1873, Heinrich admitted to a friend at the British Museum that he had made up the story of Sophia and her red shawl. He explained that Sophia was becoming a gifted archaeologist and he wanted to encourage her by including her in the story of his great discovery.

Excerpted from *The Hero Schliemann: The Dreamer Who Dug for Troy* by Laura Amy Schlitz, published by Laurel-Leaf Books.

 THINK QUESTIONS

1. What did Heinrich Schliemann hope to find, and why? Use textual evidence to support your answer.

2. How did Schliemann's archaeological methods differ from those of modern archaeologists? Support your answer with textual evidence.

3. Why did Schliemann lie about the circumstances surrounding the discovery of Troy? Cite textual evidence in your response.

4. Remember that the suffix -*ology* means "study or science of," the suffix -*ist* means "one who practices," and the Greek root *arch* means "primitive or original." Use these affix and root meanings, along with the context clues provided in the passage, to determine the meaning of **archaeologists.** Write your definition of "archaeologists" and tell how you got it.

5. Use context to determine the meaning of the word **diadem** as it is used in *The Hero Schliemann: The Dreamer Who Dug for Troy*. Write your definition of "diadem" and tell how you arrived at it.

Please note that excerpts and passages in the StudySync® library and this workbook are intended as touchstones to generate interest in an author's work. The excerpts and passages do not substitute for the reading of entire texts, and StudySync® strongly recommends that students seek out and purchase the whole literary or informational work in order to experience it as the author intended. Links to online resellers are available in our digital library. In addition, complete works may be ordered through an authorized reseller by filling out and returning to StudySync® the order form enclosed in this workbook.

Reading & Writing Companion   **157**

CLOSE READ

Reread the excerpt from *The Hero Schliemann: The Dreamer Who Dug for Troy*. As you reread, complete the Focus Questions below. Then use your answers and annotations from the questions to help you complete the Writing Prompt.

FOCUS QUESTIONS

1. Analyze the point of view the author conveys regarding Schliemann's archaeological methods in paragraph 1. How does she convey this point of view? What role does figurative language play in expressing or supporting that point of view? Highlight textual evidence and make annotations to explain your choices.

2. In paragraphs 3 and 4, the author contrasts the way Schliemann digs with the way that modern archaeologists dig. Highlight evidence from the text that helps you understand the term "archaeological dig," and use that understanding to state whether or not you think Schliemann is conducting one. Make annotations to support your ideas.

3. Highlight the claim the author makes in paragraph 4. How does she use reasons and evidence within the paragraph to support it? Make annotations and highlight textual evidence that supports your ideas.

4. In paragraph 4, the author quotes the viewpoint of modern archaeologists in reference to Heinrich Schliemann. How does the language in this paragraph compare or contrast with the figurative language used to describe Schliemann's methods in earlier paragraphs? Why are the archaeologists using the term *sacked* here? Highlight textual evidence to support your response.

5. Discuss Heinrich Schliemann's life and work in relation to the essential question for this unit: *How does history inform and inspire us?* Make annotations and highlight textual evidence that supports your ideas.

WRITING PROMPT

In *The Hero Schliemann: The Dreamer Who Dug for Troy*, the author acknowledges Schliemann's limitations as an archaeologist. Identify how the author's choice of facts to describe Schliemann's motivations, instincts, and actions reflects Schliemann's unconventional and often problematic methods of discovery. Include in your response an analysis of how the author uses language, including figurative language, to support her claims about Schliemann's work. How do both the author's choice of facts and use of language support her point of view? Support your writing with evidence from the text.

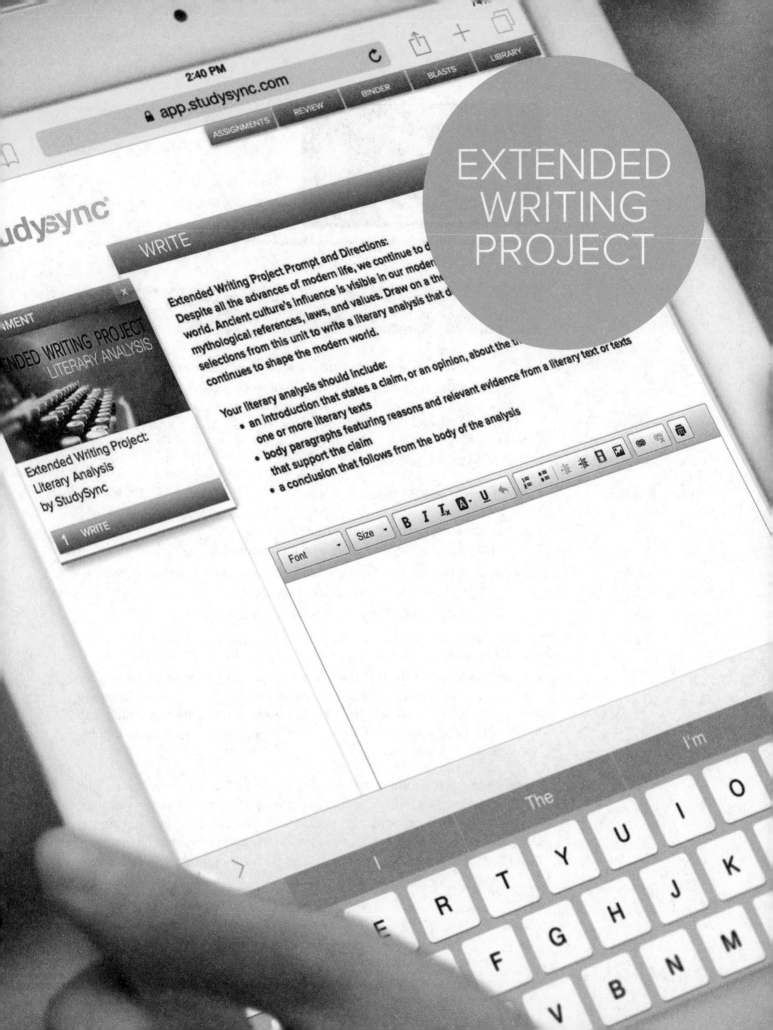

EXTENDED WRITING PROJECT

LITERARY ANALYSIS

WRITING PROMPT

Despite all the advances of modern life, we continue to draw inspiration from the ancient world. Ancient culture's influence is visible in our modern-day words and expressions, mythological references, laws, and values. Draw on a theme, idea, or lesson expressed in selections from this unit to write a literary analysis that demonstrates how ancient culture continues to shape the modern world.

Your literary analysis should include:

- an introduction that states a claim, or an opinion, about the themes or central ideas in one or more literary texts
- body paragraphs that feature reasons and relevant evidence from a literary text or texts that support the claim
- a conclusion that follows from the body of the analysis

A literary analysis considers the themes and central ideas of a piece or several pieces of literature. A literary analysis examines connections between different texts, between authors and their texts, and between literature and the world. These connections help readers better understand and identify with what they're reading.

Literary analysis is a form of argumentative writing: The writer makes a claim about the literature and then provides reasons and evidence—details, descriptions, and quotations—to support the claim. After first introducing the claim, the writer develops his or her ideas in the body of the literary analysis, using transitions to link related ideas. The purpose of the literary analysis is for the writer to convince readers that his or her claim about the literature is valid.

The features of a literary analysis include:

- an introduction that states a claim, or an opinion, about the text or texts
- a logical organizational structure with clear transitions
- embedded quotations from the text or texts that are clearly cited
- other supporting details or descriptions from the text or texts
- precise language
- a concluding statement

As you continue working on this Extended Writing Project, you'll learn more about crafting each of the elements of a literary analysis.

 STUDENT MODEL

Before you get started on your own literary analysis, begin by reading this literary analysis that one student wrote in response to the writing prompt. As you read this Student Model, highlight and annotate the features of a literary analysis that the student included.

The Consequences of Thoughtlessness

People still love reading the myths and tales of ancient Greece. By reading epics about the Trojan War, Perseus's quest, and the simple fables of Aesop, readers today can discover—and perhaps learn from—the Greeks' most deeply cherished values. The Greeks expected their heroes to be not only brave, but also intelligent and patient. To reinforce the point, ancient Greek myths and fables are full of characters who pay dearly for their foolish decisions. One theme of ancient Greek texts is clear: There can be negative consequences if people act without thinking.

Aesop was a sage whose tales were used to teach people lessons about life. Often, the lesson focused on an animal character that acts on impulse. The fox in "The Swollen Fox" was moved by hunger. He crawled into a tree to eat a meal left there by some shepherds. The fox impatiently devoured the food, and as a result became so bloated that he got stuck in the tree's trunk. Another fox told him he would have to remain there "until you become such as you were when you crept in"—in other words, until he was starving (Aesop). Similarly, the flies in "The Flies and the Honey-Pot" were greedy about food. They swarmed a jar of honey to enjoy its sweetness but became stuck and soon died. The lesson was clearly spelled out at the end: "Pleasure bought with pains, hurts" (Aesop). These fables suggest that in seeking pleasure, people may act without thinking, often with unfortunate results.

According to Greek myth, the Trojan War itself was started and concluded by a thoughtless act. When three quarreling goddesses—Hera, Athena, and Aphrodite—tossed a golden apple to a young Trojan named Paris, he caught it without thinking. Each goddess promised him something great if he would choose her as "the fairest" (Sutcliff). As the narrator of *Black Ships Before Troy* explains, instead of acting thoughtfully Paris was impulsive. He "forgot the other two with their offers of wisdom and power" (Sutcliff). He also forgot the nymph he loved and "gave the golden apple to Aphrodite" (Sutcliff). As a result, Paris received what Aphrodite had promised him, and this promise ultimately led to the war between Greece and Troy.

Unlike Paris and the fox, Perseus, as described in *Heroes Every Child Should Know*, knew that it was important to think before acting. Before he began his quest to kill the monster Medusa, Athene told him: "Be patient, and listen; for if you forget my words you will indeed die" (Mabie). Perseus listened carefully about how to use Athene's polished shield to protect himself from Medusa's deadly gaze. He followed Athene's commands even when he was afraid: "Perseus looked down the cliff and shuddered; but he was ashamed to show his dread. Then he thought of Medusa and the renown before him, and he leapt into the empty air" (Mabie). Each time Perseus faced an obstacle, he paused to consider how to go forward, and each time he was successful. Even before he cut off Medusa's head, he "thought awhile with himself, and remembered Athene's words" (Mabie). And by doing so, he successfully became a hero.

One lesson that we can learn from the literature of the ancient Greeks is to think before acting. Many tales that came to us from the Greeks emphasize the terrible consequences of acting thoughtlessly, as Paris did, or impulsively as the hungry fox and the greedy flies did. When individuals act without considering the consequences, they often end up in dire circumstances, sometimes leading to suffering or death, while those who act carefully, with patience and forethought, may become heroes. We might not all become heroes if we stop to reflect before we act, but we will be more likely to avoid trouble. That's an important lesson to think about.

THINK QUESTIONS

1. The writer of the Student Model stated an opinion that a certain theme is clear in many ancient Greek texts. What is the theme, according to the writer, and where in the first paragraph of the Model did the writer state his or her opinion about it?

2. What relevant evidence did the writer include in the Student Model to support his or her opinion? Explain why the evidence is relevant.

3. Write two or three sentences evaluating the writer's conclusion.

4. Thinking about the writing prompt, which selections or other resources would you like to use to write your own literary analysis? What are some of the selections that you may want to analyze in your own literary analysis?

5. Based on the selections you have read, listened to, or researched, how would you answer the question, *What message do ancient texts have for modern readers?* Write two or three sentences stating your opinion about some themes or messages that you might want to consider in the literary analysis you'll be developing.

Please note that excerpts and passages in the StudySync® library and this workbook are intended as touchstones to generate interest in an author's work. The excerpts and passages do not substitute for the reading of entire texts, and StudySync® strongly recommends that students seek out and purchase the whole literary or informational work in order to experience it as the author intended. Links to online resellers are available in our digital library. In addition, complete works may be ordered through an authorized reseller by filling out and returning to StudySync® the order form enclosed in this workbook.

Reading & Writing Companion   **163**

PREWRITE

WRITING PROMPT

Despite all the advances of modern life, we continue to draw inspiration from the ancient world. Ancient culture's influence is visible in our modern-day words and expressions, mythological references, laws, and values. Draw on a theme, idea, or lesson expressed in selections from this unit to write a literary analysis that demonstrates how ancient culture continues to shape the modern world.

Your literary analysis should include:

- an introduction that states a claim, or an opinion, about the themes or central ideas in one or more literary texts
- body paragraphs that feature reasons and relevant evidence from a literary text or texts that support the claim
- a conclusion that follows from the body of the analysis

You have been reading about different themes, ideas, and lessons featured in the texts of ancient civilizations. In this Extended Writing Project, you will refer to these themes and teachings as you craft your own literary analysis.

You'll first want to consider the themes, ideas, and lessons featured in the texts from this unit. What happened in each text? What conflict did the text discuss? How did the characters react? What were the consequences of the characters' actions? What lesson does the text teach?

Make a list of the answers to these questions for at least three texts from the unit. As you list the answers, look for patterns between the texts. Are any of the characters' experiences similar? Do the texts teach similar lessons? Identifying patterns can help you decide what you want to discuss in the literary analysis. Use this model to help you get started with your own prewriting:

Copyright © BookheadEd Learning, LLC

Text: *Aesop's Fables*

What Happened: A group of flies found an overturned pot of honey and ate it greedily. They became so covered with honey that they could not fly, and as a result died.

Lesson Taught: Acting hastily, without thinking, can bring about destruction.

After you have completed your prewriting, consider your thoughts and ideas as you work through the following Skills lessons to help you map out your analysis.

SKILL: THESIS STATEMENT

 ## DEFINE

In informative writing, a thesis statement expresses a writer's main idea about a topic. In argumentative writing, the thesis statement takes the form of a claim. The claim is the writer's opinion about the topic of his or her essay. When composing a literary analysis, a writer expresses an opinion about the themes or central ideas of one or more pieces of literature or informational texts. The claim typically appears in the introduction of the literary analysis, often as its last sentence. Support for the claim, such as text quotations, descriptions, and other details, appears in the body of the literary analysis.

 ## IDENTIFICATION AND APPLICATION

A thesis statement or claim in a literary analysis:

* expresses an opinion about literary or informational texts
* previews what will appear in the body of the literary analysis
* addresses all aspects of the literary analysis prompt
* appears in the introduction paragraph

 ## MODEL

The following is the introduction paragraph from the Student Model, "The Consequences of Thoughtlessness":

> People still love reading the myths and tales of ancient Greece. By reading epics about the Trojan war, Perseus's quest, and the simple fables of Aesop, readers today can discover—and perhaps learn from—the Greeks' most deeply cherished values. The Greeks expected their heroes to be not only brave, but also intelligent and patient. To reinforce the point, ancient Greek

myths and fables are full of characters who pay dearly for their foolish decisions. **One theme of ancient Greek texts is clear: There can be negative consequences if people act without thinking.**

Notice the boldfaced claim. This student's claim responds to the prompt by addressing the topic of themes in ancient texts. It also states the writer's opinion about the topic—that one clear theme of ancient Greek texts is that negative consequences can occur if someone acts without thinking.

 PRACTICE

Write a thesis statement for your literary analysis that articulates your claim in relation to the essay prompt. When you are finished, trade with a partner and offer each other feedback. How clear was the writer's claim? Is it obvious what this literary analysis will focus on? Does it specifically address the prompt? Offer each other suggestions, and remember that they are most helpful when they are constructive.

SKILL:
ORGANIZE
ARGUMENTATIVE
WRITING

DEFINE

A literary analysis is a form of argumentative writing that tries to persuade readers to accept the writer's interpretation of the theme of a literary text or the central idea of an informative text. To do so, the writer must organize and present the reasons and relevant evidence—the details and quotations from the text or texts—in a logical and convincing way. The writer must select an **organizational structure** that best suits the argument.

The writer of a literary analysis can choose from a number of organizational structures, including **compare and contrast, order of importance, problem and solution, cause-effect, and chronological order.** Experienced writers use an outline or other graphic organizer to decide how to order and convey their ideas most persuasively.

IDENTIFICATION AND APPLICATION

- When selecting an overall organizational structure for a literary analysis, a writer must consider the big idea he or she is arguing—the claim. Then the writer needs to think about the best way to present the supporting evidence. He or she can do this by asking these questions:
  - › To support my idea, will I compare and contrast ideas or details in the text?
  - › Is there an order of importance to my evidence? Is some evidence stronger than other evidence? Or does all my evidence support my idea equally well?
  - › Will I raise a question or identify a problem in my argument? Do I have supporting evidence that suggests a solution or an answer?
  - › Does my supporting evidence suggest a cause or an effect?
  - › To support my claim, does it make sense to retell the events from the text or texts in chronological order?

- Writers often use specific cue words and phrases to help readers recognize the organizational structure of their writing:
  › Compare and contrast: *like, unlike, and, both, similar to, different from, while, but, in contrast, although, also*
  › Order of importance: *most, most important, least, least important, first, finally, mainly, to begin with*
  › Problem and solution: *problem, solution, why, how*
  › Cause-effect: *because, as a consequence of, as a result, cause, effect, so*
  › Chronological order: *first, next, then, second, finally*

- Writers are not limited to using only one organizational structure throughout a text. Within a specific section or paragraph, they might use one or more different organizational structures. This does not affect the overall organization, however.

MODEL

During the prewriting stage, the writer of the Student Model discovered that several texts in this unit contained evidence to support two related ideas: The ancient Greeks admired heroes who were brave and intelligent, but they looked down on people who were foolish or thoughtless. The writer realized that he or she would need to contrast the evidence about the heroes with the evidence about the foolish characters. So a comparison-contrast organizational structure best suited this writer's argument.

In paragraph 4 of the Student Model, the writer makes the overall comparison-contrast organizational structure explicit through the use of an important cue word:

> **Unlike** Paris and the fox, Perseus, as described in *Heroes Every Child Should Know*, knew that it was important to think before acting. . . .

Once a writer has selected the most appropriate organizational structure, he or she can use an outline or a graphic organizer (for example, a Venn diagram, concept map, or flow chart) to begin organizing the supporting evidence.

The writer of the Student Model used this graphic organizer during planning to organize the evidence that supported this claim: The ancient Greeks believed that acting without thinking resulted in negative consequences.

Please note that excerpts and passages in the StudySync® library and this workbook are intended as touchstones to generate interest in an author's work. The excerpts and passages do not substitute for the reading of entire texts, and StudySync® strongly recommends that students seek out and purchase the whole literary or informational work in order to experience it as the author intended. Links to online resellers are available in our digital library. In addition, complete works may be ordered through an authorized reseller by filling out and returning to StudySync® the order form enclosed in this workbook.

Reading & Writing Companion **169**

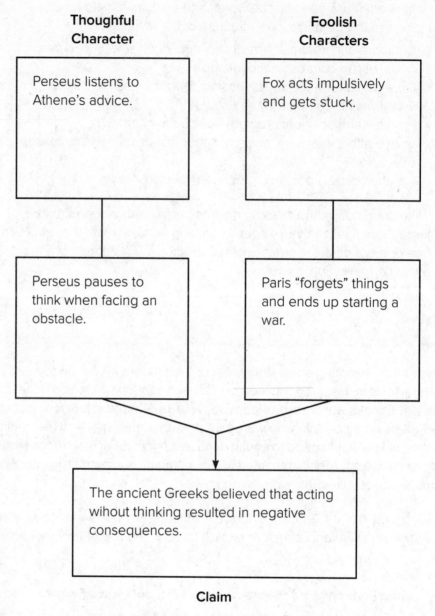

Thoughful Character

Perseus listens to Athene's advice.

Perseus pauses to think when facing an obstacle.

Foolish Characters

Fox acts impulsively and gets stuck.

Paris "forgets" things and ends up starting a war.

The ancient Greeks believed that acting wihout thinking resulted in negative consequences.

Claim

⚡ PRACTICE

Using an *Organize Argumentative Writing* graphic organizer like the one used with the Student Model, fill in the information you gathered in the prewrite stage of writing your literary analysis.

SKILL:
SUPPORTING
DETAILS

DEFINE

Because a literary analysis makes a claim about themes in literature or the central ideas in informative texts, it is a form of argumentative writing. To make his or her argument effective, the writer of a literary analysis must provide **supporting details** in the form of **reasons and relevant textual evidence** to add credibility to the claim. Reasons are statements that answer the question "Why?" Writers provide reasons to support a claim and to help readers understand their interpretation of the theme or central idea in a text. Relevant evidence includes definitions, quotations, observations, and examples from the text or texts being analyzed. Relevant evidence is the key to the success of the argument. It makes the reasons more credible and persuasive to the reader, develops the ideas, and clarifies the writer's understanding and interpretation of the text. Without reasons and relevant evidence, the writer would simply be stating his or her opinion about a theme or a central idea.

Because writers want to convince readers that their interpretations of a text's themes or central ideas are credible, they carefully select and present the evidence. Evidence is relevant only if it supports the claim and helps build the argument. If the evidence—a detail, an example, or a quotation—does not support the claim or validate the argument, it is irrelevant and should not be used.

IDENTIFICATION AND APPLICATION

Step 1:

Review your claim. To identify supporting details that are relevant to your claim, ask the following question: What am I trying to persuade my audience to believe? A writer might be making a claim about the Egyptian ruler Hatshepsut, for example:

By taking over the throne after her husband's death, Hatshepsut set an important precedent for women.

Step 2:

Ask what a reader needs to know about the topic in order to understand the claim about the theme or central idea. To understand a statement about the precedent Hatshepsut set, for example, a reader must first know what that precedent was. Why was it so significant that Hatshepsut took over the throne? The writer explains the reason for its importance in the following sentence:

Before Hatshepsut's crowning, no woman had ever been pharaoh of Egypt.

The writer then supplies additional details:

In fact, ancient Egypt did not even have a word for a female ruler.

Why is this important? The writer gives more information:

Though the word *pharaoh* meant "king," Hatshepsut nonetheless took the title because she had no other choice.

Step 3:

Look for definitions, quotations, examples, and descriptions to reinforce your claim. Use supporting details like these to build on information you've already provided, but remember to evaluate their relevance to your claim. To do this, ask yourself the following questions:

- Does this information help the reader understand the topic?
- Does this information support my claim?
- Does this information help build my argument?
- Is there stronger evidence that makes the same point?

 MODEL

In the following excerpt from *A Short Walk Around the Pyramids & Through the World of Art* Philip M. Isaacson develops the claim that the ancient Egyptian pyramids at Giza "create three unforgettable works of art."

What do we learn about art when we look at the pyramids?

First, when all of the things that go into a work—its components—complement one another, they create an object that has a certain spirit, and we can call that spirit *harmony*. The pyramids are harmonious because **limestone, a warm, quiet material, is a cordial companion for a simple, logical, pleasing shape. In fact, the stone and the shape** are so comfortable with each other that the pyramids seem inevitable—as though they were bound to have the form, color, and texture that they do have.

The pyramids also show us that simple things must be made with care. The fine workmanship that went into the building of the pyramids is a part of their beauty. Complicated shapes may conceal poor work—such shapes distract our eye—**but in something as simple as a pyramid, there is no way to hide flaws. Because any flaw would mar its beauty, the craftsmanship must be perfect** . . . Any building less beautifully designed or made with less skill would have looked awkward in the company of the dignified old structures near it.

Finally, pyramids show us that light helps to shape our feelings about art. **As the sun moves above the desert, the pyramids seem to change.** As they do, our feelings about them also change. In the **early morning** they sit squarely on the horizon, and we feel that they have **become the kings** for which they were named; by midday they have become restless and change into **silver-white clouds**; and at **dusk** they settle down and **regain their power**.

In paragraph 2, Isaacson addresses his first reason why he believes the pyramids are works of art: they're harmonious. He then gives relevant evidence that supports why.

In paragraph 3, Isaacson addresses his second reason why the pyramids are works of art: their fine workmanship. He provides relevant evidence that supports his ideas about this.

In paragraph 4, Isaacson addresses his third reason why he thinks the pyramids are works of art: they change with the light. He then gives relevant evidence that supports the different ways they do this.

The supporting details Isaacson provides add credibility to his claim.

 PRACTICE

Review a text you plan to include in your literary analysis. Then choose a detail from the text that supports the claim you plan to make. Write three or four sentences telling why this specific detail is relevant and important evidence that will support your reasons and claim in your literary analysis.

NOTES

EXTENDED WRITING PROJECT
PLAN

PLAN

WRITING PROMPT

Despite all the advances of modern life, we continue to draw inspiration from the ancient world. Ancient culture's influence is visible in our modern-day words and expressions, mythological references, laws, and values. Draw on a theme, idea, or lesson expressed in selections from this unit to write a literary analysis that demonstrates how ancient culture continues to shape the modern world.

Your literary analysis should include:

- an introduction that states a claim, or an opinion, about the themes or central ideas in one or more literary texts
- body paragraphs that feature reasons and relevant evidence from a literary text or texts that support the claim
- a conclusion that follows from the body of the analysis

Review the information you listed in your *Organize Argumentative Writing* graphic organizer detailing events and characters from different texts, along with a theme or lesson the texts share. This organized information and the claim you made in your thesis statement will help you to create a road map to use for writing your literary analysis.

Consider the following questions as you develop your main paragraph topics and their supporting details in the road map:

- What happened in the texts?
- What conflicts did the texts discuss?
- How did the characters react?
- What were the consequences of the characters' actions?
- What lesson did the texts teach, or what was their theme?
- How do the texts' lessons still shape the modern world?

When you plan your literary analysis, you want to be sure that the main topic of each paragraph supports or gives a reason for your claim. You also want to be sure that the ideas and details you include in each paragraph, such as the textual evidence you cite from your sources, are relevant to that paragraph's specific topic and help your readers understand the topic. Use this model to get started with your road map:

Literary Analysis Road Map

Claim: One theme of ancient Greek texts is that negative consequences can occur if people act without thinking.

Paragraph 1 Topic: People can discover and learn about ancient Greeks' values by reading their tales.

> **Supporting Detail #1:** Greeks expected heroes to be brave, intelligent, and patient.
>
> **Supporting Detail #2:** Characters who were foolish paid dearly for it.

Paragraph 2 Topic: Aesop's tales taught lessons about what happened to greedy characters.

> **Supporting Detail #1:** The fox in "The Swollen Fox" ate too much after finding food hidden in a tree. He got stuck in the tree.
>
> **Supporting Detail #2:** The flies in "The Flies and the Honey-Pot" swarmed a jar of honey and got stuck. They soon died.

Paragraph 3 Topic: A thoughtless act started the Trojan War.

> **Supporting Detail #1:** The goddesses Hera, Athena, and Aphrodite asked the Trojan, Paris, to choose which of them was the fairest. Paris chose Aphrodite.
>
> **Supporting Detail #2:** As a result, Paris received what Aphrodite had promised him, and this promise ultimately led to the war between Greece and Troy.

SKILL: INTRODUCTIONS

DEFINE

The **introduction** is the opening paragraph or section of a literary analysis or other nonfiction text. The introduction of a literary analysis **identifies the texts or the topic to be discussed, states the writer's claim,** and **previews the supporting evidence** that will appear in the body of the text. The introduction is also the place where most writers include a **"hook"** that is intended to connect with and engage readers.

IDENTIFICATION AND APPLICATION

- In a literary analysis, the introduction is the section in which the writer **identifies the texts or topic to be discussed.** Remember, a literary analysis examines one or more literary texts, and the writer must let readers know what the focus of the analysis will be. Once readers have that information, they can concentrate on the writer's claim.

- A literary analysis is a form of argument, so the writer's claim is an important part of the introduction. The claim is a direct statement of the writer's opinion about or interpretation of the texts under discussion. By **stating the claim** in the introduction, the writer lets readers know the ideas he or she will explore in the body of the analysis. Establishing a claim here also allows readers to form their own opinions, which they can then measure against the writer's as they read the literary analysis.

- Another use of the introduction is to provide a **preview of the supporting evidence** that will follow in the body of the text. By using the introduction to hint at key details, the writer can establish an effective argument, increasing the likelihood that readers will agree with his or her claim.

- The introduction's **"hook"** leaves readers with a first impression about what to expect from the writer. Good hooks engage readers' interest and make them want to keep reading. A hook might be an intriguing image, a surprising detail, a funny anecdote, or a shocking statistic. The hook should appeal to the audience and help readers connect to the topic in a meaningful way so that they will take the writer's claim seriously.

MODEL

The introduction of the excerpt from *A Short Walk Around the Pyramids & Through the World of Art* by Philip M. Isaacson contains key elements of an introduction:

> **At Giza, a few miles north of Saqqara, sit three great pyramids,** each named for the king—or Pharaoh—during whose reign it was built. No other buildings are so well known, yet the first sight of them sitting in their field is breathtaking. When you walk among them, you walk in a place made for giants. **They seem too large to have been made by human beings, too perfect to have been formed by nature, and when the sun is overhead, not solid enough to be attached to the sand.** In the minutes before sunrise, they are the color of faded roses, and when the last rays of the desert sun touch them, they turn to amber. But whatever the light, **their broad proportions, the beauty of the limestone, and the care with which it is fitted into place create three unforgettable works of art.**

In this introductory paragraph, the writer immediately identifies his **topic**—the pyramids of Giza. He provides a **hook** by describing the pyramids in vivid detail: they seem "too large," "too perfect," and "not solid enough to be attached to the sand." These details lead directly to the writer's **claim**—that the pyramids are "unforgettable works of art." The writer also hints at the **evidence** to follow in the analysis, referring to the pyramids' "broad proportions," "the beauty of the limestone," and "the care with which it is fitted into place."

 PRACTICE

Write an introduction for your literary analysis that includes the claim you have already worked on and a hook to capture your readers' interest. When you are finished, trade with a peer review partner. Provide helpful feedback on each other's introductions.

SKILL: BODY PARAGRAPHS AND TRANSITIONS

 DEFINE

Body paragraphs are the parts of a literary analysis that appear between the introduction and conclusion paragraphs. This is the section where you support your claim with reasons and evidence taken from the text or texts you are writing about. In general, each body paragraph should focus on one main point or idea so that the reader can easily follow along. All the main points of the body paragraphs should collectively support the claim.

It's important to structure each body paragraph clearly. One possible way to structure the body paragraph of a literary analysis is by including the following elements:

Topic sentence: The topic sentence is the first sentence of a body paragraph. It states the main point of the paragraph. The topic sentence should relate to the claim you make in your introduction.

Evidence #1: You should provide carefully selected evidence from the text or texts to support your topic sentence. Evidence can include relevant definitions, specific details, quotations, and examples.

Evidence #2: Continue to develop your topic sentence with a second piece of evidence.

Analysis/Explanation: After presenting evidence, you should explain how the evidence helps support your topic sentence—and general claim—about the text or texts.

Concluding sentence: After presenting your evidence and analysis, wrap up the main idea in a concluding sentence.

Transitions are connecting words and phrases that writers use to clarify the relationship among ideas in a text. For example, transition words and phrases can help clarify the relationship among a claim, reasons, and evidence in a literary analysis. Transitions help make connections between words in a sentence and ideas in individual paragraphs.

Copyright © BookheadEd Learning, LLC

Words such as *and, or,* and *but* help writers make connections between words in a sentence, while words and phrases such as *also, in addition to,* and *likewise* help establish relationships between ideas in body paragraphs. Adding transition words or phrases like these to the beginning or end of a paragraph can help a writer guide readers smoothly through a text.

Writers also use words and phrases such as *unlike, similarly, in contrast, most important,* and *least important* to help indicate the organizational structure in which they're presenting ideas. *Unlike, similarly,* and *in contrast,* for example, indicate a compare-and-contrast relationship among ideas. In a literary analysis, writers often compare and contrast texts in terms of the texts' similar or different approaches to a common theme, character, or other element.

 ## IDENTIFICATION AND APPLICATION

- Body paragraphs are the section of the literary analysis between the introduction and conclusion paragraphs. These paragraphs provide the main points of the literary analysis, along with their evidence and explanations. Typically, writers develop one main idea per body paragraph.
  › A topic sentence clearly states the main idea of that paragraph. The main idea always relates to the writer's claim.
  › Evidence consists of relevant definitions, specific details, quotations, and examples.
  › Analysis and explanation tell how the evidence relates to the topic sentence.
  › A conclusion sentence wraps up the paragraph's main idea.

- Certain transition words and phrases indicate specific organizational relationships within a text. Here are some examples:
  › Cause-effect: *because, accordingly, as a result, so, for, since, therefore, if, then*
  › Compare and contrast: *like, unlike, also, both, similarly, although, while, but, however, whereas, meanwhile, on the contrary, yet, still*
  › Chronological order: *first, then, next, finally, before, after, when, following, and within a few years*

 ## MODEL

Each body paragraph of the Student Model develops and supports the writer's claim with textual evidence. Just as a reader draws evidence from a literary or informational text to support ideas in a discussion, a writer also selects specific textual evidence to support ideas in his or her writing.

Please note that excerpts and passages in the StudySync® library and this workbook are intended as touchstones to generate interest in an author's work. The excerpts and passages do not substitute for the reading of entire texts, and StudySync® strongly recommends that students seek out and purchase the whole literary or informational work in order to experience it as the author intended. Links to online resellers are available in our digital library. In addition, complete works may be ordered through an authorized reseller by filling out and returning to StudySync® the order form enclosed in this workbook.

Reading & Writing Companion   **179**

Read the first body paragraph from the Student Model, "The Consequences of Thoughtlessness." Look closely at the structure and note the textual evidence as well as the transition word in bold. Think about the effectiveness of the literary analysis. Does it develop the main point made in the topic sentence? How does the transition word help you understand the relationship between the writer's claim and the ideas developed in the body paragraph?

> **Aesop was a sage whose tales were used to teach people lessons about life.** Often, the lesson focused on an animal character that acts on impulse. The fox in "The Swollen Fox" was moved by hunger. He crawled into a tree to eat a meal left there by some shepherds. The fox impatiently devoured the food, and as a result became so bloated that he got stuck in the tree's trunk. Another fox told him he would have to remain there **"until you become such as you were when you crept in"**—in other words, until he was starving (Aesop). **Similarly,** the flies in "The Flies and the Honey-Pot" were greedy about food. They swarmed a jar of honey to enjoy its sweetness but became stuck and soon died. The lesson was clearly spelled out at the end: **"Pleasure bought with pains, hurts"** (Aesop). These fables suggest that in seeking pleasure, people may act without thinking, often with unfortunate results.

The first body paragraph of the Student Model begins by stating, "Aesop was a sage whose tales were used to teach people lessons about life." This **topic sentence** clearly establishes the main idea this body paragraph will develop. It lets readers know that the writer will be discussing the lessons Aesop's tales taught.

This topic sentence is followed by **evidence.** The writer cites the example of what happens to the greedy fox in "The Swollen Fox" by including a direct quotation from the tale. The writer then cites the example of the flies in the fable "The Flies and the Honey-Pot." By using the transition word *similarly,* the writer lets readers know that the the flies are being compared to the fox. The writer chooses a direct quotation from this second fable to highlight the similarity in the lesson learned by the fox and the flies: "Pleasure bought with pains, hurts" (Aesop).

Next, the writer **explains** the significance of these ancient tales and what they tell us. The paragraph concludes by stating that Aesop's fables suggest that "in seeking gratification, people may act without thinking, often with unfortunate results." This **concluding sentence** wraps up the paragraph and relates back to the claim that a common theme in ancient Greek texts was that thoughtlessness led to bad consequences.

The writer uses additional transition words and phrases such as *also, but,* and *then* within the other body paragraphs to help guide readers as they transition from one sentence to the next.

PRACTICE

Write one body paragraph for your literary analysis that compares or contrasts the texts selected for your essay. Make sure your paragraph follows the suggested format, starting with a topic sentence. When you are finished, trade with a partner and offer each other feedback. How effective is the topic sentence at stating the main point of the paragraph? How strong is the textual evidence used to support the topic sentence? What is being compared and contrasted in the paragraph? Do transition words help make the compare-and-contrast relationship clear? Offer each other suggestions, and remember that they are most helpful when they are constructive.

Please note that excerpts and passages in the StudySync® library and this workbook are intended as touchstones to generate interest in an author's work. The excerpts and passages do not substitute for the reading of entire texts, and StudySync® strongly recommends that students seek out and purchase the whole literary or informational work in order to experience it as the author intended. Links to online resellers are available in our digital library. In addition, complete works may be ordered through an authorized reseller by filling out and returning to StudySync® the order form enclosed in this workbook.

Reading & Writing
Companion

181

SKILL: CONCLUSIONS

 DEFINE

A **conclusion** is the closing statement or section of a nonfiction text. In a literary analysis, the conclusion brings the writer's argument to a close. It follows directly from the introduction's claim and the reasons and relevant evidence provided in the body of the text. The conclusion of a literary analysis should restate the claim the writer is making about the text or texts in the analysis and also summarize the writer's main ideas. In some types of writing, the conclusion might also include a recommendation, a call to action, or an insightful comment.

 IDENTIFICATION AND APPLICATION

- An effective conclusion of a literary analysis will restate the writer's claim about the themes or central ideas of one or more texts.

- The conclusion should briefly summarize the strongest and most convincing reasons and evidence from the body paragraphs. Focusing on the strongest points makes it more likely that readers will agree with the writer's claim.

- Some conclusions offer a recommendation or some form of insight relating to the analysis. This may take any of the following forms:

  › An answer to a question first posed in the introduction
  › A question designed to elicit reflection on the part of the reader
  › A memorable or inspiring message
  › A last compelling example
  › A suggestion that readers learn more

MODEL

In the concluding paragraph of the student model "The Consequences of Thoughtlessness," the writer reinforces the claim, reminds readers of the main points of the literary analysis, and ends with a strong final message.

> **One lesson that we can learn from the literature of the ancient Greeks is to think before acting.** Many tales that came to us from the Greeks emphasize the **terrible consequences of acting thoughtlessly, as Paris did, or impulsively as the hungry fox and the greedy flies did. When individuals act without considering the consequences, they often end up in dire circumstances, sometimes leading to suffering or death,** while those who act carefully, with patience and forethought, may become heroes. We might not all become heroes **if we stop to reflect before we do something, but we will be more likely to avoid trouble. That's an important lesson to think about.**

The claim in the student model's introduction states that one theme of ancient Greek texts is that negative consequences can result if you act without thinking. The first line of the conclusion above mentions that we can learn from ancient Greek literature to think before acting. In the next few sentences, the writer includes specific examples of characters who suffered as a result of their thoughtlessness. Next, the writer states, "When individuals act without considering the consequences, they often end up suffering or dead." This statement directly supports the claim of the literary analysis. At the very end, the writer leaves us with a final message to apply to our own lives, stating that, "if we stop to reflect before we do something . . . we will be more likely to avoid trouble." This is an effective message to leave with readers.

 PRACTICE

Write a conclusion for your literary analysis. Your literary analysis should include a restatement of the claim you have already worked on and a final thought you want to leave with readers. When you are finished, trade with a peer review partner. Offer each other supportive feedback on your conclusions.

DRAFT

WRITING PROMPT

Despite all the advances of modern life, we continue to draw inspiration from the ancient world. Ancient culture's influence is visible in our modern-day words and expressions, mythological references, laws, and values. Draw on a theme, idea, or lesson expressed in selections from this unit to write a literary analysis that demonstrates how ancient culture continues to shape the modern world.

Your literary analysis should include:

- an introduction that states a claim, or an opinion, about the themes or central ideas in one or more literary texts
- body paragraphs that feature reasons and relevant evidence from a literary text or texts that support the claim
- a conclusion that follows from the body of the analysis

You've already begun working on your own literary analysis. You've considered your purpose, audience, and topic. You've carefully examined the unit's texts and selected the ones you plan to write about. Based on your analysis of textual evidence, you've identified what you want to say about lessons expressed in the texts. You've decided how to organize information, and you've gathered supporting details in the form of reasons and relevant evidence. You've practiced writing drafts of an introduction, a body paragraph, and a conclusion. Now it's time to write a whole draft of your literary analysis.

Use your road map and your other prewriting materials to help you as you write. Remember that a literary analysis begins with an introduction that features a claim. Body paragraphs then develop the claim by providing reasons and relevant evidence to support it, such as quotations, specific details, and examples. Transitional words and phrases establish an organizational structure and help the reader understand the relationships among the claim, reasons, and evidence in the literary analysis. A concluding paragraph restates or reinforces the claim and important points from the literary analysis. The conclusion may also convey a message to your readers.

When drafting, ask yourself these questions:

- How can I make my hook more effective?
- What can I do to clarify my claim?
- Which textual evidence—including relevant direct quotations, examples, and observations—best supports my claim?
- How can I improve the analysis by using better transitions?
- How can I effectively restate my claim in the conclusion?
- What final message do I want to leave with my readers?

Be sure to carefully read your draft before you submit it. You want to make sure you've addressed every part of the prompt.

REVISE

WRITING PROMPT

Despite all the advances of modern life, we continue to draw inspiration from the ancient world. Ancient culture's influence is visible in our modern-day words and expressions, mythological references, laws, and values. Draw on a theme, idea, or lesson expressed in selections from this unit to write a literary analysis that demonstrates how ancient culture continues to shape the modern world.

Your literary analysis should include:

- an introduction that states a claim, or an opinion, about the themes or central ideas in one or more literary texts
- body paragraphs that feature reasons and relevant evidence from a literary text or texts that support the claim
- a conclusion that follows from the body of the analysis

You have written a draft of your literary analysis. You have also received input from your peers about how to improve it. Now you are going to revise your draft.

Here are some recommendations to help you revise:

- Review the suggestions made by your peers.
- Focus on maintaining a formal style. A formal style suits your purpose—persuading readers to agree with your ideas about a text or texts. It is also appropriate for your audience—students, teachers, and other readers interested in learning more about your topic. Your style and tone should be consistent throughout your literary analysis.
  › As you revise, eliminate any informal language, such as slang.
  › Remove any first-person pronouns such as "I," "me," or "mine" or instances of addressing readers as "you," except when leaving readers

with a final thought or message in the conclusion. Check that you have used and punctuated all pronouns correctly.

› If necessary, incorporate a greater variety of sentence structures, and check that you aren't beginning every sentence the same way. Varying sentence lengths and patterns will make your writing style more interesting to read.

• After you have revised elements of style, review your literary analysis to see whether you can make improvements to its information or organization.

› Does your introduction present a claim that is reinforced by your conclusion?

› Have you chosen clear reasons and relevant evidence to demonstrate how ancient cultures continue to shape the modern world? What new textual evidence might you want to add, such as quotations and examples, to better support your claim?

› Can you substitute a more precise word for a word that is too general or overused?

› Is your organizational structure apparent? What transitional words and phrases might help clarify the connection among your claim, reasons, and evidence?

NOTES

SKILL: SOURCES AND CITATIONS

 DEFINE

Sources are the texts that writers use to research their writing. A **primary source** is a first-hand account of events by the person who experienced them. Another type of source is known as a **secondary source.** This is a source that analyzes or interprets primary sources. **Citations** are notes that provide information about the source texts. It is necessary for a writer to provide a citation if he or she quotes directly from a text or refers to others' ideas in a text. The citation lets readers know who stated the quoted words or originally came up with the idea.

 IDENTIFICATION AND APPLICATION

- Sources can be either primary or secondary. Primary sources are first-hand accounts or original materials, such as the following:

  › Letters or other correspondence
  › Photographs
  › Official documents
  › Diaries or journals
  › Autobiographies or memoirs
  › Eyewitness accounts and interviews
  › Audio recordings and radio broadcasts
  › Literary texts, such as novels, poems, fables, and dramas
  › Works of art
  › Artifacts

- Secondary sources are usually texts. Secondary sources are the written interpretation and analysis of primary source materials. Some examples of secondary sources include:

  › Encyclopedia articles
  › Textbooks
  › Commentary or criticisms

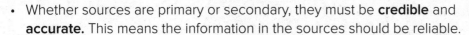

NOTES

> › Histories
> › Documentary films
> › News analyses

- Whether sources are primary or secondary, they must be **credible** and **accurate.** This means the information in the sources should be reliable.

- When a writer of a literary analysis quotes directly from a source, he or she must copy the words exactly as they appear in the source, placing them within quotation marks. Here's an example from the Student Model:

> He **"forgot the other two with their offers of wisdom and power"** (Sutcliff). He also forgot the nymph he loved and **"gave the golden apple to Aphrodite"** (Sutcliff).

- Writers of literary analyses must cite the sources they're quoting directly. One way to do this is by putting the author's name in parentheses at the end of the sentence in which the quotation appears. This is the method shown above in the excerpt from the Student Model. Another method is to cite the author's name in the context of the sentence.

- Writers must also provide citations when borrowing ideas from another source, even when writers are just paraphrasing, or putting the ideas into their own words. Citations serve both to credit the source and help readers find out where they can learn more.

 MODEL

In this excerpt from the Student Model, "The Consequences of Thoughtlessness," the writer quotes from the literary text he or she is analyzing and identifies the quotations' source.

> Aesop was a sage whose tales were used to teach people lessons about life. Often, the lesson focused on an animal character that acts on impulse. The fox in "The Swollen Fox" was moved by hunger. He crawled into a tree to eat a meal left there by some shepherds. The fox impatiently devoured the food, and as a result became so bloated that he got stuck in the tree's trunk. Another fox told him he would have to remain there **"until you become such as you were when you crept in"**—in other words, starving **(Aesop)**. Similarly, the flies in "The Flies and the Honey-Pot" were greedy about food. They

swarmed a jar of honey to enjoy its sweetness but became stuck and soon died. The lesson was clearly spelled out at the end: **"Pleasure bought with pain, hurts" (Aesop).** These fables suggest that in seeking gratification, people may act without thinking, often with unfortunate results.

Notice that only the portions of text taken directly from the source appear in quotations, and that the author's last name appears in parentheses at the end of the sentence in which the quotation appears.

 PRACTICE

Choose a body paragraph from the revised draft of your literary analysis. Be sure it is a paragraph that includes textual evidence in the form of a quotation. Review your body paragraph and add or correct citations of quoted material. Remember that you can cite the author of a source either in the context of the sentence that contains the quoted material or in parentheses at the end of the sentence.

EDIT, PROOFREAD, AND PUBLISH

WRITING PROMPT

Despite all the advances of modern life, we continue to draw inspiration from the ancient world. Ancient culture's influence is visible in our modern-day words and expressions, mythological references, laws, and values. Draw on a theme, idea, or lesson expressed in selections from this unit to write a literary analysis that demonstrates how ancient culture continues to shape the modern world.

Your literary analysis should include:

- an introduction that states a claim, or an opinion, about the themes or central ideas in one or more literary texts
- body paragraphs that feature reasons and relevant evidence from a literary text or texts that support the claim
- a conclusion that follows from the body of the analysis

Now that you have revised your literary analysis and received input from your peers, it's time to edit and proofread to produce a final version. Have you taken into consideration all the suggestions from your peers? Ask yourself these questions: Have I fully supported my claim with strong textual evidence? Have I correctly cited my sources? Does my literary analysis need additional transitions to clarify the relationship among my claim, reasons, and evidence? Have I consistently maintained a formal style? Does my conclusion follow from my analysis of the texts and reinforce my claim? What else can I do to improve my literary analysis?

Please note that excerpts and passages in the StudySync® library and this workbook are intended as touchstones to generate interest in an author's work. The excerpts and passages do not substitute for the reading of entire texts, and StudySync® strongly recommends that students seek out and purchase the whole literary or informational work in order to experience it as the author intended. Links to online resellers are available in our digital library. In addition, complete works may be ordered through an authorized reseller by filling out and returning to StudySync® the order form enclosed in this workbook.

Reading & Writing Companion **191**

Once you are satisfied with your work, proofread it for errors. For example, check that you have used correct punctuation for quotations and citations. Have you used pronouns correctly? Have you capitalized all proper nouns? Be sure to correct any misspelled words you find in your literary analysis.

After you have made all your corrections, you are ready to submit and publish your work. You can distribute your writing to family and friends, hang it on a bulletin board, or post your writing on a blog. If you do decide to publish your work online, include links to your sources and citations. This will enable readers to learn more from the sources on their own time. You might also want to adapt your writing to an oral report that you can deliver as a presentation to your class or to an audience of friends or family. As a writer, you want to share your words and thoughts with others.

studysync®

Reading & Writing Companion

When should we stand up for others and ourselves?

Facing Challenges

UNIT 3   When should we stand up for others and ourselves?

Facing Challenges

 TEXTS

TEXTS

EXTENDED WRITING PROJECT

409

Text Fulfillment
through
StudySync

A WRINKLE IN TIME

FICTION
Madeleine L'Engle
1962

INTRODUCTION

Meg Murry and her precocious younger brother Charles will do anything they can to find their father. Did their father's top-secret experiments with time-travel cause his mysterious disappearance? What evil forces are holding him hostage? The children embark on a dangerous journey to find the answers, joined by their young neighbor, Calvin. In the excerpt below, they have arrived on Camazotz, a distant planet controlled by a sinister force. There they encounter a strange man with a fixed, red-eyed gaze. Telepathically, he urges them to merge their thoughts with his.

"Look into my eyes. Look deep within them and I will tell you."

 FIRST READ

 NOTES

Excerpt from Chapter 7: The Man with Red Eyes

1 "Once ten is ten. Once eleven is eleven. Once twelve is twelve."

2 The number words pounded insistently against Meg's brain. They seemed to be **boring** their way into her skull.

3 "Twice one is two. Twice two is four. Twice three is six."

4 Calvin's voice came out in an angry shout. "Fourscore and seven years ago our fathers brought forth on this continent a new nation, conceived in liberty, and dedicated to the proposition that all men are created equal."

5 "Twice four is eight. Twice five is ten. Twice six is twelve."

6 "Father!" Meg screamed. "Father!" The scream, half involuntary, jerked her mind back out of darkness.

7 The words of the multiplication table seemed to break up into laughter. "Splendid! Splendid! You have passed your **preliminary** tests with flying colors."

8 "You didn't think we were as easy as all that, falling for that old stuff, did you?" Charles Wallace demanded.

9 "Ah, I hoped not. I most sincerely hoped not. But after all you are very young and very **impressionable,** and the younger the better, my little man. The younger the better."

Copyright © BookheadEd Learning, LLC

10 Meg looked up at the fiery eyes, at the light pulsing above them, and then away. She tried looking at the mouth, at the thin, almost colorless lips, and this was more possible, even though she had to look **obliquely,** so that she was not sure exactly what the face really looked like, whether it was young or old, cruel or kind, human or alien.

11 "If you please," she said, trying to sound calm and brave. "The only reason we are here is because we think our father is here. Can you tell us where to find him?"

12 "Ah, your father!" There seemed to be a great chortling of delight. "Ah, yes, your father! It is not *can* I, you know, young lady, but *will* I?"

13 "Will you, then?"

14 "That depends on a number of things. Why do you want your father?"

15 "Didn't you ever have a father yourself?" Meg demanded. "You don't want him for a *reason*. You want him because he's your *father*."

16 "Ah, but he hasn't been *acting* very like a father, lately, has he? Abandoning his wife and his four little children to go **gallivanting** off on wild adventures of his own."

17 "He was working for the government. He'd never have left us otherwise. And we want to see him, please. Right now."

18 "My, but the little miss is impatient! Patience, patience, young lady."

19 Meg did not tell the man on the chair that patience was not one of her virtues.

20 "And by the way, my children," he continued blandly, "you don't need to vocalize verbally with me, you know. I can understand you quite as well as you can understand me."

21 Charles Wallace put his hands on his hips defiantly. "The spoken word is one of the triumphs of man," he proclaimed, "and I intend to continue using it, particularly with people I don't trust." But his voice was shaking. Charles Wallace, who even as an infant had seldom cried, was near tears.

22 "And you don't trust me?"

23 "What reason have you given us to trust you?"

24 "What cause have I given you for distrust?" The thin lips curled slightly.

NOTES

25   Suddenly Charles Wallace darted forward and hit the man as hard as he could, which was fairly hard, as he had had a good deal of coaching from the twins.

26   "Charles!" Meg screamed.

27   The men in dark smocks moved smoothly but with swiftness to Charles. The man in the chair casually raised one finger, and the men dropped back.

28   "Hold it—" Calvin whispered, and together he and Meg darted forward and grabbed Charles Wallace, pulling him back from the platform.

29   The man gave a wince and the thought of his voice was a little breathless, as though Charles Wallace's punch had succeeded in winding him. "May I ask why you did that?"

30   "Because you aren't you," Charles Wallace said. "I'm not sure what you are, but you"—he pointed to the man on the chair—"aren't what's talking to us. I'm sorry if I hurt you. I didn't think you were real. I thought perhaps you were a robot, because I don't feel anything coming directly from you. I'm not sure where it's coming from, but it's coming through you. It isn't you."

31   "Pretty smart, aren't you?" the thought asked, and Meg had an uncomfortable feeling that she detected a snarl.

32   "It's not that I'm smart," Charles Wallace said, and again Meg could feel the palm of his hand sweating inside hers.

33   "Try to find out who I am, then," the thought probed.

34   "I have been trying," Charles Wallace said, his voice high and troubled.

35   "Look into my eyes. Look deep within them and I will tell you."

36   Charles Wallace looked quickly at Meg and Calvin, then said, as though to himself, "I have to," and focused his clear blue eyes on the red ones of the man in the chair. Meg looked not at the man but at her brother. After a moment it seemed that his eyes were no longer focusing. The pupils grew smaller and smaller, as though he were looking into an intensely bright light, until they seemed to close entirely, until his eyes were nothing but an opaque blue. He slipped his hands out of Meg's and Calvin's and started walking slowly toward the man on the chair.

37   "No!" Meg screamed. "No!"

38   But Charles Wallace continued his slow walk forward, and she knew that he had not heard her.

NOTES

39   "No!" she screamed again, and ran after him. With her inefficient flying tackle she landed on him. She was so much larger than he that he fell sprawling, hitting his head a sharp crack against the marble floor. She knelt by him, sobbing. After a moment of lying there as though he had been knocked out by the blow, he opened his eyes, shook his head, and sat up. Slowly the pupils of his eyes dilated until they were back to normal, and the blood came back to his white cheeks.

40   The man on the chair spoke directly into Meg's mind, and now there was a distinct menace to the words. "I am not pleased," he said to her. "I could very easily lose patience with you, and that, for your information, young lady, would not be good for your father. If you have the slightest desire to see your father again, you had better cooperate."

Excerpted from A Wrinkle in Time *by Madeleine L'Engle, published by Farrar, Strauss and Giroux.*

THINK QUESTIONS

1. Explain how Meg, Calvin, and Charles Wallace communicate with the man with red eyes. Support your answer with textual evidence, referring both to ideas you infer from specific details and to information that is directly stated.

2. Use details from the text to write three or four sentences describing Charles Wallace.

3. Write three or four sentences explaining how the man with red eyes is able to manipulate the children. Support your answer with textual evidence.

4. Use context to determine the meaning of the word **boring** as it is used in *A Wrinkle in Time*. Write your definition of "boring" and explain how you got it. What else can "boring" mean, and how can you tell which meaning applies here?

5. Use context clues to determine the meaning of **impressionable** as it is used in *A Wrinkle in Time*. Write your definition of "impressionable" and tell how you determined it

CLOSE READ

Reread the excerpt from *A Wrinkle in Time*. As you reread, complete the Focus Questions below. Then use your answers and annotations from the questions to help you complete the Writing Prompt.

FOCUS QUESTIONS

1. Reread paragraphs 1-7, in which the red-eyed man tries to control Meg, Charles Wallace, and Calvin by infiltrating their thoughts with the multiplication table, something that is memorized and repeated without thought. Explain how Calvin and Meg each fend off the red-eyed man's mind-control advances. How do the children's responses differ? How do their differing responses contribute to what happens next in the plot? Highlight evidence from the text and make annotations to support your answers.

2. In paragraph 8, Charles Wallace demands, "You didn't think we were as easy as all that, falling for that old stuff, did you?" How does the red-eyed man respond to the question, and what can you infer about him from his response? Highlight evidence from the text and make annotations to explain your inferences.

3. In paragraphs 11-19, what strategy does Meg use to try to find out the whereabouts of her father? How effective are her efforts? What impact does her interaction with the red-eyed man have on the developing plot? Highlight textual evidence and make annotations to explain your ideas.

4. Why does Charles Wallace strike the red-eyed man, and how does the blow relate to the man's challenge to "find out who I am, then" in paragraph 33? Highlight and annotate textual evidence to demonstrate the effect Charles Wallace's actions have on plot development.

5. In paragraphs 37-39, how does Meg stand up for Charles Wallace? How does the relationship between the children and the red-eyed man begin to change at this point in the plot? Highlight and annotate textual evidence to support your answers.

WRITING PROMPT

In this excerpt from *A Wrinkle in Time,* the red-eyed man tries to control the minds of Meg, Charles Wallace, and Calvin. In what ways do the children stand up for themselves? How do their responses contribute to the unfolding plot? Explain how the children's determination and courage shape what happens in their confrontation with the mysterious red-eyed man. Maintain a formal style in your explanation, and use clear, precise language to help your readers understand this event in the story. Cite textual evidence to support your ideas.

THE MONSTERS ARE DUE ON MAPLE STREET

DRAMA
Rod Serling
1960

INTRODUCTION

Rod Serling, creator of the science fiction television series *The Twilight Zone*, was one of the most popular writers in television history. One of his best-known scripts, "The Monsters Are Due on Maple Street" is about the reaction of a group of neighbors to a mysterious shadow that passes over their suburban street. After homes lose power and car batteries go dead, a neighborhood boy suggests that alien invaders in human form are responsible for the strange events. As power flickers back on here and there, neighbors become increasingly alarmed, turning their suspicions against one another.

"Who do I talk to? I talk to monsters from outer space."

 FIRST READ

 NOTES

1 *From Act I*

2 GOODMAN. Wait a minute now. You keep your distance—all of you. So I've got a car that starts by itself—well, that's a freak thing, I admit it. But does that make me some kind of a criminal or something? I don't know why the car works—it just does!

3 [*This stops the crowd momentarily and now* GOODMAN, *still backing away, goes toward the front porch. He goes up the steps and then stops to stand facing the mob.*

4 *We see a long shot of* STEVE *as he comes through the crowd.*]

5 STEVE. [*Quietly.*] We're all on a monster kick, Les. Seems that the general impression holds that maybe one family isn't what we think they are. Monsters from outer space or something. Different than us. Fifth columnists from the vast beyond. [*He chuckles.*] You know anybody that might fit that description around here on Maple Street?

6 GOODMAN. What is this, a gag or something? This a practical joke or something?

7 [*We see a close-up of the porch light as it suddenly goes out. There's a murmur from the group.*]

8 GOODMAN. Now I suppose that's supposed to **incriminate** me! The light goes on and off. That really does it, doesn't it? [*He look around the faces of the people.*] I just don't understand this—[*He wets his lips, looking from face to face.*] Look, you all know me. We've lived here five years. Right in this house. We're no different from any of the rest of you! We're no different at all. Really . . . this whole thing is just . . . just weird—

NOTES

9   WOMAN. Well, if that's the case, Les Goodman, explain why—[*She stops suddenly, clamping her mouth shut.*]

10 GOODMAN. [*Softly.*] Explain what?

11 STEVE. [*Interjecting*] Look, let's forget this—

12 CHARLIE. [*Overlapping him.*] Go ahead, let her talk. What about it? Explain what?

13 WOMAN. [*A little reluctantly.*] Well . . . sometimes I go to bed late at night. A couple of times... a couple of times I'd come out on the porch and I'd see Mr. Goodman here in the wee hours of the morning standing out in front of his house . . . looking up at the sky. [*She looks around the circle of faces.*] That's right, looking up at the sky as if . . . as if he were waiting for something. [*A pause.*] As if he were looking for something.

14 [*There's a murmur of reaction from the crowd again.*

15 *We cut suddenly to a group shot. As* GOODMAN *starts toward them, they back away frightened.*]

16 GOODMAN. You know really . . . this is for laughs. You know what I'm guilty of? [*He laughs.*] I'm guilty of **insomnia....**

17 *From Act II*

18 CHARLIE'S VOICE. [*Shrill, from across the street.*] You best watch who you're seen with, Steve! Until we get this all straightened out, you ain't exactly above suspicion yourself.

19 STEVE. [*Whirling around toward him.*] Or you, Charlie. Or any of us, it seems. From age eight on up.

20 WOMAN. What I'd like to know is—what are we gonna do? Just stand around here all night?

21 CHARLIE. There's nothin' else we can do! [*He turns back looking toward* STEVE *and* GOODMAN *again.*] One of 'em'll tip their hand. They got to.

22 STEVE [*Raising his voice.*] There's something you can do, Charlie. You could go home and keep your mouth shut. You could quit strutting around like a self-appointed hanging judge and just climb into bed and forget it.

23 CHARLIE. You sound real anxious to have that happen, Steve. I think we better keep our eye on you too!

Copyright © BookheadEd Learning, LLC

24 DON. [*As if he were taking the bit in his teeth, takes a hesitant step to the front.*] I think everything might as well come out now. [*He turns toward* STEVE.] Your wife's done plenty of talking, Steve, about how odd you are!

25 CHARLIE. [*Picking this up, his eyes widening.*] Go ahead, tell us what she's said. [*We see a long shot of* STEVE *as he walks toward them from across the street.*]

26 STEVE. Go ahead, what's my wife said? Let's get it all out. Let's pick out every **idiosyncrasy** of every man, woman, and child on the street. And then we might as well set up some kind of kangaroo court. How about a firing squad at dawn, Charlie, so we can get rid of all the suspects? Narrow them down. Make it easier for you.

27 DON. There's no need gettin' so upset, Steve. It's just that . . . well . . . Myra's talked about how there's been plenty of nights you spent hours down in your basement workin' on some kind of radio or something. Well, none of us have ever seen that radio—

28 [*By this time* STEVE *has reached the group. He stands there defiantly close to them.*]

29 CHARLIE. Go ahead, Steve. What kind of "radio set" you workin' on? I never seen it. Neither has anyone else. Who you talk to on that radio set? And who talks to you?

30 STEVE. I'm surprised at you, Charlie. How come you're so **dense** all of a sudden? [*A pause.*] Who do I talk to? I talk to monsters from outer space. I talk to three-headed green men who fly over here in what look like meteors.

31 [STEVE'S *wife steps down from the porch, bites her lip, calls out.*]

32 MRS. BRAND. Steve! Steve, please. [*Then looking around, frightened, she walks toward the group.*] It's just a ham radio set, that's all. I bought him a book on it myself. It's just a ham radio set. A lot of people have them. I can show it to you. It's right down in the basement.

33 STEVE. [*whirls around toward her*] Show them nothing! If they want to look inside our house—let them get a search warrant.

34 CHARLIE. Look, buddy. You can't afford to—

35 STEVE. [*Interrupting*] Charlie, don't tell me what I can afford! And stop telling me who's dangerous and who isn't and who's safe and who's a menace. [*He turns to the group and shouts.*] And you're with him, too—all of you! You're standing here all set to crucify—all set to find a scapegoat—all desperate to

NOTES

point some kind of finger at a neighbor! Well now look, friends, the only thing that's gonna happen is that we'll eat each other up alive—

36 [*He stops abruptly as CHARLIE suddenly grabs his arm.*]

37 CHARLIE. [*In a hushed voice*]That's not the only thing that can happen to us.

38 [*Cut to a long shot looking down the street. A figure has suddenly materialized in the gloom and in the silence we can hear the clickety-clack of slow, measured footsteps on concrete as the figure walks slowly toward them. One of the women lets out a stifled cry. The young mother grabs her boy as do a couple of others.*]

39 TOMMY. [*Shouting, frightened.*] It's the monster! It's the monster!

40 [*Another woman lets out a wail and the people fall back in a group, staring toward the darkness and the approaching figure.*

41 *We see a medium group shot of the people as they stand in the shadows watching. DON MARTIN joins them, carrying a shotgun. He holds it up.*]

42 DON. We may need this.

43 STEVE. A shotgun? [*He pulls it out of DON'S hand.*] Good Lord—will anybody think a thought around here? Will you people wise up? What good would a shotgun do against—

44 [*Now CHARLIE pulls the gun from STEVE's hand.*]

45 CHARLIE. No more talk, Steve. You're going to talk us into a grave! You'd let whatever's out there walk right over us, wouldn't yuh? Well, some of us won't!

46 [*He swings the gun around to point it toward the sidewalk. The dark figure continues to walk toward them.*

47 *The group stands there, fearful, apprehensive, mother's clutching children, men standing in front of wives. CHARLIE slowly raises the gun. As the figure gets closer and closer he suddenly pulls the trigger. The sound of it explodes in the stillness. There is a long angle shot looking down the figure, who suddenly lets out a small cry, stumbles forward onto his knees and then falls forward on his face. DON, CHARLIE, and STEVE race forward over to him. STEVE is there first and turns the man over. Now the crowd gathers around them.*]

48 STEVE [*Slowly looks up*] It's Pete Van Horn.

49 DON. [*In a hushed voice.*] Pete Van Horn! He was just gonna go over to the next block to see if the power was on—

50 WOMAN. You killed him, Charlie. You shot him dead!

51 CHARLIE. [*Looks around the circle of faces, his eyes frightened, his face **contorted**.*] But . . . but I didn't know who he was. I certainly didn't know who he was. He comes walkin' out of the darkness—how am I supposed to know who he was? [*He grabs* STEVE.] Steve—you know why I shot! How was I supposed to know he wasn't a monster or something? [*He grabs* DON *now.*] We're all scared of the same thing, I was just tryin' to . . . trying' to protect my home, that's all! Look, all of you, that's all I was tryin' to do. [*He looks down wildly at the body.*] I didn't know it was somebody we knew! I didn't know—

52 [*There's a sudden hush and then an intake of breath. We see a medium shot of the living room window of* CHARLIE'S *house. The window is not lit, but suddenly the house lights come on behind it.*]

53 WOMAN. [*In a very hushed voice.*] Charlie. . . Charlie. . . the lights just went on in your house. Why did the lights just go on?

54 DON. What about it, Charlie? How come you're the only one with lights now?

55 GOODMAN. That's what I'd like to know.

© 1960 by Rod Serling, *The Monsters Are Due on Maple Street.* Reproduced by permission of Carolyn Serling.

 ## THINK QUESTIONS

1. Refer to details from the text to explain why the Maple Street neighbors are suspicious of Les Goodman. Include both ideas that are directly stated and ideas that you have inferred from clues in the text.

2. Use details from the text to write two or three sentences explaining why the Maple Street neighbors are suspicious of Steve.

3. Write two or three sentences explaining why Tommy shouts, "It's the monster! It's the monster!" Support your answer with textual evidence.

4. The Latin root *tort* or *torq* means "to twist or turn." The Latin affix *con-* means "together." Use these meanings, along with context clues in the text, to determine the meaning of **contorted** as it is used in "The Monsters Are Due On Maple Street." Write your definition of "contorted" and explain how you found it.

5. The Latin prefix *in-* means "in or into," and the Latin root *crim* means "crime." The suffix *–ate,* used with a verb, often means "cause to become." Use the Latin root and affix, along with context clues provided in the passage, to determine the meaning of **incriminate** as it is used in the text. Write your definition of "incriminate" and tell how you found it.

CLOSE READ

Reread the excerpt from "The Monsters Are Due on Maple Street." As you reread, complete the Focus Questions below. Then use your answers and annotations from the questions to help you complete the Writing Prompt.

FOCUS QUESTIONS

1. How does the monster in *A Wrinkle in Time* compare and contrast with the monster in "The Monsters Are Due on Maple Street"? Support your response with textual evidence and make annotations to explain your ideas.

2. Based on Acts I and II, in what ways do Les Goodman and Charlie change roles as the plot moves toward resolution? Highlight textual evidence and make annotations to explain your response.

3. Based on Act II, how do Tommy's and Steve's responses to events contribute to the story's resolution? Highlight textual evidence and make annotations to support your explanation.

4. Compare the actions and reactions of the children in the novel *A Wrinkle in Time* with those of the adults in the teleplay "The Monsters Are Due on Maple Street," considering the way each deals with the element of fear. How do the characters' responses have an impact, either positively or negatively, on the situation they find themselves in? Highlight textual evidence and make annotations to support your explanation.

5. In "The Monsters Are Due on Maple Street," in what ways do the characters stand up for or fail to stand up for themselves? Highlight textual evidence and make annotations to explain your ideas.

WRITING PROMPT

In both *A Wrinkle in Time* and "The Monsters Are Due on Maple Street," the characters ask questions for a number of different reasons. Compare and contrast the questions asked by Meg and Charles Wallace with the questions asked by the red-eyed man in *A Wrinkle in Time* and by the neighbors in "The Monsters Are Due on Maple Street." What do these questions tell the reder about the theme of seeking the truth? How is this theme portrayed similarly and differently in the excerpts from the novel and the script? Support the claim or claims you make in your comparison and contrast with evidence from both texts.

RED SCARF GIRL:
A MEMOIR OF THE CULTURAL REVOLUTION

NON-FICTION
Ji-Li Jiang
1997

INTRODUCTION

Ji-Li Jiang grew up dedicated to the Communist Party, and was embarrassed by her family's "landlord" background during the Cultural Revolution. However, her feelings began to change when the government started attacking her family. In this excerpt, she has been pulled out of class and is being interrogated by people from her father's theater.

"We want you to testify against your father..."

 FIRST READ

1 "Sit down, sit down. Don't be afraid." Chairman Jin pointed to the empty chair. "These comrades from your father's work unit are just here to have a study session with you. It's nothing to worry about."

2 I sat down dumbly.

3 I had thought about their coming to my home but never imagined this. They were going to expose my family in front of my teachers and classmates. I would have no pride left. I would never be an **educable** child again.

4 Thin-Face sat opposite me, with a woman I had never seen before. Teacher Zhang was there too, his eyes encouraging me.

5 Thin-Face came straight to the point. "Your father's problems are very serious. " His cold eyes nailed me to my seat. "You may have read the article in the *Workers' Revolt* that exposed your family's filthy past." I slumped down in my chair without taking my eyes off his face. "In addition to coming from a landlord family, your father committed some serious mistakes during the Antirightist Movement several years ago, but he still obstinately refuses to confess." His cold manner became a little more animated. "Of course we won't tolerate this. We have decided to make an example of him. We are going to have a struggle meeting of the entire theater system to criticize him and force him to confess." He suddenly pounded the table with his fist. The cups on the table rattled.

6 I tore my eyes away from him and stared at a cup instead.

7 "As I told you before, you are your own person. If you want to make a clean break with your black family, then you can be an educable child and we will

Copyright © BookheadEd Learning, LLC

Copyright © BookheadEd Learning, LLC

welcome you to our revolutionary ranks." He gave Chairman Jin a look, and Chairman Jin chimed in, "That's right, we welcome you."

8   "Jiang Ji-li has always done well at school. In addition to doing very well in her studies, she participates in educational **reform,**" Teacher Zhang added.

9   "That's very good. We knew that you had more sense than to follow your father," Thin-Face said with a brief, frozen smile. "Now you can show your revolutionary determination." He paused. "We want you to **testify** against your father at the struggle meeting."

10   I closed my eyes. I saw Dad standing on a stage, his head bowed, his name written in large black letters, and then crossed out in red ink, on a sign hanging from his neck. I saw myself standing in the middle of the stage, facing thousands of people, **condemning** Dad for his crimes, raising my fist to lead the chant, "Down with Jiang Xi-reng." I saw Dad looking at me hopelessly, tears on his face.

11   "I...I..." I looked at Teacher Zhang for help. He looked away.

12   The Woman from the theater spoke. "It's really not such a hard thing to do. The key is your class stance. The daughter of our former Party Secretary resolved to make a clean break with her mother. When she went onstage to condemn her mother, she actually slapped her face. Of course, we don't mean that you have to slap your father's face. The point is that as long as you have the correct class stance, it will be easy to testify." Her voice grated on my ears.

13   "There is something you can do to prove you are truly Chairman Mao's child." Thin-Face spoke again. "I am sure you can tell us some things your father said and did that show his landlord and rightist mentality." I stared at the table, but I could feel his eyes boring into me. "What can you tell us?"

14   "But I don't know anything," I whispered." I don't know—"

15   "I am sure you can remember something if you think about it," Thin-Face said. "A man like him could not hide his true beliefs from a child as smart as you. He must have made comments critical of Chairman Mao and the Cultural Revolution. I am sure you are loyal to Chairman Mao and the Communist Party. Tell us!"

16   "But my father never said anything against Chairman Mao," I protested weakly. "I would tell you if he did." My voice grew stronger with **conviction.** "He never said anything against the Party."

17 "Now, you have to choose between two roads." Thin-Face looked straight into my eyes. "You can break with your family and follow Chairman Mao, or you can follow your father and become an enemy of the people." His voice grew more severe. "In that case we would have many more study sessions, with your brother and sister too, and the Red Guard Committee and the school leaders. Think about it. We will come back to talk to you again."

18 Thin-Face and the woman left, saying they would be back to get my statement. Without knowing how I got there, I found myself in a narrow passageway between the school building and the school-yard wall. The gray concrete walls closed around me and a slow drizzle dampened my cheeks. I could not go back to the classroom, and I could not go home. I felt like a small animal that had fallen into a trap, alone and helpless, and sure that the hunter was coming.

Excerpted from *Red Scarf Girl* by Ji-li Jiang, published by HarperCollins Publishers.

THINK QUESTIONS

1. How does Ji-Li feel about being called to the study session? Cite textual evidence to support your answer.

2. What problem does Ji-Li's father face? Why? Cite evidence from the text in support of your answer.

3. What choice does Ji-Li face? What will be the consequences of her choice? Support your answer with textual evidence.

4. Use context to determine the meaning of the word **condemning** as it is used in *Red Scarf Girl*. Write your definition of "condemning" and tell how you arrived at it.

5. Remembering that the Latin suffix *-able* means "able to do or to have done" and that the Latin root *educare* means "to teach, to bring up," use the context clues provided in the passage to determine the meaning of **educable.** Write your definition of "educable" and tell how you arrived at it. Can you think of any words that are related to "educable"? How might they be related to it?

CLOSE READ

Reread the excerpt from *Red Scarf Girl*. As you reread, complete the Focus Questions below. Then use your answers and annotations from the questions to help you complete the Writing Prompt.

FOCUS QUESTIONS

1. In paragraph 5, the narrator describes Thin-Face's "manner." Use context clues to determine the meaning of the word "animated," and explain what connotations "animated" has in this context. Highlight and make annotations to identify and explain any word relationships that helped you determine the word's meaning and connotations.

2. In paragraphs 9–13, as the Party officials continue talking to Ji-Li, what do they wish to achieve? How do they get their ideas across? Highlight evidence from the text and make annotations to support your answer.

3. In paragraphs 14–16, Ji-Li tells the Party officials that her father is innocent and that she doesn't know anything that would condemn him. Do key details in the text, including Ji-Li's own words, support her explanation? Why or why not? Highlight textual evidence and make annotations to support your answer.

4. In the final paragraph of the selection, Ji-Li describes the physical details of her surroundings. How do the connotations of the words she chooses contribute to your understanding of the events that have happened, and of Ji-Li's feelings about them? Highlight textual evidence and make annotations to explain your ideas.

5. The events of the study session force Ji-Li to face a new challenge. How will the decision she makes affect not only her own life but the lives of her family members as well? Highlight textual evidence and make annotations to support your answer.

WRITING PROMPT

Based on the events, facts, and details in the text, what arguments could be made for Ji-Li to condemn her father, and what arguments could be made for her to stand by him? Present at least two reasons for each side. Make sure that each reason is supported by evidence from the text. Quote at least one specific phrase, sentence, or passage from the text, and show how the connotations or denotations support a specific side of the argument. Try to make both sides of the argument as strong and convincing as possible, no matter which side you personally agree with. (You do not have to say which one you agree with.)

Please note that excerpts and passages in the StudySync® library and this workbook are intended as touchstones to generate interest in an author's work. The excerpts and passages do not substitute for the reading of entire texts, and StudySync® strongly recommends that students seek out and purchase the whole literary or informational work in order to experience it as the author intended. Links to online resellers are available in our digital library. In addition, complete works may be ordered through an authorized reseller by filling out and returning to StudySync® the order form enclosed in this workbook.

Reading & Writing Companion   **213**

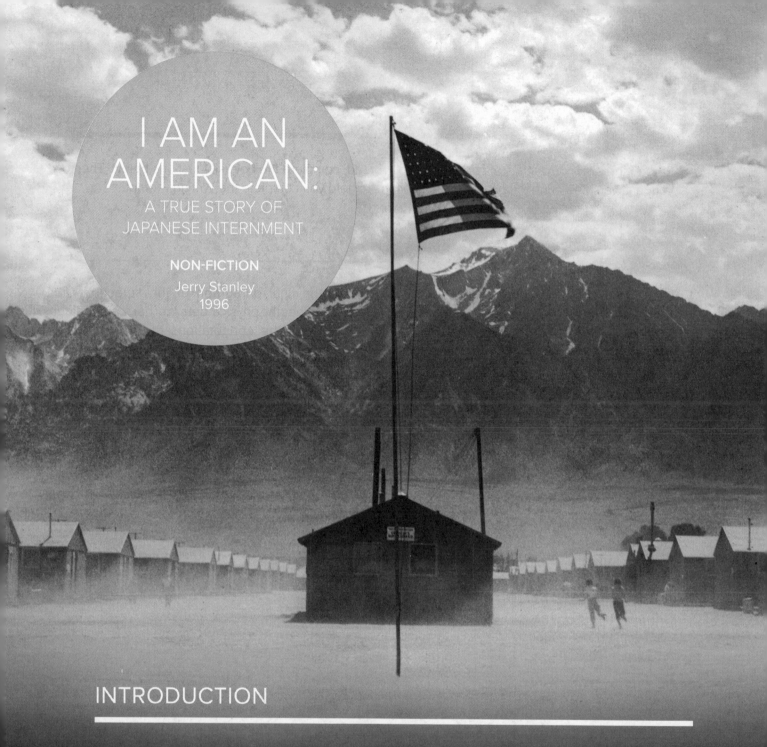

I AM AN AMERICAN:
A TRUE STORY OF JAPANESE INTERNMENT

NON-FICTION
Jerry Stanley
1996

INTRODUCTION

As described in author Jerry Stanley's non-fiction work *I Am an American*, Japanese Americans went to great lengths to show their loyalty to the United States after the Japanese attack on Pearl Harbor in 1941. However, despite initial political support for Japanese-Americans, military officials expressed concern that they might help Japan invade the West Coast. As a result of public fear and pressure, the U.S. government ordered the forced evacuation of more than 100,000 Japanese Americans from their homes to internment camps. The excerpt explores this period of war hysteria and racism in American history.

"We in our hearts know we are Americans, loyal to America."

FIRST READ

From Chapter 2: EXECUTIVE ORDER NO. 9066

1   After Pearl Harbor the Nisei went to great lengths to demonstrate their **patriotism.** They flooded the streets of San Francisco, Los Angeles, and Seattle in mass **demonstrations** of loyalty. They waved American flags and recited the pledge of the Japanese American Citizens League. They bought war bonds, donated blood, and ran ads in newspapers denouncing Japan and pledging loyalty to America. In San Francisco, Nisei started a fund-raising campaign to buy bombs for attacking Tokyo. In Los Angeles they formed committees to make sure that no person of Japanese ancestry tried to aid Japan. The day after Pearl Harbor the Japanese American Citizens League sent the following telegram to President Roosevelt:

2   In this solemn hour we pledge our fullest cooperation to you, Mr. President, and to our country. There can not be any question. . . . We in our hearts know we are Americans, loyal to America.

3   At first, the demonstrations of loyalty brought pledges of support from government officials, and Japanese **internmen**t seemed unlikely. California Congressman Leland Ford said, "These people are American-born. This is their country." United States Attorney General Francis Biddle declared, "At no time will the government engage in wholesale **condemnation** of any alien group."

4   The only action Biddle took in December was to move against enemy aliens— that is, German, Italian, and Japanese citizens living in the United States. He ordered the Federal Bureau of Investigation to arrest approximately 16,000 enemy aliens suspected of espionage or **sabotage,** but within weeks he released two-thirds of them. At the same time, the FBI and the Federal Communications Commission conducted separate investigations of the

Japanese living in America. Both investigations concluded that the Nisei were loyal citizens and that their Issei parents had taken no action to aid Japan.

5   It was a series of Japanese victories in the Pacific that started the movement to intern the Japanese. Japan captured Guam on December 13, 1941, Hong Kong on December 24, Manila on January 2, 1942, and Singapore on February 15.

6   Alarmed at the enemy's swift advance through the Pacific, military officials suggested that Japan might try to invade the west coast of America and that maybe the Issei and the Nisei who lived there would aid the invasion. The Western Defense Commander, Lieutenant General John L. DeWitt, who was responsible for the security of the Pacific coast, was influential in spreading the idea that the Japanese might be disloyal. Following the loss of Manila he said, "I have little confidence that the Japanese enemy aliens [Issei] are loyal. I have no confidence in the loyalty of the Nisei whatsoever."

7   DeWitt's distrust appeared to be confirmed in the Roberts Report, a government investigation of the bombing of Pearl Harbor. Issued at about the time Singapore fell to Japan in February, the report blamed the disaster on lack of military preparedness and on Japanese sabotage in Hawaii. It even suggested that Japanese farmers had planted their crops in the shape of arrows pointing to Pearl Harbor as the target.

8   Although the charge of Japanese sabotage on Hawaii was totally false, newspaper writers and radio broadcasters began warning of the danger of Japanese sabotage on the west coast. In Los Angeles, radio commentator John Hughes warned that "Ninety percent or more of American-born Japanese are primarily loyal to Japan."

...

9   Stunned by the growing hostility, the Nisei tried to appear as un-Japanese as possible. Slowly, sadly, all along the west coast of America, they destroyed what they possessed of their Asian heritage. Japanese books and magazines were burned because of a rumor that FBI agents had found such materials in the homes of Issei arrested on suspicion of sabotage. Priceless diaries, letters, and photographs were burned; porcelain vases, tea sets, and silk tablecloths were buried or dumped on the street.

...

10   By mid-February the entire coastline of California was designated Restricted Area Number One. DeWitt issued a stern suggestion that the Japanese living in this coastal strip should voluntarily migrate inland. But when some 4,000

tried to move, they were met with hostility. Armed men patrolled the Nevada border to turn them back while main streets in Utah sported signs reading "No Japs Wanted." Because most people in the inland states had never met a person of Japanese ancestry, they decided that if the Japanese were a threat to California then they were also a threat to them.

. . .

11 With no personal knowledge of the Japanese living in America, President Franklin D. Roosevelt yielded to pressure from the California Hotheads, the media, and the military. On February 19, 1942, Roosevelt signed Executive Order No. 9066, which gave the military the authority to remove enemy aliens and anyone else suspected of disloyalty. Although the document never mentioned the Japanese by name, it was understood that the order was meant for them alone.

"Executive Order No. 9066 (Chapter 2)" from I AM AN AMERICAN: A TRUE STORY OF JAPANESE INTERNMENT by Jerry Stanley, copyright © 1994 by Jerry Stanley. Used by permission of Crown Publishers, an imprint of Random House Children's Books, a division of Random House LLC. All rights reserved.

THINK QUESTIONS

1. Explain how and why the Nisei went to great lengths to demonstrate patriotism after the bombing of Pearl Harbor. In your response, refer to details from the text to support ideas that are directly stated and ideas that you have inferred.

2. Use details from the text to write two or three sentences explaining how U.S. Attorney Francis Biddle's public statement regarding aliens contradicted his actions.

3. Write two or three sentences explaining the reasons given for Japanese internment. Support your answer with textual evidence.

4. Use context to determine the meaning of the word **demonstrations** as it is used in the first sentence of *I Am an American: A True Story of Japanese Internment*. Write your definition of "demonstrations" here and tell how you got it. Then, use a dictionary to verify your definition.

5. Remembering that the suffix *-ism* often means "a belief in" or "a state of action" and the Latin root *pater* means "father," use the context clues provided in the passage to determine the meaning of **patriotism.** Write your definition of "patriotism" and tell how you arrived at it. Use a dictionary to verify your answer.

Please note that excerpts and passages in the StudySync® library and this workbook are intended as touchstones to generate interest in an author's work. The excerpts and passages do not substitute for the reading of entire texts, and StudySync® strongly recommends that students seek out and purchase the whole literary or informational work in order to experience it as the author intended. Links to online resellers are available in our digital library. In addition, complete works may be ordered through an authorized reseller by filling out and returning to StudySync® the order form enclosed in this workbook.

Reading & Writing Companion   **217**

CLOSE READ

Reread the excerpt from *I Am an American: A True Story of Japanese Internment*. As you reread, complete the Focus Questions below. Then use your answers and annotations from the questions to help you complete the Writing Prompt.

FOCUS QUESTIONS

1. In paragraphs 1 and 2, Stanley describes the reaction of Japanese Americans to the bombing of Pearl Harbor. How and why did Japanese Americans stand up for themselves? Highlight evidence in the text to support your ideas, and make annotations to explain your response.

2. As you reread the text of *I Am an American: A True Story of Japanese Internment,* consider the author's possible purposes for writing: to inform, to persuade, to describe, to explain, or to entertain. Remember that an author may write for more than one purpose. Based on paragraphs 3, 4, and 5, describe two possible purposes Stanley might have for writing. Highlight textual evidence that supports your response, and make annotations to explain your thinking.

3. In paragraphs 7 and 8, Stanley discusses the Roberts Report, a government investigation of the bombing of Pearl Harbor. What is Stanley's point of view regarding this report? Highlight evidence in the text to support your ideas, and make annotations to explain your thinking.

4. In paragraph 9, the author describes the destruction of cultural artifacts by Japanese Americans. Highlight textual evidence that indicates Stanley's point of view about this development, and annotate ideas that explain how he conveys it.

5. What clues in the text tell you how and why the U.S. government changed its mind about the American-born Nisei? How did this change of mind unfold? Highlight textual evidence and make annotations to explain your response.

WRITING PROMPT

Compare and contrast the points of view of the author, the government officials mentioned in the excerpt, and the Nisei themselves. How do these points of view compare? How does each party approach the question of how to deal with conflict—when to stand up and when to stand down? Support your writing with evidence from the text.

ROLL OF THUNDER, HEAR MY CRY

FICTION
Mildred D. Taylor
1976

INTRODUCTION

studysync tv

Mildred D. Taylor's gripping novel tells the story of the Logans, a landowning black family in the Deep South struggling to keep things together during a tumultuous year in the 1930's. Largely insulated from the injustices of the world around her, but raised with a strong sense of fairness, nine-year old Cassie is only beginning to realize the realities of racism, including the everyday source of fear it presents to adults in her community. In the excerpt here, neighbors bring bad news for her father.

"...he's not gonna let a few smart colored folks ruin his business."

 FIRST READ

From Chapter 9

1   When supper was ready, I eagerly grabbed the iron bell before Christopher-John or Little Man could claim it, and ran onto the back porch to summon Papa, Mr. Morrison, and Stacey from the fields. As the three of them washed up on the back porch, Mama went to the end of the porch where Papa stood alone. "What did Mr. Jamison want?" she asked, her voice barely **audible.**

2   Papa took the towel Mama handed him, but did not reply immediately. I was just inside the kitchen dipping out the butter beans. I moved closer to the window so that I could hear his answer.

3   "Don't keep anything from me, David. If there's trouble, I want to know."

4   Papa looked down at her. "Nothing to worry 'bout, honey . . . . just seems that Thurston Wallace been in town talking 'bout how he's not gonna let a few smart colored folks ruin his business. Says he's gonna put a stop to this shopping in Vicksburg. That's all."

5   Mama sighed and stared out across the plowed field to the sloping pasture land. "I'm feeling scared, David," she said.

6   Papa put down the towel. "Not yet, Mary. It's not time to be scared yet. They're just talking."

7   Mama turned and faced him. "And when they stop talking?"

8   "Then . . . then maybe it'll be time. But right now, pretty lady," he said, leading her by the hand toward the kitchen door, "right now I've got better things to think about."

Copyright © BookheadEd Learning, LLC

NOTES

9   Quickly I poured the rest of the butter beans into the bowl and hurried across the kitchen to the table. As Mama and Papa entered, I slid onto the bench beside Little Man and Christopher-John. Papa beamed down at the table.

10 "Well, look-a-here!" he exclaimed. "Good ole butter beans and cornbread! You better come on, Mr. Morrison! You too, son!" he called. "These womenfolks done gone and fixed us a feast."

11 After school was out, spring drooped quickly toward summer; yet Papa had not left for the railroad. He seemed to be waiting for something, and I secretly hoped that whatever that something was, it would never come so that he would not leave. But one evening as he, Mama, Big Ma, Mr. Morrison, and Stacey sat on the front porch while Christopher-John, Little Man, and I dashed around the yard chasing fireflies, I overheard him say, "Sunday I'm gonna have to go. Don't want to though. I got this gut feeling it ain't over yet. It's too easy."

12 I released the firefly **imprisoned** in my hand and sat beside Papa and Stacey on the steps. "Papa, please," I said, leaning against his leg, "don't go this year." Stacey looked out into the falling night, his face resigned, and said nothing.

13 Papa put out his large hand and caressed my face. "Got to, Cassie girl," he said softly. "Baby, there's bills to pay and ain't no money coming in. Your mama's got no job come fall and there's the **mortgage** and next year's taxes to think of."

14 "But, Papa, we planted more cotton this year. Won't that pay the taxes?"

15 Papa shook his head. "With Mr. Morrison here we was able to plant more, but that cotton is for living on; the railroad money is for the taxes and the mortgage."

16 I looked back at Mama wanting her to speak, to persuade him to stay, but when I saw her face I knew that she would not. She had known he would leave, just as we all had known.

17 "Papa, just another week or two, couldn't you—"

18 "I can't, baby. May have lost my job already."

19 "But Papa—"

20 "Cassie, that's enough now," Mama said from the deepening shadows.

21 I grew quiet and Papa put his arms around Stacey and me, his hands falling casually over our shoulders. From the edge of the lawn where Little Man and

Christopher-John had ventured after lightning bugs, Little Man called, "Somebody's coming!" A few minutes later Mr. Avery and Mr. Lanier emerged from the dusk and walked up the sloping lawn. Mama sent Stacey and me to get more chairs for the porch, then we settled back beside Papa still sitting on the steps, his back propped against a pillar facing the visitors.

22 "You goin' up to the store tomorrow, David?" Mr. Avery asked after all the amenities had been said. Since the first trip in January, Mr. Morrison had made one other trip to Vicksburg, but Papa had not gone with him.

23 Papa motioned to Mr. Morrison. "Mr. Morrison and me going the day after tomorrow. Your wife brought down that list of things you need yesterday."

24 Mr. Avery cleared his throat nervously. "It's—it's that list I come 'bout, David. . . . I don't want them things no more."

25 The porch grew silent.

26 When no one said anything, Mr. Avery glanced at Mr. Lanier, and Mr. Lanier shook his head and continued. "Mr. Granger making it hard on us, David. Said we gonna have to give him sixty percent of the cotton, 'stead of fifty . . . now that the cotton's planted and it's too late to plant more. . . . Don't s'pose though that it makes much difference. The way cotton sells these days, seems the more we plant, the less money we gets anyways—"

27 Mr. Avery's coughing interrupted him and he waited patiently until the coughing had stopped before he went on. "I'm gonna be hard put to pay that debt in Vicksburg, David, but I'm gonna. . . . I want you to know that."

· · ·

28 Mr. Avery's coughing started again and for a while there was only the coughing and the silence. But when the coughing ceased, Mr. Lanier said, "I pray to God there was a way we could stay in this thing, but we can't go on no chain gang, David."

29 Papa nodded. "Don't expect you to, Silas."

30 Mr. Avery laughed softly. "We sure had 'em goin' for a time though, didn't we?"

31 "Yes," agreed Papa quietly, "we sure did."

32 When the men had left, Stacey snapped, "They got no right pulling out! Just 'cause them Wallaces threaten them one time they go jumping all over themselves to get out like a bunch of scared jackrabbits—"

33 Papa stood suddenly and grabbed Stacey upward. "You, boy, don't you get so grown you go to talking 'bout more than you know. Them men, they doing

what they've gotta do. You got any idea what a risk they took just to go shopping in Vicksburg in the first place? They go on that chain gang and their families got nothing. They'll get kicked off that plot of land they tend and there'll be no place for them to go. You understand that?"

34 "Y-yessir," said Stacey. Papa released him and stared moodily into the night. "You were born blessed, boy, with land of your own. If you hadn't been, you'd cry out for it while you try to survive . . . like Mr. Lanier and Mr. Avery. Maybe even do what they doing now. It's hard on a man to give up, but sometimes it seems there just ain't nothing else he can do."

35 "I . . . I'm sorry, Papa," Stacey muttered.

36 After a moment, Papa reached out and draped his arm over Stacey's shoulder.

37 "Papa," I said, standing to join them, "we giving up too?"

38 Papa looked down at me and brought me closer, then waved his hand toward the drive. "You see that fig tree over yonder, Cassie? Them other trees all around . . . that oak and walnut, they're a lot bigger and they take up more room and give so much shade they almost **overshadow** that little ole fig. But that fig tree's got roots that run deep, and it belongs in that yard as much as that oak and walnut. It keeps on blooming, bearing good fruit year after year, knowing all the time it'll never get as big as them other trees. Just keeps on growing and doing what it gotta do. It don't give up. It give up, it'll die. There's a lesson to be learned from that little tree, Cassie girl, 'cause we're like it. We keep doing what we gotta, and we don't give up. We can't."

Excerpted from *Roll of Thunder, Hear My Cry* by Mildred D. Taylor, published by Puffin Books.

 ## THINK QUESTIONS

1. What major problems do Papa and the other characters face in this excerpt? Cite textual evidence to support your answer.

2. Why don't Mr. Avery and Mr. Lanier join in Papa's plan to try to solve the problem? Support your answer with evidence from the text.

3. In what way is the Logan family in a better economic position than their neighbors? How could that fact affect the Logans' willingness to stand up for themselves against racism? Cite textual evidence to support your answer.

4. Use context to determine the meaning of the word ventured as it is used in *Roll of Thunder, Hear My Cry*. Write your definition of "ventured" and tell how you got it.

5. The prefix *aud-* comes from the Latin word meaning "to hear," and the suffix *-ible* means "able to be." Use the word parts and the context clues in the passage to determine the meaning of audible. Write your definition of **"audible"** and tell how you got it.

CLOSE READ

Reread the excerpt from *Roll of Thunder, Hear My Cry*. As you reread, complete the Focus Questions below. Then use your answers and annotations from the questions to help you complete the Writing Prompt.

FOCUS QUESTIONS

1. What information do readers learn in the first two paragraphs of *Roll of Thunder, Hear My Cry?* Highlight evidence from the text and make annotations noting specific reasons for your answer.

2. In paragraphs 3–8, what does the dialogue between Mama and Papa reveal about the problem they face and the way they each deal with it? How does this contribute to the development of the story's plot? Highlight specific evidence from the text and make annotations to support your answer.

3. In paragraphs 11–17, what key words and phrases does the author use to indicate the passage of time and move the plot forward? What inference can readers make about why Papa has delayed leaving the farm? Highlight specific words, phrases, or sentences from the text and make annotations to explain your answer.

4. In paragraphs 22–26, how does the conversation Papa has with Mr. Avery and Mr. Lanier relate to his earlier conversation with Mama? How is the language used in this conversation different from his earlier discussion, and what does it suggest about the characters? Highlight textual evidence and make annotations to explain your ideas.

5. In paragraphs 33–38, Papa talks with Stacey, and then with Cassie. In these passages, what do Stacey and Cassie learn from Papa about the importance of standing up for themselves and for others? What theme, or message, do Papa's words express? Highlight evidence from the text and make annotations to explain your ideas.

WRITING PROMPT

Analyze how the story structure Mildred Taylor chose to use in this chapter of her novel *Roll of Thunder, Hear My Cry* helped you to understand and appreciate the text. In your analysis, be sure to include examples of particular events and characterization, including the language and dialect various characters use. Examine and explain how the examples fit into the overall structure of the text. How did they help to develop the story's plot and message? Cite evidence from the text to support your ideas.

CHILDREN OF THE DUSTBOWL
THE TRUE STORY OF THE SCHOOL AT WEEDPATCH CAMP

NON-FICTION
Jerry Stanley
1993

INTRODUCTION

In the 1930s, drought and dust storms severely damaged the prairies of the United States, resulting in a period known as the Dust Bowl. Tens of thousands of families abandoned their destroyed farms in the Midwest and migrated to California and other states looking for work, but because of the Great Depression, many were unsuccessful. *Children of the Dust Bowl: The True Story of the School at Weedpatch Camp* is a nonfiction book about the period that focuses on educator Leo Hart and his role in creating a "federal emergency school" for the children of Weedpatch Camp, one of the farm-labor camps built by the federal government to house migrant workers, commonly known as "Okies." The camp is the same one described in author John Steinbeck's *The Grapes of Wrath*.

"...the feeling of rejection was greatest among Okie children."

 FIRST READ

From Chapter Four: Okie, Go Home!

1   When they left Weedpatch Camp to find work, the Okies faced ridicule, **rejection,** and shame. "Okie use' ta mean you was from Oklahoma," an Okie says in *The Grapes of Wrath.* "Now it means . . . you're scum." A store owner in nearby Arvin called Okies "ignorant, filthy people." A local doctor said they were **"shiftless** trash who lived like dogs." One woman screamed, "There's more darn 'Okies' in California than white people," while a local newspaper, the *Kern Herald,* alarmed readers with the headline MIGRANT HORDE INVADES KERN.

2   Californians were hostile to Okies because they competed with residents for jobs and because taxpayers were forced to pay for problems that arose as a result of the Okie migration to California. For example, **epidemics** of disease in the Okievilles caused the health and **sanitation** budget for Kern County to double between 1935 and 1940. During the same period, overcrowding in the schools caused Kern County's education bill to increase by 214 percent, while property taxes rose 50 percent.

. . .

3   But the feeling of rejection was greatest among Okie children. Because they had been poor for so long and had been traveling for months to get to California, the Okie children had not been able to attend school, and many couldn't read or write. When they went to school each day, most of the teachers ignored the migrants, believing that Okie kids were too stupid to learn the alphabet, too dumb to master math . . . Other teachers forced the newcomers to sit on the floor in the back of the classroom, while the non-Okie kids, well dressed with clean faces and the best school supplies, sat at desks and poked fun at their classmates who wore dresses made out of

Copyright © BookheadEd Learning, LLC

chicken-feed sacks, baggy overalls held up by rope, and frequently no shoes at all.

. . .

From Chapter 5: Mr. Hart

4   Leo Hart liked to visit the Okie children when they played in the field next to Weedpatch Camp. He was forty years old at the time, but it did not seem unusual to the children that this tall, slender man came to their makeshift playground at least once a week. When he played tag or baseball with the Okie kids or sat in a circle with them in the field and talked, the children called him Mr. Hart. He was a caring man who always had a smile on his face, as if he knew some great secret no one else knew.

. . .

5   The **opposition** to the Okie children angered Leo. Edna Hart recalled that her husband would come home from work so upset that he couldn't eat or sleep. "I could never understand," Leo said, "why these kids should be treated differently. I could never understand why they shouldn't be given the same opportunity as others. Someone had to do something for them because no one cared about them."

6   In 1940 Leo decided that if no one wanted the Okie kids in the public schools, then maybe the Okie children should have their own school. It would be a different school, he thought. It would be more than bricks and buildings, more than lessons and homework in math and writing. It would teach practical skills, such as masonry, mechanics, and agriculture. It would also teach the children to be proud of who they were. It would instill self-confidence in them so they might succeed in life of their own. It would provide the Okie children, Leo said, "with educational experiences in a broader and richer curriculum than were present in most schools." Above all else, Leo insisted, it would be "their school."

From Chapter Six: Weedpatch School

7   In April 1940 Superintendent Hart phoned the president of the Vineland school board, who was usually hostile to Okies and to the superintendent's office. But on this day Leo was phoning to tell the school board just what it wanted to hear.

8   Leo told the president of the board that he wanted to remove the Okie children from the public school. The president enthusiastically agreed. Then Leo asked him to declare that an emergency existed. "The emergency," Leo said, "was overcrowding in the public schools." Knowing that the president

was willing to consider any idea that might solve what he thought of as the Okie problem, Leo asked him for permission to build an "emergency school" for Okie children "at no expense to the district." Swiftly the president granted permission—without asking where the school might be located or how it might come about.

""Okie, Go Home!" (Chapter Four)," "Mr. Hart (Chapter Five)," and "Weedpatch School (Chapter Six)" from CHILDREN OF THE DUST BOWL by Jerry Stanley, copyright © 1992 by Jerry Stanley. Used by permission of Crown Publishers, an imprint of Random House Children's Books, a division of Random House LLC. All rights reserved.

 THINK QUESTIONS

1. Write two or three sentences explaining why Californians were hostile toward "Okies." Support your answer with textual evidence.

2. Refer to one or more details from the text to explain how these children were treated in school—both from ideas that are directly stated and ideas that you have inferred from clues in the text.

3. Use details from the text to write two or three sentences describing how Leo Hart was different from other teachers.

4. Use context to determine the meaning of the word **rejection** as it is used in *Children of the Dust Bowl: The True Story of the School at Weedpatch Camp*. Write your definition of "rejection" and tell how you got it. Then, check your definition by using it in the context of a sentence or by looking in a dictionary.

5. Remembering that the Latin root *sanitas* means "health," use this information and the context to determine the meaning of the word **sanitation** as it is used in *Children of the Dust Bowl: The True Story of the School at Weedpatch Camp*. Write your definition of "sanitation" and tell how you got it. Then, check your definition by using it in the context of a sentence or by looking in a dictionary.

CLOSE READ

Reread the excerpt from *Children of the Dust Bowl: The True Story of the School at Weedpatch Camp.* As you reread, complete the Focus Questions below. Then use your answers and annotations from the questions to help you complete the Writing Prompt.

FOCUS QUESTIONS

1. In paragraph 3, the author makes a distinction between "Okie" and "non-Okie" kids. Discuss how the term "Okie" transforms from a neutral word meaning "someone from Oklahoma" (paragraph 1) to a negative word. Highlight textual evidence and make annotations to explain your ideas.

2. The camp in the text, based near Arvin, California, takes on the name "Weedpatch Camp." Based on paragraphs 2 and 3, make annotations about the denotation and connotation of the word "weedpatch" as it is used in the name of the camp. Support your response with textual evidence, and make annotations to explain your ideas.

3. In paragraph 4, author Jerry Stanley describes Leo Hart as "a caring man who always had a

smile on his face, as if he knew some great secret no one else knew." What do you think is the author's point of view toward Leo Hart? How does Stanley use word choice to reveal this point of view? Support your response with textual evidence, and make annotations to explain your response.

4. Use the central idea and the most important supporting details from paragraphs 7 and 8 to provide a summary of Leo Hart's plan. Highlight evidence from the text and make annotations to explain your ideas.

5. How did Leo Hart's vision for an "Okie school" show that he was standing up for others? Highlight evidence from the text and make annotations to explain your ideas.

WRITING PROMPT

What is the excerpt from *Children of the Dust Bowl: The True Story of the School at Weedpatch Camp* all about? What do the details in the text have in common? Use your understanding of a central (or main) idea and the details that support the central idea to write an objective summary of the text in your own words. Support your writing with textual evidence. Be sure not to include your feelings, opinions, or judgments in your summary.

Please note that excerpts and passages in the StudySync® library and this workbook are intended as touchstones to generate interest in an author's work. The excerpts and passages do not substitute for the reading of entire texts, and StudySync® strongly recommends that students seek out and purchase the whole literary or informational work in order to experience it as the author intended. Links to online resellers are available in our digital library. In addition, complete works may be ordered through an authorized reseller by filling out and returning to StudySync® the order form enclosed in this workbook.

Reading & Writing Companion   **229**

THE CIRCUIT:
STORIES FROM THE LIFE OF A MIGRANT CHILD

FICTION
Francisco Jimenez
1997

INTRODUCTION

When Francisco Jimenez was four years old, he and his family immigrated to the United States. At the age of six, he began working on farms, like other members of his family. Now a professor of literature at Santa Clara University in California, Jimenez said, "I came to realize that learning and knowledge were the only stable things in my life. Whatever I learned in school, that knowledge would stay with me no matter how many times we moved." *The Circuit: Stories from the Life of a Migrant Child* is Jimenez's autobiographical novel about migrant farm workers in 1950s California. It describes how migrant workers would go from farm to farm picking fruits and vegetables—also known as travelling

"... everything we owned was neatly packed in cardboard boxes."

FIRST READ

From the Chapter: The Circuit

1   It was that time of year again. Ito, the strawberry sharecropper, did not smile. It was natural. The peak of the strawberry season was over and the last few days the workers, most of them *braceros,* were not picking as many boxes as they had during the months of June and July.

2   As the last days of August disappeared, so did the number of braceros. Sunday, only one—the best picker—came to work. I liked him. Sometimes we talked during our half-hour lunch break. That is how I found out he was from Jalisco, the same state in Mexico my family was from. That Sunday was the last time I saw him.

3   When the sun had tired and sunk behind the mountains, Ito signaled us that it was time to go home. "*Ya esora,*" he yelled in his broken Spanish. Those were the words I waited for twelve hours a day, every day, seven days a week, week after week. And the thought of not hearing them again saddened me.

4   As we drove home Papá did not say a word. With both hands on the wheel, he stared at the dirt road. My older brother, Roberto, was also silent. He leaned his head back and closed his eyes. Once in a while he cleared from his throat the dust that blew in from outside.

5   Yes, it was that time of year. When I opened the front door to the shack, I stopped. Everything we owned was neatly packed in cardboard boxes. Suddenly I felt even more the weight of hours, days, weeks, and months of work. I sat down on a box. The thought of having to move to Fresno and knowing what was in store for me there brought tears to my eyes.

Please note that excerpts and passages in the StudySync® library and this workbook are intended as touchstones to generate interest in an author's work. The excerpts and passages do not substitute for the reading of entire texts, and StudySync® strongly recommends that students seek out and purchase the whole literary or informational work in order to experience it as the author intended. Links to online resellers are available in our digital library. In addition, complete works may be ordered through an authorized reseller by filling out and returning to StudySync® the order form enclosed in this workbook.

Reading & Writing Companion   **231**

6   That night I could not sleep. I lay in bed thinking about how much I hated this move.

7   A little before five o'clock in the morning, Papá woke everyone up. A few minutes later, the yelling and screaming of my little brothers and sisters, for whom the move was a great adventure, broke the silence of dawn. Shortly, the barking of the dogs accompanied them.

8   While we packed the breakfast dishes, Papá went outside to start the "*Carcachita.*" That was the name Papá gave his old black Plymouth. He bought it in a used-car lot in Santa Rosa. Papá was very proud of his little jalopy. He had a right to be proud of it. He spent a lot of time looking at other cars before buying this one. When he finally chose the *Carcachita,* he checked it thoroughly before driving it out of the car lot. He examined every inch of the car. He listened to the motor, tilting his head from side to side like a parrot, trying to **detect** any noises that spelled car trouble. After being satisfied with the looks and sounds of the car, Papá then insisted on knowing who the original owner was. He never did find out from the car salesman, but he bought the car anyway. Papá figured the original owner must have been an important man because behind the rear seat of the car he found a blue necktie.

9   Papá parked the car out in front and left the motor running. "*Listo,*" he yelled. Without saying a word, Roberto and I began to carry the boxes out to the car. Roberto carried the two big boxes and I carried the two smaller ones. Papá then threw the mattress on top of the car roof and tied it with ropes to the front and rear bumpers.

10   Everything was packed except Mamá's pot. It was on old large galvanized pot she had picked up at an army surplus store in Santa Maria. The pot had many dents and nicks, and the more dents and nicks it **acquired** the more Mamá liked it. "*Mi olla,*" she used to say proudly.

11   I held the front door open as Mamá carefully carried out her pot by both handles, making sure not to spill the cooked beans. When she got to the car, Papá reached out to help her with it. Roberto opened the rear car door and Papá gently placed it on the floor behind the front seat. All of us then climbed in. Papá sighed, wiped the sweat off his forehead with his sleeve, and said wearily: "*Es todo.*"

12   As we drove away, I felt a lump in my throat. I turned around and looked at our little shack for the last time.

13   At sunset we drove into a labor camp near Fresno. Since Papá did not speak English, Mamá asked the camp **foreman** if he needed any more workers. "We don't need no more," said the foreman, scratching his head. "Check with

Sullivan down the road. Can't miss him. He lives in a big white house with a fence around it."

14   When we got there, Mamá walked up to the house. She went through a white gate, past a row of rose bushes, up the stairs to the front door. She rang the doorbell. The porch light went on and tall husky man came out. They exchanged a few words. After the man went in, Mamá clasped her hands and hurried back to the car. "We have work! Mr. Sullivan said we can stay there the whole season," she said, gasping and pointing to an old garage near the stables.

15   The garage was worn out by the years. It had no windows. The walls, eaten by termites, strained to support the roof full of holes. The dirt floor, populated by earthworms, looked like a gray road map.

16   That night, by the light of a kerosene lamp, we unpacked and cleaned our new home. Roberto swept away the loose dirt, leaving the hard ground. Papá plugged the holes in the walls with old newspapers and tin can tops. Mamá fed my little brothers and sisters. Papá and Roberto then brought in the mattress and placed it on the far corner of the garage. "Mamá, you and the little ones sleep on the mattress. Roberto, Panchito, and I will sleep outside under the trees," Papá said.

17   Early next morning Mr. Sullivan showed us where his crop was, and after breakfast, Papá, Roberto, and I headed for the vineyard to pick.

18   Around nine o'clock the temperature had risen to almost one hundred degrees. I was completely soaked in sweat and my mouth felt as if I had been chewing on a handkerchief. I walked over to the end of the row, picked up the jug of water we had brought, and began drinking. "Don't drink too much; you'll get sick," Roberto shouted. No sooner had he said that than I felt sick to my stomach. I dropped to my knees and let the jug roll off my hands. I remained motionless with my eyes glued on the hot sandy ground. All I could hear was the drone of insects. Slowly I began to recover. I poured water over my face and neck and watched the dirty water run down my arms to the ground.

19   I still felt a little dizzy when we took a break to eat lunch. It was past two o'clock and we sat underneath a large walnut tree that was on the side of the road. While we ate, Papá jotted down the number of boxes we had picked. Roberto drew designs on the ground with a stick. Suddenly I noticed Papá's face turn pale as he looked down the road. "Here comes the school bus," he whispered loudly in alarm. Instinctively, Roberto and I ran and hid in the vineyards. We did not want to get in trouble for not going to school. The neatly dressed boys about my age got off. They carried books under their

Copyright © BookheadEd Learning, LLC

arms. After they crossed the street, the bus drove away. Roberto and I came out from hiding and joined Papá. "*Tienen que tener cuidado,*" he warned us.

20 After lunch we went back to work. The sun kept beating down. The buzzing insects, the wet sweat, and the hot dry dust made the afternoon seem to last forever. Finally the mountains around the valley reached out and swallowed the sun. Within an hour it was too dark to continue picking. The vines blanketed the grapes, making it difficult to see the bunches. "*Vámanos,*" said Papá, signaling to us that it was time to quit work. Papá then took out a pencil and began to figure out how much we had earned our first day. He wrote down numbers, crossed some out, wrote down some more, "*Quince,*" he murmured.

21 When we arrived home, we took a cold shower underneath a water hose. We then sat down to eat dinner around some wooden crates that served as a table. Mamá had cooked a special meal for us. We had rice and tortillas with *carne con chile,* my favorite dish.

22 The next morning I could hardly move. My body ached all over. I felt little control over my arms and legs. This feeling went on every morning for days until my muscles finally got used to the work.

23 It was Monday, the first week of November. The grape season was over and I could now go to school. I woke up early that morning and lay in bed, looking at the stars and **savoring** the thought of not going to work and of starting sixth grade for the first time that year. Since I could not sleep, I decided to get up and join Papá and Roberto at breakfast. I sat at the table across from Roberto, but I kept my head down. I did not want to look up and face him. I knew he was sad. He was not going to school today. He was not going tomorrow, or next week, or next month. He would not go until the cotton season was over, and that was sometime in February. I rubbed my hands together and watched the dry, acid stained skin fall to the floor in little rolls.

24 When Papá and Roberto left for work, I felt relief. I walked to the top of a small grade next to the shack and watched the *Carcachita* disappear in the distance in a cloud of dust.

25 Two hours later, around eight o'clock, I stood by the side of the road waiting for school bus number twenty. When it arrived I climbed in. Everyone was busy either talking or yelling. I sat in an empty seat in the back.

26 When the bus stopped in front of the school, I felt very nervous. I looked out the bus window and saw boys and girls carrying books under their arms. I put my hands in my pant pockets and walked to the principal's office. When I entered I heard a woman's voice say: "May I help you?" I was startled. I had not heard English for months. For a few seconds I remained speechless. I

NOTES

looked at the lady who waited for an answer. My first instinct was to answer her in Spanish, but I held back. Finally, after struggling for English words, I managed to tell her that I wanted to enroll in the sixth grade. After answering many questions, I was led to the classroom.

27 Mr. Lema, the sixth grade teacher, greeted me and assigned me a desk. He then introduced me to the class. I was so nervous and scared at that moment when everyone's eyes were on me that I wished I were with Papá and Roberto picking cotton. After taking roll, Mr. Lema gave the class the assignment for the first hour. "The first thing we have to do this morning is finish reading the story we began yesterday," he said enthusiastically. He walked up to me, handed me an English book, and asked me to read. "We are on page 125," he said politely. When I heard this, I felt my blood rush to my head; I felt dizzy. "Would you like to read?" he asked **hesitantly**. I opened the book to page 125. My mouth was dry. My eyes began to water. I could not begin. "You can read later," Mr. Lema said understandingly.

28 For the rest of the reading period I kept getting angrier and angrier with myself. I should have read, I thought to myself. During recess I went into the restroom and opened my English book to page 125. I began to read in a low voice, pretending I was in class. There were many words I did not know. I closed the book and headed back to the classroom.

29 Mr. Lema was sitting at his desk correcting papers. When I entered he looked up at me and smiled. I felt better. I walked up to him and asked if he could help me with the new words. "Gladly," he said.

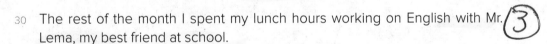

30 The rest of the month I spent my lunch hours working on English with Mr. Lema, my best friend at school.

31 One Friday, during lunch hour, Mr. Lema asked me to take a walk with him to the music room. "Do you like music?" he asked me as we entered the building. "Yes, I like *corridos*," I answered. He then picked up a trumpet, blew on it, and handed it to me. The sound gave me goose bumps. I knew that sound. I had heard it in many *corridos*."How would you like to learn how to play it?" he asked. He must have read my face because before I could answer, he added: "I'll teach you how to play it during our lunch hours."

32 That day I could hardly wait to tell Papá and Mamá the great news. As I got off the bus, my little brothers and sisters ran up to meet me. They were yelling and screaming. I thought they were happy to see me, but when I opened the door to our shack, I saw that everything we owned was neatly packed in cardboard boxes.

Please note that excerpts and passages in the StudySync® library and this workbook are intended as touchstones to generate interest in an author's work. The excerpts and passages do not substitute for the reading of entire texts, and StudySync® strongly recommends that students seek out and purchase the whole literary or informational work in order to experience it as the author intended. Links to online resellers are available in our digital library. In addition, complete works may be ordered through an authorized reseller by filling out and returning to StudySync® the order form enclosed in this workbook.

Reading & Writing Companion   235

THINK QUESTIONS

1. How does Francisco feel about moving from farm to farm? Support your response with details that are directly stated in the story and ideas that you infer.

2. In what ways are Francisco's feelings about school divided? What causes this? Support your response with textual evidence from the story.

3. Use textual evidence to describe the role that Mr. Lema plays in Francisco's life, as well as how Francisco is affected by him.

4. Use context to determine the meaning of the word **foreman** as it is used in *The Circuit: Stories From the Life of a Migrant Child*. Write your definition of "foreman" and tell how you got it.

5. Use context to determine the meaning of the word **savoring** as it is used in *The Circuit: Stories From the Life of a Migrant Child*. Write your definition of "savoring" and tell how you got it.

CLOSE READ

Reread the excerpt from *The Circuit: Stories From the Life of a Migrant Child*. As you reread, complete the Focus Questions below. Then use your answers and annotations from the questions to help you complete the Writing Prompt.

FOCUS QUESTIONS

1. In paragraph 8, Francisco describes Papá's car and tells readers the story of how Papá bought it. How does this description help you get to know Papá from Francisco's perspective? Highlight details in the paragraph that help you infer Papá's character traits, and make annotations to record your ideas.

2. In paragraph 27, Francisco meets his sixth grade teacher, Mr. Lema. Highlight textual evidence in this paragraph that indicates Francisco's impression of his teacher. Then make annotations to explain how this viewpoint supports the actions Francisco takes in the next two paragraphs.

3. In both paragraph 5 and the final paragraph, Francisco comes home to find his family's belongings "neatly packed in cardboard boxes." Why do you think he specifically uses the word "neatly" each time he describes this detail to readers? How does this description contrast with Francisco's feelings about moving? Annotate your ideas and highlight evidence from the text that supports them.

4. In the last two paragraphs, how does the mood, or emotional feeling of the story, change to reflect what Francisco is now feeling? Annotate your ideas and highlight evidence from the text that supports them.

5. In what ways does the use of first-person point of view allow readers to better understand the challenges Francisco faces in *The Circuit*? In what ways might a third-person point of view give readers a different understanding of these challenges? Annotate your ideas and highlight evidence from the text that supports them.

WRITING PROMPT

Author Francisco Jimenez chose to write his autobiographical novel *The Circuit: Stories from the Life of a Migrant Child* from the first-person point of view of a child migrant worker.

How might the story be different if told from the point of view of Francisco's mother or father? What might the reader discover about his parents' thoughts and feelings as they anticipate another move? Examine and explain how changing the point of view from the boy to one of his parents might reveal different aspects of what life was like for migrant workers as they faced challenges and hardships. Remember to support your central idea with relevant, well-organized evidence from the text, including quotations, details, and examples, to show how the point of view in a story influences readers' understanding of characters and their experiences.

Please note that excerpts and passages in the StudySync® library and this workbook are intended as touchstones to generate interest in an author's work. The excerpts and passages do not substitute for the reading of entire texts, and StudySync® strongly recommends that students seek out and purchase the whole literary or informational work in order to experience it as the author intended. Links to online resellers are available in our digital library. In addition, complete works may be ordered through an authorized reseller by filling out and returning to StudySync® the order form enclosed in this workbook.

Reading & Writing Companion   **237**

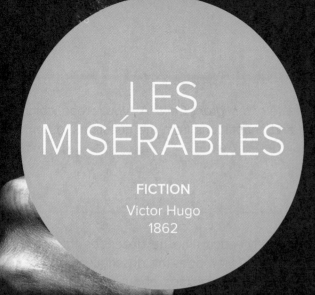

LES MISÉRABLES

FICTION

Victor Hugo

1862

INTRODUCTION

studysync tv

Victor Hugo's *Les Misérables,* set during the turbulent years after Napoleon's defeat in the early 19th Century, is the dramatic story of Jean Valjean. Valjean has spent nineteen years in prison for stealing a loaf of bread to feed his sister's family and then for numerous escape attempts. When he is at last released from prison, he is marked as an ex-convict, facing a hostile world and forced to sleep on the street. Finally, embittered and losing his spirit, he is given refuge by the good-natured Bishop Myriel, known as Monseigneur Bienvenu for his welcoming nature. Valjean has now come to a crossroads where he will face a moral challenge that will change his life and those around him forever.

"Jean Valjean, my brother, you no longer belong to evil, but to good."

FIRST READ

NOTES

Excerpt from Chapter V

TRANQUILITY

1   After bidding his sister good night, Monseigneur Bienvenu took one of the two silver candlesticks from the table, handed the other to his guest, and said to him, —

2   "Monsieur, I will conduct you to your room."

3   The man followed him.

4   As might have been observed from what has been said above, the house was so arranged that in order to pass into the oratory where the alcove was situated, or to get out of it, it was necessary to traverse the Bishop's bedroom.

5   At the moment when he was crossing this apartment, Madame Magloire was putting away the silverware in the cupboard near the head of the bed. This was her last care every evening before she went to bed.

6   The Bishop installed his guest in the alcove. A fresh white bed had been prepared there. The man set the candle down on a small table.

7   "Well," said the Bishop, "may you pass a good night. To-morrow morning, before you set out, you shall drink a cup of warm milk from our cows."

8   "Thanks, Monsieur l'Abbe," said the man.

9   Hardly had he pronounced these words full of peace, when all of a sudden, and without transition, he made a strange movement, which would have frozen the two sainted women with horror, had they witnessed it. Even at this

Please note that excerpts and passages in the StudySync® library and this workbook are intended as touchstones to generate interest in an author's work. The excerpts and passages do not substitute for the reading of entire texts, and StudySync® strongly recommends that students seek out and purchase the whole literary or informational work in order to experience it as the author intended. Links to online resellers are available in our digital library. In addition, complete works may be ordered through an authorized reseller by filling out and returning to StudySync® the order form enclosed in this workbook.

Reading & Writing
Companion   **239**

day it is difficult for us to explain what inspired him at that moment. Did he intend to convey a warning or to throw out a menace? Was he simply obeying a sort of instinctive impulse which was obscure even to himself? He turned abruptly to the old man, folded his arms, and bending upon his host a savage gaze, he exclaimed in a hoarse voice:—

10 "Ah! really! You lodge me in your house, close to yourself like this?"

11 He broke off, and added with a laugh in which there lurked something monstrous:—

12 "Have you really reflected well? How do you know that I have not been an assassin?"

13 The Bishop replied:—

14 "That is the concern of the good God."

15 Then gravely, and moving his lips like one who is praying or talking to himself, he raised two fingers of his right hand and bestowed his **benediction** on the man, who did not bow, and without turning his head or looking behind him, he returned to his bedroom.

Excerpt from Chapter XII

THE BISHOP WORKS

16 The next morning at sunrise Monseigneur Bienvenu was strolling in his garden. Madame Magloire ran up to him in utter consternation.

17 "Monseigneur, Monseigneur!" she exclaimed, "does your Grace know where the basket of silver is?"

18 "Yes," replied the Bishop.

19 "Jesus the Lord be blessed!" she resumed; "I did not know what had become of it."

20 The Bishop had just picked up the basket in a flower-bed. He presented it to Madame Magloire.

21 "Here it is."

22 "Well!" said she. "Nothing in it! And the silver?"

23 "Ah," returned the Bishop, "so it is the silver which troubles you? I don't know where it is."

24   "Great, good God! It is stolen! That man who was here last night has stolen it."

25   In a twinkling, with all the vivacity of an alert old woman, Madame Magloire had rushed to the oratory, entered the alcove, and returned to the Bishop. The Bishop had just bent down, and was sighing as he examined a plant of cochlearia des Guillons, which the basket had broken as it fell across the bed. He rose up at Madame Magloire's cry.

26   "Monseigneur, the man is gone! The silver has been stolen!"

27   As she uttered this exclamation, her eyes fell upon a corner of the garden, where traces of the wall having been scaled were visible. The coping of the wall had been torn away.

28   "Stay! yonder is the way he went. He jumped over into Cochefilet Lane. Ah, the abomination! He has stolen our silver!"

29   The Bishop remained silent for a moment; then he raised his grave eyes, and said gently to Madame Magloire:—

30   "And, in the first place, was that silver ours?"

31   Madame Magloire was speechless. Another silence ensued; then the Bishop went on:—

32   "Madame Magloire, I have for a long time detained that silver wrongfully. It belonged to the poor. Who was that man? A poor man, evidently."

33   "Alas! Jesus!" returned Madame Magloire. "It is not for my sake, nor for Mademoiselle's. It makes no difference to us. But it is for the sake of Monseigneur. What is Monseigneur to eat with now?"

34   The Bishop gazed at her with an air of amazement.

35   "Ah, come! Are there no such things as pewter forks and spoons?"

36   Madame Magloire shrugged her shoulders.

37   "Pewter has an odor."

38   "Iron forks and spoons, then."

39   Madame Magloire made an expressive grimace.

40   "Iron has a taste."

41   "Very well," said the Bishop; "wooden ones then."

Copyright © BookheadEd Learning, LLC

42 A few moments later he was breakfasting at the very table at which Jean Valjean had sat on the previous evening. As he ate his breakfast, Monseigneur Welcome remarked gayly to his sister, who said nothing, and to Madame Magloire, who was grumbling under her breath, that one really does not need either fork or spoon, even of wood, in order to dip a bit of bread in a cup of milk.

43 "A pretty idea, truly," said Madame Magloire to herself, as she went and came, "to take in a man like that! and to lodge him close to one's self! And how fortunate that he did nothing but steal! Ah, mon Dieu! it makes one shudder to think of it!"

44 As the brother and sister were about to rise from the table, there came a knock at the door.

45 "Come in," said the Bishop.

46 The door opened. A singular and violent group made its appearance on the threshold. Three men were holding a fourth man by the collar. The three men were gendarmes; the other was Jean Valjean.

47 A brigadier of gendarmes, who seemed to be in command of the group, was standing near the door. He entered and advanced to the Bishop, making a military salute.

48 "Monseigneur—" said he.

49 At this word, Jean Valjean, who was dejected and seemed overwhelmed, raised his head with an air of **stupefaction.**

50 "Monseigneur!" he murmured. "So he is not the cure?"

51 "Silence!" said the gendarme. "He is Monseigneur the Bishop."

52 In the meantime, Monseigneur Bienvenu had advanced as quickly as his great age permitted.

53 "Ah! here you are!" he exclaimed, looking at Jean Valjean. "I am glad to see you. Well, but how is this? I gave you the candlesticks too, which are of silver like the rest, and for which you can certainly get two hundred francs. Why did you not carry them away with your forks and spoons?"

54 Jean Valjean opened his eyes wide, and stared at the **venerable** Bishop with an expression which no human tongue can render any account of.

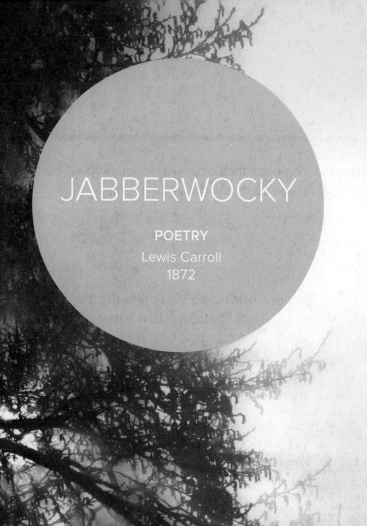

JABBERWOCKY

POETRY
Lewis Carroll
1872

INTRODUCTION

studysync📺

This whimsical poem about a heroic quest was first published in its entirety in author Lewis Carroll's *Through the Looking Glass*. Alice finds the poem in a book after she steps through the mirror into an odd new world. The poem's fantastical characters, invented language and formal structure have made it a classic in its own right.

Copyright © BookheadEd Learning, LLC

NOTES

55 "Monseigneur," said the brigadier of gendarmes, "so what this man said is true, then? We came across him. He was walking like a man who is running away. We stopped him to look into the matter. He had this silver—"

56 "And he told you," interposed the Bishop with a smile, "that it had been given to him by a kind old fellow of a priest with whom he had passed the night? I see how the matter stands. And you have brought him back here? It is a mistake."

57 "In that case," replied the brigadier, "we can let him go?"

58 "Certainly," replied the Bishop.

59 The gendarmes released Jean Valjean, who recoiled.

60 "Is it true that I am to be released?" he said, in an almost inarticulate voice, and as though he were talking in his sleep.

61 "Yes, thou art released; dost thou not understand?" said one of the gendarmes.

62 "My friend," resumed the Bishop, "before you go, here are your candlesticks. Take them."

63 He stepped to the chimney-piece, took the two silver candlesticks, and brought them to Jean Valjean. The two women looked on without uttering a word, without a gesture, without a look which could disconcert the Bishop.

64 Jean Valjean was trembling in every limb. He took the two candlesticks mechanically, and with a bewildered air.

65 "Now," said the Bishop, "go in peace. By the way, when you return, my friend, it is not necessary to pass through the garden. You can always enter and depart through the street door."

66 Then, turning to the gendarmes:—

67 "You may retire, gentlemen."

68 The gendarmes retired.

69 Jean Valjean was like a man on the point of fainting.

70 The Bishop drew near to him, and said in a low voice:—

71 "Do not forget, never forget, that you have promised to use this money in becoming an honest man."

NOTES

72   Jean Valjean, who had no recollection of ever having promised anything, remained speechless. The Bishop had emphasized the words when he uttered them. He resumed with solemnity:—

73   "Jean Valjean, my brother, you no longer belong to evil, but to good. It is your soul that I buy from you; I withdraw it from black thoughts and the spirit of **perdition,** and I give it to God."

74   It is never fastened with anything but a latch, either by day or by night."

THINK QUESTIONS

1. How does Jean Valjean react when the Bishop wishes him a good night and tells him that he'll be given a cup of warm milk in the morning? How does the Bishop respond to what Valjean says? Support your answers with textual evidence.

2. How does Valjean repay the Bishop's kindness the next morning? Support your answer with textual evidence.

3. How does the Bishop respond to Valjean's return? Support your answer both with evidence that is directly stated and with ideas that you have inferred from clues in the text.

4. The Latin root *vener-* (or *venus*) means "love" or "charm." The affix *-able* means "capable of" or "fit for." Use this, along with context clues from the text, to determine the meaning of the word **venerable** as it is used in *Les Misérables*. Write your definition of "venerable" and tell how you determined it.

5. Remembering that the Latin root *bene* means "well," and the root *dict* means "to speak," use the context clues provided in the passage to determine the meaning of benediction. Write your definition of **"benediction"** and tell how you determined it

CLOSE READ

Reread the excerpt from *Les Misérables*. As you reread, complete the Focus Questions below. Then use your answers and annotations from the questions to help you complete the Writing Prompt.

FOCUS QUESTIONS

1. After the Bishop wishes his guest good night, Valjean responds first in one way, and then in a completely different way. What do his two very different responses tell you about Valjean's character? What clues can you find in his responses that contribute to the development of the story's theme? Highlight and annotate textual evidence to support your answers.

2. Following Valjean's implied threat about having been an assassin, how does the Bishop respond? What does the Bishop's response tell you both about his character and about his view of the purpose and function of the church? Highlight and annotate textual evidence to explain your answers and inferences.

3. After Madame Magloire discovers that the silver is missing, the Bishop says, "I have for a long time detained that silver wrongfully. It belonged to the poor. Who was that man? A poor man, evidently." Why do you think the Bishop feels that he has "detained that silver wrongfully"? What clues can you find in his statement that contribute to the development of the story's theme? Highlight and annotate evidence from the text to support your answers.

4. How does Madame Magloire feel about what Valjean does, and about what the Bishop does? What clues to the story's theme can you find in her attitude and responses? Highlight evidence from the text and make annotations to support your views of Madame Magloire.

5. Valjean accepts the silver candlesticks from the Bishop. With this action, does Valjean agree to the promise that the Bishop warns him never to forget? Will he accept the Bishop's challenge? Highlight evidence from the text and make annotations to support your response.

WRITING PROMPT

The Bishop, who sees goodness in Valjean and wants him to lead an honest life, implies to the gendarmes that Valjean did not steal the silver. Does his wish to help Valjean, to stand up for him, justify what he tells the gendarmes? What other reasons might he have had for acting as he does? Write a brief essay explaining how the Bishop's words and actions in relation to Valjean, particularly in the presence of the gendarmes, help reveal the story's theme. Use relevant, well-organized textual evidence to develop your ideas.

"Beware the Jabberwock, my son!"

FIRST READ

From Chapter 1: "Looking-Glass House"

1 'Twas brillig, and the slithy toves
2 Did gyre and gimble in the wabe;
3 All mimsy were the borogoves,
4 And the mome raths outgrabe.

5 'Beware the Jabberwock, my son!
6 The jaws that bite, the claws that catch!
7 Beware the Jubjub bird, and **shun**
8 The frumious Bandersnatch!'

9 He took his vorpal sword in hand:
10 Long time the manxome foe he **sought**
11 So rested he by the Tumtum tree,
12 And stood awhile in thought.

13 And as in uffish thought he stood,
14 The Jabberwock, with eyes of flame,
15 Came whiffling through the tulgey wood,
16 And **burbled** as it came!

17 One, two! One, two! And through and through
18 The vorpal blade went snicker-snack!
19 He left it dead, and with its head
20 He went **galumphing** back.

21 'And hast thou slain the Jabberwock?
22 Come to my arms, my beamish boy!

Please note that excerpts and passages in the StudySync® library and this workbook are intended as touchstones to generate interest in an author's work. The excerpts and passages do not substitute for the reading of entire texts, and StudySync® strongly recommends that students seek out and purchase the whole literary or informational work in order to experience it as the author intended. Links to online resellers are available in our digital library. In addition, complete works may be ordered through an authorized reseller by filling out and returning to StudySync® the order form enclosed in this workbook.

Reading & Writing Companion **247**

NOTES

23 O frabjous day! Callooh! Callay!'
24 He **chortled** in his joy.

25 'Twas brillig, and the slithy toves
26 Did gyre and gimble in the wabe;
27 All mimsy were the borogoves,
28 And the mome raths out grabe.

THINK QUESTIONS

1. The person who kills the Jabberwock is related to the narrator of the poem. What is the relationship? Cite textual evidence for your answer.

2. What do you think the Jabberwock looks like? Use details from the text to write two or three sentences describing the Jabberwock.

3. Summarize the action of "Jabberwocky." For each major event, provide a piece of evidence from the text.

4. Use context to determine the meaning of the word **shun** as it is used in *Jabberwocky*. Write your definition of "shun" and tell how you found it. Then, consult a dictionary to check your definition. What is the precise meaning of "shun"?

5. Use the context clues provided in the passage to determine the meaning of **galumphing.** Write your definition of "galumphing" and tell how you got it. How do you think this word might sound aloud? Then, using a dictionary or similar resource, check your definition and determine the correct pronunciation of "galumphing."

CLOSE READ

Reread the poem "Jabberwocky." As you reread, complete the Focus Questions below. Then use your answers and annotations from the questions to help you complete the Writing Prompt.

FOCUS QUESTIONS

1. How does the poet's use of invented words in the first stanza affect the tone of the poem? Annotate the text to cite specific words and phrases as evidence of the poem's tone.

2. In "Jabberwocky," much of the fun is that a heroic adventure is described in a silly way. From the first four stanzas, highlight two examples of descriptions that use a heroic tone and a silly tone at the same time. Annotate the text with a note about how the words you highlighted contribute to the tone.

3. Many of the words that Lewis Carroll invented for this poem sound like what they seem to mean. This is called *onomatopoeia*. From the last four stanzas of the poem, highlight two words from the poem that sound like what you think they mean. Annotate the text to provide the meaning that you infer, and explain how the sound helped you find the meaning.

4. The final stanza is exactly the same as the first stanza. Highlight these stanzas and make annotations about how you think this affects the tone of the poem. Include an annotation about how you would read these two stanzas and the tone of voice you would use. Describe any differences between how you would read the first and last stanzas and refer to specific words and phrases in the text.

5. How does the young man in "Jabberwocky" stand up for himself? What effects does his action have? Highlight the text that shows evidence of this.

WRITING PROMPT

What serious point do you think Lewis Carroll might be making in "Jabberwocky"? Use your understanding of tone and connotation to support your opinion. Cite evidence from the text to develop your claim about the more serious meaning of "Jabberwocky."

Please note that excerpts and passages in the StudySync® library and this workbook are intended as touchstones to generate interest in an author's work. The excerpts and passages do not substitute for the reading of entire texts, and StudySync® strongly recommends that students seek out and purchase the whole literary or informational work in order to experience it as the author intended. Links to online resellers are available in our digital library. In addition, complete works may be ordered through an authorized reseller by filling out and returning to StudySync® the order form enclosed in this workbook.

Reading & Writing Companion   **249**

BULLYING IN SCHOOLS

NON-FICTION
2014

INTRODUCTION

The writers of these two articles each believe that bullying is a serious problem that needs to be addressed. However, the writers disagree on the issue of whether schools are currently doing enough to face the challenge. One writer argues that schools have not invested nearly enough effort in creating safeguards and programs to protect students and prevent bullying. The other writer argues that most schools now take bullying very seriously and have initiated enough programs to effectively address and begin to solve the problem. Both writers present strong arguments and support their claims with evidence. Which

"...one of three students is bullied either in school or through social media."

FIRST READ

1 **Bullying in Schools: Are We Doing Enough?**

2 **Point: Schools Are Not Doing Enough to Prevent Bullying**

3   Although the media continues to raise public awareness of student bullying, many schools are still not doing enough to face the challenge of solving the problem. Most teachers and school administrators do not witness bullying. Sometimes they don't know how to recognize it. Sometimes they ignore it. They may also hold the age-old attitude that bullying is just something children do or go through. They think it's a normal part of growing up. But we know now that the repercussions of bullying can be lasting and severe. Sometimes they even end in tragedy.

4   The simple fact that a huge amount of bullying still happens demonstrates that not enough is being done about the issue. The exact number of victims is hard to determine because many incidents go unreported. The National Center for Education Statistics reported in 2013 that one of three students is bullied either in school or through social media. This statistic includes both physical and emotional harassment. Either form can leave lasting scars on victims. Students who are bullied often become very stressed. They can have trouble sleeping and begin to do poorly in school. Furthermore, victims are at a greater risk of suffering from low self-esteem, anxiety, and depression. These effects can even continue well into adulthood.

5   One way in which schools are failing to keep pace with the problem is in adequately supervising school property. Bullying usually happens in unsupervised areas like bathrooms, cafeterias, and school buses. The simplest solution would be for schools to put teachers, monitors, or aides in these areas. Unfortunately, many schools do not have enough staff to ensure that these areas are supervised.

6   An even harder venue to monitor for bullying is the Internet. Cyber-bullying, or bullying that happens over social media, is often extremely hard to track. It is easy to delete comments or pictures before authority figures can see them. In many cases there is little evidence to go on. Students, teachers, and administrators all need to be educated about how to deal with the challenge of cyber-bullying. There are not currently enough programs that address this issue.

7   Most schools also do not have a clear procedure or policy for investigating bullying. This means that if a victim is brave enough to come forward and ask for help, he or she often does not receive it. This is because administrators and authorities do not have a set path for examining the situation. They do not have a plan for ending harmful situations.

8   In addition to educating teachers and administrators about bullying, schools need more programs to help students themselves address the problem. Top-down approaches that simply dole out punishments for bullies are not enough to solve the problem. Students need to be taught more about the ways their words and actions can hurt others. They also need to learn that cases of bullying are often more complex than a "perpetrator" and a "victim." Often, a situation of perceived "bullying" is actually made up of several smaller events. Different students may have played different roles. A student may be bullied one day and become the bully the next. These complicated interactions and behaviors can make it difficult to find a solution that will satisfy all parties.

9   Many schools have "zero-tolerance" policies regarding bullying. These policies are often not sensitive enough to students' particular needs and reasons for behaving the way they do. Every school is different, and student issues can vary widely. Teachers and administrators need to listen carefully to students' problems and perceived injustices, and be sensitive to them. If a student is punished for being a bully when he or she has a different perspective on the situation, that student may feel unfairly persecuted or "ganged-up on." Casting bullies as one-sided villains can be just as damaging to a student as being bullied.

10   Another issue with these "zero-tolerance" policies is that they can often encourage teachers and administrators to over-discipline students. Sometimes one-time or casual conflicts between students can be blown out of proportion. Students may be punished needlessly.

11   We need more policies and programs in place to educate students, teachers, administrators, and parents about what bullying is and how to recognize it. Policies and programs need to show how to end bullying, and, most importantly, what *causes* it. Most schools that do have anti-bullying strategies only deal with the surface of the problem. They don't address the underlying

causes. Without getting to the root of the situation, the problem of bullying can never truly be solved.

12 **Counterpoint: Most Schools Are Doing Their Best to Stop Bullying**

13 A group of students is playing on the playground. One boy pokes another in the back while waiting in line for the swings. "Knock it off," says the boy. "That's not nice."

14 "Oh, sorry," says the first boy, and stops. "I didn't really mean that."

15 This is the sort of response you might hear on the playground at a school in Forest Lakes, Minnesota, where Dave Seaburg is a teacher. In many schools across the country, bullying is being reduced or eliminated thanks to anti-bullying programs and policies. These programs are carried out by dedicated teachers like Mr. Seaburg. As part of an anti-bullying program, he leads workshops and provides lessons designed to teach students about the harmful effects of bullying. Students also learn ways to empower themselves against it. The school district where Dave Seaburg works has seen a steady decline in bullying since anti-bullying programs were implemented.

16 Schools across the United States are in fact doing an enormous amount to meet the challenge of bullying. As the media has heightened awareness of the issue, the attention devoted to solving the problem has been growing steadily. One example would be schools in the state of New Jersey. The first law against bullying in New Jersey schools was passed by the state legislature a little more than a decade ago. Within a few years, school districts were required to appoint an anti-bullying coordinator in every school. Today, according to the *Asbury Park Press,* each New Jersey school district spends more than thirty thousand dollars a year on supplies, software, additional personnel, and staff and teacher training devoted to anti-bullying measures.

17 How many school districts are expending this kind of effort? Certainly, many hundreds. More than forty-five states currently have laws on the books that direct school districts to adopt anti-bullying programs. Organizations from the National Education Association to the National Association of Student Councils are developing initiatives aimed at preventing bullying.

18 What exactly do school programs to prevent bullying do, and how do they work? There is no one single profile. A New Hampshire law states that all school staff must be trained to know what bullying looks like. People learn to spot the signs, and those who see bullying must report it. In Midland, Texas, police officers visit the schools to let students know that bullying is a crime. A school district in Miami, Florida has implemented several anti-bullying programs including Challenge Day and Girls Day Out. Girls Day Out teachs

NOTES

girls how they can deal with social issues in a positive way rather than resorting to bullying.

19   When it comes to cyber-bullying, it can be extremely difficult for a school to monitor and police students' activity on social media. Some of the effort needs to be made on the part of the parents. When parents take an active role in their children's social media usage, it becomes much easier to keep track of what's going on. Also, students are less likely to cyber-bully if they know their Internet activity is being supervised and they are being held accountable for their actions. Even in the arena of cyber-bullying, however, there is a role schools can and do play. In more than a dozen states, schools have been authorized to take disciplinary action against students who engage in bullying that takes place off of school property.

20   For example, the state of California recently passed Seth's Law. This new law strengthens the anti-bullying legislation that is already in place. It requires all California public schools to regularly update their anti-bullying programs and policies. There are even provisions for cyber-bullying. Seth's Law also focuses on protecting students who are victims of bullying due to their race, gender, sexual orientation, religion, or disabilities. Seth's Law makes it mandatory for teachers and authority figures to take action against any bullying behavior that they witness.

21   If school anti-bullying programs vary widely, are there any general guidelines that can be recommended? Certainly controversial issues exist where school policies are concerned. Should bullies be suspended or otherwise punished, or should they be helped with counseling and anger management programs? Should bystanders who witness bullying and fail to report it be reprimanded? Should schools be involved at all, or is bullying a family matter, as some people contend?

22   The federal government hosts a website, http://stopbullying.gov, with information for students, parents, and teachers on the issue of bullying. It suggests a number of different measures that schools can implement. For teachers and staff, these measures include finding out why, when, and where bullying takes place; launching awareness campaigns; creating school safety committees; and building information into the student curriculum. The website also recommends something that can be useful everywhere at all times— creating a culture of civility and tolerance.

23   Most schools are doing all they can to raise awareness, prevent, and ultimately eliminate bullying. If they devote any more time to anti-bullying education than they already do, it will take time away from core subjects like math and language arts. Anti-bullying programs are expensive for schools to run and they require highly trained staff.

24 Still, even with the very best anti-bullying programs and policies, it can take a long time for change to come about. It may be as many as three to ten years before an anti-bullying culture becomes standard all over the country. Though it may not seem like schools are doing enough because bullying still persists, even the most effective programs will take time to bring about the sort of change people are looking for.

 THINK QUESTIONS

1. Use details from the text to explain the "Point" author's response to the question *Bullying in Schools: Are We Doing Enough?* Cite the "Point" author's main claim and one reason why the author makes the claim. What evidence does the author use to support this position?

2. Use details from the text to explain the "Counterpoint" author's response to the question *Bullying in Schools: Are We Doing Enough?* Cite the "Counterpoint" author's main claim and one reason why the author makes this claim. What evidence does the author use to support this position?

3. The "Point" author acknowledges that some schools have "'zero-tolerance' policies," but he or she is critical of them. Explain why the author takes issue with these policies. Use textual evidence to support your answer.

4. Use context to determine the meaning of the word **venue** as it is used in "Bullying in Schools." Write your definition of "venue" and tell how you determined its meaning. Then, check your inferred definition both in context and with a dictionary.

5. Remembering that the suffix or means "person connected with," use the context clues provided in the selection to determine the meaning of **perpetrator.** Write your definition of "perpetrator" and tell how you determined its meaning. Plug your inferred meaning into the original sentence to check it, and then consult a dictionary to confirm your meaning.

Please note that excerpts and passages in the StudySync® library and this workbook are intended as touchstones to generate interest in an author's work. The excerpts and passages do not substitute for the reading of entire texts, and StudySync® strongly recommends that students seek out and purchase the whole literary or informational work in order to experience it as the author intended. Links to online resellers are available in our digital library. In addition, complete works may be ordered through an authorized reseller by filling out and returning to StudySync® the order form enclosed in this workbook.

Reading & Writing Companion 255

CLOSE READ

Reread the Point/Counterpoint debate "Bullying in Schools." As you reread, complete the Focus Questions below. Then use your answers and annotations from the questions to help you complete the Writing Prompt.

FOCUS QUESTIONS

1. The introductory first paragraph of the "Point" text presents a number of statements about bullying. Based on these statements, what is the "Point" author's opinion about schools' effectiveness in reducing bullying? What is the author's purpose for writing?

2. The introductory three paragraphs of the "Counterpoint" text focus on events at a specific school. Based on the example of this school, what is the "Counterpoint" author's opinion about schools' effectiveness in reducing bullying? What is the author's purpose for writing? Highlight evidence from the text and make annotations to explain your response.

3. Identify one claim or reason that the "Counterpoint" author makes within paragraphs

4 through 9 that is well-supported by evidence. Highlight textual evidence and make annotations to explain your analysis.

4. Identify one claim or reason that the "Point" author makes within paragraphs 4 through 6 that is not well-supported by evidence. Highlight evidence from the text and make annotations to support your analysis.

5. Based on the ideas presented in both articles, how are schools dealing with the challenges of bullying? In what ways are schools standing up or failing to stand up for the victims of bullying? Highlight textual evidence and make annotations to explain your ideas.

WRITING PROMPT

The "Point" and "Counterpoint" authors offer two points of view on whether schools are doing enough to prevent bullying. Both offer reasons and evidence to support their claims. If you trace and evaluate the argument and specific claim of each author, which author is most convincing? Which author most effectively uses reasons and evidence to support his or her claim? Does one author cite more credible sources? Use your understanding of purpose and point of view as you evaluate the argument in each passage. Support your own argument and claim with relevant and well-organized evidence from the texts.

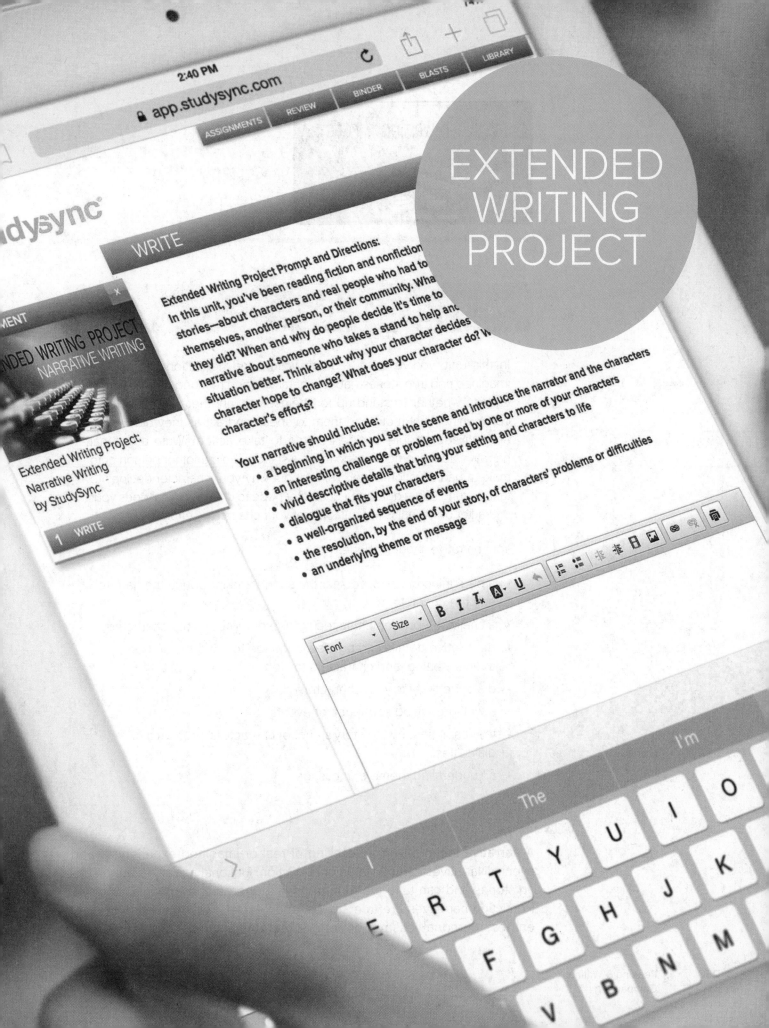

EXTENDED WRITING PROJECT

WRITE

Extended Writing Project Prompt and Directions:
In this unit, you've been reading fiction and nonfiction
stories—about characters and real people who had to
themselves, another person, or their community. Wha
they did? When and why do people decide it's time to
narrative about someone who takes a stand to help and
situation better. Think about why your character decides
character hope to change? What does your character do? W
character's efforts?

Your narrative should include:
- a beginning in which you set the scene and introduce the narrator and the characters
- an interesting challenge or problem faced by one or more of your characters
- vivid descriptive details that bring your setting and characters to life
- dialogue that fits your characters
- a well-organized sequence of events
- the resolution, by the end of your story, of characters' problems or difficulties
- an underlying theme or message

EXTENDED WRITING PROJECT NARRATIVE WRITING

Extended Writing Project:
Narrative Writing
by StudySync

1 WRITE

NARRATIVE WRITING

WRITING PROMPT

In this unit, you've been reading fiction and nonfiction narratives—imagined and true stories—about characters and real people who had to choose whether to stand up for themselves, another person, or their community. What motivated them to speak and act as they did? When and why do people decide it's time to take action? Write a fictional narrative about someone who takes a stand to help another person or to make a bad situation better. Think about why your character decides to take a stand. What does your character hope to change? What does your character do? What is the outcome of your character's efforts?

Your narrative should include:

- a beginning in which you set the scene and introduce the narrator and the characters

- a challenge or problem faced by one or more of your characters

- descriptive details and precise language to bring the story's events, setting, and characters to life

- dialogue that fits your characters

- a well-organized sequence of events

- the resolution, by the story's end, of characters' problems or difficulties

- an underlying theme or message

A **narrative** is the telling or retelling of real or imagined experiences and events. Narratives can be fiction or nonfiction. Fictional narratives are made-up stories and can take the form of novels, short stories, poems, or plays. Nonfiction narratives are true stories, often expressed in memoirs or diary entries, personal essays or letters, autobiographies or biographies, eyewitness accounts or histories. Many narratives have a clearly identified narrator who tells the story as it unfolds. In nonfiction narratives, the author usually tells the story. In fictional narratives, the narrator can be a character in the story or someone outside the story. Effective fictional narratives generally focus on a problem or conflict that needs to be resolved. The writer uses storytelling techniques such as dialogue, pacing, and description to develop events and characters. Events are generally presented in sequence, and transition words are used as needed to clarify time order.

The features of narrative writing include:

- setting—the time and place in which your story happens
- characters or real individuals
- plot—the sequence of events in a story
- point of view—the narrator's perspective on people and events
- precise language and descriptive details
- theme—the message about life that a story communicates

As you actively participate in this Extended Writing Project, you will receive more instructions and practice to help you craft each of the elements of narrative writing

STUDENT MODEL

Before you begin to write your own fictional narrative (or story), begin by reading this story that one student wrote in response to the writing prompt. As you read this Student Model, highlight and annotate the features of narrative writing that the student included in his or her fictional narrative.

Taking the Shot

I wanted to scream every time I saw it happening. My brother Kyle would get handed a basketball during gym class. He would dutifully stand in front of the net, try to line up his shot, and then wildly hurl the ball, which almost always landed in an entirely different part of the gym. Sometimes it bounced into the bleachers, catching bystanders by surprise. Sometimes it rolled into the girls' changing room. One time, it got stuck in an air vent. Then the teasing would begin. The minute the coach turned his back, the trio of mean boys would start laughing and talking trash. They'd say stuff like "Take cover, guys; Kyle is chucking the ball again. Your height is totally wasted on you, man. Your twin sister Celia has got all the athletic talent in your family, dude."

Then Kyle would shrug and say something like, "Yep. She's a great ball player. But I'm a great cook," and walk off the court.

He's right. He's a great cook! He takes after my dad, who's the head chef at the Pasta Pot. Kyle even made ribs for the whole family last week—with just a little help from my dad. And Kyle's good at other things, too—especially science. He says chemistry is like cooking with another name.

So, he can't throw a ball. Who cares? I wanted those guys to quit teasing him. It made me bonkers to see Kyle just give up and walk off the court, while those horrible kids made fun of him!

One day, when we were standing in the kitchen at our house, I asked him about it. I said, "Why don't you let me teach you how to do a free throw, so those guys will leave you alone?"

He said, "Celia, those guys don't bother me. Why do they bother you?"

Good question. Why do kids like that make me go bananas? Because they pick on the kids whose talents they don't recognize. Because it makes them feel big to say mean things about other people. That's not fair. I don't like it when things aren't fair. And that's what I told Kyle. But he just looked at me and went back to stirring a batch of vegetable soup. Sometimes I worry he'll mix-up our dinner with a science experiment, but that hasn't happened yet.

Now, here's a question my twin didn't ask me: *Why don't I stand up to those guys if I care so much?* My best friend, Mac, asked me that when we were playing basketball in the driveway.

"What do you mean?" I demanded.

Mac asked, "Are you afraid of those guys? Is that why you won't stand up for Kyle?"

I snatched the ball away from him and started dribbling. "No," I snapped. I was getting pretty angry myself. "Why would I be afraid of those guys?"

"Because they <u>are</u> mean. Because you <u>are</u> the only girl on the school basketball team. Because they could easily make you a target of their nasty comments, which would hurt. That's why."

Stunned, I tossed the ball and blew the shot. The ball bounced off the edge of the hoop with a metallic bang and into the garage. I knew that Mac was right. I was wrong. It was time to fix things. "All right," I said. "But I'm gonna need your help."

That weekend, Mac came over to our house with a new video game. It was one of those virtual sports games—basketball. Mac told Kyle that he was having trouble figuring it out. So Kyle, who is also great with computers, helped Mac set up the game. Then Mac showed Kyle how to toss a virtual basketball into a virtual hoop. Turns out, Kyle was actually very good. It seems that when Kyle isn't holding a real ball in his hands, he can line up a shot and make it. He and Mac spent all afternoon playing the computer game. I stayed out of the way.

So, the next time Kyle had to play basketball in gym class, we were both prepared, although Kyle didn't know it. He took the ball from the gym teacher and then stopped to calculate his shot—something he had learned from the video game. When he threw the ball, for the first time ever, it went toward the net. It actually bounced off the metal hoop! I could see that everyone—including the meanest boy of all—was amazed. But it wasn't like the gang suddenly turned nice or anything. "Missed again," one of them—a boy named Trey—hissed just loud enough for Kyle to hear.

I walked right up to Trey. "Give my brother a break," I shouted. That shocked the group for a couple of seconds. "He made a good shot. Deal with it."

"And besides," I told Trey in a quieter voice, "You're not so hot in science, you know. How would you feel if every time you answered a question, I yelled 'wrong!'"

He stared at me like I threw him for a loop. "Mr. Simon would never let you do that," he snarled.

By now, Kyle was tugging on my arm. "Come on," he said. "Let's just get out of here."

"True," I said to Trey. "He wouldn't. But Mr. Simon did say that my brother could help prep anybody who was failing science for the test next week. He thought it would be an okay thing to do during study hall. And aren't you kind of...well...having some trouble?"

Please note that excerpts and passages in the StudySync® library and this workbook are intended as touchstones to generate interest in an author's work. The excerpts and passages do not substitute for the reading of entire texts, and StudySync® strongly recommends that students seek out and purchase the whole literary or informational work in order to experience it as the author intended. Links to online resellers are available in our digital library. In addition, complete works may be ordered through an authorized reseller by filling out and returning to StudySync® the order form enclosed in this workbook.

Reading & Writing Companion   261

Trey shot us a dirty look and walked away. "I don't need help," he barked. "Not from a loser."

What can you do? Without another word, we began heading out the door. Then, to our shock, another one of the mean boys, George, stopped us.

"Hey," George said.

"Hey," we answered.

"I could use a little help," George said.

I could tell he was shy about asking, because he wouldn't look at us. He just kept dribbling around us in circles. But before Kyle could say yes or no, George added "Help get me ready for the test, and afterwards I'll coach you, get you up to speed in the game."

I have to admit at that second, I felt kind of envious. I wouldn't have minded some extra coaching. I love basketball, and I'm good at it. And George is a super player.

On the other hand, Kyle is Kyle. He's just himself. He paused, and I could see him thinking over the offer. I knew he didn't want to reject George's temporary kindness. After all, maybe it would turn out to be more than temporary.

"I'll tell you what," Kyle said. "Basketball on a court isn't really my thing. But basketball on a computer..."

"...is a great game," George said, finishing Kyle's sentence. "I'd do that. Maybe this Sunday afternoon?"

I sighed with relief. Standing up for my brother was both easier and harder than I thought it would be. I made a plan and took a risk and it paid off. Phew! Now I could get back to the really important things in life—winning at basketball.

THINK QUESTIONS

1. What is the setting of the story in the first four paragraphs? Cite specific descriptive details that tell you when and where the events in the first four paragraphs of the story take place.

2. Who is the story's narrator, and how do you know? What other major character is introduced at the beginning of the story? What can you infer about both of these characters from the details in the first four paragraphs?

3. What happens in the story? Use time-order (or sequence) words to summarize the sequence of key events in the plot of the Student Model.

4. Think about the writing prompt. Which ideas from selections or other resources can be used as inspiration or models for your own narrative writing? For example, which authors of fiction or nonfiction narrative texts, in your opinion, use vivid, interesting language especially effectively or handle descriptive details particularly successfully? Which selections develop events in a sequence that unfolds in a very natural or interesting way? Support your ideas with evidence from the texts you have read.

5. Based on what you have read, listened to, or researched, how would you answer the question, "How do people decide when to stand up for themselves or on behalf of others?" What are some ways that people or characters respond when they or someone they love needs help or support? Cite details from the selections you have read so far in the unit.

Please note that excerpts and passages in the StudySync® library and this workbook are intended as touchstones to generate interest in an author's work. The excerpts and passages do not substitute for the reading of entire texts, and StudySync® strongly recommends that students seek out and purchase the whole literary or informational work in order to experience it as the author intended. Links to online resellers are available in our digital library. In addition, complete works may be ordered through an authorized reseller by filling out and returning to StudySync® the order form enclosed in this workbook.

Reading & Writing Companion   **263**

PREWRITE

WRITING PROMPT

In this unit, you've been reading fiction and nonfiction narratives—imagined and true stories—about characters and real people who had to choose whether to stand up for themselves, another person, or their community. What motivated them to speak and act as they did? When and why do people decide it's time to take action? Write a fictional narrative about someone who takes a stand to help another person or to make a bad situation better. Think about why your character decides to take a stand. What does your character hope to change? What does your character do? What is the outcome of your character's efforts?

Your narrative should include:

- a beginning in which you set the scene and introduce the narrator and the characters
- a challenge or problem faced by one or more of your characters
- descriptive details and precise language to bring the story's events, setting, and characters to life
- dialogue that fits your characters
- a well-organized sequence of events
- the resolution, by the story's end, of characters' problems or difficulties
- an underlying theme or message

In addition to studying the techniques authors use to tell stories, you have been reading real and imagined stories about individuals or characters who took a risk in deciding to stand up for themselves or others. In the Extended Writing Project, you will use those storytelling techniques to compose your own made-up narrative, or story.

Because your story will be about characters who make choices about standing up for themselves or others, you will want to think about the characters or individuals you have read about in the unit texts. Think back to when you read the excerpt from *A Wrinkle in Time*: In what situation do Charles Wallace and Meg find themselves? What choices do the characters have? How do they ultimately respond to the strange man with the red eyes? How is Charles Wallace's reaction different from Meg's? How might a different character have acted?

Then consider how at least two other individuals or characters you have read about in this unit—for example, Ji-Li Jiang in *Red Scarf Girl* and Cassie and Stacey in *Roll of Thunder, Hear My Cry*—react when their families are in a tough situation. Think about similarities and differences that can help you as you begin to develop the characters, plot events—including the conflict (or problem)—and theme in your story. Think about who is telling your story and how involved he or she is.

Use the selections you have read as inspiration for getting started with a prewriting brainstorm activity to generate ideas for your own fictional narrative.

When you prewrite, you begin to develop ideas for your story, and you jot them down as they occur to you. What's important when you're prewriting is that you begin to generate ideas for your story, and that you begin to get excited about your ideas.

Remember, you're writing your story in response to the writing prompt shown at the top of this lesson. Review the writing prompt. Then, read the following list of questions to guide you in developing ideas for your story. Brainstorm and write answers to each of the questions. When you've answered all of the questions to your satisfaction, you've completed your prewriting brainstorm.

- Who are your characters?
- Who is telling the story?
- In what situation do your characters find themselves?
- What risks do your characters face if they stand up for themselves—and if they don't?
- What choices do your characters make?
- How will you organize your story's events?
- How does your story end?

Please note that excerpts and passages in the StudySync® library and this workbook are intended as touchstones to generate interest in an author's work. The excerpts and passages do not substitute for the reading of entire texts, and StudySync® strongly recommends that students seek out and purchase the whole literary or informational work in order to experience it as the author intended. Links to online resellers are available in our digital library. In addition, complete works may be ordered through an authorized reseller by filling out and returning to StudySync® the order form enclosed in this workbook.

Reading & Writing Companion   **265**

SKILL: ORGANIZE NARRATIVE WRITING

 DEFINE

The purpose of writing a narrative is to entertain readers while also guiding them to think about an important theme (or message)—a larger lesson about life or human experience. To convey the theme of a story, writers need to consider how to structure the story and organize the events in a way that makes sense.

Experienced writers carefully choose a **narrative text structure** that best suits their story. Most narratives use chronological (or sequential) text structure. To put it in simpler terms, this organization of a text is also called time order. It means that an author (or narrator) tells the events in the order in which they happen in a story. By telling what happens first, second, third, and so on, the author is giving the sequence of events. Along the way, this text structure enables the author to establish the setting, the narrator and characters, and the conflict (or problem) of the plot. Telling the events in time order also allows the characters and the action of the plot to move forward, through the middle of the story, when the main character (or characters) will attempt to resolve the conflict, or solve the problem. Finally, the story ends with the resolution of the conflict.

Sometimes instead of moving the plot forward in time and action, the plot moves the action backward in time, or even starts the action in the middle of the story. For example, if the story is character-driven, the plot might focus on the character's internal thoughts and feelings, so the writer might begin with a flashback to establish the character's issues or situation before moving into the present time. Similarly, if the story is a mystery, the writer might start the story in the middle to build suspense by making readers question why the person was murdered, for example, and "who done it."

To organize their story, writers often use a sequence-of-events chart, a timeline, or a flow chart. This type of graphic organizer will help them visualize and plot the order of events.

IDENTIFICATION AND APPLICATION

- The text structure for most narratives is sequential or chronological. However, a sequential text structure does not always mean that events are told in the exact order in which they happen. A writer might consider the following questions:

  › Should I tell the story in the order that the events happen?
  › Should I use a flashback at the beginning or start in the middle to create mystery and suspense?
  › Who are my characters and how will they grow or change?
  › What will be the most exciting moment of my story?
  › How will my story end?

- Although most stories are told in time order, writers may want to organize individual paragraphs by using a second kind of text structure:

  › For example, when a plot event leads to serious consequences for a character, the writer may use cause-and-effect text structure in the paragraph or paragraphs that tell about them.
  › A writer may use comparison-contrast text structure to tell how one character's reaction to an event was similar to or different from another's.
  › Despite these paragraph shifts in text structure (or organizational pattern) the overall structure for the story is still time order.

- Writers often use transition words and phrases to hint at the narrative's overall organization and the structure of individual sections or paragraphs:

  › Time order: *first, next, then, finally, before, after, now, soon,* in the meantime
  › Cause-effect: *because, so, therefore, as a result*
  › Compare-contrast: *like, similarly, in the same way* to compare and *although, while, but, however, on the other hand* to contrast
  › Order of importance: *mainly, most important, to begin with, first*

- In a chronological text structure, transition words and phrases also are used to signal shifts within the narrative in time and setting. Time order words and phrases are especially useful in indicating the sequence of events in a plot.

- The sequence of events in a narrative helps shape how a reader responds to what happens, and it also contributes to the overall development of the story's plot from beginning to end. You will learn more about narrative sequencing, and the elements and techniques that move the plot forward, in a later lesson.

MODEL

The writer of the Student Model understood from his or her prewriting that he or she would be telling the story in chronological order. In other words, the story would start at the beginning with the first event and end with the last event. In the first paragraph of the Model, the writer makes the organizational structure clear. The narrator, who is also a character in the story named Celia, tells about a series of events that often took place during gym class. She tells them in the order they happened. By using a mixture of the past tense (*wanted, landed, bounced, rolled*) and the past tense with the word *would* (*would get handed, would dutifully stand, would begin*) the narrator signals that she is telling about events that happened on an ongoing basis in the past. She also uses phrases such as "every time," and "almost always" to indicate that the events described in the opening paragraph were repeated more than once.

> *I wanted to scream every time I saw it happening. My brother Kyle would get handed a basketball during gym class. He would dutifully stand in front of the net, try to line up his shot, and then wildly hurl the ball, which almost always landed in an entirely different part of the gym. Sometimes it bounced into the bleachers, catching bystanders by surprise. Sometimes it rolled into the girls' changing room. One time, it got stuck in an air vent. Then the teasing would begin. The minute the coach turned his back, the trio of mean boys would start laughing and talking trash. They'd say stuff like "Take cover, guys; Kyle is chucking the ball again. Your height is totally wasted on you, man. Your twin sister Celia has got all the athletic talent in your family, dude."*

The writer of the Student Model uses time-order words and phrases such as "then" and "One time" to indicate **when** events happen. If changes in time are also accompanied by changes in place, the writer is careful to indicate **where** events happen, too. The first four paragraphs are set in the gym during the school day. The fifth and sixth paragraphs take place elsewhere:

> *One day, when we were standing in the kitchen at our house, I asked him about it. I said, "Why don't you let me teach you how to do a free throw, so those guys will leave you alone?" He said, "Celia, those guys don't bother me. Why do they bother you?"*

Throughout the story, the writer provides words and phrases that tell readers when and where the story's events are happening: "when we were playing basketball in the driveway," "that weekend," and "so, the next time Kyle had to play basketball in gym class."

In order to organize the order of the story's events, the writer used an Organize Narrative Writing Timeline. He or she listed the events and then numbered them in the order in which they would appear in the story. If the place changed, the writer noted that as well.

Event #1: Kyle always throws the basketball badly in gym class, and the mean boys tease him.
Event #2: Celia offers to teach Kyle how to throw a basketball, but Kyle declines.
Event #3: One day, Mac asks Celia when they're playing basketball in the driveway why she is too afraid of the mean boys to stand up for her brother.
Event #4: Mac gives her some good reasons, and Celia decides to make a plan to help her brother.
Event #5: That weekend, Mac comes over to the house with a video game and asks Kyle to show him how it works.
Event #6: Kyle helps set up the game and learns how to throw a basketball well.
Event #7: Kyle gets another chance to throw a basketball in gym class. He almost makes the shot.
Event #8: The mean boys tease Kyle anyway.
Event #9: Celia shouts at the boys. She says she doesn't tease them when they make mistakes in science class. She says Kyle could help them on the upcoming science test.
Event #10: Trey storms off, but George asks for help. He and Kyle might become friends.

Please note that excerpts and passages in the StudySync® library and this workbook are intended as touchstones to generate interest in an author's work. The excerpts and passages do not substitute for the reading of entire texts, and StudySync® strongly recommends that students seek out and purchase the whole literary or informational work in order to experience it as the author intended. Links to online resellers are available in our digital library. In addition, complete works may be ordered through an authorized reseller by filling out and returning to StudySync® the order form enclosed in this workbook.

Reading & Writing
Companion

269

PRACTICE

By using an Organize Narrative Writing timeline, you'll be able to fill in the events for your story that you began to consider during the prewriting stage of your Extended Writing Project. When you have completed your organizer, trade with a partner and offer each other feedback on the structure of events the writer has planned, and the use of transitions to make shifts in time order and setting clear for the reader.

DESCRIPTIVE DETAILS

sync•skills
Writing

SKILL:
DESCRIPTIVE
DETAILS

 ## DEFINE

One way a writer develops the setting, characters, and plot in a narrative is by using description and descriptive details. In a story, the descriptive details help readers imagine the world in which the story takes place and the characters who live in it.

Descriptive details often use precise language—specific nouns and action verbs—to convey experiences or events. Many descriptive details use sensory language to appeal to one or more of the reader's five senses. Sensory words tell how something looks, sounds, feels, smells, or tastes.

Descriptive details should be relevant to the story, such as a character's actions or the setting. In a story, it is easy to include many interesting details, but not every detail is relevant. For example, what a character smells might be less relevant than how he or she feels or what he or she sees or hears during a key moment in the story. Too many details can make the reader feel overwhelmed. Plus, they can slow the pace of a story. It's a good idea to select only the most important, or relevant, details for your story. Think about what the reader really needs to know in order to understand or picture what is happening. Consider what your narrator actually knows and can share with the reader, especially if he or she is a character in the story. Then choose the details that will most help the readers imagine what the setting looks like, what the characters are experiencing, or how the events are happening.

 ## IDENTIFICATION AND APPLICATION

- Description and descriptive details help a reader understand story elements such as:
  › characters (how they look, what they are wearing, what emotions their facial expressions reveal, what they are thinking versus what they say, what they do and how they behave)
  › setting (time, location, appearance of the place, atmosphere)

> conflict (the severity of the problem, whether the problem is getting better or worse)

- Authors use specific nouns and strong verbs, adjectives and adverbs as appropriate, to help create vivid details
- Sensory details in a narrative appeal to readers' five senses. They help draw a reader into a story and create an engaging experience.
- Figurative language such as similes and metaphors can enhance description of what the characters are seeing, experiencing, or feeling
- Description and descriptive details can help an author build the point of view or tone of the story.

 ## MODEL

In the following excerpt from the Student Model, the writer has the narrator use vivid, precise language and specific details to describe her brother's experience in gym class. Think about how the words and details add to your understanding of the story.

> I wanted to scream every time I saw it happening. My brother Kyle would get handed a basketball during gym class. He would dutifully stand in front of the net, try to line up his shot, and then wildly hurl the ball, which almost always landed in an entirely different part of the gym. Sometimes it bounced into the bleachers, catching bystanders by surprise. Sometimes it rolled into the girls' changing room. One time, it got stuck in an air vent. Then the teasing would begin. The minute the coach turned his back, the trio of mean boys would start laughing and talking trash. They'd say stuff like "Take cover, guys; Kyle is chucking the ball again. Your height is totally wasted on you, man. Your twin sister Celia has got all the athletic talent in your family, dude."

The paragraph uses sports terminology ("line up his shot"), active verbs (*hurl, landed, bounced, chucking*), and specific nouns (*bleachers, bystanders, trio*) to describe what happens when Kyle tries to toss a basketball in gym class. Are all the details relevant? Do any of the details distract you from the scene or do they all help create a picture of Kyle and the mean boys?

One way to generate description and descriptive details is to use a graphic organizer. It can help you choose the most relevant descriptive details about your setting, characters, and plot events. Read the excerpt from the student model, "Taking the Shot." Then look at the organizer.

Copyright © BookheadEd Learning, LLC

Now, here's a question my twin didn't ask me: *Why don't I stand up to those guys if I care so much?* My best friend, Mac, asked me that when we were playing basketball in the driveway.

"What do you mean?" I demanded.

Mac asked, "Are you afraid of those guys? Is that why you won't stand up for Kyle?"

I snatched the ball away from him and started dribbling. "No," I snapped. I was getting pretty angry myself. "Why would I be afraid of those guys?"

"Because they <u>are</u> mean. Because you <u>are</u> the only girl on the school basketball team. Because they could easily make you a target of their nasty comments, which would hurt. That's why."

Stunned, I tossed the ball and blew the shot. The ball bounced off the edge of the hoop with a metallic bang and into the garage. I knew that Mac was right. I was wrong. It was time to fix things. "All right," I said. "But I'm gonna need your help."

DESCRIPTIVE DETAILS	
Precise words and phrases	**Stunned,** I **tossed** the ball and **blew** the shot. The ball **bounced** off the edge of the hoop with a metallic bang and into the garage. [This language is precise. It uses sports terms and active verbs.]
Relevant descriptive details	"No," I snapped. **I was getting pretty angry myself.** "Why would I be afraid of those guys?" [This detail is relevant. It reveals what the character is feeling.]
Sensory language	**I snatched the ball away** from him and started dribbling. [This detail appeals to one's sense of touch.]

NOTES

As the writer planned the Student Model, he or she asked some questions to determine which descriptive details would be the most relevant:

- Will this detail help the reader understand who the character is, and why he or she thinks, says, feels, or acts a certain way?
- Will this detail help the reader understand what the character is experiencing?
- Does this detail use language that is interesting and will appeal to one or more of the reader's five senses?
- Will this detail add to the story and help it move forward, or will it slow down the pace of the story?

 PRACTICE

Use a Descriptive Details graphic organizer like the one in the model to create some descriptive details for your story that appeal to the senses. Then trade your details with a partner when you are finished. Offer feedback about the details. Engage in a peer review to determine which details are strong enough to help readers visualize your setting, understand your characters, follow events, and remember your message.

PLAN

In this unit, you've been reading fiction and nonfiction narratives—imagined and true stories—about characters and real people who had to choose whether to stand up for themselves, another person, or their community. What motivated them to speak and act as they did? When and why do people decide it's time to take action? Write a fictional narrative about someone who takes a stand to help another person or to make a bad situation better. Think about why your character decides to take a stand. What does your character hope to change? What does your character do? What is the outcome of your character's efforts?

Your narrative should include:

- a beginning in which you set the scene and introduce the narrator and the characters
- a challenge or problem faced by one or more of your characters
- descriptive details and precise language to bring the story's events, setting, and characters to life
- dialogue that fits your characters
- a well-organized sequence of events
- the resolution, by the story's end, of characters' problems or difficulties
- an underlying theme or message

Review the ideas you brainstormed in the prewrite activity and then take another look at the events you listed in your *Organize Narrative Writing* Graphic Organizer and at the details you listed on your *Descriptive Details Graphic* Organizer. Think about what you have learned about audience and purpose and about creating details to develop your setting and characters.

Remember all the stories you have read. A story's plot has a beginning, middle, and end. These ideas will help you create a Story Road Map to use for writing your story.

Consider the following questions as you develop the Road Map for your narrative:

- Where and when does your story take place?
- Who are your characters? What are they like?
- Who is telling your story? Is the narrator a character in the story? Or is the narrator telling the story from outside the text?
- What challenge or problem do your characters face?
- How do your characters deal with the challenge, or problem? Do they stand up for themselves or for someone else?
- How do your characters grow or change as the story moves forward?
- What is the most exciting moment in your story?
- What happens to your characters at the end?
- What theme (or message) do you want your readers to take away from your story?

This Story Road Map has been completed with details from the Student Model, "Taking the Shot." Use it as a model for creating a Road Map for your own story.

Story Road Map

Character(s):

Characters: Celia (the narrator), Kyle (Celia's twin brother), Mac, the three mean boys. Kyle is bad at basketball but great at other things—cooking, school. Celia cares about him a lot!

Setting(s):

Middle school gymnasium, Celia and Kyle's house and driveway

Beginning:

Celia tells about how her brother Kyle gets teased by three mean boys when he can't throw a basketball properly during gym class.

Middle:

At home, Celia offers to teach Kyle how to throw a basketball, but he declines. Mac asks Celia why she is upset by the mean boys. She figures out that she is actually kind of afraid of them herself. She makes a plan with Mac to help Kyle. Mac brings over a video game. By playing it, Kyle learns some tips for throwing a basketball.

End:

Back in gym class, Kyle does better at basketball, but the mean boys tease him anyway. Celia yells at them and tells them that she doesn't tease the boys when they make mistakes in science class. She says that Kyle can tutor them. The boy named Trey refuses, but George accepts the offer. He and Kyle might become friends.

SKILL: INTRODUCTION/ STORY BEGINNING

DEFINE

The beginning of a fictional narrative is the opening passage in which the writer provides the exposition, or the important details about the story's setting, narrator, characters, plot, conflict, and even the theme. A strong introduction captures the attention of readers, making them want to read on to find out what happens next.

IDENTIFICATION AND APPLICATION

- The beginning of a narrative (or story) includes **exposition**. The exposition establishes the setting, the characters, the narrator, the narrator's point of view, the plot, and even the theme. As in other forms of writing, writers use a "hook" to grab readers' interest. In a narrative, a hook can be an exciting moment, a detailed description, or a surprising or thoughtful comment made by the narrator or the main character.

- The beginning of a narrative also establishes the **structure** of the story. Remember: a story does not have to open with the start of the action. It can begin in the middle. This strategy "grabs" the reader's attention and builds suspense by making the reader wonder what's going on. Some stories even begin at the end and work their way backward in time. These strategies use flashbacks to capture the reader's attention, but they are not necessary. Most good stories start at the beginning of the action and tell the events in time order. They use descriptive supporting details, engaging characters, and unexpected plot twists to keep readers interested.

- The beginning of a story might also offer clues about the **theme**. The theme is the message or "big idea" about life that the writer wants readers to understand. The theme is developed over the course of the story as the characters grow, change, and make decisions about life. Good writers drop hints at the beginning of the story so that readers can consider the "big idea" as they read.

- Many features of a narrative, including some aspects of the introduction, are the same in fiction and nonfiction. You have already read that writers use a "hook" in the beginning of both types of narrative in order to engage readers' attention. In the beginning of a nonfiction narrative, readers usually also learn who the narrator is, when and where the narrative takes place, what the text structure will be (usually sequential), and what the narrative generally will be about.

 MODEL

Reread the introduction to the excerpt from *Red Scarf Girl: A Memoir of the Cultural Revolution* by Ji-Li Jiang. The narrative is nonfiction, but the opening section of this excerpt includes a hook designed to capture readers' attention: the words "Don't be afraid." As soon as readers hear a phrase like that, they know they will be reading about something a little scary.

> "Sit down, sit down. Don't be afraid." Chairman Jin pointed to the empty chair. "These comrades from your father's work unit are just here to have a study session with you. It's nothing to worry about."
>
> I sat down dumbly.
>
> I had thought about their coming to my home but never imagined this. They were going to expose my family in front of my teachers and classmates. I would have no pride left. I would never be an educable child again.
>
> Thin-Face sat opposite me, with a woman I had never seen before. Teacher Zhang was there too, his eyes encouraging me.
>
> Thin-Face came straight to the point. "Your father's problems are very serious. " His cold eyes nailed me to my seat.

Ji-Li herself is the narrator and the central figure in this narrative, which tells part of her real-life story. Her use of first-person pronouns tells the reader that events will be recounted from her perspective or point of view. This section of the narrative introduces not only the narrator but also other important individuals in the story, along with the disturbing situation Ji-Li faces. Chairman Jin's words, "Don't be afraid," instantly create a feeling of danger. The problem Ji-Li experiences in the narrative is clear—her family is about to be "exposed" in front of her teachers and classmates. Her own pride will be destroyed by the accusations. Readers can infer what will happen next: she will have to choose between being considered an "educable child" and standing by her

NOTES

family. From the start of the excerpt, readers can guess that one of the themes of the narrative will be about loyalty and betrayal.

Although Ji-Li does not provide a lot of details about the setting, she seems to be the only child in a room full of adults. The sense of a bleak setting accentuates a feeling of her powerlessness. She feels "nailed to her seat." The beginning of this excerpt sets up a tense and unpredictable situation.

 PRACTICE

Write a beginning for your fictional story. It should introduce your setting, narrator, and main character (or characters), as well as the conflict (or problem) of the plot. Include a "hook" that will grab readers' attention.

SKILL:
NARRATIVE
TECHNIQUES AND
SEQUENCING

 PLAN

When writing a story, authors use a variety of narrative techniques to develop both the plot and the characters, explore the setting, and engage the reader. These techniques include dialogue, a sequencing of events, pacing, and description. **Dialogue**, what the characters say to one another, is often used to develop characters and move the events of the plot forward. Every narrative contains a **sequence of events**, which is carefully planned and controlled by the author as the story unfolds. Writers often manipulate the **pacing** of a narrative, or the speed with which events occur, to slow down or speed up the action at certain points in a story. This can create tension and suspense. Writers use **description** to build story details and reveal information about the characters, setting, and plot.

The beginning of a story is called the **introduction** or **exposition**. This is the part of the story in which the writer provides the reader with essential information, introducing the characters, the time and place in which the action occurs, and the problem or conflict the characters must face and attempt to solve.

As the story continues, the writer includes details and events to develop the conflict and move the story forward. These events—known as the **rising action** of the story—build until the story reaches its **climax**. This is a turning point in the story, where the most exciting and intense action usually occurs. It is also the point at which the characters begin to find a solution to the problem or conflict in the plot.

The writer then focuses on details and events that make up the **falling action** of the story. This is everything that happens after the climax, leading to a **resolution.** These elements make up a story's **conclusion,** which often contains a message or final thought for the reader.

Please note that excerpts and passages in the StudySync® library and this workbook are intended as touchstones to generate interest in an author's work. The excerpts and passages do not substitute for the reading of entire texts, and StudySync® strongly recommends that students seek out and purchase the whole literary or informational work in order to experience it as the author intended. Links to online resellers are available in our digital library. In addition, complete works may be ordered through an authorized reseller by filling out and returning to StudySync® the order form enclosed in this workbook.

Reading & Writing
Companion

281

IDENTIFICATION AND APPLICATION

- Most narratives are written in sequential order. However, arranging events in time order is not the only skill involved in narrative sequencing. Writers group events to shape both a reader's response to what happens and the development of the plot from beginning to end.
  - › *Exposition refers* to the essential information at the start of a story.
  - › *Rising action* refers to the sequence of events leading up to a story's turning point.
    - › The turning point is called the climax, and it's usually the most suspenseful moment in the story.
    - › During the rising action, readers may experience anticipation, curiosity, concern, or excitement.
  - › *Falling action* refers to the sequence of events following the story's turning point, or climax, and leading to the resolution of the story's conflict or problem.
    - › During the falling action, readers may look forward to finding out how the story will end.

- Pacing is a technique writers use to control the speed with which events are revealed. Description and dialogue can help writers vary the pacing in a narrative.

- Description uses specific details, precise language, and sensory words to develop characters, setting, and events. It can be used to slow down pacing.

- Dialogue, or the exchange of words between two or more characters, can reveal character traits and important plot details. Dialogue can be used to speed up or slow down pacing. A short, snappy line of dialogue might speed up a story. A long speech might slow it down.

  - › Dialogue is set in its own paragraph and inside quotation marks. A line of dialogue might look like this: "My name is Jeannette."
  - › Dialogue is usually followed by a tag, such as *she said* or *he asked,* to indicate who is speaking.
  - › Dialogue should suit the character who speaks it. Business executives at an important meeting would speak differently from teenagers playing a game at a friend's house.

 MODEL

Following its introduction or beginning section, the Student Model develops the characters and events of the story, including the conflict (or problem) that the main character faces. In these paragraphs, the rising action moves the first-person narrator, Celia, to the point of recognizing that she has to stand up for her brother. The writer uses description and dialogue to enrich the story and to vary the pacing of events. Some paragraphs are longer than others. Some include dialogue, and some don't. Some include more descriptive details than others or different types of sentences. By varying the pacing, writers hold readers' interest.

Reread paragraphs 3-9 from the middle of the Student Model, "Taking the Shot." Look closely at the text structure and at the way in which the sequence of events consists of rising action that builds toward a change in Celia.

He's right. He's a great cook! He takes after my dad, who's the head chef at the Pasta Pot. Kyle even made ribs for the whole family last week—with just a little help from my dad. And Kyle's good at other things, too—especially science. He says chemistry is like cooking with another name.

So, he can't throw a ball. Who cares? I wanted those guys to quit teasing him. It made me bonkers to see Kyle just give up and walk off the court, while those horrible kids made fun of him!

One day, when we were standing in the kitchen at our house, I asked him about it. I said, "Why don't you let me teach you how to do a free throw, so those guys will leave you alone?"

He said, "Celia, those guys don't bother me. Why do they bother you?"

Good question. Why do kids like that make me go bananas? Because they pick on the kids whose talents they don't recognize. Because it makes them feel big to say mean things about other people. That's not fair. I don't like it when things aren't fair. And that's what I told Kyle. But he just looked at me and went back to stirring a batch of vegetable soup. Sometimes I worry he'll mix-up our dinner with a science experiment, but that hasn't happened yet.

Now, here's a question my twin didn't ask me: Why don't I stand up to those guys if I care so much? My best friend, Mac, asked me that when we were playing basketball in the driveway.

"What do you mean?" I demanded.

Please note that excerpts and passages in the StudySync® library and this workbook are intended as touchstones to generate interest in an author's work. The excerpts and passages do not substitute for the reading of entire texts, and StudySync® strongly recommends that students seek out and purchase the whole literary or informational work in order to experience it as the author intended. Links to online resellers are available in our digital library. In addition, complete works may be ordered through an authorized reseller by filling out and returning to StudySync® the order form enclosed in this workbook.

Reading & Writing Companion **283**

Notice how the third paragraph of the story (the first paragraph above) focuses on one thing—details that tell what the character of Kyle is like. (The choice of details that Celia, the narrator, includes says something about her character, too.) The fourth paragraph of the story tells readers how the narrator feels. The fifth and sixth paragraphs of the story feature dialogue, or words spoken by the characters. The author places the words within quotation marks and uses tags, such as "I said" and "He said" to indicate who is speaking and to whom. Dialogue reveals directly what the characters are thinking. The short, conversational sentences also tend to speed up the pace of the story. Notice also the vivid descriptive detail in the seventh paragraph: "stirring a batch of vegetable soup."

Most important, notice what happens in the story. Celia offers to help her brother, but he turns down her offer. The action continues to rise toward a turning point when Max asks Celia a question that makes her realize she has her own reasons for not yet taking a stand.

 PRACTICE

Write one paragraph of rising action for your narrative. Use your paragraph to develop an event that helps lead to your story's climax. Include elements such as dialogue, sensory language, and specific details. Be sure that the text structure of your paragraph is clear, and that transitions clarify any changes in time or setting. When you are finished, trade with a partner and offer each other feedback. Remember that comments are most helpful when they are constructive.

SKILL:
CONCLUSION/
STORY ENDING

DEFINE

The **conclusion** is the final section of a narrative (or story). It is where the readers find out what happens to the characters. The plot winds down, and the main character's conflict (or problem) is resolved. The ending of a narrative is called the resolution. In some stories, the narrator or a character leaves readers with a final lesson about life or human experience. More often, however, readers have to figure out the lesson, or theme, on their own by drawing inferences from the end of the story.

IDENTIFICATION AND APPLICATION

- An effective ending brings the story to a satisfying close. It follows from the story's events, resolves the conflict, ties up loose ends, and may hint at what happens to the characters when the story is over.

    › The way a problem is resolved (the resolution) should be logical and feel like a natural part of the plot, but it can still be a surprise.
    › The resolution should tell clearly how the characters resolved the conflict (or problem)—or how it was resolved for them.
    › The concluding statement may sum up the story and leave readers feeling as if they were thoroughly entertained and thinking "That was a great story!"

- The conclusion might also include a memorable comment from the narrator or a character that helps readers understand the theme–the larger lesson about life or human experience that the story conveyed.

MODEL

In the conclusion to the nonfiction excerpt from *Red Scarf Girl: A Memoir of the Cultural Revolution,* the narrator Ji-Li Jiang is faced with a terrible choice.

Copyright © BookheadEd Learning, LLC

A local Communist official has told Ji-Li that she must choose between defending her father, who the officials say betrayed the Communist Party, and continuing with her education and being accepted as a good Communist. Either way, Ji-Li will lose. What will she decide to do? Will she stand up for herself? Will she defend her father? Will she give in to the local officials' demands?

> "Now, you have to choose between two roads." Thin-Face looked straight into my eyes. "You can break with your family and follow Chairman Mao, or you can follow your father and become an enemy of the people." His voice grew more severe. "In that case we would have many more study sessions, with your brother and sister too, and the Red Guard Committee and the school leaders. Think about it. We will come back to talk to you again."

> Thin-Face and the woman left, saying they would be back to get my statement. Without knowing how I got there, I found myself in a narrow passageway between the school building and the school-yard wall. The gray concrete walls closed around me and a slow drizzle dampened my cheeks. I could not go back to the classroom, and I could not go home.

Ji-Li does not make her decision, but it is clear that her loyalties are torn and she is frightened. Readers can only guess at the decision that Ji-Li will make in the sections that follow. Is her father's love worth the risk? Can she help her family more if she agrees to condemn her father but can get her education? These struggles are what eventually will lead her to a resolution of her conflict or problem. As you have noticed in your own reading, very few real-life or made-up stories end with the characters in the middle of a conflict. The conflict or problem must be resolved in some way for the story to be satisfying for the reader.

Now, read this section from the last few paragraphs of the Student Model:

> *"I'll tell you what," Kyle said. "Basketball on a court isn't really my thing. But basketball on a computer…"*

> *"…is a great game," George said, finishing Kyle's sentence. "I'd do that. Maybe this Sunday afternoon?"*

> *I sighed with relief.*

With the resolution of Celia's conflict and Kyle's problem, the story is moving toward its conclusion. One of the mean boys has offered to become friendly with Kyle. Kyle remains true to himself while at the same time accepting George's offer of friendship. And Celia, who has at last bravely stood up for her brother, experiences a moment of relief that everything seems to be working out. The resolution is satisfying to main characters and to the reader as well.

The last sentences of the very last paragraph of the Student Model flow naturally from the story's events and ends on an amusing note:

> *I made a plan and took a risk and it paid off. Phew! Now I could get back to the really important things in life—winning at basketball.*

 PRACTICE

Write an ending for your fictional story. It should let your readers know how the main character (or characters) resolved the conflict (or problem). Your ending might also hint at what happens to the character after the story is over. In your conclusion (or ending), try to include a thoughtful statement about life or human experience. Your message might be something that the narrator or a character says, or it might be an inference about the theme that the reader can draw from specific evidence in the text.

Please note that excerpts and passages in the StudySync® library and this workbook are intended as touchstones to generate interest in an author's work. The excerpts and passages do not substitute for the reading of entire texts, and StudySync® strongly recommends that students seek out and purchase the whole literary or informational work in order to experience it as the author intended. Links to online resellers are available in our digital library. In addition, complete works may be ordered through an authorized reseller by filling out and returning to StudySync® the order form enclosed in this workbook.

Reading & Writing Companion **287**

DRAFT

WRITING PROMPT

In this unit, you've been reading fiction and nonfiction narratives—imagined and true stories—about characters and real people who had to choose whether to stand up for themselves, another person, or their community. What motivated them to speak and act as they did? When and why do people decide it's time to take action? Write a fictional narrative about someone who takes a stand to help another person or to make a bad situation better. Think about why your character decides to take a stand. What does your character hope to change? What does your character do? What is the outcome of your character's efforts?

Your narrative should include:

- a beginning in which you set the scene and introduce the narrator and the characters
- a challenge or problem faced by one or more of your characters
- descriptive details and precise language to bring the story's events, setting, and characters to life
- dialogue that fits your characters
- a well-organized sequence of events
- the resolution, by the story's end, of characters' problems or difficulties
- an underlying theme or message

You've already made progress toward writing your own fictional narrative. You've thought about your characters and their conflict (or problem), setting, plot, and theme. You've considered your audience and purpose, determined an appropriate text structure to organize your ideas and events, and generated plenty of supporting details. You've practiced writing a beginning

Copyright © BookheadEd Learning, LLC

section and ending for your story. Now it's time to write a full draft of your story.

Use your timeline of events and other graphic organizers to help you as you write. Remember that a fictional narrative has an introduction, a middle, and a conclusion. The introduction (or beginning) establishes the setting, the narrator, the characters, and conflict (or problem) of the story. The middle section develops the characters and plot by using narrative techniques such as description, pacing, and dialogue. Transitions enable readers to follow the sequence of events by signalling changes in time or setting. Throughout the story, precise language—including specific nouns, strong verbs, and descriptive and sensory details—allows readers to picture the characters and events. The conclusion (or ending) tells how the characters resolve their problem, or how it is resolved for them. It ties up loose ends and hints at the theme of the story and its important message. An effective ending can also do more—it can leave a lasting impression on your readers.

When drafting your story, ask yourself these questions:

- How can I improve my introduction to "hook" my readers?
- Who is the narrator of my story?
- What relevant supporting details, description, and precise or sensory words can I add to fully develop the characters, experiences, and events in my story?
- Have I included dialogue that fits the characters?
- Have I ordered the events of the plot so that my body paragraphs move the characters and action forward? Have I varied the pacing of events to hold readers' interest?
- What transition words and phrases might make the order of events clearer?
- Is the end of my story interesting or surprising? Is the resolution of the conflict believable?
- Will my readers understand the theme? What changes can I make to present a clearer theme (or message) to my readers?
- Have I corrected errors in grammar, punctuation, and spelling?

Before you submit your draft, read it over carefully. You want to be sure that you have responded to all aspects of the prompt.

Please note that excerpts and passages in the StudySync® library and this workbook are intended as touchstones to generate interest in an author's work. The excerpts and passages do not substitute for the reading of entire texts, and StudySync® strongly recommends that students seek out and purchase the whole literary or informational work in order to experience it as the author intended. Links to online resellers are available in our digital library. In addition, complete works may be ordered through an authorized reseller by filling out and returning to StudySync® the order form enclosed in this workbook.

Reading & Writing Companion 289

REVISE

WRITING PROMPT

In this unit, you've been reading fiction and nonfiction narratives—imagined and true stories—about characters and real people who had to choose whether to stand up for themselves, another person, or their community. What motivated them to speak and act as they did? When and why do people decide it's time to take action? Write a fictional narrative about someone who takes a stand to help another person or to make a bad situation better. Think about why your character decides to take a stand. What does your character hope to change? What does your character do? What is the outcome of your character's efforts?

Your narrative should include:

- a beginning in which you set the scene and introduce the narrator and the characters
- a challenge or problem faced by one or more of your characters
- descriptive details and precise language to bring the story's events, setting, and characters to life
- dialogue that fits your characters
- a well-organized sequence of events
- the resolution, by the story's end, of characters' problems or difficulties
- an underlying theme or message

You have written a draft of your narrative. You have also received input and advice from your peers about how to improve it. Now you are going to revise your draft. Here are some recommendations to help you revise:

- Review the suggestions made by your peers.

- Focus on your use of transitions. Transitions are words or phrases that help your readers follow the flow of events and ideas.

  › As you revise, look for places where you can add transition words or phrases to help make the order of events or the relationship between ideas clearer. Do transition words indicate shifts in time and setting?

  › Test the transitions you have used or want to add. Make sure they reflect the relationship that you want to convey. Review the types of transition words you can use—chronological (sequential or time order), cause-effect, compare-contrast, problem-solution, spatial, order of importance, and so on.

- After you have revised your body paragraphs for transitions, think about whether there is anything else you can do to improve your introduction and conclusion.

  › Do you need a better "hook" at the beginning of your story to grab readers' interest?

  › Do you need to add or subtract details or events from the middle of your story? Does your story drag a little in the middle or does it skip over important details or events readers need to know?

  › Does your conclusion wrap up the story in a satisfying way? Or do you need to provide more details about what happens to the characters?

  › Does your conclusion leave readers with a message about life? Do you need to have a character or the narrator state this theme directly? Or can you add details that hint at the theme?

- As you revise, be aware of how you are using language to express characters' thoughts, words, and actions, along with the events that make up the narrative.

  › Are you varying the types of sentences you're using? Writing becomes boring when it sounds the same. Incorporating a variety of simple, compound, and complex sentences into your writing adds interest. Remember, a simple sentence has one subject and one predicate; a compound sentence contains two or more simple sentences joined by a comma and a coordinating conjunction (such as *and, but* or *or*) or by a semicolon. A complex sentence has an independent clause and one or more dependent clauses.

  › Are you choosing words carefully? Remember that in writing, less is often more. Look for ideas or sentences that you can combine or delete to avoid unnecessary repetition, and make your word choice as precise as it can be.

Please note that excerpts and passages in the StudySync® library and this workbook are intended as touchstones to generate interest in an author's work. The excerpts and passages do not substitute for the reading of entire texts, and StudySync® strongly recommends that students seek out and purchase the whole literary or informational work in order to experience it as the author intended. Links to online resellers are available in our digital library. In addition, complete works may be ordered through an authorized reseller by filling out and returning to StudySync® the order form enclosed in this workbook.

Reading & Writing Companion   **291**

NOTES

› Are you using a mixture of standard and conversational English? Use the language that best suits your narrator and characters, but also keep in mind that your readers need to be able to understand the writing or they will lose interest.

› Does your dialogue sound believable? Avoid using a lot of slang that readers won't know, but don't make your characters sound pretentious by using ornate language, or they won't sound believable.

› Are you using pronouns properly? If it is not clear to what or to whom your pronouns refer, your readers could get confused. Don't let small errors get in the way of telling an effective story.

› Are you you carefully checking your spelling and punctuation?

EDIT, PROOFREAD AND PUBLISH

WRITING PROMPT

In this unit, you've been reading fiction and nonfiction narratives—imagined and true stories—about characters and real people who had to choose whether to stand up for themselves, another person, or their community. What motivated them to speak and act as they did? When and why do people decide it's time to take action? Write a fictional narrative about someone who takes a stand to help another person or to make a bad situation better. Think about why your character decides to take a stand. What does your character hope to change? What does your character do? What is the outcome of your character's efforts?

Your narrative should include:

- a beginning in which you set the scene and introduce the narrator and the characters

- a challenge or problem faced by one or more of your characters

- descriptive details and precise language to bring the story's events, setting, and characters to life

- dialogue that fits your characters

- a well-organized sequence of events

- the resolution, by the story's end, of characters' problems or difficulties

- an underlying theme or message

You have revised your narrative and received input from your peers on your revised writing. Now it's time to edit and proofread your story to produce a final version. Have you included all the valuable suggestions from your peers? Ask yourself: Have I effectively introduced and fully developed my setting, characters, plot, conflict (or problem), and theme? What more can I do to improve my story's

Please note that excerpts and passages in the StudySync® library and this workbook are intended as touchstones to generate interest in an author's work. The excerpts and passages do not substitute for the reading of entire texts, and StudySync® strongly recommends that students seek out and purchase the whole literary or informational work in order to experience it as the author intended. Links to online resellers are available in our digital library. In addition, complete works may be ordered through an authorized reseller by filling out and returning to StudySync® the order form enclosed in this workbook.

Reading & Writing Companion   **293**

NOTES

supporting descriptive details? Did I use transitions well to move from event to event? Did I provide an engaging ending that follows from the story's events? Did I use varied sentence structure, realistic dialogue, and appropriate variations on standard English to make my writing more interesting?

When you are satisfied with your work, proofread it for errors. Use this list to check for correct:

- capitalization
- punctuation
- spelling
- grammar
- usage

In addition, check for correct punctuation in the dialogue, particularly for nonrestrictive elements. Check that you matched the number and gender of each pronoun to the person or thing it referred to; for example: *The dog wagged its tail at the arrival of its owner. Don checked for his smart phone, while Donna clutched her keys.*

Once you have made your corrections to your writing, you are ready to submit and publish your work. You can distribute your story to family and friends, attach it to a bulletin board, or post it to your blog. If you publish online, create links to the stories that have inspired you in this unit. That way, readers can read more stories that they might enjoy. Remember, too, that another way to have your story reach an audience is by becoming a storyteller. Tell your story to friends and classmates. Presenting a narrative orally can be fun both for the writer who created the story and for the audience who listens to it.

studysync®

Reading & Writing Companion

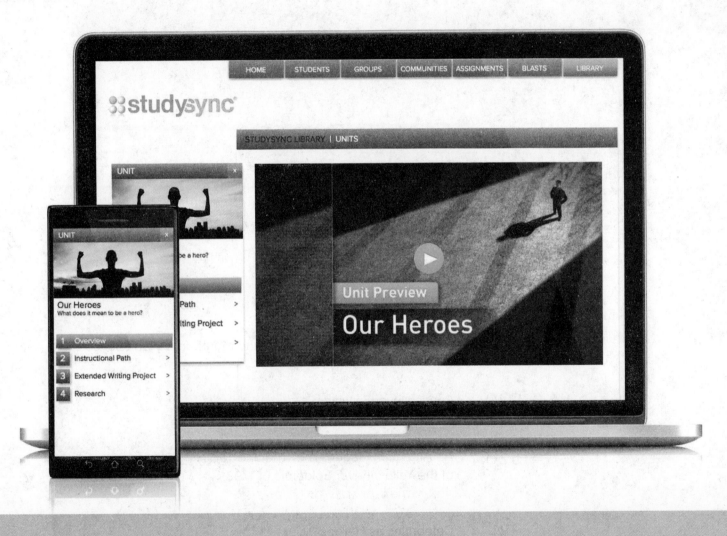

What does it mean to be a hero?

Our Heroes

UNIT 4   What does it mean to be a hero?

Our Heroes

TEXTS

TEXTS

EXTENDED WRITING PROJECT

ROSA PARKS: MY STORY

NON-FICTION
Rosa Parks
1992

INTRODUCTION

studysync tv

n 1955, racial segregation on buses was common throughout the American South. Municipal laws in many cities required that African Americans sit at the back of the bus, and, when requested, give up their seats to white passengers. In Montgomery, Alabama, where sixty-six percent of bus riders were black, no segregation law was more hated. When Rosa Parks challenged the law on December 1 and refused an order to give up her seat, her arrest sparked a year-long bus boycott that left the Montgomery public transit system financially crippled. Ms. Parks describes the simple act of civil disobedience that changed history.

"I saw a vacant seat in the middle section of the bus and took it."

 FIRST READ

 NOTES

Excerpt from Chapter 8: "You're Under Arrest"

1   When I got off from work that evening of December 1, I went to Court Square as usual to catch the Cleveland Avenue bus home. I didn't look to see who was driving when I got on, and by the time I recognized him, I had already paid my fare. It was the same driver who had put me off the bus back in 1943, twelve years earlier. He was still tall and heavy, with red, rough-looking skin. And he was still mean-looking. I didn't know if he had been on that route before—they switched the drivers around sometimes. I do know that most of the time if I saw him on a bus, I wouldn't get on it.

2   I saw a vacant seat in the middle section of the bus and took it. I didn't even question why there was a vacant seat even though there were quite a few people standing in the back. If I had thought about it at all, I would probably have figured maybe someone saw me get on and did not take the seat but left it vacant for me. There was a man sitting next to the window and two women across the aisle.

3   The next stop was the Empire Theater, and some whites got on. They filled up the white seats, and one man was left standing. The driver looked back and noticed the man standing. Then he looked back at us. He said, "Let me have those front seats," because they were the front seats of the black section. Didn't anybody move. We just sat right where we were, the four of us. Then he spoke a second time: "Y'all better make it light on yourselves and let me have those seats."

4   The man in the window seat next to me stood up, and I moved to let him pass by me, and then I looked across the aisle and saw that the two women were also standing. I moved over to the window seat. I could not see how standing up was going to "make it light" for me. The more we gave in and **complied**, the worse they treated us.

Please note that excerpts and passages in the StudySync® library and this workbook are intended as touchstones to generate interest in an author's work. The excerpts and passages do not substitute for the reading of entire texts, and StudySync® strongly recommends that students seek out and purchase the whole literary or informational work in order to experience it as the author intended. Links to online resellers are available in our digital library. In addition, complete works may be ordered through an authorized reseller by filling out and returning to StudySync® the order form enclosed in this workbook.

Reading & Writing Companion   299

NOTES

5   I thought back to the time when I used to sit up all night and didn't sleep, and my grandfather would have his gun right by the fireplace, or if he had his one-horse wagon going anywhere, he always had his gun in the back of the wagon. People always say that I didn't give up my seat because I was tired, but that isn't true. I was not tired physically, or no more tired than I usually was at the end of a working day. I was not old, although some people have an image of me as being old then. I was forty-two. No, the only tired I was, was tired of giving in.

6   The driver of the bus saw me still sitting there, and he asked was I going to stand up. I said, "No." He said, "Well, I'm going to have you arrested." Then I said, "You may do that." These were the only words we said to each other. I didn't even know his name, which was James Blake, until we were in court together. He got out of the bus and stayed outside for a few minutes, waiting for the police.

7   As I sat there, I tried not to think about what might happen. I knew that anything was possible. I could be **manhandled** or beaten. I could be arrested. People have asked me if it occurred to me then that I could be the test case the NAACP had been looking for. I did not think about that at all. In fact if I had let myself think too deeply about what might happen to me, I might have gotten off the bus. But I chose to remain.

8   Meanwhile there were people getting off the bus and asking for transfers, so that began to loosen up the crowd, especially in the back of the bus. Not everyone got off, but everybody was very quiet. What conversation there was, was in low tones; no one was talking out loud. It would have been quite interesting to have seen the whole bus empty out. Or if the other three had stayed where they were, because if they'd had to arrest four of us instead of one, then that would have given me a little support. But it didn't matter. I never thought hard of them at all and never even bothered to criticize them.

9   Eventually two policemen came. They got on the bus, and one of them asked me why I didn't stand up. I asked him, "Why do you all push us around?" He said to me, and I quote him exactly, "I don't know, but the law is the law and you're under arrest." One policeman picked up my purse, and the second one picked up my shopping bag and escorted me to the squad car. In the squad car they returned my personal belongings to me. They did not put their hands on me or force me into the car. After I was seated in the car, they went back to the driver and asked him if he wanted to swear out a **warrant**. He answered that he would finish his route and then come straight back to swear out the warrant. I was only in **custody**, not legally arrested, until the warrant was signed.

Copyright © BookheadEd Learning, LLC

10   As they were driving me to the city desk, at City Hall, near Court Street, one of them asked me again, "Why didn't you stand up when the driver spoke to you?" I did not answer. I remained silent all the way to City Hall.

11   As we entered the building, I asked if I could have a drink of water, because my throat was real dry. There was a fountain, and I was standing right next to it. One of the policemen said yes, but by the time I bent down to drink, another policeman said, "No, you can't drink no water. You have to wait until you get to the jail." So I was denied the chance to drink a sip of water. I was not going to do anything but wet my throat. I wasn't going to drink a whole lot of water, even though I was quite thirsty. That made me angry, but I did not respond.

12   At the city desk they filled out the necessary forms as I answered questions such as what my name was and where I lived. I asked if I could make a telephone call and they said, "No." Since that was my first arrest, I didn't know if that was more **discrimination** because I was black or if it was standard practice. But it seemed to me to be more discrimination. Then they escorted me back to the squad car, and we went to the city jail on North Ripley Street.

13   I wasn't frightened at the jail. I was more resigned than anything else. I don't recall being real angry, not enough to have an argument. I was just prepared to accept whatever I had to face. I asked again if I could make a telephone call. I was ignored.

14   They told me to put my purse on the counter and to empty my pockets of personal items. The only thing I had in my pocket was a tissue. I took that out. They didn't search me or handcuff me.

15   I was then taken to an area where I was fingerprinted and where mug shots were taken. A white matron came to escort me to my jail cell, and I asked again if I might use the telephone. She told me that she would find out.

16   She took me up a flight of stairs (the cells were on the second level), through a door covered with iron mesh, and along a dimly lighted corridor. She placed me in an empty dark cell and slammed the door closed. She walked a few steps away, but then she turned around and came back. She said, "There are two girls around the other side, and if you want to go over there with them instead of being in a cell by yourself, I will take you over there."

Excerpted from Rosa Parks: My Story by Rosa Parks, published by Puffin Books.

THINK QUESTIONS

1. Refer to one or more details in the text to explain how Rosa's previous interaction with the bus driver may have contributed to her actions on December 1—both from ideas that are directly stated and ideas that you have inferred from evidence in the text.

2. Use details from the text to explain other factors Parks believes contributed to her actions on December 1, 1955. What do other people seem to think contributed, and does Parks agree?

3. Based on the historical context, how do the law enforcement officials behave in expected and unexpected ways during Rosa's arrest? What inferences can you make from this behavior? Support your answer with textual evidence.

4. Use context to determine the meaning of the word **complied** as it is used in *Rosa: Parks: My Story*. Write your definition of *complied* and tell how you got it.

5. The Latin word *discriminare*, from which *discrimination* comes, means "to separate." Use this knowledge along with the context clues provided in the passage to determine the meaning of **discrimination**. Write your definition of *discrimination* and tell how you got it.

CLOSE READ

Reread the excerpt from *Rosa Parks: My Story*. As you reread, complete the Focus Questions below. Then use your answers and annotations from the questions to help you complete the Writing Prompt.

FOCUS QUESTIONS

1. Based on paragraphs 1 and 2, analyze how Rosa Parks introduced herself. What additional information do you learn about Parks' character from the details she shares? Highlight evidence from the text and make annotations to explain your analysis.

2. In paragraph 5, Parks used the word *tired* repeatedly. Why does she repeat the word? What effect does this create? Discuss the denotations and connotations of this word as Parks used it. Highlight textual evidence and make annotations to explain your response.

3. In paragraph 13, Parks said that she was not frightened or angry but "resigned" to the consequences of the situation. Which details in previous paragraphs illustrate this attitude? Support your answer with textual evidence and make annotations to explain your response.

4. In paragraph 16, explain how Parks used word denotation and connotation to create the mood of the jail. Highlight evidence from the text and make annotations to support your explanation.

5. Based on the text, is Rosa Parks a hero? Why or why not? Highlight textual evidence and make annotations to explain your evaluation.

WRITING PROMPT

The excerpt you read from *Rosa Parks: My Story* is part of Parks's autobiography, a non-fiction narrative she wrote to tell about her life. In it, she introduces and elaborates on a time when she behaved in a very courageous way. Using the excerpt as a model, write a real-life story, or personal narrative, about a time when you responded to a conflict or problem in a brave, kind, or generous way. What was the problem or conflict? Was anyone else involved in the experience or situation? How was the problem or conflict resolved? Remember that your personal narrative should be told from the first-person point of view. Introduce and elaborate on your experience with details and examples, and use transitions to help readers follow the sequence of events. Include description, dialogue, and precise or sensory language to capture and hold readers' attention. Try to use words with connotations that support the overall mood and tone of your narrative. Finally, consider what you learned from your experience. What theme or message might you want to share with your readers in your personal narrative?

Please note that excerpts and passages in the StudySync® library and this workbook are intended as touchstones to generate interest in an author's work. The excerpts and passages do not substitute for the reading of entire texts, and StudySync® strongly recommends that students seek out and purchase the whole literary or informational work in order to experience it as the author intended. Links to online resellers are available in our digital library. In addition, complete works may be ordered through an authorized reseller by filling out and returning to StudySync® the order form enclosed in this workbook.

Reading & Writing Companion   **303**

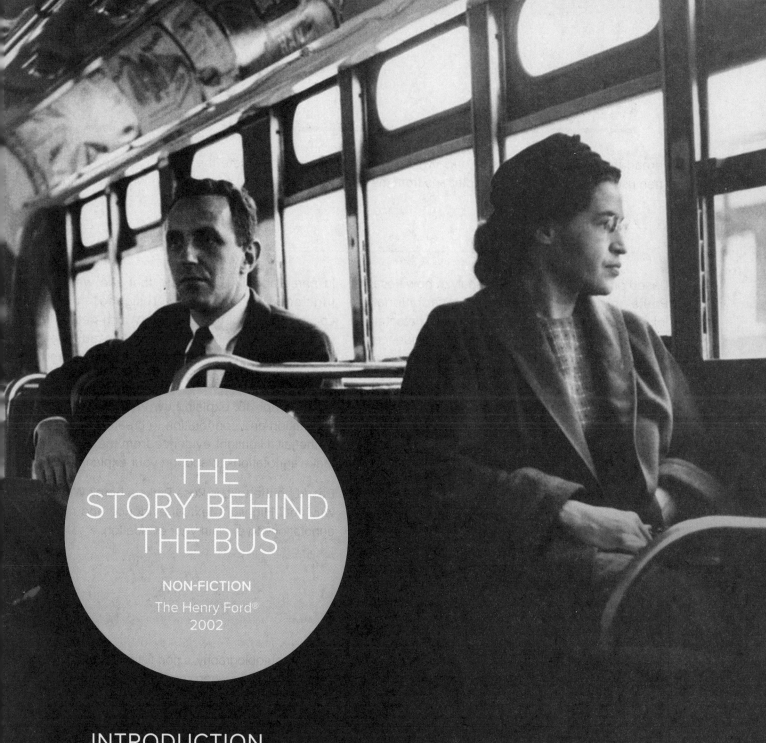

THE STORY BEHIND THE BUS

NON-FICTION
The Henry Ford®
2002

INTRODUCTION

The Henry Ford® museum houses a large collection of items of historical significance, including John F. Kennedy's presidential limousine, Abraham Lincoln's seat from Ford's Theatre, and the bus on which civil rights activist Rosa Parks took her famous stand against segregation. This excerpt from the museum's website offers background information on Rosa Parks and the circumstances surrounding her December 1955 arrest in Montgomery, Alabama.

"...Rosa Parks initiated a new era in the American quest for freedom and equality."

FIRST READ

NOTES

1   On December 1, 1955, Rosa Parks, a 42-year-old African American woman who worked as a seamstress, boarded this Montgomery City bus to go home from work. On this bus on that day, Rosa Parks initiated a new era in the American quest for freedom and equality.

2   She sat near the middle of the bus, just behind the 10 seats reserved for whites. Soon all of the seats in the bus were filled. When a white man entered the bus, the driver (following the standard practice of **segregation**) insisted that all four blacks sitting just behind the white section give up their seats so that the man could sit there. Mrs. Parks, who was an active member of the local NAACP, quietly refused to give up her seat.

3   Her action was spontaneous and not premeditated, although her previous civil rights involvement and strong sense of justice were obvious influences. "When I made that decision," she said later, "I knew that I had the strength of my ancestors with me."

4   She was arrested and convicted of violating the laws of segregation, known as "Jim Crow laws." Mrs. Parks appealed her conviction and thus formally challenged the legality of segregation.

5   At the same time, local civil rights activists initiated a boycott of the Montgomery bus system. In cities across the South, segregated bus companies were daily reminders of the **inequities** of American society. Since African Americans made up about 75 percent of the riders in Montgomery, the boycott posed a serious economic threat to the company and a social threat to white rule in the city.

6   A group named the Montgomery Improvement Association, composed of local activists and ministers, organized the boycott. As their leader, they chose a young Baptist minister who was new to Montgomery: Martin Luther

King, Jr. Sparked by Mrs. Parks' action, the boycott lasted 381 days, into December 1956 when the U.S. Supreme Court ruled that the segregation law was **unconstitutional** and the Montgomery buses were **integrated.** The Montgomery Bus Boycott was the beginning of a revolutionary era of non-violent mass protests in support of civil rights in the United States.

7 It was not just an accident that the civil rights movement began on a city bus. In a famous 1896 case involving a black man on a train, *Plessy v. Ferguson,* the U.S. Supreme Court enunciated the "separate but equal" rationale for Jim Crow. Of course, facilities and treatment were never equal.

8 Under Jim Crow customs and laws, it was relatively easy to separate the races in every area of life except transportation. Bus and train companies couldn't afford separate cars and so blacks and whites had to occupy the same space.

9 Thus, transportation was one of the most **volatile** arenas for race relations in the South. Mrs. Parks remembers going to elementary school in Pine Level, Alabama, where buses took white kids to the new school but black kids had to walk to their school.

10 "I'd see the bus pass every day," she said. "But to me, that was a way of life; we had no choice but to accept what was the custom. *The bus was among the first ways I realized there was a black world and a white world"* (emphasis added).

11 Montgomery's Jim Crow customs were particularly harsh and gave bus drivers great latitude in making decisions on where people could sit. The law even gave bus drivers the authority to carry guns to enforce their edicts. Mrs. Parks' attorney Fred Gray remembered, "Virtually every African-American person in Montgomery had some negative experience with the buses. But we had no choice. We had to use the buses for transportation."

12 Civil rights advocates had outlawed Jim Crow in interstate train travel, and blacks in several Southern cities attacked the practice of segregated bus systems. There had been a bus boycott in Baton Rouge, Louisiana, in 1953, but black leaders compromised before making real gains. Joann Robinson, a black university professor and activist in Montgomery, had suggested the idea of a bus boycott months before the Parks arrest.

13 Two other women had been arrested on buses in Montgomery before Parks and were considered by black leaders as potential clients for challenging the law. However, both were rejected because black leaders felt they would not gain white support. When she heard that the well-respected Rosa Parks had been arrested, one Montgomery African American woman exclaimed, "They've messed with the wrong one now."

14 In the South, city buses were lightning rods for civil rights activists. It took someone with the courage and character of Rosa Parks to strike with lightning. And it required the commitment of the entire African American community to fan the flames ignited by that lightning into the fires of the civil rights revolution.

 © 2002 by The Henry Ford®, "The Story Behind the Bus".
www.thehenryford.org. Reproduced by permission of The Henry Ford®.

 THINK QUESTIONS

1. Refer to one or more details from the text to support your understanding of Rosa Parks's statement, "When I made that decision [not to give up my bus seat], I knew that I had the strength of my ancestors with me." Base your explanation both on ideas that are directly stated and ideas that you infer from clues in the text.

2. Use details from the text to explain why the Montgomery bus boycott was particularly effective.

3. Write several sentences explaining why buses were such an important setting for protesters to use for their stance in favor of civil rights. Support your answer with textual evidence.

4. Use context to determine the meaning of the word **segregation** as it is used in "The Story Behind the Bus." Write your definition of *segregation* and tell how you determined it. Then, use a dictionary to check your definition.

5. Use the context clues provided in the passage to determine the meaning of **inequities.** Write your definition of *inequities* and tell how you determined it. Check your definition in context, by using it in place of *inequities* in the sentence.

CLOSE READ

Reread the text "The Story Behind the Bus." As you reread, complete the Focus Questions below. Then use your answers and annotations from the questions to help you complete the Writing Prompt.

FOCUS QUESTIONS

1. Which text—*Rosa Parks: My Story* or "The Story Behind the Bus"—does a better job of introducing readers to the character of Rosa Parks? Which text does a better job of helping readers understand the significance of Rosa Parks's actions? Highlight textual evidence in "The Story Behind the Bus" to illustrate what this text accomplishes that is different from what *Rosa Parks: My Story* accomplishes. Make annotations to explain your evaluations.

2. In paragraph 6 of "The Story Behind the Bus," the writer says that Rosa Parks's actions "sparked" the Montgomery bus boycott that followed. Using evidence from the text as well as inferences based on clues in the text, and Parks's own words in paragraph 5 of *Rosa Parks: My Story*, explain why Rosa Parks's actions helped inspire the Montgomery Improvement Association to take action of its own. Make annotations to explain your analysis.

3. In referring to Rosa Parks, an African American woman is quoted as saying, "They've messed with the wrong one now." What do you think she meant by this comment? Base your answer on textual evidence and inferences drawn from clues in the text. Make annotations to explain your conclusions and inferences.

4. In paragraph 10 of "The Story Behind the Bus," Rosa Parks is quoted as saying, "The bus was among the first ways I realized there was a black world and a white world." How does her experience on the bus reflect the wider experience of African Americans in the segregated South? How does Parks describe a similar type of experience in *Rosa Parks: My Story?* Highlight textual evidence and make annotations in "The Story Behind the Bus" and *Rosa Parks: My Story* to support your conclusions and inferences.

5. In what ways have the achievements of the Civil Rights Movement depended not only on heroes such as Rosa Parks and Martin Luther King, Jr., who have achieved recognition for their contributions, but also on heroes such as the African Americans who boycotted the buses for more than a year, yet whose names may not be known to the public or mentioned in accounts such as "The Story Behind the Bus"? Highlight textual evidence and make annotations to explain your ideas.

WRITING PROMPT

Rosa Parks: My Story and "The Story Behind the Bus" both tell about Rosa Parks's famous refusal to give up her seat on a Montgomery bus. However, each author writes for a different purpose and from a different point of view. How are the two presentations of the same event similar and different? Use your understanding of the content as well as purpose, style, and point of view to compare and contrast the two texts. Introduce your writing with a thesis statement. Support your thesis statement with well-organized evidence from the texts, including facts, details, and quotations. Use precise language to explain information, and include transitions as needed to connect ideas. Remember to maintain a formal style in your writing and to reinforce your thesis statement in your conclusion.

Please note that excerpts and passages in the StudySync® library and this workbook are intended as touchstones to generate interest in an author's work. The excerpts and passages do not substitute for the reading of entire texts, and StudySync® strongly recommends that students seek out and purchase the whole literary or informational work in order to experience it as the author intended. Links to online resellers are available in our digital library. In addition, complete works may be ordered through an authorized reseller by filling out and returning to StudySync® the order form enclosed in this workbook.

Reading & Writing Companion   **309**

ROSA

POETRY
Rita Dove
1986

INTRODUCTION

Rita Dove is highly regarded African-American poet and author who won the 1987 Pulitzer Prize for Poetry. Dove's poetic works explore a variety of topics, including historical and political events, and she is known for capturing complex emotions succinctly. Her poem "Rosa" is a tribute to Rosa Parks, the activist who helped end segregation by quietly refusing to leave her seat on the bus.

"Doing nothing was the doing..."

 ## FIRST READ

1 How she sat there,
2 the time right inside a place
3 so wrong it was ready.

4 That **trim** name with
5 its dream of a bench
6 to rest on. Her **sensible** coat.

7 Doing nothing was the doing:
8 the clean flame of her gaze
9 **carved** by a camera flash.

10 How she stood up
11 when they bent down to **retrieve**
12 her purse. That **courtesy**.

"Rosa", from ON THE BUS WITH ROSA PARKS by Rita Dove. Copyright © 1999 by
Rita Dove. Used by permission of W. W. Norton & Company, Inc.

THINK QUESTIONS

1. Refer to one or more details from the poem to explain how the setting described in the first stanza is "right" in its wrongness. Base your answer both on ideas that are directly stated and ideas that you infer from the title.

2. Use details from the third stanza and your inferences to explain the speaker's characterization of Parks's action on the bus.

3. Write two or three sentences explaining what happens in the fourth stanza. What does Parks do, and why? What do the officers do, and why? Support your answer with textual evidence and with inferences you make based on textual clues.

4. The word **trim** is an example of a word with multiple meanings. Use context clues from the poem to determine which meaning is being used in "Rosa." Write your definition of *trim* here and tell how you determined it.

5. Remembering that the Latin suffix *-ible* means "able to be," and given that the base word *sense* means "understanding or logic," use these word parts and the context clues provided in the poem to determine the meaning of **sensible.** Write your definition of *sensible* and tell how you determined it.

CLOSE READ

Reread the poem "Rosa." As you reread, complete the Focus Questions below. Then use your answers and annotations from the questions to help you complete the Writing Prompt.

FOCUS QUESTIONS

1. In lines 2 and 3, the speaker uses the antonyms *right* and *wrong.* Discuss how the multiple meanings of each word enhance this word relationship and the meaning of the poem. Highlight textual evidence and make annotations to support your analysis.

2. In lines 4, 5, and 6, Dove makes use of personification—a figure of speech in which an animal, an object, a force of nature, or an idea is given human characteristics—when she suggests that the "name" has a "dream." Discuss the effect of this, and any other, figurative language on Dove's poem. Support your answer with textual evidence and make annotations to explain your analysis.

3. In lines 6 and 12, Dove employs short sentence fragments. Discuss the effect of these elements of poetic structure on Dove's poem. Highlight textual evidence and make annotations to explain your analysis.

4. In line 8, the speaker describes the "clean flame" of Rosa Parks's gaze. Discuss the connotations of these words as they affect the reader's understanding of the image. What other words in this stanza are related to this description, and how? How do these relationships develop the image? Highlight textual evidence and make annotations to explain your analysis.

5. Do you think that Rita Dove believes that Rosa Parks is a hero? Why or why not? How does the structure of the poem support the author's feelings about Rosa Parks? Highlight textual evidence and make annotations to explain your thinking.

WRITING PROMPT

At first glance, Rita Dove's poem "Rosa" appears simple. However, once readers begin to unpack Dove's compact use of poetic structure and language, they find that looks are deceiving. How does Dove use structure and language to create a portrait of the subject of her poem, Rosa Parks? Use your understanding of poetic structure, denotation and connotation, and word relationships to discuss the relationships among form, language, and meaning. Support your writing with textual evidence.

FREEDOM WALKERS:
THE STORY OF THE MONTGOMERY BUS BOYCOTT

NON-FICTION
Russell Freedman
2006

INTRODUCTION

Rosa Parks's famous refusal to give up her seat on a Montgomery, Alabama bus was part of a planned civil action. Nine months earlier, fifteen-year-old Claudette Colvin spontaneously made the same decision, confronting a

"It was against the law for blacks to sit in the same row as a white person."

FIRST READ

Excerpt from Chapter Two

CLAUDETTE COLVIN

1   "It's my constitutional right!"

2   Two youngsters from New Jersey—sixteen-year-old Edwina Johnson and her brother Marshall, who was fifteen—arrived in Montgomery to visit relatives during the summer of 1949. No one told them about the city's segregation laws for buses, and one day they boarded a bus and sat down by a white man and boy.

3   The white boy told Marshall to get up from the seat beside him. Marshall refused. Then the bus driver ordered the black teenagers to move, but they continued to sit where they were. Up North, they were accustomed to riding integrated buses and trains. They didn't see now why they should give up their seats.

4   The driver called the police, and Edwina and Marshall were arrested. Held in jail for two days, they were convicted at a court hearing of violating the city's segregation laws. Judge Wiley C. Hill threatened to send them to reform school until they were twenty-one, but relatives managed to get them an attorney. They were fined and sent back to New Jersey.

5   During the next few years, other black riders were arrested and convicted for the same offense—sitting in seats reserved for whites. They paid their fines quietly and continued to ride the public buses. It took a spunky fifteen-year-old high school student to bring matters to a head.

6   Claudette Colvin was an A student at all-black Booker T. Washington High. She must have been paying attention in her **civics** classes, for she insisted on applying the lessons she had learned after boarding a city bus on March 2, 1955.

7   Claudette was on her way home from school that day. She found a seat in the middle of the bus, behind the section reserved for whites. As more riders got on, the bus filled up until there were no empty seats left. The aisle was jammed with passengers standing, mostly blacks and a few whites.

8   The driver stopped the bus and ordered black passengers seated behind the white section to get up and move farther back, making more seats available for whites. Reluctantly, black riders gave up their seats and moved into the crowded aisle as whites took over the vacated seats.

9   Claudette didn't move. She knew she wasn't sitting in the **restricted** white section. She felt that she was far enough back to be **entitled** to her seat. A pregnant black woman was sitting next to her: When the driver insisted that the woman get up and stand in the aisle, a black man in the rear offered her his seat, then quickly left the bus to avoid trouble.

10   Claudette was now occupying a double seat alone. "Hey, get up!" the bus driver ordered. Still she refused to move. None of the white women standing would sit in the empty seat next to Claudette. It was against the law for blacks to sit in the same row as a white person.

11   The driver refused to move the bus. "This can't go on," he said. "I'm going to call the cops." He did, and when the police arrived, he demanded that Claudette be arrested.

12   "No," Claudette replied. "I don't have to get up. I paid my fare, so I don't have to get up." At school, Claudette had been studying the U.S. Constitution and the Bill of Rights, and she had taken those lessons to heart. "It's my constitutional right to sit here just as much as that [white] lady," she told the police. "It's my constitutional right!"

13   Blacks had been arrested before for talking back to white officials. Now it was Claudette's turn. She was crying and madder than ever when the police told her she was under arrest. "You have no right to do this," she protested. She struggled as they knocked her books aside, grabbed her wrists, and dragged her off the bus, and she screamed when they put on the handcuffs.

14   "I didn't know what was happening," she said later. "I was just angry. Like a teenager might be, I was just downright angry. It felt like I was helpless." She remained locked up at the city jail until she was bailed out later that day by the pastor of her church.

15   Under Montgomery's segregation laws, Claudette was in fact entitled to her seat behind the whites-only section. If no seats were available for blacks to move back to as additional white passengers boarded the bus, then they were not required to give up their seats. That was the official **policy**. But in

actual practice, whenever a white person needed a seat, the driver would order blacks to get up and move to the back of the bus, even when they had to stand in the aisle.

16   Prosecutors threw the book at Claudette. She was charged not only with violating the segregation laws, but also with assault and **battery** for resisting arrest. "She insisted she was colored and just as good as white," the surprised arresting officer told the judge at the court hearing.

17   Claudette's arrest galvanized the black community. E.D. Nixon, an influential black leader, came to the teenager's defense. Nixon was employed as a railroad sleeping car porter, but his passion was working to advance human rights. A rugged man with a forceful manner and commanding voice, he founded the Montgomery chapter of the National Association for the Advancement of Colored People (NAACP). Nixon was recognized by blacks and whites alike as a powerful presence in the black community, a vital force to be reckoned with. It was said that he knew every white policeman, judge, and government clerk in town, and he was always ready to help anyone in trouble.

18   When Nixon heard about Claudette Colvin's arrest, he got in touch with Clifford Durr, a liberal white attorney in Montgomery. Together they contacted Fred Gray, a twenty-four-year-old black lawyer who agreed to represent Colvin in court. Gray had grown up in Montgomery, attended Alabama State, and gone to Ohio for law school, because Alabama didn't have a law school for blacks. He was one of only two black attorneys in town.

19   After a brief trial in juvenile court, Claudette was found guilty of assault. She was fined and placed on probation in her parents' custody. She had expected to be cleared, and when the judge announced his verdict, she broke into agonized sobs that shook everyone in the crowded courtroom.

20   "The verdict was a bombshell!" Jo Ann Robinson recalled. "Blacks were as near a breaking point as they had ever been."

21   E.D. Nixon and other blacks leaders wanted to take the entire bus segregation issue into federal court. They hoped to demonstrate that segregated buses were illegal under the U.S. Constitution. But first they needed the strongest possible case-the arrest of a black rider who was above reproach, a person of unassailable character and reputation who could withstand the closest scrutiny. Claudette Colvin, Nixon felt, was too young and immature, too prone to emotional outbursts, to serve as standard-bearer for a long and expensive constitutional test case. As Nixon pointed out, she had fought with police, she came from the poorer side of black Montgomery, and it was later rumored that she was pregnant. "I had to be sure I had somebody I could win with...to ask people to give us a half million dollars to fight discrimination on a bus line," Nixon said later.

NOTES

22 In October 1955, several months after Claudette was convicted, Mary Louise Smith, an eighteen-year-old black girl, was arrested when she refused to move to the back of the bus so a white woman could take her seat. "[The driver] asked me to move three times," Smith recalled. "And I refused. I told him, 'I am not going to move out of my seat. I am not going to move anywhere. I got the privilege to sit her like anybody else does.'"

23 Smith's case did not create the furor that the Colvin case did, because Smith chose to plead guilty. She was fined five dollars. Once again, Nixon decided that Smith, like Colvin, wasn't the right person to inspire a battle against bus segregation.

24 Two months later, on December 1, 1955, another black woman boarded a city bus and found an empty seat just behind the white section. She was Rosa Parks.

Excerpted from *Freedom Walkers: The Story of the Montgomery Bus Boycott* by Russell Freedman, published by Holt McDougal.

 THINK QUESTIONS

1. Use details from the text to explain why Edwina and Marshall Johnson have trouble with the Montgomery bus laws.

2. Refer to one or more details from the text to explain what Claudette Colvin learns about the difference between Montgomery's segregation laws and actual practice on buses at that time. Base your answer both on evidence that is directly stated and ideas that you infer from clues in the text.

3. Write several sentences explaining how Claudette Colvin hurts her case by struggling with her arresting officers. Support your answer with textual evidence.

4. The Latin root *civis* means "citizen." Using this information and the context from the text, determine the meaning of the word **civics** as it is used in this excerpt from *Freedom Walkers: The Story of the Montgomery Bus Boycott*. Write your definition of *civics* and explain how you got it.

5. The Greek root *polis* means "city" and is also the root for words such as *police*. Use these origins, along with the context clues provided in the passage, to determine the meaning of **policy.** Write your definition of *policy* and tell how you determined the word's meaning.

Copyright © BookheadEd Learning, LLC

CLOSE READ

Reread the excerpt from *Freedom Walkers: The Story of the Montgomery Bus Boycott*. As you reread, complete the Focus Questions below. Then use your answers and annotations from the questions to help you complete the Writing Prompt.

FOCUS QUESTIONS

1. Note that Freedman's text begins with the words "It's my constitutional right," a sentence that is repeated in paragraph 12. Why does Freedman structure the text in this way, and how does this repetition contribute to the development of ideas? Highlight evidence from the text and make annotations to explain your analysis.

2. How does paragraph 5 form a transitional bridge between the stories of the Johnson siblings and Claudette Colvin as well as state a main idea of the text? Support your answer with textual evidence and make annotations to explain your analysis.

3. Freedman brings attention to Claudette Colvin's education in paragraphs 6 and 12. How does this repeated reference contribute to the development of ideas in the text? Highlight textual evidence and make annotations to explain your analysis.

4. In paragraph 13, how does Freedman use text structure to connect Colvin's experience to other African Americans? Highlight textual evidence and make annotations to support your analysis.

5. In what ways are Edwina and Marshall Johnson and Claudette Colvin heroes? Highlight textual evidence and make annotations to explain your ideas.

WRITING PROMPT

In this chapter, Russell Freedman informs readers about a sequence of events that preceded the Montgomery bus boycott, and he also makes a connection between the actions of Edwina and Marshall Johnson in 1949, other African American bus riders in Montgomery over the next few years, and Claudette Colvin in 1955. How does each section of the text fit into the overall structure and contribute to Freedman's development of ideas? Use your understanding of informational text structure to analyze the excerpt. Support your writing with textual evidence, including facts, details, and quotations. Use precise vocabulary as appropriate to explain the topic, including words specifically related to the issues and laws of the time.

Please note that excerpts and passages in the StudySync® library and this workbook are intended as touchstones to generate interest in an author's work. The excerpts and passages do not substitute for the reading of entire texts, and StudySync® strongly recommends that students seek out and purchase the whole literary or informational work in order to experience it as the author intended. Links to online resellers are available in our digital library. In addition, complete works may be ordered through an authorized reseller by filling out and returning to StudySync® the order form enclosed in this workbook.

Reading & Writing Companion   **319**

SUNRISE OVER FALLUJAH

FICTION
Walter Dean Myers
2008

INTRODUCTION

Robin Perry doesn't know exactly why he joined the Army after 9/11, but he knows he is headed to the Mideast to take part in Operation Iraqi Freedom. As part of a unit meant to stabilize the country and interact with the Iraqi people, it isn't long before he realizes that good intentions take a backseat to survival. In the excerpt below, Robin has just arrived in Kuwait.

"'So what are you doing in Kuwait?' I asked."

FIRST READ

Excerpt from Chapter 1

1   We left the tent and drifted out into the bright Kuwaiti sun. The intense direct light was always a bit of a shock and I saw guys going for their water bottles. I wasn't sure whether I should drink as much water as possible or try to train myself to drink less.

2   Since Kuwait was right next to Iraq, I thought things would be tense here, but they're not. Our living quarters are in a warehouse area; the mess hall is really good and it even has a coffee shop. There are also fast food places, a theater, and a library that was built after the first Gulf War. After two weeks in the country, I was still trying to get used to the heat and even complaining like everybody else, but down deep this is a little exciting, too. I'm also wondering if there really is going to be a war. There is a huge amount of guys and heavy equipment already here and more being brought in every day.

3   "Hey, Birdy!"

4   I turned around and a tall blonde caught up with me. I'm six-two and we were almost eye to eye when she reached me. I glanced at her name tape. Kennedy.

5   "Say, Birdy, weren't you at Fort Dix?" she asked.

6   "Yeah, and the name is Robin, not Birdy," I said.

7   "Whatever," she said. "I like Birdy better."

8   "Kennedy, I knocked out the last person who got my name wrong," I said.

9   "Really? I'm impressed," she said; a grin spread across her face. "What kind of weapon was she carrying?"

NOTES

10   Kennedy flipped the sling of her M-16 over her shoulder and **sauntered** off toward the women's quarters.

11   I had come down with measles at Fort Dix, New Jersey, with only two weeks left to go in my **infantry** training cycle. After a week in **isolation** at the hospital I spent three weeks hanging around the dayroom watching television and shooting pool while it was being decided if I would have to repeat the whole cycle again. I ended up with another training group and then received orders to report to the Civil Affairs **detachment** at Camp Doha in Kuwait.

12   I went to dinner in the main mess. The tables actually had flowers and napkins on them and we ate off regular plates instead of the trays we had used at Fort Dix. I grabbed some meat loaf, mashed potatoes, and string beans, and found a table. One of the guys who had been at the meeting with Major Sessions came over and asked if he could join me.

13   "Sure," I said. The guy was about five-seven with smooth brown skin and a round face. Solidly built, he looked like he could take care of himself. But when I saw his **camouflage** do-rag and dark shades I knew he was a little different.

14   "So what you about, man?" he asked.

15   "Same thing everybody else is," I answered, "getting ready to go to war. What are you about?"

16   "I'm about the blues," he answered. "You know, the blues is what's real. Everything else is just messing around waiting until you get back to the blues."

17   "So what are you doing in Kuwait?" I asked. I glanced down at his name tape. It read JONES.

18   "Yeah, I'm Jones," he said. "But everybody back home calls me 'Jonesy.' What I'm doing here is getting some experience, getting to see some stuff, and saving my money so I can open up a blues club. When I get that club going I'm going to play blues guitar six nights a week. Then on Sundays I'll jam with God because me and him is like this."

19   Jones held up two crossed fingers.

20   "Yeah, okay."

21   "Yeah, yeah. Look, you and me got to stick together," he said. "That way I can watch your back and you can watch mine."

22   "Okay."

23 "You play guitar?"

24 "No."

25 "You sing?"

26 "No."

27 Jones looked away and I got the feeling he had already lost interest in watching my back. He talked some more about the club he was going to open. He didn't sound as if he had much of an education, but he seemed sincere about wanting to play his guitar. He said he practiced it at least two hours a day.

28 "Yo, Jones, that's good," I said.

29 "'Jonesy,' you got to call me 'Jonesy,'" he said. "That way I know you looking out."

30 I liked Jonesy even though I wasn't sure what he was talking about sometimes. Like when he asked me if I was a hero.

31 "No," I answered.

32 "You tall—how tall are you?"

33 "Six foot two."

34 "A lot of tall dudes are hero types," Jonesy said. "You go crazy trying to watch their backs. You know what I mean?"

35 "Yeah, but I'm not the hero type," I said.

Excerpted from *Sunrise Over Fallujah* by Walter Dean Myers, published by Scholastic Inc.

Please note that excerpts and passages in the StudySync® library and this workbook are intended as touchstones to generate interest in an author's work. The excerpts and passages do not substitute for the reading of entire texts, and StudySync® strongly recommends that students seek out and purchase the whole literary or informational work in order to experience it as the author intended. Links to online resellers are available in our digital library. In addition, complete works may be ordered through an authorized reseller by filling out and returning to StudySync® the order form enclosed in this workbook.

Reading & Writing Companion 323

THINK QUESTIONS

1. Use details from the text to explain how Kuwait is different from the narrator's expectations.

2. Refer to one or more details from the text to explain how Kennedy uses humor to lighten the conversation with the narrator. Base your answer both on evidence that is directly stated and ideas that you have inferred from clues in the text.

3. Write two or three sentences explaining how the narrator and Jonesy have different attitudes toward their time in Kuwait. Support your answer with textual evidence.

4. Use context to determine the meaning of the word **isolation** as it is used in *Sunrise Over Fallujah*. Write your definition of *isolation* and tell how you determined the word's meaning.

5. Remembering that the prefix *de* often means "opposite of," and that the suffix *ment* forms a noun from a verb, use the context clues provided in the passage to determine the meaning of **detachment**. Write your definition of *detachment* and tell how you determined the word's meaning.

CLOSE READ

Reread the excerpt from *Sunrise Over Fallujah*. As you reread, complete the Focus Questions below. Then use your answers and annotations from the questions to help you complete the Writing Prompt.

FOCUS QUESTIONS

1. Explain how the author, Walter Dean Myers, develops the narrator's point of view in the first two paragraphs of the excerpt from *Sunrise Over Fallujah*. What tone does Meyers communicate through Robin's comments? Is this tone consistent, and if so, what does the author do to maintain it? Support your answer with textual evidence and make annotations to explain your analysis.

2. In paragraph 11, Robin is isolated in the hospital for measles. What tone does Myers's choice of words establish toward military decision making? Highlight textual evidence and make annotations to explain your analysis.

3. In paragraphs 12 and 13, what does Robin notice about the mess hall and about Jonesy? How do his observations add to what readers already know about Robin and about his point of view on life in a military camp? In paragraph 15, what does Robin's reply tell you about his point of view?

4. In paragraph 16, Jonesy explains that he's "about" the blues, and the characters go on to talk more about the blues and playing music in paragraphs 18 through 28. What tone does the author convey toward the blues through the characters' conversation? What words, phrases, or sentence structures help maintain this tone? Highlight textual evidence and make annotations to support your analysis.

5. In paragraphs 30, 34, and 35 Jonesy and Robin each use the term *hero*. How does Jonesy use the word? How does Robin use the word? Do the two characters define *hero* in the same way? Highlight textual evidence and make annotations to explain your analysis.

WRITING PROMPT

By using a first-person narrator, Walter Dean Myers ensures that readers will experience *Sunrise Over Fallujah* only through what Robin is able to see, hear, think, and observe. How might the story's point of view be different if a different character, Jonesy for example, was the first-person narrator who told the story? How might the tone of the story be different? Using details from the text, write an essay explaining how the excerpt would be different if told from Jonesy's point of view. What might Jonesy notice that would be different from what Robin observes? What would Jonesy's attitude be toward life in the camp? Would he share Robin's excitement or have other feelings? What would Jonesy have to say about Robin himself? Would his point of view on Robin be favorable? Use what you have learned about tone to establish a formal tone in your essay, and maintain it. Use textual evidence to support your ideas.

Please note that excerpts and passages in the StudySync® library and this workbook are intended as touchstones to generate interest in an author's work. The excerpts and passages do not substitute for the reading of entire texts, and StudySync® strongly recommends that students seek out and purchase the whole literary or informational work in order to experience it as the author intended. Links to online resellers are available in our digital library. In addition, complete works may be ordered through an authorized reseller by filling out and returning to StudySync® the order form enclosed in this workbook.

Reading & Writing Companion   325

AN AMERICAN PLAGUE:

THE TRUE AND TERRIFYING STORY OF
THE YELLOW FEVER EPIDEMIC OF 1793

NON-FICTION
Jim Murphy
2003

INTRODUCTION

Thought to have originated in Africa, yellow fever spread to the Americas in the 17th and 18th centuries on trading ships. In 1793, the plague struck inhabitants of quayside neighborhoods in Philadelphia with gruesome and heartbreaking results. Author Jim Murphy takes an unflinching look at the scourge, including the doctors who labored to save the afflicted and discover the causes and cures, the politicians who sought to govern the panicked city,

"...her skin took on the pale-yellow color that gave the disease its name."

FIRST READ

Excerpt from Chapter 2: All Was Not Right

1   "*8 or 10 persons buried out of Water St. between Race and Arch Sts.; many sick in our neighborhood, and in ye City generally.*"
—Elizabeth Drinker, August 21, 1793

2   **Monday, August 19.** It was clear that thirty-three-year-old Catherine LeMaigre was dying, and dying horribly and painfully. Between agonized gasps and groans she muttered that her stomach felt as if it were burning up. Every ten minutes or so her moaning would stop abruptly and she would vomit a foul black bile.

3   Her husband, Peter, called in two neighborhood doctors to save his young wife. One was Dr. Hugh Hodge, whose own daughter had been carried off by the same fever just days before. Hodge had been an army surgeon during the Revolutionary War, and while stubborn and crusty in his ways, he was a respected physician. The other was Dr. John Foulke, who was a fellow of Philadelphia's **prestigious** College of Physicians and a member of the Pennsylvania Hospital board.

4   Hodge and Foulke did what they could for their patient. They gave her cool drinks of barley water and apple water to reduce the fever, and red wine with laudanum to help her rest. Her forehead, face, and arms were washed regularly with damp cloths.

5   Nothing worked, and Catherine LeMaigre's condition worsened. Her pulse slowed, her eyes grew bloodshot, her skin took on the pale-yellow color that gave the disease its name. More black vomit came spewing forth. In desperation, the two physicians sent for their esteemed colleague Dr. Benjamin Rush.

NOTES

6　Rush was forty-seven years old and so highly respected that he was often called in by colleagues when they were baffled by a case. His medical training had been extensive, consisting of five years of apprenticeship with the pre-eminent doctor in the United States, John Redman. After this he had gone to Europe to study under the most skilled surgeons and doctors in the western world.

7　He was passionate and outspoken in his beliefs, no matter what the subject. He opposed slavery, felt that alcohol and tobacco should be avoided, urged that the corporal punishment of children be stopped, and thought that the best way to keep a democracy strong was by having universal education. Along with his beliefs went an unimaginable amount of energy. Despite a persistent cough and weak lungs that often left him gasping for air, he worked from early in the morning until late at night—writing letters and papers, visiting patients, rereading the latest medical literature, or attending to any one of a number of institutions and charities he belonged to.

8　Hodge and Foulke told Rush about Catherine LeMaigre's **symptoms** and what they had done to help her. There was nothing much else they could do, Rush said, after the three men left her bedchamber to discuss the case. Rush then noted that in recent days he had seen "an unusual number of bilious fevers, accompanied with symptoms of uncommon malignity." In a grave voice, his seriousness reflected in his intense blue eyes, he added that "all was not right in our city."

9　The two other doctors agreed, and then all three recounted the symptoms they had seen. The sickness began with chills, headache, and a painful aching in the back, arms, and legs. A high fever developed, accompanied by constipation. This stage lasted around three days, and then the fever suddenly broke and the patient seemed to recover.

10　But only for a few short hours.

11　The next stage saw the fever shoot up again. The skin and eyeballs turned yellow, as red blood cells were destroyed, causing the bile pigment bilirubin to accumulate in the body; nose, gums, and intestines began bleeding; and the patient vomited stale, black blood. Finally, the pulse grew weak, the tongue turned a dry brown, and the victim became depressed, confused, and delirious.

12　Rush noted another sign as well: tiny reddish eruptions on the skin. "They appeared chiefly on the arms, but they sometimes extended to the breast." Physicians called these sores petechiae, which is Latin for skin spots, and Rush observed that they "resembled moscheto bites."

Copyright © BookheadEd Learning, LLC

13 Hodge then pointed out that the deaths, including his daughter's, had all happened on or near Water Street. Foulke told of other deaths along the street and said he knew the origin of the fevers: the repulsive smell in the air caused by the rotting coffee on Ball's Wharf.

14 The idea that illness was caused by **microscopic organisms,** such as **bacteria** and **viruses,** was not known at the time. Instead, doctors based their medical thinking on the 2,500-year-old Greek humoral theory. This concept stated that good health resulted when body fluids, called humors, were in balance. The humors were phlegm, choler, bile, and blood.

15 Disease arose from an imbalance of these humors—too much of one, not enough of another. Any number of things could cause this condition, such as poor diet, excess drinking, poison, or a dog bite, to name just a few. Even bad news could unsettle the humors and cause illness. So it made sense to Rush, Hodge, and Foulke that the putrid-smelling air could upset people enough to cause an outbreak of violent, fatal fevers.

16 Rush, however, sensed something else. The symptoms he was seeing reminded him of a sickness that had swept through Philadelphia back in 1762, when he was sixteen years old and studying under Dr. Redman. Rush was never shy with his opinions, and standing there in the LeMaigres' parlor, he boldly announced that the disease they now confronted was the dreaded yellow fever.

Excerpted from *An American Plague* by Jim Murphy, published by Clarion Books.

 THINK QUESTIONS

1. Use details from the text to describe three symptoms that indicated a patient had yellow fever.

2. Refer to one or more details from the text to explain both the suspected and the true causes of yellow fever. Why was Benjamin Rush suspicious of the suspected cause?

3. Write two or three sentences explaining how Dr. Rush was able to diagnose the yellow fever. Support your answer with textual evidence.

4. The Greek word root *symptoma* means "happening." Use this root, along with the context, to determine the technical meaning of the word **symptoms** as it is used in *An American Plague: The True and Terrifying Story of the Yellow Fever Epidemic of 1793*. Write your definition of *symptoms* and tell how you determined it.

5. The Greek prefix *micro* means "small" and the Greek root *scop* means "to see." Use these word parts along with the context clues provided in the passage to determine the technical meaning of **microscopic.** Write your definition of *microscopic* here and tell how you determined it.

CLOSE READ

Reread the excerpt from *An American Plague: The True and Terrifying Story of the Yellow Fever Epidemic of 1793*. As you reread, complete the Focus Questions below. Then use your answers and annotations from the questions to help you complete the Writing Prompt.

FOCUS QUESTIONS

1. How do the details of Catherine LeMaigre's illness in paragraphs 2 and 5 connect to the details of Dr. Hodge's daughter's illness in paragraph 3, and the illnesses of other patients in the city in paragraphs 8–13? How do they help convey the central idea of the text? Highlight evidence from the text and make annotations to explain your ideas.

2. What details in paragraphs 4 and 5 cause Drs. Hodge and Foulke to send for Dr. Rush? How does the decision to consult with Dr. Rush prove key in diagnosing Catherine LeMaigre and support the central idea of the text? Support your answer with textual evidence and make annotations to explain your ideas.

3. In paragraphs 14–15, readers may note that the passage describes the medical thinking prevalent during the late 1700s. Identify the key details in the passage. What do they have in common? Use the central idea and key details to summarize this passage. Highlight important details in the text and make annotations to explain your reasoning.

4. What do the ways in which Drs. Hodge and Foulke respond to the mysterious illness of their patient, Catherine LeMaigre, reveal about their character? Highlight details from the text and make annotations to provide evidence for your answer.

5. In what ways is Dr. Rush a hero? Highlight textual evidence and make annotations to explain your ideas.

WRITING PROMPT

Notice that the text says that Dr. Rush "worked from early in the morning until late at night" on a number of tasks, including "writing letters and papers." Physicians often write papers about health-related topics for publication in medical journals. Imagine that you are Dr. Hodge, Dr. Foulke, or Dr. Rush. Summarize for city politicians the health situation in Philadelphia in 1793. What might you say? Write an objective summary introducing the central or main idea and the most important details that support it, such as facts, definitions, and examples. Be sure not to include irrelevant details or your feelings or judgments. Use precise language and specific vocabulary, such as scientific and medical terms, as appropriate in your summary, and include transitions to connect your ideas. Maintain a formal style, and provide a conclusion that follows from the information you present. Support your writing with textual evidence.

CELEBRITIES AS HEROES

NON-FICTION
2015

INTRODUCTION

There is no question that celebrities are frequently idolized as heroes, especially by young people. But do they deserve such admiration? The authors of these two articles have different opinions. One claims that most celebrities are not heroic because they have not done enough to change the world in positive ways. The other argues that many celebrities do qualify as heroes because of their outstanding achievements and influence as role models. Both writers present strong arguments and support their claims with evidence.

"...money, notoriety, and flamboyant behavior don't make someone a hero."

NOTES

FIRST READ

Celebrities as Heroes

Point: Celebrities Should Not Be Idolized as Heroes

1 "Did you read what he said on Twitter? He's my hero!"

2 "Do you know what she did on vacation? She's my hero!"

3 "Did you hear how they finally tracked down the gang in the latest podcast? They're my heroes!"

4 "Did you see what she wore to that awards show? She's my hero!"

5 Today, many people use the word "hero" too lightly. They confuse the word "hero" with the word "celebrity." Right now, almost anyone can be a celebrity just because his or her name or face can be recognized. But money, notoriety, and flamboyant behavior don't make someone a hero. Neither does playing the role of a hero on TV or in the movies. In fact, most celebrities don't deserve to be called heroes because they aren't heroes. They're people who are "celebrities" or "celebrated" for no other reason than because their fame has spread by word of mouth, the press, or social media.

6 What makes a hero? Heroes have been defined as people who have demonstrated admirable qualities such as strength, honesty, courage, and **perseverance,** sometimes at great risk to themselves. They have accomplished something that helped others in some way. For example, by refusing to give up her seat on a bus, Rosa Parks became a hero for civil rights. Her action inspired others to fight for equality in peaceful ways. Firefighters, police officers, soldiers, and regular citizens have often acted heroically when they have saved people from attacks and natural disasters. Heroes can also be individuals who have made a difference in people's lives, such as teachers, parents, coaches, and mentors.

Copyright © BookheadEd Learning, LLC

7   When celebrities are **idolized** just because they play heroes in movies and on television or are famous for dangerous or inappropriate publicity stunts, they end up overshadowing real heroes. They may get our attention, but they certainly don't do much to positively change the world. This leaves young people with poor role models and heroes with little substance.

8   Psychologist Abby Aronowitz, Ph.D., says that the media is partly to blame for the hero worship of celebrities. She says that the media devotes a lot of attention to celebrities and little time to reporting on true heroes. However, many who work in the media claim that news about their idols is what people want to watch and read about, and so that's what they give them. Celebrity sells.

9   Dr. Stuart Fischoff of the American Psychological Association says it's normal for people to idolize those who have fame and fortune. "We are **sociologically** preprogrammed to 'follow the leader,'" he says. However, if young people choose to idolize a celebrity who indulges in risky behavior, then they might be inspired to do the same. They may think that if they themselves act like their idol, they too will become famous.

10 While many celebrities love that the media turns them into heroes, other celebrities criticize these false images. They don't want to be heroes. They don't want the pressure of being seen as role models for young fans. They know that their mistakes will be widely reported and will likely upset and disappoint those who idolize them. However, the price of fame is that young fans will continue to idolize celebrity superstars and consider them heroes.

11 Convincing young people that celebrities do not make good role models or heroes will be difficult if there are no real heroes to replace the celebrities. So the media and parents need to focus on real heroes. Many can be found in history. Examples include Martin Luther King Jr., Eleanor Roosevelt, Gandhi, and Abraham Lincoln. There are also many everyday men and women who have acted heroically by facing danger to help people. Even though they have flaws as all humans do, their courage can inspire others. Such heroes will still be heroes long after celebrities are no longer remembered.

Counterpoint: Celebrities Can Be Cultural Heroes

12 After the baseball game is over, young fans line up to get autographs from their favorite players. The player who hit the home run that won the game is greeted with cheers. One fan yells, "You're my hero!"

13 Many actors, singers, and television stars are idolized with the same adoration that many fans show sports stars. They are all famous celebrities, but are they also heroes? Do they deserve or even want such admiration?

14 Society is very quick to sneer at celebrities who are idolized and very ready to say that any contribution a celebrity makes is minor. Many people are **dismissive** of celebrities just because they are celebrities. Yet, there are many celebrities who are true heroes. These individuals may have struggled courageously to reach their goals and made outstanding achievements in their fields—sports, movies, music, fashion—that can inspire others.

15 Striving to be the best one can be at a sport or in science, medicine, or another profession can require extraordinary skill, determination, self-sacrifice, and dedication. Celebrities who set good examples as role models for striving and achieving at the very highest levels in their chosen fields and beyond can at times be considered heroic in their struggle, commitment, and accomplishment.

16 Dr. Eric Hollander at the Mt. Sinai School of Medicine in New York City says "Celebrities can have a positive influence on our lives, with positive messages." This is especially true when fans appreciate a celebrity's abilities and achievements. They may idolize a soccer player's genuine ability to play well and score points in nearly every game. This admiration may lead young fans to work harder when they play soccer because they want to be like their hero.

17 In addition, some celebrities have made outstanding contributions to charitable causes. Paul Newman was called one of the best actors of his time, but he also founded a food company that donates all of its profits to charity. Other celebrities like Derek Jeter have attained greatness in their chosen fields and are also very active in charitable work. Jeter created an organization that helps kids turn away from drugs and alcohol. As a result, celebrities like Derek Jeter have a positive effect on people, especially their young fans, who are inspired to live healthier lives. Helping people is definitely something that heroes do.

18 Because many celebrities deserve admiration for their achievements in or beyond their chosen fields, it's really up to the fans to choose their heroes carefully. Fans need to know what qualities real heroes have and to look for these qualities in the celebrities they are attracted to. They need to ask themselves if they are worshiping celebrities just because these people are famous or because they are true heroes. If fans confuse mere celebrities with real heroes, they rob themselves of good role models. If the only celebrities young people are exposed to do nothing but go to parties, wear expensive clothes, appear on television gossip programs, and act rudely, then that is who will be a major influence on young people.

19 It's also up to the media to pay more attention to celebrities who are true role models. This is not always easy because these celebrities are not necessarily

looking for the media to shine a spotlight on their actions. They are involved in helping refugees, fighting for conservation, or working to improve people's health because these issues are important to them. They aren't doing these things to increase their fame or to be admired as heroes.

20 We all need heroes; people we can look up to and strive to imitate. If we are clear about the qualities we admire, we will be able to find many true role models among that diverse group of people we categorize simply as "celebrities. But the individuals we choose to call our "heroes" can't be just any celebrities. They should be people who, by example or action, are trying to make a difference in other people's lives.

 THINK QUESTIONS

1. Cite the "Point" author's main claim and one reason why the author makes the claim. What evidence does the author provide to support this position? Use details from the text to support your answer.

2. Use details from the text to explain the "Counterpoint" author's main claim and one reason why the author makes this claim. What evidence does the author provide to support this position?

3. The "Point" author acknowledges that some celebrities, particularly sports stars, do not want to be heroes or role models, but he or she insists that these desires are irrelevant. Explain the author's position on this issue. Use textual evidence to support your answer.

4. Use context clues from the text to determine the meaning of the word **perseverance** as it is used in "Celebrities as Heroes" Write your definition of *perseverance* here and tell how you determined the word's meaning.

5. Remembering that the Latin root *socio* means "friend or companion" and the suffix *-ology* means "a branch of learning," use the context clues provided in the selection to determine the meaning of **sociologically**. Write your definition of *sociologically* and tell how you determined the word's meaning.

Please note that excerpts and passages in the StudySync® library and this workbook are intended as touchstones to generate interest in an author's work. The excerpts and passages do not substitute for the reading of entire texts, and StudySync® strongly recommends that students seek out and purchase the whole literary or informational work in order to experience it as the author intended. Links to online resellers are available in our digital library. In addition, complete works may be ordered through an authorized reseller by filling out and returning to StudySync® the order form enclosed in this workbook.

Reading & Writing Companion   **335**

CLOSE READ

Reread the text "Celebrities as Heroes." As you reread, complete the Focus Questions below. Then use your answers and annotations from the questions to help you complete the Writing Prompt.

FOCUS QUESTIONS

1. Review the "Point" author's claim in paragraph 5 of the "Point" section that "most celebrities don't deserve to be called heroes because they aren't heroes." What reason does the author give in the same paragraph for making his or her claim? What evidence is missing to support the word *most* in the claim? Then review the "Counterpoint" author's claim in paragraph 14 of the "Counterpoint" section that "there are many celebrities who are true heroes." What reason does this author give in the same paragraph for making his or her claim? What evidence is missing to support the word *many* in the claim? Highlight textual evidence and make annotations to explain your ideas.

2. In paragraph 7, the "Point" author states that celebrities "end up overshadowing real heroes" and that this "leaves young people with poor role models and heroes with little substance." What evidence does the "Point" author include in paragraph 8 to support this statement? What additional information could the author have included to make his or her argument more effective? Highlight textual evidence and make annotations to support your evaluation.

3. Evaluate the evidence provided by the expert quoted in paragraph 9 of the "Point" section. How well does it support the "Point" author's claim that celebrities should not be considered heroes? Highlight textual evidence and make annotations to support your evaluation.

4. Identify a reason that the "Counterpoint" author provides in paragraph 16 of "Celebrities Can Be Cultural Heroes" to support his or her claim. What evidence supports the reason and claim? Evaluate the strength of the evidence. Highlight textual evidence and make annotations to explain your analysis.

5. Do you agree or disagree with the "Point" author that historical figures, firefighters, police officers, soldiers, teachers, parents, coaches, and mentors are more heroic than most celebrities? Why or why not? Highlight textual evidence and make annotations to explain your ideas.

WRITING PROMPT

The "Point" and "Counterpoint" authors offer two points of view regarding whether celebrities are heroes. Both offer reasons and evidence to support their claims. If you trace and evaluate the argument of each author, which author is most convincing? Which author most effectively uses reasons and evidence to support his or her claim? Is each claim fully supported by reasons and evidence? If not, which aspect of the particular claim remains unsupported? Use your understanding of purpose and point of view as you evaluate the argument in each passage. Support your opinion with textual evidence.

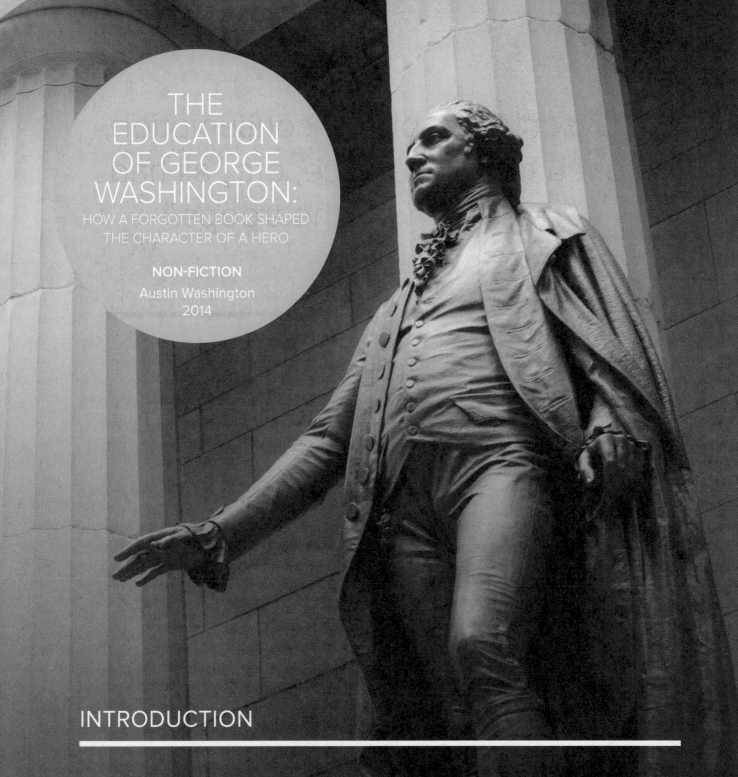

THE EDUCATION OF GEORGE WASHINGTON:

HOW A FORGOTTEN BOOK SHAPED THE CHARACTER OF A HERO

NON-FICTION
Austin Washington
2014

INTRODUCTION

The Education of George Washington, a biography of the American hero written by his great-nephew Austin Washington, offers a lively and humorous account of Washington's life. The book focuses on how a forgotten 200-year-old text and other experiences helped shape Washington into a man who represents honor, courage, and integrity. In the excerpt, Washington and his troops face a desperate situation at Valley Forge, and receive assistance from Baron von

"Dysentery, typhoid, consumption, pneumonia, jaundice, etc., all had their way with the troops."

 FIRST READ

Excerpt from Chapter Eleven: Valley Forge

1 Most of us have heard about the hard, cold winter at Valley Forge. The bloody feet in the snow and all the rest.

2 For those of you for whom the details are a bit hazy, war was a summer thing in those days. No major battles were expected to be fought in the off season. Both armies would hunker down for the winter. Valley Forge, Pennsylvania, was selected as the winter home for the twelve thousand or so soldiers directly under George's control in the fall of 1777, a year after the crossing of the Delaware had given the Americans their first unambiguous victory.

3 Although the first months of Valley Forge were a hellish struggle—if hell can be freezing, that is—there are no contemporary images of the cadaverous survivors to remind us of the horror.

4 The most famous image, which is both fictional and trite, is a painting made 198 years after the (non) incident, depicting George Washington, fully clothed and shod (as he of course would have been), praying alone in the snow (as he never did). For those of a less Norman Rockwellesque frame of mind—it was actually a guy named Friberg who made that particularly falsely iconic, Rockwellesque image—Valley Forge is seen most often as a metaphor for the entire revolutionary struggle: against impossible odds, impossibly undersupplied troops suffered and sacrificed with no realistic hope in sight.

5 But they soldiered on.

6 Without any evocative images to remind us, though, the true horror is often forgotten. As fall turned into winter in 1777, two-thirds of the twelve thousand soldiers camped in Valley Forge still had no shoes. No shoes! At one point, a third were listed as unfit for duty—well, four thousand or so, which was more

NOTES

than a third once you subtract the twenty-five hundred who had died by the spring from the horrific diseases that sliced through the camp, all of them untreatable at the time and most of them contagious.

7   Dysentery, typhoid, consumption, pneumonia, jaundice, etc., all had their way with the troops. It didn't help that the conditions were horrifyingly unsanitary by modern standards (and by contemporaneous Prussian standards, but we'll get to that in a minute). Nor, of course, did the freezing cold offer any comfort.

8   In short, George Washington's army was in desperate conditions—even more desperate than the circumstances of the Duke of Schonberg's army that, as George had read in the Panegyrick, once suffered "an incredible scarcity of all things; and the rage of Hunger, more cruel than that of the Sword. . . weaken'd below by Mortal Diseases; consum'd from within with want; and fac'd without, with a numerous Army. . . ." This was warfare in the era before modern technology, when the difference between defeat and victory wasn't who had stealth fighters and bunker-busting bombs, but who was best able to rise above hunger and disease to fight on.

9   Lack of adequate shelter, at least at first, contributed to the misery, suffering, and disease of George's men. Hobbit homes would have been a step up from the accommodations originally available at Valley Forge. Malnutrition didn't help. The soldiers survived, at times, on nothing but "fire bread," made from flour, melted snow, and nothing else. Occasionally their diet would be supplemented by fallen animals, which were butchered where they fell. They would let what little might remain rot, although the rotting was, as some small consolation, limited by the cold.

10 They relieved themselves where they were, the germ theory of disease being a century in the future. The cold therefore prevented at least some incidents of illness by freezing things that might otherwise putrefy.

11 But the cold also killed throughout the winter.

12 This suffering, **epitomized** by shoeless soldiers' bloody footprints in the snow, is the darkest image that comes to us from that winter at Valley Forge, Pennsylvania.

13 What most people don't see is why and how the American soldiers—those who survived, that is—overcame all of this. They emerged tougher, stronger, and better, rather than weaker, crippled, and dispirited, as would surely have been the case without the entrance, towards the end of that winter, of someone almost more **prototypically** American—or at least more self-made— than George Washington.

NOTES

14 Lieutenant General Friedrich Wilhelm Rudolf Gerhard Augustin Baron von Steuben—Baron von Steuben for short—was little of what his name would suggest. For one, he seems to have been a self-appointed baron. Then again, Michael Jackson was a self-anointed King (of Pop). Self-anointing, rather than inheriting titles, seems to be the American fashion, so von Steuben fit right in.

15 Nor, going a little deeper, had he been a lieutenant general in the Prussian army, as the Americans believed. He had risen to the rank of major there and later been given the honorary title of lieutenant general in a prince's court, after he had been downsized out of the Prussian army. Von Steuben was, though, **indisputably** a Friedrich, a Wilhelm, a Rudolf, and a Gerhard, all at once, which is more than most people can say for themselves.

16 Von Steuben is often given short shrift for his inflated credentials, but as he was to make his biggest mark in a land in which no one of importance had any credentials—the most notable of all, such as Washington and Benjamin Franklin, lacking even university degrees—an observer might ask a big, historical so what? Okay, he was a captain and then major, never a general in the Prussian army, but it *was* the Prussian *army*, widely considered the best in Europe. And he wasn't just any staff officer, he had been aide-de-camp to the King of Prussia. The King!

17 Von Steuben was even one of thirteen officers selected for a *Spezialklasse der Kriegskunst,* a kind of warfare class conducted by the King. Presumably the baron—or whatever he was—was chosen for that class by the King himself. As von Steuben didn't speak English very well, the whole "lieutenant general in the Prussian army" thing was very possibly a misunderstanding. Meanwhile the title, if incorrect, did arguably convey his background and skill in a kind of shorthand.

18 Anyway, the somewhat inflated background is what Benjamin Franklin conveyed in a letter he wrote to George Washington (who was later to repeat the characterization), when Franklin was in Europe scouting out potential officers.

19 If the inflated military rank was of the same provenance as the "baron" title—which might, to be fair, have been the fault of faulty genealogical work by his father, not deliberate **mendacity** on the part of either von Steuben fils or père—or if they were both puffery, we still won the war, which we might not have done otherwise.

20 Von Steuben proved himself by his actions, just as George Washington and Benjamin Franklin (and all great Americans since) have done.

21 Von Steuben, after all, started his life in a land where a "baron" title would open up vistas—promotions, positions at court—that would be otherwise

closed to him. He then came to a land where a convenient conflation of ranks advanced his career to the level where his skills and talents naturally should have placed him. We are here today, most would agree, because von Steuben overcame the limitations of his birth by the only means reasonably available, puffery. It sounds unpleasant. But it worked.

22　Von Steuben, who loved the pomp of the army as much as anything else, traveled to America, somewhat exotically, not with a wife but with a greyhound. Von Steuben's dog, whether by nature or nurture, had learned to howl when someone sang out of tune (but to wag his tail when the singing was in tune). The dog's short-legged, jowly master wore "a splendid medal of gold and diamonds" on his chest, which was the outward sign of an honorary knighthood. How could he be ignored?

23　George Washington rode out especially to meet him, and was, if not instantly taken, then very soon impressed. The "baron" may have been **eccentric**, but then geniuses often are, aren't they? He was, as George was soon to see, exactly the man George needed to supply the order and discipline the American army so desperately needed.

24　Possibly von Steuben's most important contribution to the American army— don't laugh, it saved countless lives—was putting the latrines *down* hill from where the soldiers lived. Sounds obvious, doesn't it? The Americans hadn't thought of it.

25　Oh, and he also came up with the idea of the latrines themselves. Someone had to suggest them, and that someone was the little "baron" himself. He had picked up his ideas in Germany, where latrines were standard issue.

26　Despite his Prussian background, von Steuben was American enough to particularly point out what he found a refreshing—if at first infuriating— difference between American soldiers and their European counterparts. Ultimately, the difference in American soldiers was the spirit of the Revolution, itself, its *raison d'etre*. Or, as Von Steuben put it, "The genius"—that is, the inherent spirit—"of this nation is not in the least to be compared with the Prussians, the Austrians, or French." While you could say to a European soldier, "'Do this,' and he doeth it," in America, von Steuben discovered, "I am obliged to say, 'This is the reason why you ought to do that,' and then he does it."

27　In other words, Americans thought for themselves. Even the common soldiers didn't let themselves be pushed around.

From the book *The Education of George Washington*, by Austin Washington. Copyright © 2014. Published by Regnery Publishing. All rights reserved. Reprinted by special permission of Regnery Publishing, Washington, DC.

THINK QUESTIONS

1. Use details from the text to write two or three sentences describing the conditions at Valley Forge.

2. Write two or three sentences explaining whom the author credits for not only the survival but the toughness and strength of the American soldiers at Valley Forge. Support your answer with textual evidence.

3. Refer to one or more details from the text to explain what Baron von Steuben credits for not only the soldiers' survival at Valley Forge but ultimately for the American victory in the war—both from ideas that are directly stated and ideas that you have inferred from clues in the text.

4. Use context to determine the meaning of the word **indisputably** as it is used in *The Education of George Washington: How a Forgotten Book Shaped the Character of a Hero*. Write your definition of *indisputably* and tell how you determined the word's meaning. How might you pronounce this word? Use a dictionary to confirm the word's precise meaning and pronunciation.

5. Remembering that the prefix *proto-* means "original" and the suffix *-ly* means "in a particular manner," use the context clues provided in the passage to determine the meaning of **prototypically,** and make an inference about its pronunciation. Write your definition of *prototypically* and tell how you determined the word's meaning. Then, check your definition and pronunciation in a dictionary.

CLOSE READ

Reread the excerpt from *The Education of George Washington: How a Forgotten Book Shaped the Character of a Hero.* As you reread, complete the Focus Questions below. Then use your answers and annotations from the questions to help you complete the Writing Prompt.

FOCUS QUESTIONS

1. What point does Austin Washington make in paragraph 3 that helps you understand his point of view about the Friberg painting in paragraph 4? Highlight textual evidence and use the annotation tool to explain your reasoning.

2. Highlight examples of personification used in paragraph 8. Then use the annotation tool to explain how the personification helps you understand what is being described.

3. In paragraphs 4, 8, and 26, how does the author convey his point of view regarding the spirit of the American soldiers at Valley Forge? Highlight textual evidence and make annotations to explain your analysis.

4. In paragraph 13, the author suggests that Baron von Steuben is the perfect person to lead American soldiers in the Revolutionary War because he is "self-made." Highlight textual evidence and make annotations to explain Washington's point of view.

5. According to the author's point of view, in what ways is von Steuben a hero? Highlight textual evidence and make annotations to explain your evaluation.

WRITING PROMPT

In *The Education of George Washington: How a Forgotten Book Shaped the Character of a Hero,* how effectively does the author, Austin Washington, convey his point of view regarding the events at Valley Forge and the role of Baron von Steuben in the American war effort? How do both the presentation of facts and details, as well as the use of figurative language and personification, support the author's point of view? Do you find the author's point of view convincing? Why or why not? How clear and convincing are the reasons and evidence provided by the author? Cite specific evidence from the text to support your own claim or claims in your writing.

Please note that excerpts and passages in the StudySync® library and this workbook are intended as touchstones to generate interest in an author's work. The excerpts and passages do not substitute for the reading of entire texts, and StudySync® strongly recommends that students seek out and purchase the whole literary or informational work in order to experience it as the author intended. Links to online resellers are available in our digital library. In addition, complete works may be ordered through an authorized reseller by filling out and returning to StudySync® the order form enclosed in this workbook.

Reading & Writing Companion   **343**

ELEANOR ROOSEVELT:
A LIFE OF DISCOVERY

NON-FICTION
Russell Freedman
1993

INTRODUCTION

nitially reluctant to be a president's wife, "poor little rich girl" Eleanor Roosevelt rose to the challenge. Bright, energetic and courageous, she became the most celebrated and admired First Lady the White House had ever known. As an invaluable researcher for her husband during the years of the Great Depression, and later a representative of the United Nations, Eleanor raised the bar of possibilities for all First Ladies who followed her.

"She dreaded the prospect of living in the White House."

FIRST READ

NOTES

Excerpt from Chapter One: First Lady

1   Eleanor Roosevelt never wanted to be a president's wife. When her husband Franklin won his campaign for the presidency in 1932, she felt deeply troubled. She dreaded the prospect of living in the White House.

2   Proud of her accomplishments as a teacher, a writer, and a political power in her own right, she feared that she would have to give up her hard-won independence in Washington. As First Lady, she would have no life of her own. Like other presidential wives before her, she would be assigned the traditional role of official White House hostess, with little to do but greet guests at receptions and preside over formal state dinners.

3   "From the personal standpoint, I did not want my husband to be president," she later confessed. "It was pure selfishness on my part, and I never mentioned my feelings on the subject to him."

4   Mrs. Roosevelt did her duty. During her years in the White House, the executive mansion bustled with visitors at teas, receptions, and dinners. At the same time, however, she cast her fears aside and seized the opportunity to transform the role of America's First Lady. Encouraged by her friends, she became the first wife of a president to have a public life and career.

5   Americans had never seen a First Lady like her. She was the first to open the White House door to reporters and hold on-the-record press conferences, the first to drive her own car, to travel by plane, and to make many official trips by herself. "My missus goes where she wants to!" the president boasted.

6   She was the first president's wife to earn her own money by writing, lecturing, and broadcasting. Her earnings usually topped the president's salary. She gave most of the money to charity.

7   When she insisted on her right to take drives by herself, without a chauffeur or a police escort, the Secret Service, worried about her safety, gave her a pistol and begged her to carry it with her. "I [took] it and learned how to use it," she told readers of her popular newspaper column. "I do not mean by this that I am an expert shot. I only wish I were. . . . My opportunities for shooting have been far and few between, but if the necessity arose, I do know how to use a pistol."

8   She had come a long way since her days as an obedient society matron, and, before then, a **timid** child who was "always afraid of something." By her own account, she had been an "ugly duckling" whose mother told her, "You have no looks, so see to it that you have manners." Before she was ten, both of her unhappy parents were dead. She grew up in a time and place where a woman's life was ruled by her husband's interests and needs, and dominated by the domestic duties of wife and mother. "It was not until I reached middle age," she wrote, "that I had the courage to develop interests of my own, outside of my duties to my family."

9   Eleanor Roosevelt lived in the White House during the Great Depression and the Second World War. In her endless travels through America, she served as a fact-finder and trouble-shooter for her husband and an impassioned publicist for her own views about social justice and world peace. She wanted people to feel that their government cared about them. After Franklin Roosevelt's death, she became a major force at the United Nations, where her efforts on behalf of human rights earned her the title, First Lady of the World.

10   People meeting her for the first time often were startled by how "unjustly" the camera treated her. Photographs had not prepared them for her warmth and dignity and **poise.** An unusually tall woman, she moved with the grace of an athlete, and when she walked into a room, the air seemed charged with her **vibrancy.** "No one seeing her could fail to be moved," said her friend Martha Gellhorn. "She gave off light, I cannot explain it better."

11   For thirty years from the time she entered the White House until her death in 1962, Eleanor Roosevelt was the most famous and at times the most **influential** woman in the world. And yet those who knew her best were most impressed by her simplicity, by her total lack of **self-importance**.

12   "About the only value the story of my life may have," she wrote, "is to show that one can, even without any particular gifts, overcome obstacles that seem insurmountable if one is willing to face the fact that they must be overcome; that, in spite of timidity and fear, in spite of a lack of special talents, one can find a way to live widely and fully."

Excerpted from *Eleanor Roosevelt: A Life of Discovery* by Russell Freedman, published by Clarion Books.

 THINK QUESTIONS

1. Use details from the text to write two or three sentences describing how Eleanor Roosevelt expected her life to change when she became First Lady.

2. Write two or three sentences explaining how Eleanor Roosevelt both fulfilled the traditional duties of the First Lady and transformed the role. Support your answer with textual evidence.

3. Refer to one or more details from the text to explain how Eleanor Roosevelt transformed from an "ugly" child to a beautiful adult—both from ideas that are directly stated and ideas that you infer from clues in the text.

4. Use context to determine the meaning of the word **timid** as it is used in *Eleanor Roosevelt: A Life of Discovery*. Write your definition of *timid* and tell how you determined the word's meaning. Then, use a dictionary to check your inferred meaning. Does the dictionary meaning change your understanding of the word?

5. Use context to determine the meaning of the word **poise** as it is used in *Eleanor Roosevelt: A Life of Discovery*. Write your definition of *poise* and tell how you determined it. Then, check your meaning in a dictionary or other reference work. Was your inferred meaning accurate?

Please note that excerpts and passages in the StudySync® library and this workbook are intended as touchstones to generate interest in an author's work. The excerpts and passages do not substitute for the reading of entire texts, and StudySync® strongly recommends that students seek out and purchase the whole literary or informational work in order to experience it as the author intended. Links to online resellers are available in our digital library. In addition, complete works may be ordered through an authorized reseller by filling out and returning to StudySync® the order form enclosed in this workbook.

Reading & Writing Companion   **347**

CLOSE READ

Reread the excerpt from *Eleanor Roosevelt: A Life of Discovery*. As you reread, complete the Focus Questions below. Then use your answers and annotations from the questions to help you complete the Writing Prompt.

FOCUS QUESTIONS

1. In paragraphs 3, 7, 8, and 12, Freedman quotes Eleanor Roosevelt. What might be Freedman's purpose for doing so? Highlight textual evidence and make annotations to explain your analysis.

2. In paragraphs 5 and 10, Freedman quotes others speaking about Eleanor Roosevelt. What might be his purpose for doing so? Support your response with textual evidence and make annotations to explain your analysis.

3. In paragraph 8, the author uses the phrase "ugly duckling" to describe Eleanor Roosevelt as a child. What does the phrase mean? Is it an appropriate description of Roosevelt? Why or why not? What purpose does the author have for including this detail? Highlight your textual evidence and make annotations to explain your analysis.

4. In paragraph 8, Freedman describes Eleanor Roosevelt as "an obedient society matron." In paragraph 9, she is "First Lady of the World." Discuss Freedman's use of the words "matron," and "lady. How does the connotative meaning of each word affect Freedman's description of Roosevelt? Highlight textual evidence and make annotations to support your analysis.

5. In what ways is Eleanor Roosevelt a hero? Highlight textual evidence and make annotations to support your answer.

WRITING PROMPT

Russell Freedman subtitles his biographical portrait of Eleanor Roosevelt "a life of discovery." What does Freedman suggest Eleanor Roosevelt discovered about herself over the course of a lifetime, and what impact do you think her process of self-discovery had on America and the world? Looking to the excerpt from Chapter One, introduce a claim about what Roosevelt discovered about herself, and why Freedman chose to write not just about discovery but also about self-discovery. Support your claim with clear reasons and relevant evidence from the text, including facts, details, and quotations. Organize your information logically and use transitions as needed to clarify relationships among your claim, reasons, and evidence.

ELEANOR ROOSEVELT AND MARIAN ANDERSON

NON-FICTION

Franklin D. Roosevelt Presidential
Library and Museum
2014

INTRODUCTION

Eleanor Roosevelt, First Lady of the United States for 12 years, was an outspoken advocate for social justice. Like many women of her class and background, she belonged to the Daughters of the American Revolution, known as the DAR, a women's organization founded in the nineteenth century to promote American patriotism. Roosevelt's DAR membership came into sharp conflict with her ideals in 1939 when the DAR refused to allow world famous opera singer Marian Anderson to sing in Constitution Hall because Anderson was African American. This web feature by the staff of the FDR Museum and Library describes

"To remain as a member implies approval of that action, therefore I am resigning."

FIRST READ

Eleanor Roosevelt first met African American **contralto** opera singer Marian Anderson in 1935 when the singer was invited to perform at the White House.

1 Ms. Anderson had performed throughout Europe to great praise, and after the White House concert the singer focused her attentions on a lengthy concert tour of the United States. Beginning in 1936, Anderson sang an annual concert to benefit the Howard University School of Music in Washington, DC. These benefit concerts were so successful that each year larger and larger **venues** had to be found.

2 In January 1939, Howard University petitioned the Daughters of the American Revolution (DAR) to use its Washington, DC auditorium called Constitution Hall for a concert to be scheduled over Easter weekend that year. Constitution Hall was built in the late 1920s to house the DAR's national headquarters and host its annual conventions. It seated 4,000 people, and was the largest auditorium in the capital. As such, it was the center of the city's fine arts and music events universe.

3 However, in 1939, Washington, DC was still a racially segregated city, and the DAR was an all-white heritage association that promoted an aggressive form of American patriotism. As part of the original funding arrangements for Constitution Hall, major donors had insisted that only whites could perform on stage. This unwritten white-performers-only policy was enforced against African American singer/actor Paul Robeson in 1930. Additionally, blacks who attended events there were seated in a segregated section of the Hall.

4 The organizers of Marian Anderson's 1939 concert hoped that Anderson's fame and reputation would encourage the DAR to make an exception to its restrictive policy. But the request was denied anyway, and despite pressure from the press, other great artists, politicians, and a new organization called

Copyright © BookheadEd Learning, LLC

NOTES

the Marian Anderson Citizens Committee (MACC), the DAR held fast and continued to deny Anderson use of the Hall.

5   As the controversy grew, First Lady Eleanor Roosevelt carefully weighed the most effective manner to protest the DAR's decision. Mrs. Roosevelt had been issued a DAR membership card only after the 1932 election swept her husband Franklin Roosevelt into the presidency. As such, she was not an active member of the DAR. She initially chose not to challenge the DAR directly because, as she explained, the group considered her to be "too radical" and "this situation is so bad that plenty of people will come out against it."

6   Rather, Mrs. Roosevelt first led by **enlightened** example. She agreed to present the Spingarn Medal to Marian Anderson at the upcoming national convention of the National Association for the Advancement of Colored People (NAACP). And she invited Anderson to again perform at the White House, this time for the King and Queen of England when they came to the United States later in the year. But as the weeks went on, Mrs. Roosevelt grew increasingly frustrated that more active DAR members than she were not challenging the group's policy.

Roosevelt Resigns from the DAR

7   On February 26, 1939, Mrs. Roosevelt submitted her letter of **resignation** to the DAR president, declaring that the organization had "set an example which seems to me unfortunate" and that the DAR had "an opportunity to lead in an enlightened way" but had "failed to do so." That same day, she sent a telegram to an officer of the Marian Anderson Citizens Committee publicly expressing for the first time her disappointment that Anderson was being denied a concert venue.

8   On February 27, Mrs. Roosevelt addressed the issue in her *My Day* column, published in newspapers across the country. Without mentioning the DAR or Anderson by name, Mrs. Roosevelt couched her decision in terms everyone could understand: whether one should resign from an organization you disagree with or remain and try to change it from within. Mrs. Roosevelt told her readers that in this situation, "To remain as a member implies approval of that action, therefore I am resigning."

Groundbreaking 1939 Lincoln Memorial Concert

9   Mrs. Roosevelt's resignation thrust the Marian Anderson concert, the DAR, and the subject of racism to the center of national attention. As word of her resignation spread, Mrs. Roosevelt and others quietly worked behind the scenes promoting the idea for an outdoor concert at the Lincoln Memorial, a symbolic site on the National Mall overseen by the Department of the Interior.

10   Interior Secretary Harold Ickes, himself a past president of the Chicago NAACP, was excited about such a display of democracy, and he met with President Roosevelt to obtain his approval. After the President gave his assent, Ickes announced on March 30th that Marian Anderson would perform at the Lincoln Memorial on Easter Sunday.

11   Fearing that she might upstage Anderson's triumphant moment, Mrs. Roosevelt chose not to be publicly associated with the sponsorship of the concert. Indeed, she did not even attend, citing the burdens of a nationwide lecture tour and the forthcoming birth of a grandchild. However, she and others lobbied the various radio networks to broadcast the concert to the nation.

12   On April 9th, seventy-five thousand people, including dignitaries and average citizens, attended the outdoor concert. It was as diverse a crowd as anyone had seen—black, white, old, and young—dressed in their Sunday finest. Hundreds of thousands more heard the concert over the radio. After being introduced by Secretary Ickes who declared that "Genius knows no color line," Ms. Anderson opened her concert with *America*. The operatic first half of the program concluded with *Ave Maria*. After a short intermission, she then sang a selection of spirituals familiar to the African American members of her audience. And with tears in her eyes, Marian Anderson closed the concert with an encore, *Nobody Knows the Trouble I've Seen*.

13   The DAR's refusal to grant Marian Anderson the use of Constitution Hall, Eleanor Roosevelt's resignation from the DAR in protest, and the resulting concert at the Lincoln Memorial combined into a **watershed** moment in civil rights history, bringing national attention to the country's color barrier as no other event had previously done.

14   Mrs. Roosevelt and Marian Anderson remained friends for the rest of Mrs. Roosevelt's life. Marian Anderson continued to sing in venues around the world, including singing the National Anthem at President Kennedy's inauguration in 1961. She died in 1993 at the age of 96.

"Eleanor Roosevelt and Marian Anderson", Franklin D. Roosevelt Presidential Library and Museum, http://www.fdrlibrary.marist.edu/

THINK QUESTIONS

1. Refer to one or more details from the text to explain why organizers at Howard University wanted to use Constitution Hall as a venue for Marian Anderson's annual benefit concert.

2. Use details from the text to write two or three sentences explaining why the Daughters of the American Revolution refused to allow Marian Anderson to perform at Constitution Hall.

3. Explain the strategies that Eleanor Roosevelt used to support Marian Anderson and bring national attention to the country's color barrier. Support your answer by citing textual evidence and making inferences.

4. Use context to determine the meaning of the word **venues** as it is used in "Eleanor Roosevelt and Marian Anderson." Write your definition of *venues* and tell how you determined the word's meaning. Then use a dictionary to determine the precise definition and pronunciation of the word.

5. Use context clues provided in the passage to determine the meaning of the word **enlightened**. Write your definition of *enlightened* and tell how you determined the word's meaning. Then use a dictionary to determine the precise definition and pronunciation of the word.

Please note that excerpts and passages in the StudySync® library and this workbook are intended as touchstones to generate interest in an author's work. The excerpts and passages do not substitute for the reading of entire texts, and StudySync® strongly recommends that students seek out and purchase the whole literary or informational work in order to experience it as the author intended. Links to online resellers are available in our digital library. In addition, complete works may be ordered through an authorized reseller by filling out and returning to StudySync® the order form enclosed in this workbook.

Reading & Writing
Companion

353

CLOSE READ

Reread the text "Eleanor Roosevelt and Marian Anderson." As you read, complete the Focus Questions below. Then use your answers and annotations from the questions to help you complete the Writing Prompt.

FOCUS QUESTIONS

Questions 1, 2, and 4 ask you to use documents located on the web. Ask your teacher for URLs to find these documents.

1. Reread paragraphs 5–7 of "Eleanor Roosevelt and Marian Anderson" and reread Eleanor Roosevelt's DAR resignation letter. Compare and contrast Roosevelt's response to the event as described in both media. How does each medium inform the other? Highlight textual evidence in paragraph 5 through 7 and annotate ideas from the letter to show the development of your understanding.

2. Read Mrs. Roosevelt's newspaper column "My Day". How does the column illustrate the claim that the article makes in paragraph 8. "Mrs. Roosevelt couched her decision in terms everyone could understand"? What information do you learn from the column about Mrs. Roosevelt's persuasive techniques? Highlight textual evidence in paragraph 8 and annotate ideas from the column to show the development of your understanding of enlightened leadership.

3. What additional information can a reader gain about Eleanor Roosevelt's character from reading about her decision to resign from the DAR in paragraphs 3 and 4 of the "My Day" column that can't be gained from the article? Highlight textual evidence and make annotations to show your understanding.

4. View the video from the Lincoln Memorial concert. Compare the video to the details in the article about the event. As a reader, what did you visualize about the scene? How did this visualization compare with what you viewed in the video? How does viewing the video contribute to your understanding of the event you read about in the text? Highlight textual evidence in paragraph 12 and annotate ideas from the video to support your ideas.

5. In what ways are Eleanor Roosevelt and Marian Anderson heroes? Highlight textual evidence and make annotations to explain your ideas.

WRITING PROMPT

By integrating the information presented in the primary and secondary sources as well as the audio file, you may develop a coherent understanding of Eleanor Roosevelt's resignation from the DAR and the events that followed. Compare and contrast the secondary authors' presentation of events with the primary sources from Roosevelt herself. Which details are emphasized or absent in each medium? What are the possible reasons behind these choices? How does each source contribute to your understanding of the issue? Support your writing with textual evidence.

Please note that excerpts and passages in the StudySync® library and this workbook are intended as touchstones to generate interest in an author's work. The excerpts and passages do not substitute for the reading of entire texts, and StudySync® strongly recommends that students seek out and purchase the whole literary or informational work in order to experience it as the author intended. Links to online resellers are available in our digital library. In addition, complete works may be ordered through an authorized reseller by filling out and returning to StudySync® the order form enclosed in this workbook.

Reading & Writing
Companion

355

MY FATHER IS A SIMPLE MAN

POETRY
Luis Omar Salinas
1987

INTRODUCTION

Luis Omar Salinas was a highly regarded Mexican American poet. Considered one of the founding founders of Chicano poetry in America, Salinas worked alongside other well-known poets like Gary Soto to produce works that have inspired generations of Chicanos. In the words of Soto, Salinas possessed "a powerful imagination, a sensitivity to the world, and an intuitive feel for handling language." In "My Father Is a Simple Man," which comes from Salinas's work, *The Sadness of Days: Selected and New Poems*, the speaker of the poem honors a

"He has taken me on this journey and it's been lifelong."

 FIRST READ

 NOTES

1 I walk to town with my father
2 to buy a newspaper. He walks slower
3 than I do so I must slow up.
4 The street is filled with children.
5 We argue about the price of **pomegranates.** I convince
6 him it is the fruit of **scholars.**
7 He has taken me on this journey
8 and it's been lifelong.
9 He's sure I'll be healthy
10 so long as I eat more oranges,
11 and tells me the orange
12 has seeds and so is **perpetual;**
13 and we too will come back
14 like the orange trees.
15 I ask him what he thinks
16 about death and he says
17 he will gladly face it when
18 it comes but won't jump
19 out in front of a car.
20 I'd gladly give my life
21 for this man with a sixth
22 grade education, whose kindness
23 and patience are true. . .
24 The truth of it is, he's the scholar,
25 and when the bitter-hard reality
26 comes at me like a punishing
27 evil stranger, I can always
28 remember that here was a man
29 who was a worker and provider,
30 who learned the simple facts
31 in life and lived by them,

Please note that excerpts and passages in the StudySync® library and this workbook are intended as touchstones to generate interest in an author's work. The excerpts and passages do not substitute for the reading of entire texts, and StudySync® strongly recommends that students seek out and purchase the whole literary or informational work in order to experience it as the author intended. Links to online resellers are available in our digital library. In addition, complete works may be ordered through an authorized reseller by filling out and returning to StudySync® the order form enclosed in this workbook.

Reading & Writing Companion   **357**

32 who held no **pretense.**
33 And when he leaves without
34 benefit of **fanfare** or applause
35 I shall have learned what little
36 there is about greatness.

"My Father Is a Simple Man" is reprinted with permission from the publisher of "The Sadness of Days: Selected and New Poems" by Luis Omar Salinas (© 1987 Arte Público Press–University of Houston).

THINK QUESTIONS

1. Refer to one or more details from the text to explain the disagreement between the speaker and his father over fruit. Base your answer both on evidence that is directly stated and ideas that you infer from clues in the text.

2. Use textual evidence to write three or four sentences that establish the father's age.

3. Use details from the text to explain how the speaker's use of the word *scholar* changes between lines 6 and 24.

4. Use context to determine the meaning of the word **perpetual** as it is used in "My Father Is a Simple Man." Write your definition of *perpetual* and tell how you determined the word's meaning.

5. The French word *fanfarer* means "to blow trumpets." Use this root meaning and the context clues provided in the passage to determine the meaning of **fanfare.** Write your definition of *fanfare* and tell how you determined the word's meaning.

CLOSE READ

Reread the poem "My Father Is a Simple Man." As you reread, complete the Focus Questions below. Then use your answers and annotations from the questions to help you complete the Writing Prompt.

FOCUS QUESTIONS

1. In lines 11–12, 15–19, 20, and 33, how does the speaker make death one theme of the poem? What is his message regarding death? Highlight evidence from the text and make annotations to explain your analysis.

2. In lines 1 and 29, how does the speaker make family one theme of the poem? What is his message regarding family? Support your answer with textual evidence and make annotations to explain your analysis.

3. Note that Salinas structures his poem as a single free verse stanza. Remember that free verse describes poetry that does not rhyme or have a regular rhythm or meter. How does this poetic structure contribute to the development of the poem's theme? Highlight your textual evidence and make annotations to explain your analysis.

4. Listen to the audio reading of lines 20 through 26. How does the speaker use pacing, guided by the ellipsis in the print text, to show a new understanding of his father? Highlight textual evidence in the lines and annotate ideas from the audio recording to show the development of your understanding of media techniques.

5. In what ways is the speaker's father a hero? Highlight textual evidence and make annotations to explain your ideas.

6. Use your understanding of the theme of the poem to summarize the speaker's feelings about his father. Highlight textual evidence and make annotations to explain your ideas.

WRITING PROMPT

The poem "My Father Is a Simple Man" ends with the speaker saying that he will "have learned what little/ there is about greatness" when his father dies. What has the speaker learned about greatness from his father? Do you agree with the speaker that greatness is a topic about which there is "little" to learn? Why or why not? Use your understanding of theme and poetic structure to analyze the message of the poem. Support the ideas you express in your response to the literature with textual evidence, including details, descriptions, and quotations from the poem.

Please note that excerpts and passages in the StudySync® library and this workbook are intended as touchstones to generate interest in an author's work. The excerpts and passages do not substitute for the reading of entire texts, and StudySync® strongly recommends that students seek out and purchase the whole literary or informational work in order to experience it as the author intended. Links to online resellers are available in our digital library. In addition, complete works may be ordered through an authorized reseller by filling out and returning to StudySync® the order form enclosed in this workbook.

Reading & Writing
Companion

359

EXTENDED WRITING PROJECT

StudySync

WRITE

Extended Writing Project Prompt and Directions:
Every day the media run headlines celebrating heroes amon...
charges into the burning building to save an infant is a hero...
life to help patients with infectious diseases—she's a hero to...
have in common? What makes one person more heroic than...

In this unit, you have been reading both nonfiction and fiction...
considered American heroes—George Washington, Eleanor Roos...
Freedom Walkers, Dr. Benjamin Rush, Gulf War soldiers.

Recognizing that not everyone agrees on what it means to be a hero or who our heroes are,
write an argumentative essay that identifies an individual from the selections in this unit
who you feel best exemplifies the qualities of a hero.

To support your ideas you will include textual evidence from at least one selection in unit 4
and research from three other print or digital sources.

Your argumentative essay with research should include:

- an explicitly stated claim about the individual who you think is the most heroic
- a logically organized argument supported by persuasive reasons and relevant textual evidence
- information from one unit text and at least three print or digital sources
- citations of your sources and a works cited page
- a conclusion that restates your claim, sums up your evidence, and leaves your readers with an original thought about the topic

ASSIGNMENT

EXTENDED WRITING PROJECT
ARGUMENTATIVE WRITING

Extended Writing Project:
Argumentative Essay
by StudySync

1 WRITE

NOTES

ARGUMENTATIVE WRITING

WRITING PROMPT

Every day the media runs headlines celebrating heroes among us. The firefighter who charges into the burning building to save an infant is a hero. The nurse who risks her own life to help patients with infectious diseases—she's a hero too. What qualities do all heroes have in common? What makes one person more heroic than another?

In this unit, you have been reading both non-fiction and fiction texts about people who are considered American heroes—George Washington, Eleanor Roosevelt, Rosa Parks, the Freedom Walkers, Dr. Benjamin Rush, Gulf War soldiers.

Recognizing that not everyone agrees on what it means to be a hero or who our heroes are, write an argumentative essay that identifies an individual from the selections in this unit who you feel best exemplifies the qualities of a hero.

To support your ideas you will include textual evidence from at least one selection in unit 4 and research from three other print or digital sources.

Your argumentative essay with research should include:

- an explicitly stated claim about the individual who you think is the most heroic
- a logically organized argument supported by persuasive reasons and relevant textual evidence
- information from one unit text and at least three other print or digital sources

Please note that excerpts and passages in the StudySync® library and this workbook are intended as touchstones to generate interest in an author's work. The excerpts and passages do not substitute for the reading of entire texts, and StudySync® strongly recommends that students seek out and purchase the whole literary or informational work in order to experience it as the author intended. Links to online resellers are available in our digital library. In addition, complete works may be ordered through an authorized reseller by filling out and returning to StudySync® the order form enclosed in this workbook.

Reading & Writing Companion   **361**

WRITING PROMPT

- citations of your sources and a Works Cited page
- a conclusion that restates your claim, sums up your reasons and evidence, and leaves your readers with an original thought about the topic

An **argumentative essay** is a form of persuasive writing. The writer's job is to make a claim about a topic, present logical reasons for making the claim, and then provide evidence—facts, details, and quotations—to support the claim. After first introducing the claim, the writer develops his or her ideas in the body of the argument, maintaining a formal style and using transitions to link related ideas. The purpose of the argument is for the writer to convince readers that his or her claim is valid. After presenting all the evidence to support his or her claim, the writer provides a concluding statement that follows from the argument presented.

In order to provide convincing supporting evidence, the writer must often do outside research, either because it is assigned or because it is essential to understanding a complex topic. That means the writer looks at print or digital sources of information related to the topic—books, articles, Web pages, diaries, letters, interviews, and other documents—and incorporates the information he or she finds into the argument. The writer cites these sources so that readers know where the supporting evidence was found and can confirm credibility. (In later Extended Writing Project Lessons, you will learn more about how to research a topic, including selecting appropriate material, effectively incorporating your research, and citing your sources.)

The features of an argumentative essay include:

- an introduction that states a claim, or an opinion, about the topic
- reasons and evidence that support the claim or claims
- a logical organizational structure with clear transitions
- embedded quotations from credible sources that are clearly cited
- a formal style that is maintained throughout the essay
- a concluding statement that follows from the argument presented

As you continue working on this Extended Writing Project, you'll learn more about crafting each of the elements of an argumentative essay with research.

STUDENT MODEL

Before you get started on your own argumentative essay, begin by reading one that a student wrote in response to the writing prompt. As you read this Student Model, highlight and annotate the features of an argumentative essay that the student included.

Rosa Parks: A True American Hero

Who is a hero? Many people might think that heroes have special powers and can save the world. But the superheroes we see in blockbuster movies and on TV are make-believe, and fighting monsters and stopping meteors are not real-life problems. As many of the selections in this unit show, true heroes live in the real world, take risks, and act as role models. For example, George Washington led a rebel army because he believed in an independent United States. Eleanor Roosevelt voiced the concerns of the poor during the Great Depression.

Both Washington and Roosevelt, who are considered heroes for good reasons, were also important leaders of their time. Washington was a general in the Continental Army and later president of the United States. Roosevelt was the First Lady of the United States. While they each had to confront huge obstacles, they were already respected citizens when they took up their causes. Rosa Parks, however, was an ordinary woman when she courageously refused to give up her bus seat and so changed American history. In defying authorities and the law, she committed an incredibly brave and even dangerous act. She did so with determination, grace, and dignity. The consequences of Parks's action—her arrest—and the African American community's response to it, helped launch the civil rights movement. This movement would make the United States a fairer place for everyone. Because, as an ordinary woman, she took great risks and acted peacefully and bravely on behalf of herself and others, I think she is the greatest hero we have read about in unit 4.

It's clear that Parks knew what she might face if she didn't obey the law. African Americans who defied the laws of segregation could face potential violence. As a child living in the South, she had seen her grandfather prepare to defend his family against the Ku Klux Klan ("Remembering Rosa Parks"). As an adult living in the segregated city of Montgomery, Alabama, in 1955, Parks understood the dangers of disobeying bus segregation policies. Civil rights leader Reverend

Joseph Lowery explained the possibilities in a 2005 interview: "The buses were particularly vicious in their policies . . . and it was especially humiliating to all the citizen[s] of Montgomery" ("Remembering Rosa Parks"). According to Parks's obituary in the *New York Times*, African Americans "had been arrested, even killed, for disobeying bus drivers" (Shipp). Indeed, her bravery surely was fed in part by anger and frustration that had built up over the years. As she wrote in her autobiography, she never considered obeying the bus driver: "I could not see how standing up was going to 'make it light' for me. The more we gave in and complied, the worse [whites] treated us" (Parks). Because of this history and her personal feelings, Parks decided to take action.

After her arrest, Parks continued to show great courage. She says she 'wasn't afraid," and yet she must have felt some fear (Parks). She knew that there was no guarantee she would get through the experience without physical harm. As a result, Parks really had a terrible choice to make: continuing to be treated as a second-class citizen or risking her freedom and perhaps even her life to reject segregation. She chose not to surrender to injustice.

What happened next was amazing, and it changed the course of American history. Parks's arrest did not go unnoticed. Congresswoman Eleanor Holmes Norton later called it "a quiet revolutionary act" that inspired a city and then a nation ("Remembering Rosa Parks"). Parks was "convicted of violating segregation laws and fined $4 in court fees" (Shipp). The law said Parks was in the wrong. However, more than 40,000 African Americans in Montgomery thought otherwise, and they took action. They did not react violently, but instead engaged in civil disobedience. In other words, they took lawful and peaceful steps toward making their voices heard. They struck back at the bus company by boycotting, or refusing to ride, the buses for 381 days (Shipp). The boycott was a great hardship for the people, but by not paying to ride buses, the African American community made its point.

During this time, lawyers contested bus segregation in court. The case went all the way to the Supreme Court, which finally banned segregation throughout the United States. So thanks to Rosa Parks, African Americans could ride a bus and sit wherever they chose without being harassed. According to Reverend Lowery, Parks's refusal to move her seat on a bus "triggered the greatest revolution in American history in terms of nonviolent protest against segregation and discrimination" ("Remembering Rosa Parks"). The movement she inspired caused many Americans to go on to fight peacefully, by way of marches and sit-ins, for African American voting rights and other social justice causes.

In standing up against a powerful segregated society, Rosa Parks reminded all Americans what equality means. In her autobiography, she summed up why she refused to move from her seat on the bus: "People always say that I didn't give up my seat because I was tired, but that isn't true . . . No, the only tired I was, was tired of giving in" (Parks). She channeled her anger peacefully. She took a huge risk and still maintained her dignity, serving as a model for others. I think in the end she made this country a better place to live for all people. Because of her efforts, among all the heroic men and women we have read about, she deserves to be honored as one of the greatest of American heroes.

Works Cited

Parks, Rosa, and James Haskins. *Rosa Parks: My Story*. New York: Dial Books, 1990. Print.

"Remembering Rosa Parks." PBS Newshour. 25 Oct. 2005. Web. 12 Dec. 2014. <http://www.pbs.org/newshour/bb/social_issues-july-dec05-parks_10-25>

Shipp, E.R. "Rosa Parks, 92, Founding Symbol of Civil Rights Movement, Dies." *New York Times*. 25 Oct. 2005. Web. 12 Dec. 2014. <http://www.nytimes.com/2005/10/25/us/25parks.html>

"Today in History: December 1." *The Library of Congress*. Web. 12 Dec. 2014 <http://memory.loc.gov/ammem/today/dec01.html>

Please note that excerpts and passages in the StudySync® library and this workbook are intended as touchstones to generate interest in an author's work. The excerpts and passages do not substitute for the reading of entire texts, and StudySync® strongly recommends that students seek out and purchase the whole literary or informational work in order to experience it as the author intended. Links to online resellers are available in our digital library. In addition, complete works may be ordered through an authorized reseller by filling out and returning to StudySync® the order form enclosed in this workbook.

Reading & Writing Companion   **365**

THINK QUESTIONS

1. The writer of the Student Model stated a claim about one of the individuals he or she read about in the unit. What is the writer's opinion about this person? What reason or reasons does the writer give? Where in the second paragraph of the Model did the writer state this claim and reasons?

2. What relevant textual evidence did the writer include in the Student Model to support his or her claim? Explain why the evidence is relevant.

3. Write two or three sentences evaluating the writer's conclusion in relation to the essay's claim, reasons, and evidence.

4. Thinking about the writing prompt, which selections or other resources would you like to use to write your own argumentative essay? What are some of the selections that you may want to consider as you think about which individual is the greatest hero?

5. Based on the selections you have read, listened to, or researched, how would you answer the question, *What does it mean to be a hero*? What are some ideas that you might consider in the argument you'll be developing?

PREWRITE

WRITING PROMPT

Every day the media runs headlines celebrating heroes among us. The firefighter who charges into the burning building to save an infant is a hero. The nurse who risks her own life to help patients with infectious diseases—she's a hero too. What qualities do all heroes have in common? What makes one person more heroic than another?

In this unit, you have been reading both non-fiction and fiction texts about people who are considered American heroes—George Washington, Eleanor Roosevelt, Rosa Parks, the Freedom Walkers, Dr. Benjamin Rush, Gulf War soldiers.

Recognizing that not everyone agrees on what it means to be a hero or who our heroes are, write an argumentative essay that identifies an individual from the selections in this unit who you feel best exemplifies the qualities of a hero.

To support your ideas you will include textual evidence from at least one selection in unit 4 and research from three other print or digital sources.

Your argumentative essay with research should include:

- an explicitly stated claim about the individual who you think is the most heroic
- a logically organized argument supported by persuasive reasons and relevant textual evidence
- information from one unit text and at least three other print or digital sources

Please note that excerpts and passages in the StudySync® library and this workbook are intended as touchstones to generate interest in an author's work. The excerpts and passages do not substitute for the reading of entire texts, and StudySync® strongly recommends that students seek out and purchase the whole literary or informational work in order to experience it as the author intended. Links to online resellers are available in our digital library. In addition, complete works may be ordered through an authorized reseller by filling out and returning to StudySync® the order form enclosed in this workbook.

Reading & Writing
Companion

367

WRITING PROMPT

- citations of your sources and a Works Cited page
- a conclusion that restates your claim, sums up your reasons and evidence, and leaves your readers with an original thought about the topic

Your first step—even before you start thinking about the person or group from the unit that you will write about—is to define what a hero is. Now is the time to start thinking about the qualities of a hero. You can use any of the prewriting strategies you have learned, including list making, brainstorming, freewriting, concept mapping, sketching, and so on. Begin by writing this sentence starter at the top of a blank sheet of paper: "I think a hero is someone who . . . ." Then fill the page with your ideas. You can jot words or phrases or draw pictures. After you have thought about what a hero is, write a complete sentence at the bottom of the page. Here's what the writer of the Student Model wrote: "I think a hero is someone who takes risks in order to make the world a better place to live."

Now flip over your sheet of paper. Use the back to answer these questions about the people you read about in the unit. As you answer the questions, think about your ideas about heroism. You can add your own questions to the list below, too.

- Which person from the unit was the bravest? What did he or she do that was brave? Did he or she feel brave at the time?
- Which person from the unit made the greatest sacrifice? What did he or she give up? Why?
- Which person from the unit did the most to make the world a better place to live? Give an example of that person's actions.
- Which person from the unit do I admire most? Why?

Look at the answers to your questions. Did you mention one person from the unit more than any other? Does that person exemplify your ideas about heroism? If so, you might have found the person who will be the topic of your argumentative essay.

Once you have identified your topic, the next step is to make a list of research questions. You want to ask questions that will lead you to evidence that supports your claim. The answers you uncover during your research will help you build an effective argument.

Copyright © BookheadEd Learning, LLC

Use a graphic organizer like this one to help you get started with your own research. It shows some of the research questions that the writer of the Student Model asked about Rosa Parks. Notice how the student's questions try to get beyond the basic *who, what, where, when,* and *how questions.* The questions ask about how Parks felt, what she was thinking, and what kind of impact she had on the world. The questions show that the writer is trying to figure out why Parks was a heroic figure.

As you write your own questions in the left-hand column, think about the possible sources you might consult—history books, encyclopedia articles, news articles, memoirs, interviews, Web pages—for the answers. List the possible sources in the other column. (Later in the writing process, you can add a third column for the answers you find as you research your questions.)

Topic: Rosa Parks

Claim: Rosa Parks is a hero because she took serious risks to help make the world a fairer place for everyone.

RESEARCH QUESTIONS	POSSIBLE SOURCES
Why do most people consider Rosa Parks to be a hero?	history books, books and articles about the civil rights movement, Web pages
What risks did Rosa Parks face in refusing to give up her seat on a bus?	autobiography/memoir, interviews, civil rights memoirs and histories, newspaper articles
Why did Rosa Parks disobey the bus driver?	autobiography/memoir, interviews, history books
What impact did Rosa Parks's action have on history?	history books, encyclopedia articles, newspaper articles, news analyses
What are civil disobedience and the civil rights movement?	American history books, encyclopedia articles
What happened to Rosa Parks after she was arrested? After segregation was outlawed?	autobiography/memoir, interviews, history books
What was Rosa Parks really like as a person?	autobiography/memoir, interviews, history books

Please note that excerpts and passages in the StudySync® library and this workbook are intended as touchstones to generate interest in an author's work. The excerpts and passages do not substitute for the reading of entire texts, and StudySync® strongly recommends that students seek out and purchase the whole literary or informational work in order to experience it as the author intended. Links to online resellers are available in our digital library. In addition, complete works may be ordered through an authorized reseller by filling out and returning to StudySync® the order form enclosed in this workbook.

Reading & Writing Companion **369**

NOTES

SKILL:
RESEARCH
AND
NOTE-TAKING

 ## DEFINE

If you have already completed the Research presentations for previous units or have been working on a Research presentation for this unit, you have already learned something about how to do research. **Research** is how you find new information or double-check facts or ideas that you don't know for sure. Research can be as straightforward as checking a word's meaning in the dictionary or as challenging as trying a new activity to get first-hand experience.

Unless you have a perfect memory (and few of us do), **note-taking** is essential to good research. Each time you check a source, you should take notes. A **source** might be a textbook, a newspaper article, a website, a dictionary, or an authority on a subject. Your **notes** should include the title of the source, its author's name, its date of publication, and any information and ideas you learned from it relevant to your research.

Why do you need all this in your notes? You might need to go back later to double-check a fact. You also need this information in order to prepare citations and a Works Cited section in your writing. Finally, your readers can use the information about your sources to do their own research.

Remember your purpose for doing research. In this unit, you are writing an argumentative essay. The point of your research is to find facts, details, and quotations that help support your claim about your topic.

 ## IDENTIFICATION AND APPLICATION

- Your topic might be one that's assigned or one that you choose. Before you start your research, ask, *What don't I know about the topic?*
- Keep in mind questions you asked during prewriting as you think about your topic and do research. More questions should come up as you

research to help you determine what you really need to know and want to say.

- Enter specific keywords and phrases when researching online. You will likely have to experiment with the words and phrases in order to find accurate and reliable sources.

- Think about the accuracy and reliability of your sources. To choose sources carefully:

  › Look for reputable sources, such as fact-based newspapers, magazines, and academic journals.

  › Try to stick to educational and government websites (those ending in .*edu* and .*gov*).

- Remember the difference between primary sources (firsthand accounts) and secondary sources (secondhand accounts).

  › Autobiographies, journals, diaries, letters, interviews, and memoirs are primary sources.

  › Textbooks, encyclopedias articles, history books, and most newspaper articles are secondary sources.

- Stay focused when you take notes. To stay focused:

  › Look for the answers to your research questions.

  › Think about your purpose and audience.

  › Don't get distracted by irrelevant information.

- Take careful notes. If you prefer to write your notes on index cards, use one card for each source:

  › Be sure to include the title, author, and publication information on the card.

  › Number multiple cards for the same source in order.

- You can take notes digitally using note-taking apps, software, or a word processing program. To take digital notes using a word processing program, do the following:

  › Open a new document for each source.

  › At the top of the page, identify the title, author, and publication information.

  › Use bullets or new paragraphs for each new set of facts and information.

- If they are available, as in a book, include page numbers in your notes so you can remember where you found specific items of information.

- If you want to quote a source, write down the words exactly as they appear in the source and place them within quotation marks. Be sure to credit the source.

- Sometimes you might want to restate or paraphrase in your own words the ideas and words from a source. But you still must cite the original source so that readers know where you got the information.

- Cite your sources very carefully to avoid plagiarizing, or presenting other people's words and ideas as your own. Here's a rule of thumb: Anytime you use information from a researched source, give the writer credit.

 MODEL

Consider the following paragraph from the Student Model essay "Rosa Parks: A True American Hero":

> What happened next was amazing and **it changed the course of American history.** Parks's arrest did not go unnoticed. **Congresswoman Eleanor Holmes Norton later called it "a quiet revolutionary act"** that inspired a city and then a nation ("Remembering Rosa Parks"). Parks was **"convicted of violating segregation laws and fined $4 in court fees"** (Shipp). The law said Parks was in the wrong. However, more than 40,000 African Americans in Montgomery thought otherwise, and they took action. They did not react violently, but instead engaged in civil disobedience. In other words, they took lawful and peaceful steps toward making their voices heard. **Then they struck back at the bus company by boycotting, or refusing to ride, the buses for 381 days** (Shipp). The boycott was a great hardship for the people, but by not paying to ride buses, the African American community made its point.

Notice the research that the writer has included and the purpose it serves. After learning more about Parks from reading different sources, the writer decided to say that Parks's act helped "change the course of American history." To support this idea with evidence, the writer quotes a congresswoman, someone the writer discovered in the course of doing research. The congresswoman called what Parks did "a quiet revolutionary act," a comment that affirms the writer's own statement that history was changed. The writer tells readers the name of the congresswoman who made the remark and provides a parenthetical citation: ("Remembering Rosa Parks"). A quick glance at the Works Cited tells readers that the source is a reliable news program's website (*PBS Newshour,* at www.pbs.org). Later in the paragraph, the writer quotes from and also paraphrases information from Rosa Parks's obituary in the *New York Times,* written by E.R. Shipp. The writer has cited this source several times throughout the essay, so he or she does not need to introduce it every time.

PRACTICE

Research a quotation about the person you will be discussing in your essay on heroism. Write down the quotation exactly as it appears in the source. Then for practice, restate the quotation in your own words and cite its source. As always, record the source's title, author, date, and publication information in your notes.

Please note that excerpts and passages in the StudySync® library and this workbook are intended as touchstones to generate interest in an author's work. The excerpts and passages do not substitute for the reading of entire texts, and StudySync® strongly recommends that students seek out and purchase the whole literary or informational work in order to experience it as the author intended. Links to online resellers are available in our digital library. In addition, complete works may be ordered through an authorized reseller by filling out and returning to StudySync® the order form enclosed in this workbook.

Reading & Writing
Companion

373

SKILL: THESIS STATEMENT

DEFINE

The thesis of an argumentative essay takes the form of a claim. A claim is the writer's opinion about the topic of the essay. It is a statement of position, belief, or judgment. A claim might be introduced with certain phrases that make the writer's point of view clear, such as "I believe...," "I think...," "We should...," or "One must..." An opinion cannot be proven to be true, but it can be supported with relevant evidence—facts, statistics, quotations from experts, examples, and so on. The claim of an argument typically appears in the introductory section, often as the last sentence.

IDENTIFICATION AND APPLICATION

A thesis statement or claim in an argumentative essay:

- states an opinion about the topic of the essay
- previews the ideas and evidence that will be presented in the body paragraphs of the essay
- gets stated in the introductory section, which usually consists of one paragraph but may consist of two. You will learn more about crafting an introductory section in a later Extended Writing Project lesson.

MODEL

The following are the two introductory paragraphs from the Student Model argumentative essay, "Rosa Parks: A True American Hero":

Who is a hero? Many people might think that heroes have special powers and can save the world. But the superheroes we see in blockbuster movies and on TV are make-believe, and fighting monsters and stopping meteors

Copyright © BookheadEd Learning, LLC

are not real-life problems. As many of the selections in this unit show, true heroes live in the real world, take risks, and act as role models. For example, George Washington led a rebel army because he believed in an independent United States. Eleanor Roosevelt voiced the concerns of the poor during the Great Depression.

Both Washington and Roosevelt, who are considered heroes for good reasons, were also important leaders of their time. Washington was a general in the Continental Army and later president of the United States. Roosevelt was the First Lady of the United States. While they each had to confront huge obstacles, they were already respected citizens when they took up their causes. Rosa Parks, however, was an ordinary woman when she courageously refused to give up her bus seat and so changed American history. In defying authorities and the law, she committed an incredibly brave and even dangerous act. She did so with determination, grace, and dignity. The consequences of Parks's action—her arrest—and the African American community's response to it, helped launch the civil rights movement, which would make the United States a fairer place for everyone. **Because, as an ordinary woman, she took great risks and acted peacefully and bravely on behalf of herself and others, I think she is the greatest hero we have read about in unit 4.**

Notice the boldfaced claim at the end of the essay's second paragraph. This student's claim responds to the writing prompt by identifying the individual from the unit who the writer thinks best exemplifies the qualities of a hero. By using the words "I think," the writer makes clear that the thesis or claim expresses an opinion. Notice how the writer previews the ideas to be discussed in the body of the paper. He or she will present evidence to support the idea that Rosa Parks "took great risks and acted peacefully and bravely on behalf of herself and others."

 PRACTICE

Write a thesis statement in the form of a claim for your argumentative essay. Your statement should identify the individual you consider a hero and state a reason why you believe so. When you are finished writing your claim, exchange your work with a partner for peer review. How clear is your partner's claim? Is it obvious why he or she thinks the individual is a hero? How well does the claim address all the parts of the prompt? Offer suggestions and make constructive comments that will help your partner develop an effective thesis.

Copyright © BookheadEd Learning, LLC

SKILL: ORGANIZE ARGUMENTATIVE WRITING

 DEFINE

As you have learned, the purpose of argumentative writing is to persuade readers to accept the writer's thesis statement, or claim. To do so, the writer must organize and present his or her reasons and relevant evidence—the facts, examples, statistics, and quotations found during research —in a logical and convincing way. The writer must also select an **organizational structure** that best suits the argument.

The writer of argument can choose from a number of organizational structures, including **compare and contrast, order of importance, problem and solution, cause-effect, and chronological (or sequential) order.** Experienced writers use **transition words and phrases** in their writing to help readers understand which organizational structure is being used. As they plan, writers often use an outline or other graphic organizer to determine the best way to present their ideas and evidence most persuasively.

Writers are not limited to using only one organizational structure throughout a text. Within a specific section or paragraph, they might use one or more different organizational structures. This does not affect the overall organization, however.

 IDENTIFICATION AND APPLICATION

- When selecting an overall organizational structure for an argument, a writer must consider the claim he or she is making. Then the writer needs to think about the best way to present the evidence that supports it. Do this by asking:

  › To support my claim, should I compare and contrast ideas or details in the text?

  › Is there an order of importance to my evidence? Is some evidence stronger than other evidence or does all my evidence support my claim equally well?

- › In my claim, have I raised a question or identified a problem? Do I have supporting evidence that suggests a solution or an answer?
  - › Does my supporting evidence suggest a cause or an effect?
  - › To support my claim, does it make sense to retell an events or series of events in chronological, or time, order?
- Writers often use specific transition words and phrases to help readers recognize the organizational structure of their writing:
  - › Compare and contrast: *like, unlike, and, both, similar to, different from, while, but, in contrast, although, also*
  - › Order of importance: *most, most important, least, least important, first, finally, mainly, to begin with*
  - › Problem and solution: *problem, solution, why, how*
  - › Cause-effect: *because, as a consequence of, as a result, cause, effect, so, in order to*
- Chronological order: *first, next, then, second, finally, before, after*

MODEL

During the prewriting stage, the writer of the Student Model figured out that Rosa Parks's actions had many causes and several important effects. The writer decided the best approach would be to use a cause-effect organizational structure for the argument.

At several points in the Student Model, the author uses transition words to show cause-effect relationships:

Because of this history and her personal feelings, Parks decided to take action.

As a result, Parks really had a terrible choice to make...

So thanks to Rosa Parks, African Americans could ride a bus and sit wherever they chose without being harassed.

Because of her efforts, among all the heroic men and women we have read about, she deserves to be honored as one of the greatest of American heroes.

Once a writer has selected the most appropriate organizational structure, he or she can use an outline or a graphic organizer (for example, a Venn diagram, flow chart, concept map, or timeline) to begin organizing the supporting evidence.

The writer of the Student Model argument used the following graphic organizer during planning to organize the evidence that supports this claim:

Because, as an ordinary woman, she took great risks and acted peacefully and bravely on behalf of herself and others, I think she is the greatest hero we have read about in unit 4.

CAUSE	EFFECT
Parks took risks for others, was brave, acted peacefully	Parks is the greatest hero of all in the unit.
The South was segregated. The bus laws were vicious and humiliating. Parks was angry.	Parks refused to give up seat on bus.
Parks faced danger.	Parks had a tough choice to make.
Parks inspired the bus boycott.	Segregation was banned. A great peaceful revolution began.

 PRACTICE

Use an *Organize Argumentative Writing* graphic organizer like the one used with the Student Model, or choose one that better suits your organizational strategy. Fill in the organizer with evidence you gathered in the Prewrite stage of writing your argument.

SUPPORTING DETAILS

sync•skills
Writing

SKILL: SUPPORTING DETAILS

DEFINE

The writer of an effective argument must provide **supporting details** in the form of reasons and relevant evidence. **Reasons** are statements that answer the question "Why?" They tell why the writer thinks his or her claim is true. A writer provides reasons to support a claim, which makes it more believable. **Relevant evidence** includes facts, statistics, definitions, quotations from experts, observations from eyewitnesses, and examples. Evidence that supports the reasons and the claim is often found through research.

Research can be the key to a successful argument. While researching, the writer deepens his or her understanding of the topic and finds evidence that supports the reasons and the claim. (Just as important—if the writer can't find enough evidence that supports the claim, then he or she knows it's time to change the claim or rethink the reasons.) Without solid supporting evidence, the writer would simply be stating his or her opinion about a topic—and that is rarely convincing to readers.

Because writers want to convince readers that their claims are credible, or believable, they carefully select and present the supporting details. A detail is **relevant** only if it supports the claim and helps build the argument. If the detail does not support the claim or strengthen the argument, it is irrelevant and should not be used.

IDENTIFICATION AND APPLICATION

Step 1:

Review your claim. In your research, you want to find supporting details that are relevant to your claim. Ask the following question: "What am I trying to persuade my audience to believe?" That's what the writer of the Student Model did. Here's the claim:

Because as an ordinary woman [Parks] took great risks and acted peacefully and bravely on behalf of herself and others, I think she is the greatest hero we have read about in unit 4.

Step 2:

Ask what a reader needs to know about the topic in order to accept the claim. To understand a claim about the risks Parks took, for example, a reader must first know something about the world in which she lived. Why was it so dangerous for Rosa Parks to refuse to give up her seat on a bus? Here's the reason the writer gives:

> African Americans who defied the laws of segregation could face potential violence.

The writer provides several supporting details that back up that reason:

1. As a child living in the South, she had seen her grandfather prepare to defend his family against the Ku Klux Klan ("Remembering Rosa Parks").

2. As an adult living in the segregated city of Montgomery, Alabama, in 1955, Parks understood the dangers of disobeying bus segregation policies.

3. Civil rights leader Reverend Joseph Lowery explained the possibilities in a 2005 interview: "The buses were particularly vicious in their policies . . . and it was especially humiliating to all the citizen[s] of Montgomery" ("Remembering Rosa Parks").

4. According to Parks's obituary in the *New York Times,* African Americans "had been arrested, even killed, for disobeying bus drivers" (Shipp).

Most of these supporting details came from the writer's research. The details definitely support the writer's claim that Parks took risks.

Step 3:

You might find lots of details in your research, and you might want to use them all to support your claim, but it is important to evaluate each detail before you use it to make sure it is relevant and convincing. To do this, ask yourself the following questions:

• Does this information help the reader deepen his or her understanding of the topic?

• Does this information support my claim?

• Does this information help build my argument?

• Do I have stronger evidence that makes the same point?

If you can answer *yes* to the first three questions and *no* to the fourth, then definitely use the supporting detail in your argument.

 ## MODEL

The Student Model writer used evidence found during his or her research to support the part of the claim that says Parks acted peacefully and on behalf of others.

> What happened next was amazing, and it changed the course of American history. Parks's arrest did not go unnoticed. Congresswoman Eleanor Holmes Norton later called it "a quiet revolutionary act" that inspired a city and then a nation ("Remembering Rosa Parks"). Parks was "convicted of violating segregation laws and fined $4 in court fees" (Shipp). The law said Parks was in the wrong. However, more than 40,000 African Americans in Montgomery thought otherwise, and they took action. They did not react violently but instead engaged in civil disobedience. In other words, they took lawful and peaceful steps toward making their voices heard. They struck back at the bus company by boycotting, or refusing to ride, the buses for 381 days (Shipp). The boycott was a great hardship for the people, but by not paying to ride buses, the African American community made its point.

What supporting details does the writer use here? The writer provides a direct quotation from an expert, along with facts about the terms of Parks's conviction and fine. The writer also provides details about the African American community's peaceful but forceful boycott to support the claim about Parks taking peaceful action on behalf of others.

 ## PRACTICE

Write your claim. Below it, write some supporting details for your argumentative essay. Draw on the research you completed earlier in the Extended Writing Project. Then exchange your work with a partner. Use what you have learned about relevant supporting details to evaluate his or her work. Be constructive in your comments.

PLAN

WRITING PROMPT

Every day the media runs headlines celebrating heroes among us. The firefighter who charges into the burning building to save an infant is a hero. The nurse who risks her own life to help patients with infectious diseases—she's a hero too. What qualities do all heroes have in common? What makes one person more heroic than another?

In this unit, you have been reading both non-fiction and fiction texts about people who are considered American heroes—George Washington, Eleanor Roosevelt, Rosa Parks, the Freedom Walkers, Dr. Benjamin Rush, Gulf War soldiers.

Recognizing that not everyone agrees on what it means to be a hero or who our heroes are, write an argumentative essay that identifies an individual from the selections in this unit who you feel best exemplifies the qualities of a hero.

To support your ideas you will include textual evidence from at least one selection in unit 4 and research from three other print or digital sources.

Your argumentative essay with research should include:

- an explicitly stated claim about the individual who you think is the most heroic
- a logically organized argument supported by persuasive reasons and relevant textual evidence
- information from one unit text and at least three other print or digital sources

WRITING PROMPT

- citations of your sources and a Works Cited page
- a conclusion that restates your claim, sums up your reasons and evidence, and leaves your readers with an original thought about the topic

Review the organizational structure and information you used to complete your *Organize Argumentative Writing* graphic organizer. This organized information and your claim will help you create a road map to use for writing your argumentative essay.

Consider the following questions as you develop your main paragraph topics and their supporting details in the road map:

- Who is the subject of your essay?
- What claim (or argument) are you making about this subject? (How does this person best exemplify the qualities of a hero?)
- What are your reasons for making this claim?
- What specific reasons and relevant evidence from the unit selections and from your research can you use to support your claim?
- How can you best present the evidence so that it persuades your audience to accept your claim?

Use this model to get started with your road map:

Argumentative Essay Road Map

Claim: Rosa Parks is the greatest hero of all the people we have read about in unit 4 because she was an ordinary woman who took great risks and acted bravely on behalf of herself and others.

Paragraph 1 Topic: Rosa Parks bravely did not give up her seat even though she risked physical harm.

Supporting Detail #1: Parks remembered the danger her family faced from the Ku Klux Klan when she was a girl.

Supporting Detail #2: Quote from interview with Reverend Joseph Lowery about how Montgomery's bus segregation laws were "especially humiliating"

Please note that excerpts and passages in the StudySync® library and this workbook are intended as touchstones to generate interest in an author's work. The excerpts and passages do not substitute for the reading of entire texts, and StudySync® strongly recommends that students seek out and purchase the whole literary or informational work in order to experience it as the author intended. Links to online resellers are available in our digital library. In addition, complete works may be ordered through an authorized reseller by filling out and returning to StudySync® the order form enclosed in this workbook.

Reading & Writing Companion

383

Supporting Detail #3: Quote from the obituary of Parks in the *New York Times* about how African Americans were treated when they disobeyed bus drivers

Supporting Detail #4: Despite the risks, Parks was angry and frustrated with segregation laws, so she resisted them. Quote from Parks about how whites treated African Americans.

Paragraph 2 Topic: Parks showed great courage even after being arrested.

Supporting Detail #1: Quote from Parks about how she "wasn't afraid," but she must have known she might face physical harm at the hands of the police

Supporting Detail #2: Parks preferred to face arrest and possible violence than be treated as a second-class citizen any longer.

Paragraph 3 Topic: Parks's courageous action spurred a nonviolent revolution to end segregation in the United States.

Supporting Detail #1: Quote from the *New York Times* about how after Parks's arrest, thousands of African Americans refused to ride the Montgomery city buses for 381 days

Supporting Detail #2: The Supreme Court ruled that bus segregation laws were unconstitutional throughout the country.

Supporting Detail #3: Quote from Reverend Lowery about how Parks's arrest and the bus boycott led to other acts of civil disobedience that helped fight segregation and other kinds of social injustice

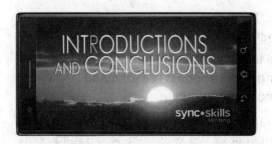

SKILL:
INTRODUCTIONS
AND
CONCLUSIONS

 DEFINE

The **introduction** is the opening paragraph or section of an argumentative essay or other non-fiction text. The introduction of an argumentative essay **identifies the topic to be discussed, states the writer's claim,** and **previews the supporting details** (reasons and evidence found during research) that will appear in the body of the text. The introduction is also the place where most writers include a **"hook"** that engages readers and helps them connect to the topic.

A **conclusion** is the closing paragraph or section of an argumentative essay or other type of non-fiction text. The conclusion is where the writer brings the argument to a close. The ideas presented in a conclusion follow directly from the introduction's claim and the supporting details provided in the body of the argument. In other words, it's where the writer restates the claim and sums up his or her evidence and research. In addition, the conclusion of an argument might also end with a call to action or an insightful comment.

 IDENTIFICATION AND APPLICATION

- In an argument, the introduction is the opening section in which the writer **identifies the topic to be discussed** and **directly states the claim.** The claim expresses the writer's opinion about the topic. By presenting the claim at the beginning of an argument, the writer lets readers know his or her position on the topic.

- The introduction is also where the writer provides a **preview of the reasons and evidence supporting the claim.** By doing so, the writer can establish an effective argument and increase the likelihood that readers will agree with the claim.

- An effective introduction has a "hook." A good hook engages readers' interest and makes them want to keep reading. A hook might be an intriguing image, a surprising detail, an interesting question, a funny anecdote, or a shocking statistic. The hook should also help readers connect to the topic in a meaningful way.

- An effective conclusion **restates the writer's claim** and **briefly summarizes the most convincing and strongest reasons and researched evidence** from the body paragraphs.

- Some conclusions offer some form of **insight** relating to the argument. The insightful comment is the last chance the writer has to persuade and even inspire readers to think or believe something. The insight may take any of the following forms:

  › An answer to a question first posed in the introduction
  › A question designed to elicit reflection on the part of the reader
  › A memorable or inspiring message
  › A last compelling example
  › A suggestion that readers learn more

 MODEL

The introduction and conclusion of the Student Model, "Rosa Parks: A True American Hero," contain many of the key elements discussed above. Consider the introduction:

> **Who is a hero? Many people might think that heroes have special powers and can save the world. But the superheroes we see in blockbuster movies and on TV are make-believe, and fighting monsters and stopping meteors are not real-life problems.** As many of the selections in this unit show, true heroes live in the real world, take risks, and act as role models. For example, George Washington led a rebel army because he believed in an independent United States. Eleanor Roosevelt voiced the concerns of the poor during the Great Depression.

> Both Washington and Roosevelt, who for good reasons are considered heroes, were also important leaders of their time. Washington was a general in the Continental Army and later president of the United States. Roosevelt was the First Lady of the United States. While they each had to confront huge obstacles, they were already respected citizens when they took up their causes. **Rosa Parks, however, was an ordinary woman when she courageously refused to give up her bus seat and so changed American history.** In defying authorities and the law, **she committed an incredibly brave and even dangerous act.** She did so with determination, grace, and

dignity. Moreover, she accepted the consequences of her action—arrest—and went through legal channels to protest and change the law. In addition, **her so-called "crime" and her arrest helped launch the civil rights movement. This movement would make the United States a fairer place for everyone. Because, as an ordinary woman, she took great risks and acted peacefully and bravely on behalf of herself and others, I think she is the greatest hero we have read about in unit 4.**

The introductory section of the Student Model consists of two paragraphs. Paragraph 1 of the introduction **"hooks"** readers by asking a question and by referring to "heroes" with "special powers," "superheroes," and "summer blockbuster movies." Then, in paragraph 2, the writer identifies the **topic**—Rosa Parks. The details about Parks not only hint at the evidence that will follow in the body of the argument, they also lead directly to the writer's **claim**—that Parks "is the greatest hero we have read about in unit 4." The sentence that includes the claim also previews some of the reasons the writer will discuss in the body of the essay.

Now consider the concluding paragraph of the Student Model:

In standing up against a powerful segregated society, Rosa Parks reminded Americans what equality means. In her autobiography, she summed up why she refused to move from her seat on the bus: "People always say that I didn't give up my seat because I was tired, but that isn't true . . . No, the only tired I was, was tired of giving in" (Parks). **She channeled her anger peacefully. She took a huge risk and still maintained her dignity, serving as a model for others. I think in the end she made this country a better place to live for all people. Because of her efforts, among all the heroic men and women we have read about, she deserves to be honored as one of the greatest of American heroes.**

The concluding paragraph **restates the claim, sums up the most important reasons,** and includes this **insightful comment:** "In standing up against a powerful segregated society, Parks reminded all Americans about what equality means."

 PRACTICE

Write an introduction and a conclusion for your argument. Your introduction should include a "hook," identify your topic, state your claim, and hint at the

Please note that excerpts and passages in the StudySync® library and this workbook are intended as touchstones to generate interest in an author's work. The excerpts and passages do not substitute for the reading of entire texts, and StudySync® strongly recommends that students seek out and purchase the whole literary or informational work in order to experience it as the author intended. Links to online resellers are available in our digital library. In addition, complete works may be ordered through an authorized reseller by filling out and returning to StudySync® the order form enclosed in this workbook.

Reading & Writing Companion   387

supporting details (reasons and evidence from your research) that will appear in the body of the essay. Then draft a conclusion that mirrors your introduction by restating your claim and summing up your research. Try to include an insightful comment about your topic or your claim. Finally, trade your work with a peer for review. Provide helpful feedback on your peer's introductions and conclusion.

SKILL: BODY PARAGRAPHS AND TRANSITIONS

 DEFINE

Body paragraphs appear between the introduction and conclusion of an argumentative essay. Together, they form the section in which a writer supports his or her claim with reasons and evidence collected during research. In general, each body paragraph should focus on one idea or reason so that the reader can easily follow along. The ideas in each body paragraph should support the claim.

It's important to structure a body paragraph clearly. Here is one way to structure the body paragraph of an argumentative essay:

- **Topic sentence:** The topic sentence is the first sentence of a body paragraph. It states the main point of the paragraph. The topic sentence should relate to your claim.
- **Evidence #1:** You should provide evidence that supports your topic sentence. Evidence can include relevant facts, definitions, observations, quotations, and examples.
- **Evidence #2:** Continue to develop your claim with a second piece of evidence.
- **Analysis/Explanation:** After presenting evidence, you should explain how the evidence helps support your topic sentence—and general claim—about the topic. Analysis is important in an argumentative essay. It is how you make sure that readers understand the connections you are making between the supporting evidence and the claim.
- **Concluding sentence:** After presenting your evidence and analysis, wrap up the main idea in a concluding sentence.

As you write body paragraphs, think carefully about how to incorporate your evidence. **Quotations** are an excellent form of evidence, but they need to be integrated into your writing carefully, or they will sound awkward. Always place the exact words of the quotations within quotation marks. Then end the sentence with a citation, so readers know where the quoted material comes from.

Copyright © BookheadEd Learning, LLC

Compare these examples of a poorly integrated and well-integrated quotation:

Poorly integrated quotation:

Parks's arrest did not go unnoticed. It was "a quiet revolutionary act." That was what Congresswoman Eleanor Holmes Norton said about Parks's arrest at a later time.

Well integrated quotation:

Congresswoman Eleanor Holmes Norton later called it "a quiet revolutionary act" that inspired a city and then a nation ("Remembering Rosa Parks").

Remember, if a full quotation is too long, you can use **ellipses** (...) to show the parts that you left out—like this:

"People always say that I didn't give up my seat because I was tired, but that isn't true... No, the only tired I was, was tired of giving in" (Parks).

You can also **paraphrase** the quotation—or any of your evidence. Paraphrasing involves restating information in your own words. For example, the writer of the Student Model used specific facts and figures from one of Parks's obituaries but used his or her own words to present the information and also cited the source:

The law said Parks was in the wrong, but more than 40,000 African Americans in Montgomery thought otherwise, *and they took action. However, they did not react violently, but rather engaged in civil disobedience. In other words, they took lawful and peaceful steps toward making their voices heard. Then* **they struck back at the bus company by boycotting, or refusing to ride, the buses for 381 days (Shipp).**

Transitions are connecting words and phrases that writers use to clarify the relationships between ideas in a text. Transitions help make connections between words in a sentence and ideas in individual paragraphs. They also help indicate the organizational structure of a text. Adding transition words or phrases to the beginning or end of a paragraph can help a writer guide readers smoothly through a text.

IDENTIFICATION AND APPLICATION

- Body paragraphs are the section of the argumentative essay between the introduction and conclusion. These paragraphs provide reasons and supporting evidence. Typically, writers of arguments focus on one main idea in each body paragraph.
  - › A topic sentence clearly states the main idea of that paragraph. The main idea should support and relate to the writer's main claim. The main idea may provide one of the reasons for making the claim.
  - › Evidence consists of relevant facts, definitions, observations, quotations, and examples.
  - › Analysis and explanation tell how the evidence supports the topic sentence and the claim.
  - › A conclusion sentence wraps up the paragraph's main idea.

- Certain transition words and phrases indicate specific organizational relationships within a text. Here are some examples:
  - › Cause-effect: *because, accordingly, as a result, so, for, since, therefore, if, then*
  - › Compare and contrast: *like, unlike, also, both, similarly, although, while, but, however, whereas, meanwhile, on the contrary, yet, still*
  - › Chronological order: *first, then, next, finally, before, after, when, following, within a few years*

- Transition words and phrases also help readers connect ideas and information in a text, as well as understand the relationship among the claim, reasons, and evidence. A phrase like *for example* can help show the relationship between a main point and its evidence. The phrase *in addition* to can help link similar ideas.

- Quotations are an excellent form of evidence. You can include direct quotes from sources in your writing or paraphrase a quote in your own words. To avoid **plagiarism,** be sure to introduce the source of the quotation before you quote it.
  - › When using a direct quote, always place the exact words of the quotations within quotation marks.
  - › Whenever you paraphrase or provide a direct quote, always end the sentence with a citation, so readers know where the paraphrased or quoted material comes from.

Please note that excerpts and passages in the StudySync® library and this workbook are intended as touchstones to generate interest in an author's work. The excerpts and passages do not substitute for the reading of entire texts, and StudySync® strongly recommends that students seek out and purchase the whole literary or informational work in order to experience it as the author intended. Links to online resellers are available in our digital library. In addition, complete works may be ordered through an authorized reseller by filling out and returning to StudySync® the order form enclosed in this workbook.

Reading & Writing Companion   **391**

MODEL

The Student Model uses a body paragraph structure to develop the claim. It also includes transitions to help the reader understand the relationship between ideas and to indicate the text's organizational structure.

Read the second body paragraph from the Student Model, "Rosa Parks: A True American Hero." Look closely at the structure and think about how the writer incorporated his or her research. Look at the transition words and phrases in bold. How effective is the paragraph's structure? Does it develop ideas related to the claim? How do the transition words and phrases help you understand the text's organizational structure and the relationships between and among ideas?

> **After** her arrest, Parks continued to show great courage. **She says she "wasn't afraid,"** and yet she must have felt some fear (Parks). She knew that there was no guarantee she would get through the experience without physical harm. **As a result,** Parks really had a terrible choice to make: continuing to be treated as a second-class citizen or risking her freedom and perhaps even her life to reject segregation. **She chose not to surrender to injustice.**

The **topic sentence** of this paragraph presents one reason the writer has claimed that Rosa Parks is a great hero. Even after her arrest, she showed courage. The topic sentence is immediately followed by **evidence** in the form of a **quotation.** The writer neatly **integrates** the quotation. He or she makes clear whose words are used and follows them with his or her own ideas. The word *after* acts as a **transition** from the previous paragraph; it lets readers know they are reading about events in a sequence. The phrase *as a result* indicates a cause-effect relationship between Parks's fear and her action. The paragraph wraps up with the writer's **analysis.** The **concluding sentence** sums up what happened.

 PRACTICE

Write one of the body paragraphs of your essay following the format above. When you finish writing, take a few minutes to think about what you've written. Then go back and edit your paragraph. Make sure you used clear transitions and check that you have chosen strong facts, details, and quotations to support your topic sentence. Ask yourself whether you have integrated your research smoothly and correctly. When you are finished, exchange your work with a partner. Offer each other constructive feedback by answering the following questions:

- How well does the topic sentence introduce the topic of the paragraph?

- How effectively does the topic sentence refer back to the claim?

- How strong is the evidence and analysis used to support the topic sentence?

- How well did the writer integrate quotes and paraphrased evidence? Did the writer cite this evidence properly?

- How do transitions help guide readers through the text? What functions do they serve?

- How well did the writer sum up ideas in the concluding sentence?

DRAFT

WRITING PROMPT

Every day the media runs headlines celebrating heroes among us. The firefighter who charges into the burning building to save an infant is a hero. The nurse who risks her own life to help patients with infectious diseases—she's a hero too. What qualities do all heroes have in common? What makes one person more heroic than another?

In this unit, you have been reading both non-fiction and fiction texts about people who are considered American heroes—George Washington, Eleanor Roosevelt, Rosa Parks, the Freedom Walkers, Dr. Benjamin Rush, Gulf War soldiers.

Recognizing that not everyone agrees on what it means to be a hero or who our heroes are, write an argumentative essay that identifies an individual from the selections in this unit who you feel best exemplifies the qualities of a hero.

To support your ideas you will include textual evidence from at least one selection in unit 4 and research from three other print or digital sources.

Your argumentative essay with research should include:

- an explicitly stated claim about the individual who you think is the most heroic

- a logically organized argument supported by persuasive reasons and relevant textual evidence

- information from one unit text and at least three other print or digital sources

WRITING PROMPT

- citations of your sources and a Works Cited page
- a conclusion that restates your claim, sums up your reasons and evidence, and leaves your readers with an original thought about the topic

You've already begun working on your own argumentative essay. So far, you've thought about your purpose, audience, and topic. You've carefully examined the unit texts and selected the individual you consider to be the greatest hero. You have also completed some outside research to gather information and evidence that supports your claim. If the evidence you found did not support your claim, you have refocused your ideas and claim as necessary. You've decided how to organize information, and you've gathered supporting details in the form of reasons and relevant evidence. You've carefully evaluated the argument you plan to make in order to ensure that you can support it fully with facts, details, and quotations. Now it's time to write a draft of your argument.

Use your road map and your other prewriting materials to help you as you write. Remember that an argument begins with an introduction that features a claim. Body paragraphs then develop the claim by providing clear reasons and relevant supporting details such as facts, details, quotations, and examples. Body paragraphs also provide your analysis of the evidence. Transitions signal an organizational structure and help the reader understand how the claim, reasons, and evidence are connected. A concluding paragraph restates or reinforces the claim and important points from the argument you have made. The conclusion may also share an original thought with your readers.

When drafting, ask yourself these questions:

- How can I make my hook more effective?
- What can I do to clarify my claim?
- Which relevant evidence from the unit text (or texts) and outside sources—including facts, direct quotations, examples, and observations—best supports my claim?
- How can I improve the structure of my argument by using better transitions?
- How convincing is my analysis of the evidence in support of my claim?

Please note that excerpts and passages in the StudySync® library and this workbook are intended as touchstones to generate interest in an author's work. The excerpts and passages do not substitute for the reading of entire texts, and StudySync® strongly recommends that students seek out and purchase the whole literary or informational work in order to experience it as the author intended. Links to online resellers are available in our digital library. In addition, complete works may be ordered through an authorized reseller by filling out and returning to StudySync® the order form enclosed in this workbook.

Reading & Writing Companion   395

- How can I effectively restate my claim in the conclusion?
- What final message do I want to leave with my readers?

Be sure to carefully read your draft before you submit it. You want to make sure you've addressed every part of the prompt.

SKILL:
SOURCES AND
CITATIONS

DEFINE

Sources are the texts that writers use to research their writing. A **primary source** is a first-hand account of events by the person who experienced them. Another type of source is known as a **secondary source.** This is a source that analyzes or interprets primary sources. **Citations** are notes that provide information about the source texts. It is necessary for a writer to provide a citation if he or she quotes a source directly, refers to ideas from a source, or includes specific facts and figures from a source. The citation lets readers know where the information originally came from.

IDENTIFICATION AND APPLICATION

- Sources can be either primary or secondary. Primary sources are first-hand accounts or original materials such as the following:

  › Letters or other correspondence
  › Photographs
  › Official documents
  › Diaries or journals
  › Autobiographies or memoirs
  › Eyewitness accounts and interviews
  › Audio recordings and radio broadcasts
  › Literary texts, such as novels, poems, fables, and dramas
  › Works of art
  › Artifacts

- Secondary sources are usually texts. These texts are the written interpretation and analysis of primary source materials. Some examples of secondary sources include:

  › Encyclopedia articles
  › Textbooks
  › Commentary or criticisms

Please note that excerpts and passages in the StudySync® library and this workbook are intended as touchstones to generate interest in an author's work. The excerpts and passages do not substitute for the reading of entire texts, and StudySync® strongly recommends that students seek out and purchase the whole literary or informational work in order to experience it as the author intended. Links to online resellers are available in our digital library. In addition, complete works may be ordered through an authorized reseller by filling out and returning to StudySync® the order form enclosed in this workbook.

Reading & Writing
Companion

397

> Histories
> Documentary films
> News analyses

- Whether sources are primary or secondary, they must be **credible** and **reliable.**

- When a writer quotes directly from a source, he or she must copy the words exactly as they appear in the source, placing them within quotation marks. The writer must also cite the source of the quotation. Here's an example from the Student Model:

    Civil rights leader Reverend Joseph Lowery explained the possibilities in a 2005 interview, **"The buses were particularly vicious in their policies . . . and it was especially humiliating to all the citizen[s] of Montgomery"** ("Remembering Rosa Parks").

- One way to cite the source of a quotation is to put the information in parentheses at the end of the sentence. Another way is to mention the source in the context of the sentence. Sometimes the speaker of a quotation is different from the source where it was found. In that case, the speaker usually is mentioned in the sentence itself and the source in parentheses, as in the example of Reverend Lowry's quotation above.

- Information in parentheses includes either the last name of the source's author or the source's title, if an author is not named. If a page number is available, for example from a book, also cite the page number.

- Writers must also provide citations when borrowing ideas or specific facts and figures from another source, even when writers are paraphrasing, or putting the information into their own words. Citations serve both to credit the source and help readers find out where they can learn more.

- There are several styles of citation in addition to the parenthetical style. Ask your teacher to identify the style he or she prefers.

    > Writers who cite from sources in the body of their writing need to provide a **Works Cited** section that lists all the sources the writer used. As with citations, there are different styles of Works Cited lists, but the sources are always listed in alphabetical order by author's name. If the source has no author, then it is alphabetized by title.

 MODEL

Writers do research in order to answer questions they may have about a topic or to learn about a topic in greater depth or detail than what they already know. When they conduct research, writers should draw on credible and

Copyright © BookheadEd Learning, LLC

reliable sources, both to check the accuracy of information and add to their knowledge. They should always cite their sources. In this excerpt from the Student Model, "Rosa Parks: A True American Hero," the writer quotes from two different sources and identifies each quotations' source.

> What happened next was amazing, and it changed the course of American history. Parks's arrest did not go unnoticed. **Congresswoman Eleanor Holmes Norton later called it "a quiet revolutionary act"** that inspired a city and then a nation **("Remembering Rosa Parks")**. Parks was **"convicted of violating segregation laws and fined $4 in court fees" (Shipp)**. The law said Parks was in the wrong. However, more than 40,000 African Americans in Montgomery thought otherwise, and they took action. They did not react violently, but instead engaged in civil disobedience. In other words, they took lawful and peaceful steps toward making their voices heard. **They struck back at the bus company by boycotting, or refusing to ride, the buses for 381 days (Shipp).** The boycott was a great hardship for the people, but by not paying to ride buses, the African American community made its point.

Notice that only the portions of text taken directly from the source appear in quotations and that the author's last name or the title of the source appears in parentheses after each quotation. Also notice that the author's last name appears in parentheses after the paraphrased ideas in sentence 9.

Here is how the writer's sources appear in the Works Cited section that follows the argumentative essay:

Works Cited

Parks, Rosa, and James Haskins. *Rosa Parks: My Story*. New York: Dial Books, 1990. Print.

"Remembering Rosa Parks." *PBS Newshour*. 25 Oct. 2005. Web. **12 Dec. 2014.**
<http://www.pbs.org/newshour/bb/social_issues-july-dec05-parks_10-25>

Shipp, E.R. "Rosa Parks, 92, Founding Symbol of Civil Rights Movement, Dies." *New York Times*. 25 Oct. 2005. Web. **12 Dec. 2014.**
<http://www.nytimes.com/2005/10/25/us/25parks.html>

NOTES

"**Today** in History: December 1." *The Library of Congress.* Web. **12 Dec. 2014.**
<http://memory.loc.gov/ammem/today/dec01.html>

Notice how the sources are listed alphabetically by the author's last name (or by the title if the source has no author). The author's name is followed by the title and the publication information. When a source is published online, the writer needs to identify its URL and give the date of when he or she accessed it. From this Works Cited section, you can tell that the writer accessed all three online sources on the same day.

 PRACTICE

If you have not yet written your Works Cited section, do so now. Go back to your draft and check that you have cited your sources correctly. Edit your citations, making sure they follow the conventions your teacher recommended. Then exchange your Works Cited section with a partner and provide each other with feedback. Look carefully at how your partner formatted and punctuated the citations. Edit and provide constructive feedback.

EXTENDED WRITING PROJECT
REVISE

REVISE

WRITING PROMPT

Every day the media runs headlines celebrating heroes among us. The firefighter who charges into the burning building to save an infant is a hero. The nurse who risks her own life to help patients with infectious diseases—she's a hero too. What qualities do all heroes have in common? What makes one person more heroic than another?

In this unit, you have been reading both non-fiction and fiction texts about people who are considered American heroes—George Washington, Eleanor Roosevelt, Rosa Parks, the Freedom Walkers, Dr. Benjamin Rush, Gulf War soldiers.

Recognizing that not everyone agrees on what it means to be a hero or who our heroes are, write an argumentative essay that identifies an individual from the selections in this unit who you feel best exemplifies the qualities of a hero.

To support your ideas you will include textual evidence from at least one selection in unit 4 and research from three other print or digital sources.

Your argumentative essay with research should include:

- an explicitly stated claim about the individual who you think is the most heroic

- a logically organized argument supported by persuasive reasons and relevant textual evidence

- information from one unit text and at least three other print or digital sources

Copyright © BookheadEd Learning, LLC

NOTES

WRITING PROMPT

- citations of your sources and a Works Cited page
- a conclusion that restates your claim, sums up your reasons and evidence, and leaves your readers with an original thought about the topic

You have written a draft of your argumentative essay. You have also received input from your peers about how to improve it. Now you are going to revise your draft.

Here are some recommendations to help you revise:

- Review the suggestions made by your peers. You don't have to implement every suggestion, but think seriously about your peers' comments as you revise.

- Focus on maintaining a formal style and tone. A formal style suits your purpose—persuading readers to agree with your ideas about a topic. It is also appropriate for your audience—students, teachers, and other readers interested in learning more about your topic. Your tone, or attitude toward your topic, should be serious, thoughtful, and respectful. It should help indicate that you fully understand your topic.

  › Use standard English in your writing. As you revise, eliminate any informal language, particularly slang, unless it is included in quoted material or is essential to readers' understanding.

  › Review your language. Look for words and phrases that are too general or overused. Think of more precise words or specialized vocabulary to replace them. Provide definitions, if you think your readers will need them.

  › Pay attention to pronouns. Make sure you have used the proper pronoun (same number and case) to replace the noun it refers to in a sentence. Check that you have punctuated all possessive pronouns properly.

  › Incorporate a variety of sentence structures into your writing. Check that you aren't beginning every sentence the same way. A mixture of sentence lengths and types will create an interesting pattern that will keep readers engaged in your writing.

- After you have revised for elements of style and tone, use these questions to review your argument for ways you could improve its organization and supporting details:

> Is your organizational structure apparent? Would your argument flow better if you added more transitions between sentences and paragraphs? What transition words best suit your organizational structure?

> What additional evidence, such as quotations and facts, might you want to add in order to fully support your claim and reasons for making the claim?

> How well have you incorporated quotations into your sentences and paragraphs? Are the quotations clearly introduced and punctuated properly? Have you double-checked your citations to make sure you have correctly cited the source of the quotation in the body of the paper and in the Works Cited section?

Please note that excerpts and passages in the StudySync® library and this workbook are intended as touchstones to generate interest in an author's work. The excerpts and passages do not substitute for the reading of entire texts, and StudySync® strongly recommends that students seek out and purchase the whole literary or informational work in order to experience it as the author intended. Links to online resellers are available in our digital library. In addition, complete works may be ordered through an authorized reseller by filling out and returning to StudySync® the order form enclosed in this workbook.

Reading & Writing Companion   **403**

EDIT, PROOFREAD, AND PUBLISH

WRITING PROMPT

Every day the media runs headlines celebrating heroes among us. The firefighter who charges into the burning building to save an infant is a hero. The nurse who risks her own life to help patients with infectious diseases—she's a hero too. What qualities do all heroes have in common? What makes one person more heroic than another?

In this unit, you have been reading both non-fiction and fiction texts about people who are considered American heroes—George Washington, Eleanor Roosevelt, Rosa Parks, the Freedom Walkers, Dr. Benjamin Rush, Gulf War soldiers.

Recognizing that not everyone agrees on what it means to be a hero or who our heroes are, write an argumentative essay that identifies an individual from the selections in this unit who you feel best exemplifies the qualities of a hero.

To support your ideas you will include textual evidence from at least one selection in unit 4 and research from three other print or digital sources.

Your argumentative essay with research should include:

- an explicitly stated claim about the individual who you think is the most heroic
- a logically organized argument supported by persuasive reasons and relevant textual evidence
- information from one unit text and at least three other print or digital sources

WRITING PROMPT

- citations of your sources and a Works Cited page
- a conclusion that restates your claim, sums up your reasons and evidence, and leaves your readers with an original thought about the topic

Now that you have revised your argumentative essay and received feedback from your peers, it's time to edit and proofread to produce a final version. Have you taken into consideration all the suggestions from your peers? Ask yourself these questions:

- Have I presented a persuasive argument?
- Have I fully supported my claim with strong reasons and relevant textual evidence?
- Is the organization of information clear and easy for the reader to follow?
- Have I correctly cited my sources?
- Would my argument benefit from additional transitions?
- Have I used a variety of effective sentence structures? Have I used a formal style and tone throughout?
- What else can I do to improve my essay's information and organization?

Once you are satisfied with your work, proofread it for grammatical and mechanical errors. For example:

- Are all your pronouns in the proper case?
- Have you used the correct punctuation for quotations and citations?
- Have you capitalized all proper nouns?

Be sure to correct any misspelled words you find in your argument. If you're uncertain about the spelling of a word, double-check your work by looking in a dictionary.

Once you have made all your corrections, you are ready to submit and publish your work. You can distribute your writing to family and friends, or post it at school or online. If you do decide to publish online, include links to your sources and citations. This will enable readers to learn more from the sources on their own time. You might also take an opportunity to deliver your argumentative essay as an oral presentation to friends, family, or classmates. They might welcome the chance to hear your ideas about someone you consider to be a hero.

Please note that excerpts and passages in the StudySync® library and this workbook are intended as touchstones to generate interest in an author's work. The excerpts and passages do not substitute for the reading of entire texts, and StudySync® strongly recommends that students seek out and purchase the whole literary or informational work in order to experience it as the author intended. Links to online resellers are available in our digital library. In addition, complete works may be ordered through an authorized reseller by filling out and returning to StudySync® the order form enclosed in this workbook.

Reading & Writing Companion

405

Text Fulfillment
Through StudySync

If you are interested in specific titles, please fill out the form below and we will check availability through our partners.

ORDER DETAILS

Date:

TITLE	AUTHOR	Paperback/ Hardcover	Specific Edition *If Applicable*	Quantity

SHIPPING INFORMATION

Contact:

Title:

School/District:

Address Line 1:

Address Line 2:

Zip or Postal Code:

Phone:

Mobile:

Email:

BILLING INFORMATION   ☐ SAME AS SHIPPING

Contact:

Title:

School/District:

Address Line 1:

Address Line 2:

Zip or Postal Code:

Phone:

Mobile:

Email:

PAYMENT INFORMATION

☐ CREDIT CARD

Name on Card:

Card Number: Expiration Date: Security Code:

☐ PO

Purchase Order Number:

StudySync Text Fulfillment, BookheadEd Learning, LLC
610 Daniel Young Drive | Sonoma, CA 95476